Professional Examinati

CW01213004

Operational Level

Paper F1

Financial Operations

EXAM PRACTICE KIT

CIMA
PUBLISHING

KAPLAN
PUBLISHING

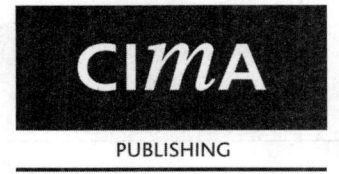

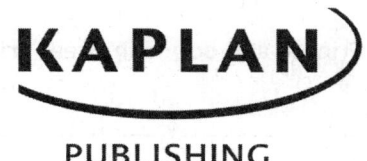

PAPER F1 : FINANCIAL OPERATIONS

Published by: Kaplan Publishing UK

Unit 2 The Business Centre, Molly Millars Lane, Wokingham, Berkshire RG41 2QZ

Copyright © 2013 Kaplan Financial Limited. All rights reserved.

No part of this publication may be reproduced, stored in a retrieval system or transmitted in any form or by any means electronic, mechanical, photocopying, recording or otherwise without the prior written permission of the publisher.

Acknowledgements

We are grateful to the Chartered Institute of Management Accountants for permission to reproduce past examination questions. The answers to CIMA Exams have been prepared by Kaplan Publishing, except in the case of the CIMA November 2010 and subsequent CIMA Exam answers where the official CIMA answers have been reproduced.

Notice

The text in this material and any others made available by any Kaplan Group company does not amount to advice on a particular matter and should not be taken as such. No reliance should be placed on the content as the basis for any investment or other decision or in connection with any advice given to third parties. Please consult your appropriate professional adviser as necessary. Kaplan Publishing Limited and all other Kaplan group companies expressly disclaim all liability to any person in respect of any losses or other claims, whether direct, indirect, incidental, consequential or otherwise arising in relation to the use of such materials.

British Library Cataloguing in Publication Data

A catalogue record for this book is available from the British Library

ISBN: 978-0-85732-996-7

Printed and bound in Great Britain.

CONTENTS

	Page
Index to questions and answers	v
Analysis of past exam papers	xi
Exam technique	xiii
Paper specific information	xv
Approach to revision	xix
The detailed revision plan	xxiii

Section

1	Section A-type Questions	1
2	Section B-type Questions	65
3	Section C-type Questions	111
4	Answers to Section A-type Questions	187
5	Answers to Section B-type Questions	233
6	Answers to Section C-type Questions	293
7	Specimen exam questions Reproduced with the kind permission of CIMA	459
8	Answers to specimen exam questions Reproduced with the kind permission of CIMA	471
9	November 2013 questions and answers Reproduced with the kind permission of CIMA	485

Key features in this edition

In addition to providing a wide ranging bank of real past exam questions, we have also included in this edition:

- Paper specific information and advice on **exam technique**.
- Our **recommended approach** to make your revision for this particular subject as effective as possible.

  This includes step by step guidance on how best to use our Kaplan material (Complete Text, Kaplancards and Exam Kit) at this stage in your studies.

- Enhanced **tutorial answers** packed with specific key answer tips, technical tutorial notes and exam technique tips from our experienced tutors.

PAPER F1 : FINANCIAL OPERATIONS

You will find a wealth of other resources to help you with your studies on the following sites:

www.mykaplan.co.uk

www.cimaglobal.com

INDEX TO QUESTIONS AND ANSWERS

INTRODUCTION

Paper F1: Financial Operations will be first tested in May 2010 as part of the new CIMA syllabus. The syllabus for paper F1 is almost identical to that of the old syllabus paper P7: Financial Accounting and Tax, and indeed it has the same examiner.

This Exam Practice Kit includes an extensive selection of questions that entirely cover the syllabus – this ensures that your knowledge is tested across all syllabus areas. Wherever possible questions have been grouped by syllabus topics.

All questions are of exam standard and format – this enables you to master the exam techniques. Section 1 contains Section A-type questions you will come across in your exam; Section 2 contains Section B-type questions and Section 3 contains Section C-type questions.

We have worked closely with experienced CIMA tutors and lecturers to ensure that our Kits are exam-focused and user-friendly.

The specimen paper for the new syllabus can be found at the end of the book – try this under timed conditions and this will give you an exact idea of the way you will be tested in your exam.

KEY TO THE INDEX

PAPER ENHANCEMENTS

We have added the following enhancements to the answers in this exam kit:

Key answer tips

Many answers include key answer tips to help your understanding of each question.

Tutorial note

Many answers include more tutorial notes to explain some of the technical points in more detail.

Top tutor tips

For selected questions, we "walk through the answer" giving guidance on how to approach the questions with helpful 'tips from a top tutor', together with technical tutor notes.

These answers are indicated with the "footsteps" icon in the index.

v

PAPER F1 : FINANCIAL OPERATIONS

	Page number		
	Question	*Answer*	*Past exam*

SECTION A-TYPE QUESTIONS

Principles of business taxation (Questions 1 to 88)	1	187	–
Principles of regulation of financial reporting (Questions 89 to 130)	22	204	–
Single company financial accounts (Questions 131 to 222)	31	207	–
Group company financial accounts (Questions 223 to 242)	58	226	–

SECTION B-TYPE QUESTIONS
PRINCIPLES OF BUSINESS TAXATION

243	Adjusted profits (1)	65	233	*May 07*
244	Adjusted profits (2)	66	234	*May 08*
245	Tax charge (1)	67	235	*May 10*
246	Tax charge (2)	68	236	*Nov 11*
247	HG	69	237	*Feb 13*
248	MT	69	237	*May 13*
249	DG	70	238	*Nov 06*
250	GJ	71	239	*Nov 08*
251	Deferred tax	71	239	*Sep 11*
252	FG	71	240	*May 11*
253	TY	72	240	*Mar 12*
254	TX	72	241	*May 12*
255	KQ	73	241	*Nov 12*
256	GH	73	242	*May 13*
257	PU	74	243	*Aug 13*
258	Sales tax (1)	74	244	*Nov 07*
259	Excise duties (1)	74	244	*May 09*
260	Sales tax (2)	75	244	*May 10*
261	Sales tax (3)	75	245	*Sep 11*
262	Sales tax (4)	76	245	*Nov 11*
263	Sales tax (5)	76	246	*Mar 12*
264	Sales tax (6)	77	246	*Nov 12*
265	Excise duties (2)	77	247	*Feb 13*
266	Sales tax (7)	77	248	*May 13*
267	Sales tax (8)	78	248	*Aug 13*
268	Indirect tax	78	249	*May 12*
269	Capital gains	78	249	*May 11*
270	Avoidance v evasion	79	250	*May 10*
271	Tax base	79	250	*Nov 11*
272	Imputation system	79	250	*Mar 12*
273	Losses	79	251	*Nov 10*

INDEX TO QUESTIONS AND ANSWERS

		Page number		
		Question	*Answer*	*Past exam*
274	Powers	80	251	*Nov 12*
275	Benefits in kind	80	252	*Aug 13*
276	Withholding tax	80	252	*May 06*
277	Overseas (1)	80	253	*May 10*
278	Overseas (2)	81	253	*Nov 10*
279	Underlying tax	81	254	*May 11*
280	Double tax relief (1)	81	254	*Sep 11*
281	Double tax relief (2)	82	254	*Nov 12*

PRINCIPLES OF REGULATION OF FINANCIAL REPORTING

282	Development	82	255	*May 06*
283	Framework (1)	82	255	*May 07*
284	Framework (2)	82	256	*Nov 09*
285	External audit	83	256	*May 10*
286	Principle-based standards	83	256	*May 11*
287	Elements of financial statements	83	257	*May 05*
288	Assets and liabilities	83	257	*Sep 11*
289	Objectives and underlying assumptions	84	257	*May 11*
290	Influences on regulation	84	258	*Sep 11*
291	Ethics	84	259	*May 11*
292	Capital maintenance	84	259	*Nov 11*
293	Audit	85	260	*Nov 11*
294	Ethical problems (1)	85	260	*Nov 11*
295	Roles (1)	85	261	*Mar 12*
296	Audit objective and report	85	261	*Mar 12*
297	Ethical problems (2)	86	262	*Mar 12*
298	Benefits of external audit	86	262	*May 12*
299	Roles (2)	86	263	*Nov 12*
300	Purpose of the framework	86	263	*Feb 13*
301	Ethical dilemma	87	264	*May 13*
302	Ethical issues	87	264	*Aug 13*

SINGLE COMPANY FINANCIAL ACCOUNTS

303	DF	87	264	*Nov 06*
304	Statement of profit or loss	88	265	*May 06*
305	BJ	88	266	*Nov 05*
306	Tangible non-current assets	89	267	–
307	DW	90	267	–
308	BI	90	268	*Nov 05*
309	Revaluation	91	269	*Nov 06*

vii

PAPER F1 : FINANCIAL OPERATIONS

		Page number		
		Question	Answer	Past exam
310	Useful economic life	91	270	–
311	Decommissioning	92	270	–
312	Hotels	92	271	–
313	Development costs (1)	93	272	May 06
314	Development costs (2)	93	273	May 08
315	HF errors	94	273	May 09
316	Redeemable shares (1)	94	273	May 06
317	Redeemable shares (2)	95	274	May 08
318	Redeemable shares (3)	95	275	May 13
319	Share issues	95	275	Aug 13
320	CB importers	96	275	May 06
321	Related parties	96	276	Nov 07
322	AE	96	276	May 05
323	HS	97	277	May 09
324	CC	97	278	May 10
325	Intangibles	98	278	Nov 09
326	Earthquake	98	279	Nov 10
327	Shoe factory	99	279	May 10
328	Operating segments	99	280	Nov 12
329	Finance lease (1)	100	280	–
330	Finance lease (2)	100	281	May 05
331	Finance lease (3)	100	282	May 07
332	Closure (1)	101	283	May 07
333	Closure (2)	101	283	Nov 07
334	WZ	102	284	Sep 11
335	LP	103	284	Feb 13
336	Revenue recognition (1)	103	285	Nov 07
337	Revenue recognition (2)	104	285	Nov 09
338	Direct method	104	286	May 08
339	GK	105	287	Nov 08
340	Benefits of cash flow	107	288	May 12
341	Investing activities	107	289	May 13
342	Financing activities	108	290	Aug 13

GROUP COMPANY FINANCIAL ACCOUNTS

343	Goodwill	109	290	Nov 10
344	Investments	109	291	Nov 10

INDEX TO QUESTIONS AND ANSWERS

SECTION C-TYPE QUESTIONS
SINGLE COMPANY FINANCIAL ACCOUNTS

345	AF		111	293	*May 05*
346	DZ		113	296	*May 07*
347	EY		115	302	*Nov 07*
348	FZ		118	308	*May 08*
349	GZ		121	313	*Nov 08*
350	JZ		123	321	*Nov 09*
351	EZ		125	327	*May 10*
352	XB		127	331	*Nov 10*
353	MN		129	336	*May 11*
354	ZY		131	341	*Sep 11*
355	ABC		133	346	*Nov 11*
356	RTY		135	353	*Mar 12*
357	DFG		137	359	*May 12*
358	QWE		139	365	*Aug 12*
359	YZ		141	370	*Nov 12*
360	CQ		143	375	*Feb 13*
361	SA		145	380	*May 13*
362	BVQ		147	385	*Aug 13*
363	CJ		148	391	*May 06*
364	DN		151	394	*Nov 06*
365	HZ		153	397	*May 09*
366	YG		156	402	*Nov 10*
367	OP		158	405	*May 11*
368	UV		161	408	*Sep 11*

GROUP COMPANY FINANCIAL ACCOUNTS

369	Jasper		164	412	–
370	Hot		165	415	–
371	AX group		166	417	*May 10*
372	PH group		169	422	*Nov 11*
373	Tree group		171	426	*Mar 12*
374	Loch group		173	430	*May 12*
375	Wood group		175	434	*Aug 12*
376	AZ group		178	441	*Nov 12*
377	TX group		180	446	*Feb 13*
378	Club group		182	450	*May 13*
379	Road group		184	454	*Aug 13*

ANALYSIS OF PAST EXAM PAPERS

The table below summarises the key topics that have been tested in the new syllabus examinations to date.

	Specimen	May 10	Nov 10	May 11	Sept 11	Nov 11	Mar 12	May 12	Aug 12	Nov 12	Feb 13	May 13	Aug 13
Principles of Business Taxation													
1 Explain the types of tax that can apply to incorporated businesses, their principles and potential administrative requirements.	Q1	Q1, 2	Q1	Q1	Q1	Q1, 2	Q1, 2	Q1, 2	Q1	Q1, 2	Q1, 2	Q1, 2	Q1, 2
2 Explain fundamental concepts in international taxation of incorporated businesses.	Q2	Q2	Q2	Q1, 2	Q2		Q1	Q2	Q1, 2	Q2	Q1	Q1	Q1
3 Prepare corporate income tax calculations.	Q1, 2	Q2	Q3	Q2		Q1, 2	Q2	Q1	Q1, 2	Q2	Q2	Q1, 2	Q1
4 Apply the accounting rules for current and deferred taxation.	Q3	Q3, 4	Q3	Q2, 3	Q2, 3	Q2, 3	Q2, 3	Q2, 3	Q2, 3	Q1, 2, 3	Q1, 3	Q2, 3	Q2
Regulation and Ethics of Financial Reporting													
1 Explain the need for and methods of regulating accounting and financial reporting.	Q1, 2	Q1, 2	Q1, 2	Q2	Q2	Q2	Q2	Q1, 2	Q1, 2	Q1, 2	Q1, 2	Q1, 2	Q1
2 Apply the provisions of the CIMA Code of Ethics for Professional Accountants.	Q1	Q2	Q4	Q2	Q2	Q2	Q2	Q1	Q1	Q1	Q1	Q2	Q2
Financial Accounting and Reporting													
1 Preparation of the financial statements of a single company, as specified in IAS 1 (revised), including statement of changes in equity.	Q3	Q3	Q3	Q3	Q3	Q3	Q3	Q3	Q3	Q3	Q3	Q3	Q3
2 Preparation of the statement of cash flows (IAS 7).		Q1	Q4	Q4	Q4			Q2		Q1	Q1	Q2	Q2
3 Preparation of the consolidated statement of financial position and statement of comprehensive income where: interests are directly held by the acquirer (parent) company; any subsidiary is fully controlled; and all interests were acquired at the beginning of an accounting period (IFRS3 and IAS 27, to the extent that their provisions are relevant to the specified learning outcome).	Q1, 4	Q4	Q2	Q1	Q1	Q4	Q4	Q4	Q4	Q4	Q4	Q3	Q3

xi

PAPER F1 : FINANCIAL OPERATIONS

		Specimen	May 10	Nov 10	May 11	Sept 11	Nov 11	Mar 12	May 12	Aug 12	Nov 12	Feb 13	May 13	Aug 13
4	Apply international standard dealing with a range of matters and items:													
	IAS 2 – Inventory	Q1				Q3						Q3		
	IAS 8 – Accounting policies, changes and errors				Q1									
	IAS 10 – Events after the reporting period		Q3	Q2		Q3	Q1, 3	Q3			Q1			
	IAS 11 – Construction contracts		Q2				Q3			Q2				
	IAS 16 – Non-current assets	Q3	Q1,3	Q3	Q3	Q3,4	Q3	Q3	Q3	Q3	Q3	Q3	Q3	Q3
	IAS 17 – Leases	Q2	Q1, 3		Q4	Q3					Q3	Q3		Q3
	IAS 18 – Revenue recognition		Q1				Q1	Q1	Q3	Q1	Q1	Q1		
	IAS 24 – Related party transactions	Q1		Q1		Q1	Q1	Q1				Q1		
	IAS 32 – Financial Instruments	Q2		Q1		Q1, 3							Q2	Q2
	IAS 36 – Impairment		Q3											Q3
	IAS 37 – Provisions and contingencies			Q2		Q3		Q3		Q1, 3	Q2, 3			
	IAS 38 – Intangibles		Q1				Q1	Q3	Q3	Q3	Q3	Q3		
	IFRS 5 – Discontinuing operations and non-current assets held for sale	Q2	Q1, 2			Q3			Q1	Q1		Q2	Q3	Q3
	IFRS 8 – Operating segments			Q1	Q1		Q1	Q1		Q1	Q2			

EXAM TECHNIQUE

- Use the allocated **20 minutes reading and planning time** at the beginning of the exam to:
  - read the questions and examination requirements carefully, and
  - begin planning your answers.
- **Divide the time** you spend on questions in proportion to the marks on offer:
  - there are 1.8 minutes available per mark in the examination
  - within that, try to allow time at the end of each question to review your answer and address any obvious issues

  Whatever happens, always keep your eye on the clock and **do not over run on any part of any question!**
- Spend the last **five minutes** of the examination:
  - reading through your answers, and
  - **making any additions or corrections.**
- If you **get completely stuck** with a question:
  - leave space in your answer book, and
  - **return to it later.**
- Stick to the question and **tailor your answer** to what you are asked.
  - pay particular attention to the verbs in the question.
- If you do not understand what a question is asking, **state your assumptions**.

  Even if you do not answer in precisely the way the examiner hoped, you should be given some credit, if your assumptions are reasonable.
- You should do everything you can to make things easy for the marker.

  The marker will find it easier to identify the points you have made if your **answers are legible**.
- **Written questions**:

  Your answer should have:
  - a clear structure
  - a brief introduction, a main section and a conclusion.

  Be concise. It is better to write a little about a lot of different points than a great deal about one or two points.
- **Computations**:

  It is essential to include all your workings in your answers. Many computational questions require the use of a standard format e.g. net present value, adjusted present value.

  Be sure you know these formats thoroughly before the exam and use the layouts that you see in the answers given in this book and in model answers.
- **Reports, memos and other documents**:

  Some questions ask you to present your answer in the form of a report, a memo, a letter or other document.

  Make sure that you use the correct format – there could be easy marks to gain here.

PAPER F1 : FINANCIAL OPERATIONS

PAPER SPECIFIC INFORMATION

THE EXAM

FORMAT OF THE EXAM

		Number of marks
Section A:	A variety of compulsory objective test questions, each work 2 to 4 marks. Mini-scenarios may be given, to which a group of questions relate.	20
Section B:	Six compulsory short questions, each worth five marks. Short scenarios will be given, to which some or all questions relate.	30
Section C:	One or two compulsory questions.	50
		100

Total time allowed: 3 hours plus 20 minutes reading and planning time.

Note that questions will be drawn from all areas of the syllabus.

PASS MARK

The pass mark for all CIMA Qualification examination papers is 50%.

READING AND PLANNING TIME

Remember that all three hour CIMA examinations have an additional 20 minutes reading time.

CIMA GUIDANCE

CIMA guidance on the use of this time is as follows:

> This additional time is allowed at the beginning of the examination to allow candidates to read the questions and to begin planning their answers before they start to write in their answer books.
>
> This time should be used to ensure that all the information and, in particular, the exam requirements are properly read and understood.
>
> During this time, candidates may only annotate their question paper. They may not write anything in their answer booklets until told to do so by the invigilator.

PAPER F1 : FINANCIAL OPERATIONS

FURTHER GUIDANCE

During the 20 minutes of reading time you should be able to review the questions in the paper and decide which ones are most appealing. All students have different strengths and preferred topics, so it is impossible to give general advice on which questions should be chosen to do first. However, it is worth noting that numerical questions can often be more time consuming than written questions, so you are more likely to over run on numerical questions.

In relation to paper F1, we recommend that you take the following approach with your reading time:

- **Skim through Section B**, assessing the level of difficulty of each question. Try to decide which questions looks most appealing. Although all questions are compulsory it is important that you begin with your stronger areas, working towards your weaker areas.

- **Now focus on the Section C questions**. Work out how much time you should spend on each part of the requirements (using the measure of 1.8 minutes per mark). Decide which techniques you will need to attack each of the questions. These questions are generally the most time consuming so use your reading time to prepare yourself, i.e. read through the notes and write down what you will need to do, for example, "this is a non-current asset held for sale – value at the lower of carrying value or net selling price" You may find a highlighter useful to highlight the key points so you don't forget, for example, the question may tell you to charge all depreciation to cost of sales.

- **Turn to Section A**. If you have any time left skim through the requirement and decide what topics are being tested. As you skim through you may be able to answer some of the "wordy" questions.

- **Decide the order** in which you think you will attempt the questions:

    This is a personal choice and you have time on the revision phase to try out different approaches, for example, if you sit mock exams.

    A common approach is to tackle the question you think is the easiest and you are most comfortable with first.

    Others may prefer to tackle the longest question first, or conversely leave them to the last.

    It is usual however that students tackle their least favourite topic and/or the most difficult question in their opinion last. It is sensible to try to attack the preferred questions before attempting the difficult looking ones.

    Whatever you approach, you must make sure that you leave enough time to attempt all questions fully and be very strict with yourself in timing each question.

- **For each question** in turn, read the requirements and then the detail of the question carefully.

    Always read the requirement first as this enables you to **focus on the detail of the question with the specific task in mind**. Bear in mind the CIMA verb hierarchy.

    For computational questions:

    Highlight key numbers/information and key words in the question, scribble notes to yourself on the question paper to remember key points in your answer.

PAPER SPECIFIC INFORMATION

> **For written questions:**
>
> Take notice of the format required (e.g. letter, memo, notes) and identify the recipient of the answer. You need to do this to judge the level of financial sophistication required in your answer and whether the use of a formal reply or informal bullet points would be satisfactory.
>
> Plan your beginning, middle and end and the key areas to be addressed and your use of titles and sub-titles to enhance your answer.
>
> **For all questions:**
>
> Spot the easy marks to be gained in a question and parts which can be performed independently of the rest of the question.
>
> Make sure that you do these parts first when you tackle the question.
>
> Don't go overboard in terms of planning time on any one question – you need a good measure of the whole paper and a plan for all of the questions at the end of the 20 minutes.
>
> By covering all questions you can often help yourself as you may find that facts in one question may remind you of things you should put into your answer relating to a different question.
>
> - With your plan of attack in mind, **start answering your chosen question** with your plan to hand, as soon as you are allowed to start.

DETAILED SYLLABUS

The detailed syllabus and study guide written by CIMA can be found at:

www.CIMAGlobal.com

POST EXAM GUIDES (PEGs)

After each sitting, the examiners and lead markers produce a report for each paper outlining what they were looking for in the exam, how it related to the syllabus and highlights in detail what students did well and the areas that caused problems. This feedback is extremely useful to help you to focus on producing what the examiners want and thus increase your chances of passing the exams. The PEGs for F1 can be found here

http://www.cimaglobal.com/Students/Exam-preparation/Operational-level/F1-financial-operations/Post-exam-guides/

APPROACH TO REVISION

QUESTION PRACTICE IS THE KEY TO SUCCESS

Success in professional examinations relies upon you acquiring a firm grasp of the required knowledge at the tuition phase. In order to be able to do the questions, knowledge is essential.

However, the difference between success and failure often hinges on your exam technique on the day and making the most of the revision phase of your studies.

The **study text** is the starting point, designed to provide the underpinning knowledge to tackle all questions. However, in the revision phase, pouring over text books is not the answer.

The **online fixed tests** help you consolidate your knowledge and understanding and are a useful tool to check whether you can remember key topic areas.

Revision cards are designed to help you quickly revise a topic area; however you then need to practise questions. There is a need to progress to full exam standard questions as soon as possible, and to tie your exam technique and technical knowledge together.

The importance of question practice cannot be over-emphasised.

The recommended approach below is designed by expert tutors in the field, in conjunction with their knowledge of the examiner and their recent real exams.

The approach taken for the lower level papers is to revise by topic area. However, with the strategic level papers, a multi topic approach is required to answer the scenario based questions.

You need to practise as many questions as possible in the time you have left.

OUR AIM

Our aim is to get you to the stage where you can attempt exam standard questions confidently, to time, in a closed book environment, with no supplementary help (i.e. to simulate the real examination experience).

Practising your exam technique on real past examination questions, in timed conditions, is also vitally important for you to assess your progress and identify areas of weakness that may need more attention in the final run up to the examination.

In order to achieve this we recognise that initially you may feel the need to practise some questions with open book help and exceed the required time.

The approach below shows you which questions you should use to build up to coping with exam standard question practice, and references to the sources of information available should you need to revisit a topic area in more detail.

Remember that in the real examination, all you have to do is:

- attempt all questions required by the exam
- only spend the allotted time on each question, and
- get them at least 50% right!

Try to practise this approach on every question you attempt from now to the real exam.

THE F1 REVISION PLAN

Stage 1: Assess areas of strengths and weaknesses

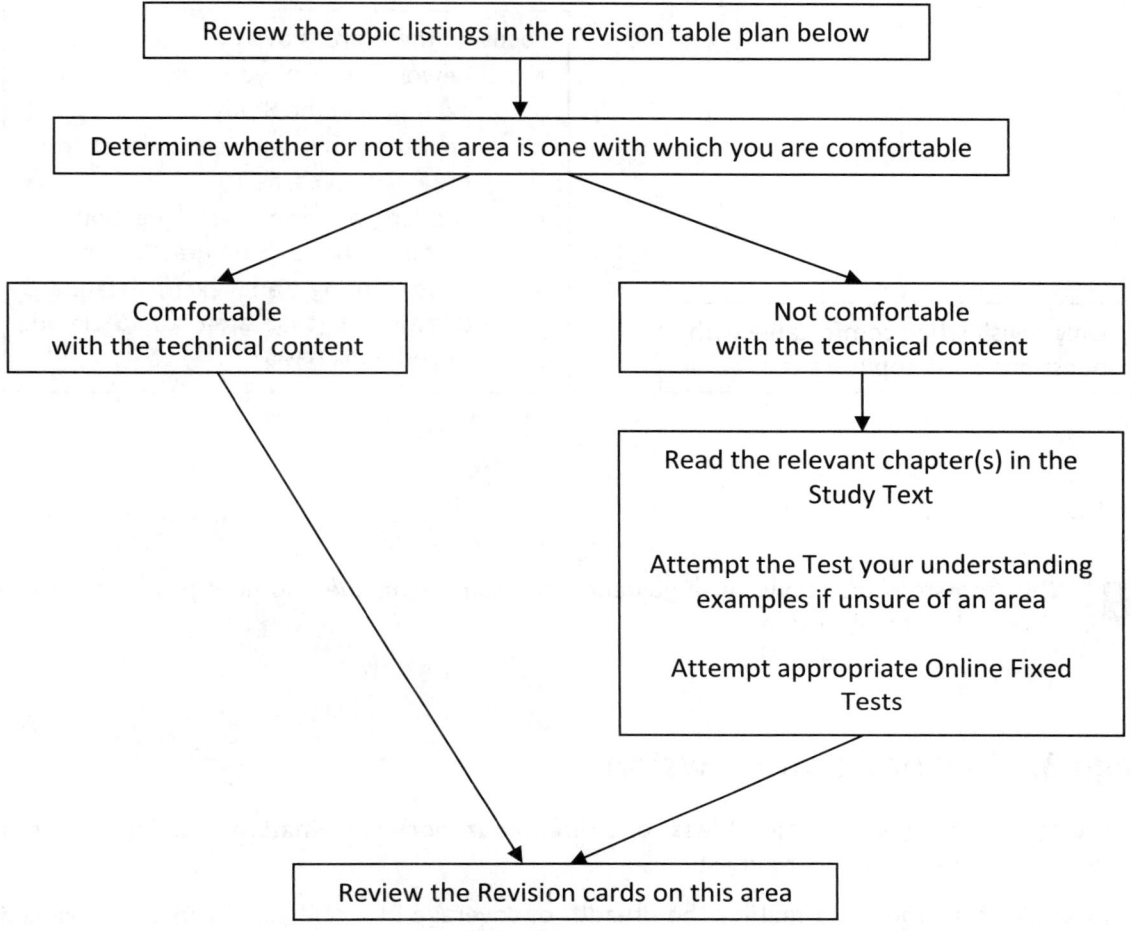

Stage 2: Practice questions

Follow the order of revision of topics as recommended in the revision table plan below and attempt the questions in the order suggested.

Try to avoid referring to text books and notes and the model answer until you have completed your attempt.

Try to answer the question in the allotted time.

Review your attempt with the model answer and assess how much of the answer you achieved in the allocated exam time.

PAPER F1 : FINANCIAL OPERATIONS

Fill in the self-assessment box below and decide on your best course of action.

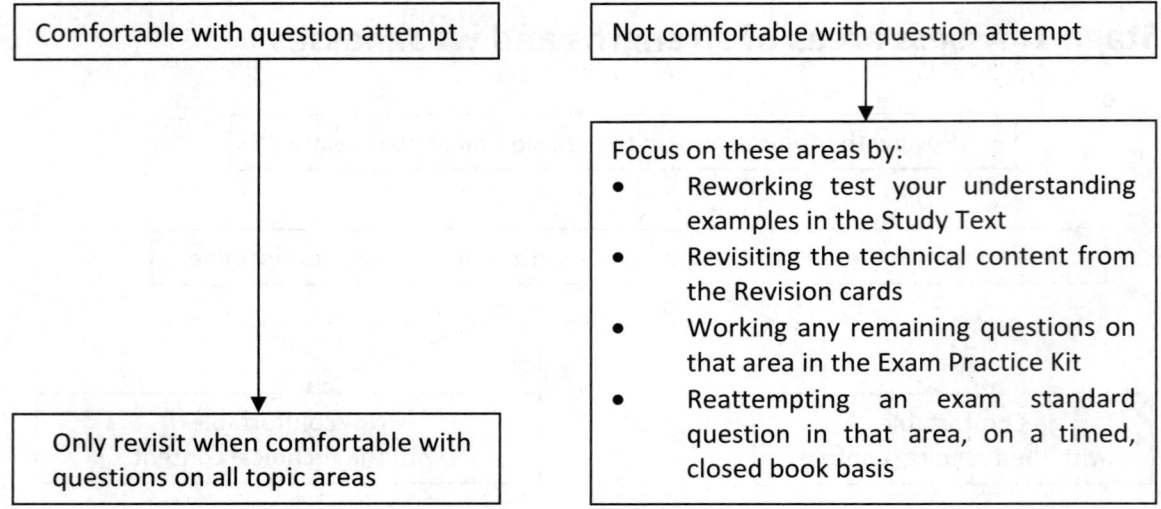

Note that :

 The "footsteps questions" give guidance on exam technique and how you should have approached the question.

Stage 3: Final pre-exam revision

We recommend that you **attempt at least one three hour mock examination** containing a set of previously unseen exam standard questions.

It is important that you get a feel for the breadth of coverage of a real exam without advanced knowledge of the topic areas covered – just as you will expect to see on the real exam day.

Ideally a mock examination offered by your tuition provider should be sat in timed, closed book, real exam conditions.

THE DETAILED REVISION PLAN

Module 1: Section A and B-style questions

Topic	Complete Text Chapter	Questions to attempt	Tutor guidance	Date attempted	Self assessment
Verbs	1	–	Before you start, remind yourself of the meaning of the key verbs you are likely to encounter. This will ensure that you always provide the level of detail that the examiner is looking for.		
Business Taxation	2	**Section A** 15, 17, 20–22, 24, 29, 32, 42–44, 46–50, 52–56, 67, 80, 86 **Section B** 243, 244, 248, 258-267, 269, 270, 273–277,	These questions will give you practice on the key topic areas of business taxation, i.e. adjusted profits, VAT and overseas taxation.		
Regulation and Conceptual Framework	8–9	**Section A** 89, 93, 94 **Section B** 284, 287, 299, 300	This is a difficult topic to revise as theory based and has quite a wide scope. Use these questions to grasp the key topic areas.		

xxiii

PAPER F1: FINANCIAL OPERATIONS

Topic	Complete Text Chapter	Questions to attempt	Tutor guidance	Date attempted	Self assessment
External Audit and Ethics	10–11	**Section A** 96, 99, 109 **Section B** 285, 291, 293, 297, 298, 301	Not a big topic area. Focus on the "objective of an audit" and the different types of audit reports.		
IAS 2 – Inventory	12	**Section A** 173–175	Not a big topic area, don't forget inventory is valued at the lower of cost or net realisable value,		
IAS 8 – Accounting Policies, changes and errors	12	**Section A** 143–148	Make sure you learn the difference between a change in policy, estimate and errors with examples.		
IAS10 – Events after the reporting date	12	**Section A** 194–199	Learn the examples of adjusting and non-adjusting events.		
IAS 18 – Revenue Recognition	12	**Section A** 218–222 **Section B** 336, 237	Learn the criteria to be met in order to recognise revenue from the sales of goods or services. In a section B question you will be required to state the criteria and then apply it to the given scenario.		
IAS 24 – Related Parties	12	**Section A** 183–185 **Section B** 320, 321	Learn the different types of related parties and the disclosure requirements.		
IAS 37 – Provisions and contingencies	12	**Section A** 200–203	Make sure you know the difference between a provision and a contingency. Learn the criteria for recognising a provision.		
IFRS 8 – Operating Segments	12	**Section B** 328	Not a big topic area. Learn the 10% and 75% rules.		

Topic	Complete Text Chapter	Questions to attempt	Tutor guidance	Date attempted	Self assessment
IAS 16 – Property, Plant and Equipment	13	**Section A** 150, 151, 156–158, 160, 162, 165, 172 **Section B** 306, 309	This is an important topic area and likely to be examined in all areas of the paper. Focus on revaluation adjustments and disposals of an asset.		
IAS 38 – Intangible assets	13	**Section A** 166–168, 171 **Section B** 313, 314	Focus on the criteria to be met to capitalise a development cost and the difference between development and research.		
IFRS 5 – Assets held for sale and discontinued operations	14	**Section B** 327, 332, 333, 335	This is a popular area in section C questions but these questions will cover the basics you need to know.		
IAS 11 – Construction contracts	15	**Section A** 188–193 **Section B** 322–324	These questions will give you practice on loss making and profit making contracts. Make sure you learn how to disclose information in the income statement and statement of financial position.		
IAS 12 – Taxation	16	**Section A** 75–78, 81, 84, 85, 87 **Section B** 250–257	This is an important topic area likely to be examined in all sections of the paper. Ensure you know how to calculate deferred tax and the extracts for the income statement and statement of financial position.		

PAPER F1 : FINANCIAL OPERATIONS

Topic	Complete Text Chapter	Questions to attempt	Tutor guidance	Date attempted	Self assessment
IAS17 – Leases and IAS 32 – Financial Instruments	17	**Section A** 1479, 204–209 **Section B** 317–319, 329, 331	Focus on the different treatment of an operating and finance lease. Make sure you read the question, are payments made in areas or advance?		

Module 2: Section C-style questions

Topic	Complete Text Chapter	Questions to attempt	Tutor guidance	Date attempted	Self assessment
Published Accounts	7	345–349, 351–353, 355, 357, 359, 361	These questions should be attempted once you have revised all of the accounting standards. Work through the notes first, thinking about the entries you need to make and then complete the proforma. Don't waste time on areas you are uncertain of, leave them and go back to them at the end if you have time.		
Group Accounts	3–6	371–379	Make sure you learn the standard workings 1–5 before you attempt these questions. Remember the difference between the treatment of a subsidiary and an associate.		
IAS 7 – Statement of Cash Flows	18	363–365, 367, 368	Although this topic could be examined in any section of the paper it is good practice to attempt the longer section C questions. Any questions set in sections A or B will be on part of the statement of cash flows.		

Note that not all of the questions are referred to in the programme above. The remaining questions are available in the kit for extra practice for those who require more questions on some areas.

Section 1

SECTION A-TYPE QUESTIONS

PRINCIPLES OF BUSINESS TAXATION

1   In no more than 15 words, define the meaning of 'competent jurisdiction'. **(2 marks)**

2   In no more than 20 words, define a taxable person. **(2 marks)**

3   Briefly define the meaning of "tax evasion"? **(2 marks)**

4   Double tax treaties provide for the relief of foreign tax by one of three methods. List TWO of the methods used to provide double tax relief. **(2 marks)**

5   Which ONE of the following could be said to be a progressive tax?

   A   Property sales tax of 1% of the selling price of all properties sold

   B   Value added tax at a rate of 0%, 10% or 15% depending on the type of goods or services provided

   C   Corporate wealth tax at 2% of total net assets up to $10 million then at 0.5% on net assets greater than $10 million

   D   Personal income tax of 10% on earnings up to $10,000, then at 15% from $10,001 up to $100,000 and 25% over $100,000 **(2 marks)**

6   An ideal tax system should conform to certain principles. Which one of the following statements IS NOT generally regarded as a principle of an ideal tax?

   A   It should be fair to different individuals and should reflect a person's ability to pay

   B   It should not be arbitrary, it should be certain

   C   It should raise as much money as possible for the government

   D   It should be convenient in terms of timing and payment **(2 marks)**

7   In no more than 15 words, complete the following sentence:

   'A direct tax is one that ….' **(2 marks)**

PAPER F1 : FINANCIAL OPERATIONS

8 List (using no more than five words per item) the four main sources of tax rules in a country.
(4 marks)

9 CR is resident in Country X. CR makes a taxable profit of $750,000 and pays an equity dividend of $350,000. CR pays tax on profits at a rate of 25%.

Equity shareholders pay tax on their dividend income at a rate of 30%.

If CR and its equity shareholders pay a total of $205,000 tax between them, what method of corporate income tax is being used in Country X?

- A The classical system
- B The imputation system
- C The partial imputation system
- D The split rate system

(2 marks)

10 Which ONE of the following is NOT a benefit of pay-as-you-earn (PAYE) method of tax collection?

- A It makes payment of tax easier for the tax payer as it is in instalments
- B It makes it easier for governments to forecast tax revenues
- C It benefits the tax payer as it reduces the tax payable
- D It improves government's cash flow as cash is received earlier

(2 marks)

11 Which ONE of the following is NOT a reason for governments to set deadlines for filing tax returns and payment of taxes?

- A To enable governments to enforce penalties for late payments
- B To ensure tax deducted at source by employers is paid over promptly
- C To ensure tax payers know when they have to make payment
- D To ensure that the correct amount of tax revenue is paid

(2 marks)

12 Which ONE of the following powers is a tax authority least likely to have granted to them?

- A Power of arrest
- B Power to examine records
- C Power of entry and search
- D Power to give information to other countries' tax authorities

(2 marks)

13 The OECD model tax convention defines a permanent establishment to include a number of different types of establishments:

(i) a place of management

(ii) a warehouse

(iii) a workshop

(iv) a quarry

(v) a building site that was used for nine months.

Which of the above are included in the OECD's list of permanent establishments?

A (i), (ii) and (iii) only

B (i), (iii) and (iv) only

C (ii), (iii) and (iv) only

D (iii), (iv) and (v) only **(2 marks)**

14 In Country Y, A earns $75,000 profit for the year and receives a tax bill for $17,000.

B earns $44,000 profit for the year and receives a tax bill for $4,800.

Country Y's income tax could be said to be a:

A Regressive tax

B Proportional tax

C Progressive tax

D Fixed rate tax **(2 marks)**

15 List THREE possible reasons why governments set deadlines for filing returns and/or paying taxes. **(3 marks)**

16 In 1776, Adam Smith proposed that an acceptable tax should meet four characteristics. Three of these characteristics were certainty, convenience and efficiency.

Identify the FOURTH characteristic.

A Neutrality

B Transparency

C Equity

D Simplicity **(2 marks)**

17 Country X uses a Pay-As-You-Earn (PAYE) system for collecting taxes from employees. Each employer is provided with information about each employee's tax position and tables showing the amount of tax to deduct each period. Employers are required to deduct tax from employees and pay it to the revenue authorities on a monthly basis.

From the perspective of the government, list THREE advantages of the PAYE system.

(3 marks)

PAPER F1 : FINANCIAL OPERATIONS

18 Excise duties are deemed to be most suitable for commodities that have certain specific characteristics.

List THREE characteristics of a commodity that, from a revenue authority's point of view, would make that commodity suitable for an excise duty to be imposed. **(3 marks)**

19 Tax deducted at source by employers from employees' earnings and paid to government, often called pay-as-you-earn (PAYE) has a number of advantages.

(i) Most of the administration costs are borne by the employer.

(ii) Employers may delay payment or fail to pay over PAYE deducted from employees.

(iii) Employers may be inefficient and not deduct any tax or deduct the wrong amount from employees.

(iv) Government receives a higher proportion of the tax due as defaults and late payments are fewer.

Which TWO of the above are NOT likely to be seen as an advantage of PAYE by the government?

A (i) and (ii)

B (ii) and (iii)

C (ii) and (iv)

D (iii) and (iv) **(2 marks)**

20 What is 'Hypothecation'?

A Process of earmarking tax revenues for specific types of expenditure

B Estimation of tax revenue made by the tax authorities for budget purposes

C Refund made by tax authorities for tax paid in other countries

D Payment of taxes due to tax authorities, net of tax refunds due from tax authorities **(2 marks)**

21 The 'tax gap' is the difference between:

A when a tax payment is due and the date it is actually paid

B the tax due calculated by the entity and the tax demanded by the tax authority

C the amount of tax due to be paid and the amount actually collected

D the date when the entity was notified by the tax authority of the tax due and the date the tax should be paid **(2 marks)**

22 Developed countries generally use three tax bases. One tax base widely used is income.

List the other TWO widely used tax bases **(2 marks)**

23 Which TWO of the following are most likely to encourage an increase in incidence of tax avoidance or tax evasion?

- (i) High penalties for tax evasion.
- (ii) Imprecise and vague tax laws.
- (iii) A tax system that is seen as fair to everyone.
- (iv) Very high tax rates.

A (i) and (ii)
B (ii) and (iii)
C (ii) and (iv)
D (iii) and (iv)

(2 marks)

24 Which ONE of the following is NOT an advantage for the tax authority of deduction of tax at source?

A The total amount of tax due for the period is easier to calculate
B Tax is collected earlier
C Administration costs are borne by the entity deducting tax
D Tax is deducted before income is paid to the taxpayer

(2 marks)

25 HD sells office stationery and adds a sales tax to the selling price of all products sold. A customer purchases goods from HD has to pay the cost of the goods plus the sales tax. HD pays the sales tax collected to the tax authorities.

From the perspective of HD the sales tax would be said to have:

A formal incidence
B effective incidence
C informal incidence
D ineffective incidence

(2 marks)

26 Which ONE of the following defines the meaning of "tax gap"?

A The difference between the tax an entity expects to pay and the amount notified by the tax authority
B The difference between the total amount of tax due to be paid and the amount actually collected by the tax authority
C The difference between the due date for tax payment and the date it is actually paid
D The difference between the amount of tax provided in the financial statements and the amount actually paid

(2 marks)

PAPER F1 : FINANCIAL OPERATIONS

27 Which ONE of the following would be considered to be an example of an indirect tax?

    A   An entity assessed for corporate income tax on its profit

    B   An individual purchases goods in a shop, the price includes VAT

    C   An employee has tax deducted from salary through the PAYE system

    D   An individual pays capital gains tax on a gain arising on the disposal of an investment

(2 marks)

28 Which ONE of the following would cause a deferred tax balance to be included in the statement of financial position for an entity, as required by IAS 12 *Income Taxes*?

    A   An expense that is included in the statement of profit or loss and other comprehensive income but is not allowed for tax

    B   A non-current asset that does not qualify for tax depreciation

    C   Tax depreciation being allowed on a non-current asset at a different annual rate to that used for depreciation in the financial statements

    D   Impairment of goodwill that arose on the acquisition of a subsidiary entity **(2 marks)**

29 CFP, an entity resident in Country X, had an accounting profit for the year ended 31 December 20X1 of $860,000. The accounting profit was after charging depreciation of $42,000 and amortisation of development costs of $15,000 which should be treated as disallowable expenses.

CFP was entitled to a tax depreciation allowance of $51,000 for the year to 31 December 20X1.

Tax is charged at 25%.

CFP's tax payable for the year ended 31 December 20X1 is:

    A $202,250

    B $206,500

    C $212,750

    D $216,500 **(2 marks)**

30 Which ONE of the following defines the meaning of "hypothecation"?

    A   A new tax law has to be passed each year to allow taxes to be legally collected

    B   The difference between the total amount of tax due to be paid and the amount actually collected by the tax authority

    C   Tax is deducted from amounts due before they are paid to the recipient

    D   The products of certain taxes are devoted to specific types of public expenditure

(2 marks)

SECTION A-TYPE QUESTIONS : SECTION 1

31 Which ONE of the following would NOT normally be considered a principle of a modern tax system?

    A   Efficiency

    B   Equity

    C   Economic impact

    D   Raise revenues   (2 marks)

32 Complete the following sentence.

Under the OECD model tax convention an entity will generally have residence for tax purposes in ………………………………………………………………………… .   (2 marks)

33 An entity earns a profit of $60,000 for the year to 31 March 20X2. The entity is assessed as owing $15,000 tax for the year.

Which ONE of the following types of tax would best describe the tax due?

    A   Capital tax

    B   Income tax

    C   Wealth tax

    D   Consumption tax   (2 marks)

34 List TWO possible powers that a tax authority may be granted to enable it to enforce tax regulations.   (2 marks)

35 Taxes commonly used by many countries include:

    (i)   import duty payable on specific types of imported goods

    (ii)   individual income tax, usually deducted at source

    (iii)   corporate income tax

    (iv)   value added tax.

Which of the above would normally be defined as direct taxation?

    A   (i) and (ii)

    B   (i) and (iv)

    C   (ii) and (iii)

    D   (ii) and (iv)   (2 marks)

36 An entity makes a taxable profit of $500,000 and pays corporate income tax at 25%.

The entity pays a dividend to its shareholders. A shareholder receiving $5,000 dividend then pays the standard personal income tax rate of 15% on the dividend, paying a further $750 tax.

The tax system could be said to be:

A   A classical system

B   An Imputation system

C   A partial imputation system

D   A split rate system   (2 marks)

37 **Tax authorities use various methods to reduce tax avoidance and tax evasion.**

(i)   Increase tax rates to compensate for losses due to evasion.

(ii)   Make the tax structure as complicated as possible.

(iii)   Increase the perceived risk by auditing tax returns.

(iv)   Simplify the tax structure, minimising allowances and exemptions.

Which of the above methods could be used to help reduce tax evasion and avoidance?

A   (i) and (ii)

B   (i) and (iv)

C   (ii) and (iii)

D   (iii) and (iv)   (2 marks)

38 **Define the term "tax avoidance"**   (2 marks)

39 **Accounting depreciation is usually disallowed when calculating tax due by an entity and a deduction for tax depreciation is given instead.**

Explain ONE reason why accounting depreciation is replaced with tax depreciation in a tax computation?   (2 marks)

40 **A customer purchases goods for $115, inclusive of VAT. From the customer's point of view the VAT could be said to be:**

A   a direct tax with formal incidence

B   an indirect tax with formal incidence

C   a direct tax with effective incidence

D   an indirect tax with effective incidence   (2 marks)

SECTION A-TYPE QUESTIONS : SECTION 1

41 AE purchases products from a foreign entity and imports them into a country A. On import, the products are subject to an excise duty of $5 per item and sales tax of 15% on cost plus excise duty.

AE purchased 200 items for $30 each and after importing them sold all of the items for $50 each plus sales tax at 15%.

How much sales tax is due to be paid to the tax authorities for these transactions?

- A $450
- B $1,450
- C $2,050
- D $2,500

(3 marks)

42 **Country Z has a VAT system which allows entities to reclaim input tax paid.**

In Country Z, the VAT rates are:

Zero rated   0%

Standard rated   15%

FE owns and runs a small retail store. The store's sales include items that are zero rated, standard rated and exempt.

FE's electronic cash register provides an analysis of sales. The figures for the three months to 30 April 20X8 were:

	Sales value, including VAT where appropriate $
Zero rated	13,000
Standard rated	18,400
Exempt	11,000
Total	42,400

FE's analysis of expenditure for the same period provided the following:

	Expenditure, excluding VAT $
Zero rated purchases	6,000
Standard rated purchases relating to standard rate outputs	10,000
Standard rated purchases relating to zero rate outputs	4,000
Standard rated purchases relating to exempt outputs	5,000
	25,000

Calculate the VAT due to/from FE for the three months ended 30 April 20X8.   **(3 marks)**

43 Country Z has a VAT system where VAT is charged on all goods and services. Registered VAT entities are allowed to recover input VAT paid on their purchases.

VAT operates at three different levels in Z:

- Standard rate   15%
- Luxury rate   22%
- Zero rate   0%

During the last VAT period, an entity, GW, purchased materials and services costing $138,000, including VAT. All materials and services were at standard rate VAT.

GW converted the materials into two products A and B; product A is zero-rated and product B is luxury-rated for VAT purposes.

During the VAT period, GW made the following sales, including VAT:

A $70,000

B $183,000

At the end of the period, GW paid the net VAT due to the tax authorities.

Assume no opening or closing inventory balances.

Assuming GW had no other VAT-related transactions, calculate GW's profit and the amount of VAT that GW paid? **(4 marks)**

44 HN purchases products from a foreign country. The products cost $14 each and are subject to excise duty of $3 per item and VAT at 15%.

If HN imports 1,000 items, how much does it pay to the tax authorities for this transaction?

A $2,100

B $5,100

C $5,550

D $19,550 **(2 marks)**

45 P is a trader resident in Country X. P imports products from a foreign country. Each unit costs $15.00 to purchase and on import is subject to excise duty of $3.00 per unit. P also has to pay VAT at 15% on all imports. If P imports 2,000 units how much would the tax authorities be due on import?

A $4,500

B $6,000

C $10,500

D $11,400 **(2 marks)**

46 UF manufactures clothing and operates in Country X. UF and ZF are both registered for VAT.

UF manufactures a batch of clothing and pays expenses (taxable inputs at standard rate) of $1,000 plus VAT. UF sells the batch of clothing to a retailer ZF for $2,875 including VAT at standard rate. ZF sells the clothing items separately to various customers for a total of $6,900 including VAT at 15%.

Calculate how much VAT UF and ZF each has to pay in respect of the above transactions? **(2 marks)**

SECTION A-TYPE QUESTIONS : SECTION 1

47 CU manufactures clothing and operates in a country that has a sales tax system. The sales tax system allows entities to reclaim input tax that they have paid on taxable supplies. Sales tax is at 15% of the selling price at all stages of the manufacturing and distribution chain.

CU manufactures a batch of clothing and pays expenses (taxable inputs) of $100,000 plus sales tax. CU sells the batch of clothing to a retailer CZ for $250,000 plus sales tax. CZ unpacks the clothing and sells the items separately to various customers for a total of $600,000 plus sales tax.

How much sales tax do CU and CZ each have to pay in respect of this one batch of clothing?

(2 marks)

Data for Questions 48 and 49

Country D uses a sales tax system whereby sales tax is charged on all goods and services at a rate of 15%. Entities registered for sales tax are allowed to recover input sales tax paid on their purchases.

Country E uses a multi-stage sales tax system, where a cumulative tax is levied every time a sale is made. The tax rate is 7% and tax paid on purchases is not recoverable.

DA is a manufacturer and sells products to DB, a retailer, for $500 excluding tax. DB sells the products to customers for a total of $1,000 excluding tax.

DA paid $200 plus sales tax for the manufacturing cost of its products.

---

48 Assume DA operates in Country D and sells products to DB in the same country.

Calculate the net sales tax due to be paid by DA and DB for the products. **(2 marks)**

49 Assume DA operates in Country E and sells products to DB in the same country.

Calculate the **total** sales tax due to be paid on all of the sales of the products. **(2 marks)**

50 Country Y has a sales tax system which allows entities to reclaim input tax paid.

In Country Y the sales tax rates are:

Zero rated   0%

Standard rated   15%

DE runs a small retail store. DE's sales include items that are zero rated, standard rated and exempt.

DE's electronic cash register provides an analysis of sales. The figures for the three months to 30 April 20X7 were:

	Sales value, excluding sales tax
	$
Zero rated	11,000
Standard rated	15,000
Exempt	13,000
Total	39,000

DE's analysis of expenditure for the same period provided the following:

	Expenditure, excluding sales tax $
Zero rated purchases	5,000
Standard rated purchases relating to standard rate outputs	9,000
Standard rated purchases relating to exempt outputs	7,000
Standard rated purchases relating to zero rated outputs	3,000
	24,000

Calculate the sales tax due to be paid to/from DE for the three months ended 30 April 20X7.

(2 marks)

51 **Trading losses in any period can be carried back and set off against profits in the previous 12-month period, and any unrelieved losses can be carried forward to set against profits in future years. Trading losses cannot be set off against capital gains. Capital losses can be set off against capital gains in the same tax year, but unrelieved capital losses cannot be carried back. Unrelieved capital losses may be carried forward and set against capital gains in future years.**

QWE had the following taxable profits, gains and losses in years 1 to 4.

	Trading profits/(losses) $	Capital gains/(losses) $
Year 1	50,000	6,000
Year 2	(90,000)	(8,000)
Year 3	30,000	5,000
Year 4	70,000	6,000

What are its taxable profits and gains in each year?

Year 1 _____

Year 2 _____

Year 3 _____

Year 4 _____

(4 marks)

52 **What is the nature of group loss relief?**

A Profits and losses of all companies in the same group are consolidated and taxed at the same rate

B Losses of subsidiaries must be set off against the profits of the parent company in the group

C Members of the group may surrender their losses to any other member of the group

D Companies in the same group are required by the tax authorities to surrender their losses to any other subsidiary in the group

(2 marks)

53 Country B has a corporate income tax system that treats capital gains/losses separately from trading profits/losses. Capital gains/losses cannot be offset against trading profits/losses. All losses can be carried forward indefinitely, but cannot be carried back to previous years. Trading profits and capital gains are both taxed at 20%.

BD had no brought forward losses on 1 October 20X2. BD's results for 20X3 to 20X5 were as follows:

	Trading profit/(loss)	Capital gains/(loss)
	$000	$000
Year to September 20X3	200	(100)
Year to September 20X4	(120)	0
Year to September 20X5	150	130

Calculate BD's corporate income tax due for each of the years ended 30 September 20X3 to 20X5. **(3 marks)**

54 State TWO reasons why a group of entities might want to claim group loss relief rather than use the loss in the entity to which it relates. Group loss relief is where, for tax purposes, the loss for the year of one entity in the group is offset against the profit of the year of one or more other entities in the group. **(2 marks)**

55 BCF purchased an asset for $600,000 on 1 September 20X4. BCF incurred additional purchase costs of $5,000.

Indexation of the cost of BCF's asset is allowed in Country X. The relevant index increased by 60% in the period from 1 September 20X4 to 31 August 20Y1.

BCF sold the asset on 1 September 20Y1 for $1,200,000. BCF incurred selling costs of $9,000.

Assume all purchase and selling costs are tax allowable.

Tax is charged at 25%.

How much tax was due from BCF on disposal of its asset?

A $55,750

B $56,500

C $64,250

D $146,500 **(2 marks)**

56 EG purchased a property for $630,000 on 1 September 20X0. EG incurred additional costs for the purchase of $3,500 surveyors' fees and $6,500 legal fees. EG then spent $100,000 renovating the property prior to letting it. All of EG's expenditure was classified as capital expenditure according to the local tax regulations.

Indexation of the purchase and renovation costs is allowed on EE's property. The index increased by 50% between September 20X0 and October 20X7. Assume that acquisition and renovation costs were incurred in September 20X0. EG sold the property on 1 October 20X7 for $1,250,000, incurring tax allowable costs on disposal of $2,000.

Calculate EG's tax due on disposal assuming a tax rate of 30%. **(3 marks)**

57 CG purchased an asset on 1 April 20X6 for $650,000, exclusive of import duties of $25,000. CG is resident in Country X where the indexation factor increased by 50% in the period from 1 April 20X6 to 31 March 20Y3.

CG sold the asset on 31 March 20Y3 for $1,200,000 incurring transaction charges of $17,000.

Capital gains are taxed at 25%.

Calculate the capital gains tax due from CG on disposal of the asset. **(2 marks)**

58 RS purchased an asset on 1 April 20X0 for $375,000, incurring legal fees of $12,000. RS is resident in Country X. There was no indexation allowed on the asset.

RS sold the asset on 31 March 20X3 for $450,000 incurring transaction charges of $15,000.

Tax is charged at 25%.

Calculate the capital gains tax due from RS on disposal of the asset. **(2 marks)**

59 The OECD Model tax convention defines a permanent establishment.

Which ONE of the following is not specifically listed as a "permanent establishment" by the OECD Model tax convention?

- A An office
- B A factory
- C An oil well
- D A site of an 11 month construction project **(2 marks)**

60 Where a resident entity runs an overseas operation as a branch of the entity, certain tax implications arise.

Which ONE of the following does **not** usually apply in relation to an overseas branch?

- A Assets can be transferred to the branch without triggering a capital gain
- B Corporate income tax is paid on profits remitted by the branch
- C Tax depreciation can be claimed on any qualifying assets used in the trade of the branch
- D Losses sustained by the branch are immediately deductible against the resident entity's income **(2 marks)**

61 A withholding tax is:

- A tax withheld from payment to the tax authorities
- B tax paid less an amount withheld from payment
- C tax deducted at source before payment of interest or dividends
- D tax paid on increases in value of investment holdings **(2 marks)**

62 An entity, DP, in Country A receives a dividend from an entity in Country B. The gross dividend of $50,000 is subject to a withholding tax of $5,000 and $45,000 is paid to DP. Country A levies a tax of 12% on overseas dividends.

Country A and Country B have both signed a double taxation treaty based on the OECD model convention and both apply the credit method when relieving double taxation.

How much tax would DP be expected to pay in Country A on the dividend received from the entity in Country B?

- A $400
- B $1,000
- C $5,400
- D $6,000

(2 marks)

63 ASD is a company resident in Country X. It has declared a dividend of $3 million. FGH, a company resident in Country Y owns 80% of ASD's share capital. Withholding tax is levied at 15%.

What is the amount of withholding tax that should be deducted from the dividend paid to FGH?

(2 marks)

64 The Organisation of Economic Co-operation and Development's (OECD) model tax convention defines corporate residence.

In no more than 15 words complete the following sentence:

Under the OECD model an entity will have residence ....

(2 marks)

65 Corporate residence for tax purposes can be determined in a number of ways, depending on the country concerned.

Which ONE of the following is NOT normally used to determine corporate residence for tax purposes?

- A The country from which control of the entity is exercised
- B The country of incorporation of the entity
- C The country where the management of the entity holds its meetings
- D The country where most of the entity's products are sold

(2 marks)

66 **The following details relate to EA:**

- it was incorporated in Country A
- it carries out its main business activities in Country B
- its senior management operate from Country C and effective control is exercised from Country C.

Assume countries A, B and C have all signed double tax treaties with each other, based on the OECD model tax convention.

In which country will EA be deemed to be resident for tax purposes?

A   Country A
B   Country B
C   Country C
D   Both Countries B and C   (2 marks)

67 **EB has an investment of 25% of the equity shares in XY, an entity resident in a foreign country.**

EB receives a dividend of $90,000 from XY, the amount being after the deduction of withholding tax of 10%.

XY had profits before tax for the year of $1,200,000 and paid corporate income tax of $200,000.

How much underlying tax can EB claim for double taxation relief?   (3 marks)

68 **Double tax relief is used to:**

A   ensure that you do not pay tax twice on any of your income
B   mitigate taxing overseas income twice
C   avoid taxing dividends received from subsidiaries in the same country twice
D   provide relief where a company pays tax at double the normal rate   (2 marks)

69 **The following details are relevant:**

- HC carries out its main business activities in Country A
- HC is incorporated in Country B
- HC's senior management exercise control from Country C, but there are no sales or purchases made in Country C
- HC raises its finance and is quoted on the stock exchange in Country D.

Assume Countries A, B, C and D have all signed double taxation treaties with each other, based on the OECD model tax convention.

Which country will HC be deemed to be resident in for tax purposes?

A   Country A
B   Country B
C   Country C
D   Country D   (2 marks)

70 AB made a profit of $320,000 for the year ended 31 December 20X2 and paid $80,000 tax on its profits. AB pays a gross dividend of $150,000 to its holding company, which operates in a foreign country. When AB pays the dividend it deducts a 10% tax. This 10% tax is called:

    A   underlying tax

    B   corporate income tax

    C   foreign tax

    D   withholding tax   **(2 marks)**

71 List TWO of the main methods of giving double taxation relief.   **(2 marks)**

72 Which ONE of the following gives the meaning of rollover relief?

    A   Trading losses can be carried forward to future years

    B   Inventory can be valued using current values instead of original cost

    C   Capital losses made in a period can be carried forward to future years

    D   Payment of tax on a capital gain can be delayed if the full proceeds from the sale of an asset are reinvested in a replacement asset   **(2 marks)**

73 FD purchased an item of plant and machinery costing $600,000 on 1 April 20X5, which qualified for 50% capital allowances in the first year and 25% per year thereafter, on the reducing balance basis.

FD's policy in respect of plant and machinery is to charge depreciation on a straight line basis over five years, with no residual value.

On 1 April 20X7, FD carried out an impairment review of all its non-current assets. This item of plant and machinery was found to have a value in use of $240,000. FD adjusted its financial records and wrote the plant and machinery down to its value in use on 1 April 20X7.

Assuming there are no other temporary differences in the period and a tax rate of 25% per annum over the five years, calculate the amount of any deferred tax balances outstanding at 31 March 20X7 and 31 March 20X8. (work to the nearest $1,000).   **(4 marks)**

74 A company purchased an item of plant on 1 July 20X2 for $600,000. This asset is eligible for tax depreciation (capital allowances) at 20% each year, calculated by the reducing balance method. In the financial accounts, the annual depreciation charge is $80,000. On 1 July 20X5, the plant was sold for $300,000. The rate of tax on company profits is 40%. The company's year end is 30 June.

By how much will the tax charge for the year be increased or reduced as a consequence of the asset disposal?   **(3 marks)**

PAPER F1 : FINANCIAL OPERATIONS

75 CY had the following amounts for 20X3 to 20X5:

Year ended 31 December:	20X3	20X4	20X5
	$	$	$
Accounting depreciation for the year	1,630	1,590	1,530
Tax depreciation allowance for the year	2,120	1,860	1,320

At 31 December 20X2, CY had the following balances brought forward:

	$
Cost of property, plant and equipment qualifying for tax depreciation	20,000
Accounting depreciation	5,000
Tax depreciation	12,500

CY had no non-current asset acquisitions or disposals during the period 20X3 to 20X5.

Assume the corporate income tax rate is 25% for all years.

Calculate the deferred tax provision required by IAS 12 *Income Taxes* at 31 December 20X5.

(3 marks)

76 HF purchased an asset on 1 April 20X7 for $220,000. HF claimed a first year tax allowance of 30% and then an annual 20% writing down allowance, using the reducing balance method.

HF depreciates the asset over eight years using straight line depreciation, assuming no residual value.

On 1 April 20X8, HF revalued the asset and increased the carrying value by $50,000. The asset's useful life was not affected.

Assume there are no other temporary differences in the period and a rate of tax of 25% per annum.

Calculate the amount of deferred tax movement in the year ended 31 March 20X9 and the deferred tax balance at 31 March 20X9, in accordance with IAS 12 *Income Taxes*. **(4 marks)**

77 On 31 March 20X6, CH had a credit balance brought forward on its deferred tax account of $642,000. There was also a credit balance on its corporate income tax account of $31,000, representing an over-estimate of the tax charge for the year ended 31 March 20X5.

CH's taxable profit for the year ended 31 March 20X6 was $946,000. CH's directors estimated the deferred tax provision required at 31 March 20X6 to be $759,000 and the applicable income tax rate for the year to 31 March 20X6 as 22%.

Calculate the income tax expense that CH will charge in its statement of profit or loss for the year ended 31 March 20X6, as required by IAS 12 *Income Taxes*. **(3 marks)**

78 DZ recognised a tax liability of $290,000 in its financial statements for the year ended 30 September 20X5. This was subsequently agreed with and paid to the tax authorities as $280,000 on 1 March 20X6. The directors of DZ estimate that the tax due on the profits for the year to 30 September 20X6 will be $320,000. DZ has no deferred tax liability.

What is DZ's statement of profit or loss tax charge for the year ended 30 September 20X6?

A $310,000

B $320,000

C $330,000

D $600,000 (2 marks)

79 An item of equipment cost $60,000 on 1 April 20X7. The equipment is depreciated at 20% per annum on a reducing basis. Tax depreciation is calculated as 50% in the year of purchase and 25% thereafter on a reducing balance basis.

Corporate tax is charged at 25%.

The amount of deferred tax relating to this asset that should be recognised in the statement of financial position as at 31 March 20Y0 is:

A $1,781

B $3,461

C $3,975

D $13,845 (2 marks)

80 The tax year runs from 1 May to 30 April. An individual's accounting year ends on 31 December. Its taxable profits for the year to 31 December 20X4 were $75,000.

The rate of tax chargeable on company profits is as follows:

Year to 30 April 20X4   20%
Year to 30 April 20X5   25%

On the basis of this information, what amount of tax is payable for the tax year to 30 April 20X5? (2 marks)

81 JC purchases an item of plant and machinery costing $900,000 on 1 October 20X7, which qualifies for 50% tax allowances in the first year and 25% thereafter, on the reducing balance basis.

JC'S policy in respect of plant and machinery is to charge depreciation on a straight line basis over eight years. The residual value is estimated at $100,000.

Assume there are no other temporary differences in the period and a tax rate of 25%.

Calculate the amount of any deferred tax balance at 30 September 20X9. (3 marks)

PAPER F1 : FINANCIAL OPERATIONS

82 E has an accounting profit before tax of $95,000. The tax rate on trading profits applicable to E for the year is 25%. The accounting profit included non-taxable income from government grants of $15,000 and non-tax allowable expenditure of $10,000 on entertaining expenses.

How much tax is E due to pay for the year? **(2 marks)**

83 D purchased a non-current asset on 1 April 20X1 for $200,000. The asset attracted writing down tax allowances at 25% on the reducing balance. Depreciation was 10% on the straight-line basis. Assume income tax is at 30%.

The deferred tax balance for this asset at 31 March 20X4 is:

- A $9,000
- B $16,688
- C $27,000
- D $55,625 **(2 marks)**

84 BC, a small entity, purchased its only non-current tangible asset on 1 October 20X3. The asset cost $900,000, all of which qualified for tax depreciation.

BC's asset qualified for an accelerated first year tax allowance of 50%. The second and subsequent years qualified for tax depreciation at 25% per year on the reducing balance method.

BC's accounting depreciation policy is to depreciate the asset over its useful economic life of five years, assuming a residual value of $50,000.

Assume that BC pays tax on its income at the rate of 30%.

Calculate BC's deferred tax balance required in the statement of financial position as at 30 September 20X5 according to IAS 12 *Income Taxes.* **(4 marks)**

85 DD purchased an item of plant and machinery costing $500,000 on 1 April 20X4, which qualified for 50% capital allowances in the first year, and 20% each year thereafter, on the reducing balance basis.

DD's policy in respect of plant and machinery is to charge depreciation on a straight line basis over five years, with no residual value. On 1 April 20X6, DD decided to revalue the item of plant and machinery upwards, from its carrying value, by $120,000.

Assuming there are no other capital transactions in the three year period and a tax rate of 30% throughout, calculate the amount of deferred tax to be shown in DD's statement of profit or loss for the year ended 31 March 20X7, and the deferred tax provision to be included in its statement of financial position at 31 March 20X7. **(4 marks)**

86 EE reported accounting profits of $822,000 for the period ended 30 November 20X7. This was after deducting entertaining expenses of $32,000 and a donation to a political party of $50,000, both of which are disallowable for tax purposes.

EE's reported profit also included $103,000 government grant income that was exempt from taxation. EE paid dividends of $240,000 in the period.

Assume EE had no temporary differences between accounting profits and taxable profits.

Assume that a classical tax system applies to EE's profits and that the tax rate is 25%.

What would EE's tax payable be on its profits for the year to 30 November 20X7?

(2 marks)

87 A government wanted to encourage investment in new non-current assets by entities and decided to change tax allowances for non-current assets to give a 100% first year allowance on all new non-current assets purchased after 1 January 20X5.

ED purchased new machinery for $400,000 on 1 October 20X5 and claimed the 100% first year allowance. For accounting purposes ED depreciated the machinery on the reducing balance basis at 25% per year. The rate of corporate income tax to be applied to ED's taxable profits was 22%.

Assume ED had no other temporary differences.

Calculate the amount of deferred tax that ED would show in its statement of financial position as at 30 September 20X7.

(3 marks)

88 At 1 October 20X1 DX had the following balances in respect of property, plant and equipment:

Cost $220,000

Tax written down value $82,500

Statement of financial position: Carrying value $132,000

DX depreciates all property, plant and equipment over 5 years using the straight line method and no residual value. All assets were less than 5 years old at 1 October 20X1.

No assets were purchased or sold during the year ended 30 September 20X2.

Tax depreciation is deductible as follows:

- 50% of additions to property, plant and equipment in the accounting period in which they are recorded
- 25% per year of the written-down value (i.e. cost minus previous allowances) in subsequent accounting periods except that in which the asset is disposed of.

The corporate tax on profits is at a rate of 25%.

DX's deferred tax balance (to the nearest $) in its statement of financial position at 30 September 20X2 will be:

A $5,843

B $6,531

C $12,375

D $23,375

(2 marks)

PAPER F1 : FINANCIAL OPERATIONS

PRINCIPLES OF REGULATION OF FINANCIAL REPORTING

89 The IASB's *The Conceptual Framework for Financial Reporting* defines elements of financial statements.

In no more than 30 words define an asset. **(2 marks)**

90 In connection with the role of the external auditor, which of the following statements are CORRECT?

- (i) The auditor certifies that the financial statements of an enterprise give a true and fair view.
- (ii) It is not a primary duty of the auditor to seek out fraud.
- (iii) The directors, not the auditor have the primary responsibility for the preparation of annual financial statements and the setting up of a suitable internal control system.
- (iv) The auditor has the right of access at all times to the books, records, documents and accounts of the company.

A All four statements

B (ii), (iii) and (iv) only

C (iii) and (iv) only

D (iv) only **(2 marks)**

91 When an external auditor is unable to agree the accounting treatment of a material item with the directors of an enterprise, but the financial statements are not seriously misleading, he will issue:

A an unmodified audit report

B an adverse opinion

C a modified audit report using 'except for'

D an unmodified audit report using 'except for' **(2 marks)**

92 According to the International Accounting Standards Board's *The Conceptual Framework for Financial Reporting*, what is the objective of financial statements?

Write your answer in no more than **35** words. **(2 marks)**

93 Financial statements prepared using International Standards and the International Accounting Standards Board's (IASB) *The Conceptual Framework for Financial Reporting* are presumed to apply two of the following four underlying assumptions:

(i) relevance

(ii) going concern

(iii) prudence

(iv) accruals

Which TWO of the above are underlying assumptions according to the IASB's *Framework*?

A (i) and (ii) only

B (ii) and (iii) only

C (iii) and (iv) only

D (ii) and (iv) only **(2 marks)**

94 What is the main function of the IFRS Interpretations Committee?

A Issuing International Financial Reporting Standards

B Withdrawing International Financial Reporting Standards

C Overseeing the development of International Financial Reporting Standards

D Interpreting the application of International Financial Reporting Standards **(2 marks)**

95 In the organisation structure for the regulation and supervision of International Accounting Standards, which of the bodies listed below acts as the overall supervisory body?

A IFRS Foundation

B International Accounting Standards Board

C IFRS Advisory Council

D IFRS Interpretations Committee **(2 marks)**

96 An auditor disagrees with the accounting treatment adopted by a company. The impact of the item concerned is seen to be material, but not pervasive.

Which of the following types of audit opinion would be appropriate?

A Unmodified opinion

B Qualified opinion

C Disclaimer of opinion

D Adverse opinion **(2 marks)**

PAPER F1 : FINANCIAL OPERATIONS

97 An external auditor gives a modified audit report that is a 'disclaimer of opinion'.

This means that the auditor:

- A has been unable to agree with an accounting treatment used by the directors in relation to a material item
- B has been prevented from obtaining sufficient appropriate audit evidence
- C has found extensive errors in the financial statements and concludes that they do not show a true and fair view
- D has discovered a few immaterial differences that do not affect the auditor's opinion

(2 marks)

98 An external auditor has completed an audit and is satisfied that proper records have been maintained and that the financial statements reflect those transactions. However the auditor has one disagreement with the management of the entity. The disagreement involves the treatment of one large item of expenditure that has been classified by management as an increase in non-current assets. The auditor is of the opinion that the item should have been classified as maintenance and charged as an expense to the statement of profit or loss and other comprehensive income. The amount is material in the context of the reported profit for the year.

Assuming that the management refuse to change their approach, which ONE of the following modified audit reports should the auditor use?

- A Emphasis of matter
- B Qualified opinion
- C Adverse opinion
- D Disclaimer of opinion

(2 marks)

99 The external auditor has a duty to report on the truth and fairness of the financial statements and to report any reservations. The auditor is normally given a number of powers by statute to enable the statutory duties to be carried out.

List THREE powers that are usually granted to the auditor by statute. **(3 marks)**

100 Which ONE of the following is NOT a topic included in the International Accounting Standards Board's (IASB) *The Conceptual Framework for Financial Reporting*?

- A The objective of financial statements
- B Concepts of capital maintenance
- C Regulatory bodies governing financial statements
- D Measurement of the elements of financial statements

(2 marks)

101 The International Accounting Standards Board's *The Conceptual Framework for Financial Reporting* defines five elements of financial statements. Three of the elements are asset, liability and income.

List the other TWO elements. **(2 marks)**

SECTION A-TYPE QUESTIONS : SECTION 1

102 Which ONE of the powers listed below is unlikely to be granted to the auditor by legislation?

- A The right of access at all times to the books, records, documents and accounts of the entity
- B The right to be notified of, attend, and speak at meetings of equity holders
- C The right to correct financial statements if the auditor believes the statements do not show a true and fair view
- D The right to require officers of the entity to provide whatever information and explanations thought necessary for the performance of the duties of the auditor

(2 marks)

103 Which ONE of the following statements would be correct when an independent auditor's report gives an adverse opinion?

- A The effect of the disagreement with management is so pervasive that the financial statements are misleading and, in the opinion of the auditor, do not give a true and fair view
- B A disagreement with management over material items needs to be highlighted using an 'except for' statement
- C An opinion cannot be given because insufficient information or access to records has been given to the auditor
- D A disagreement with management over material items means that an unqualified report must be issued

(2 marks)

104 Which of the following are functions of the IFRS Committee Foundation?

- (i)   Issuing International Accounting Standards.
- (ii)   Approving the annual budget of the IASB and its committees.
- (iii) Enforcing International Accounting Standards.
- (iv)   Reviewing the strategy of the IASB.
- (v)   Publishing an annual report on the activities of the IASB.

- A (i), (ii) and (v)
- B (ii) and (iv)
- C (i), (iii) and (v)
- D (ii), (iv) and (v)

(2 marks)

PAPER F1 : FINANCIAL OPERATIONS

105 The external auditors have completed the audit of GQ for the year ended 30 June 2008 and have several outstanding differences of opinion that they have been unable to resolve with the management of GQ. The senior partner of the external auditors has reviewed these outstanding differences and concluded that individually and in aggregate the differences are not material.

Which ONE of the following audit opinions will the external auditors use for GQ's financial statements for the year ended 30 June 2008?

- A An unmodified opinion
- B An adverse opinion
- C An emphasis of matter
- D A qualified opinion   (2 marks)

106 State the TWO concepts of capital referred to in the International Accounting Standards Board's (IASB's) *The Conceptual Framework for Financial Reporting*.   (2 marks)

107 The IASB's *Framework* identifies eight categories of users of financial statements. Investors, employees and government are three of the eight categories of users of financial statements.

List TWO of the other categories.   (2 marks)

108 State the TWO underlying assumptions outlined in the International Accounting Standard Board's (IASB) *The Conceptual Framework for Financial Reporting*.   (2 marks)

109 In no more than 25 words, state the objective of an external audit.   (2 marks)

110 Which of the following gives the best description of the objectives of financial statements as set out by the International Accounting Standards Board's (IASB) *The Conceptual Framework for Financial Reporting*?

- A To fairly present the financial position and performance of an enterprise
- B To fairly present the financial position, performance and changes in financial position of an enterprise
- C To provide information about the financial position and performance of an enterprise that is useful to a wide range of users in making economic decisions
- D To provide information about the financial position, performance and changes in financial position of an enterprise that is useful to a wide range of users in making economic decisions   (2 marks)

111 The IASB's *The Conceptual Framework for Financial Reporting* defines a liability as:

- A an amount owed to another entity
- B a present obligation arising as a result of past events, the settlement of which is expected to result in an outflow of economic benefits
- C expenditure that has been incurred but not yet charged to the statement of profit or loss
- D an obligation that may arise in the future   (2 marks)

SECTION A-TYPE QUESTIONS : SECTION 1

112 Under the IASB's *The Conceptual Framework for Financial Reporting* the 'threshold quality' of useful financial information is:

- A relevance
- B reliability
- C materiality
- D understandability

(2 marks)

113 The International Accounting Standards Board's (IASB) *The Conceptual Framework for Financial Reporting* provides definitions of the elements of financial statements. One of the elements defined by the *Framework* is 'expenses'.

In no more than 35 words, give the IASB *Framework's* definition of expenses. (2 marks)

114 Which of the following is NOT a function of the IASB?

- A Enforcing international financial reporting standards
- B Issuing international financial reporting standards
- C Approving International Financial Reporting Interpretations Committee's interpretations of international financial reporting standards
- D Issuing exposure drafts for public comment

(2 marks)

115 The International Accounting Standards Board's (IASB) *The Conceptual Framework for Financial Reporting* is the IASB's conceptual framework. Which ONE of the following does the *Framework* NOT cover?

- A The format of financial statements
- B The objective of financial statements
- C Concepts of capital maintenance
- D The elements of financial statements

(2 marks)

116 According to the IASB's *The Conceptual Framework for Financial Reporting*, 'equity' is described as:

- A the amount paid into the enterprise by the owner
- B accumulated profits less amounts withdrawn
- C the residual interest in the assets less liabilities
- D owner's capital investment in the enterprise

(2 marks)

117 The IASB's *Framework* lists two fundamental qualitative characteristics of financial statements, one of which is faithful representation.

Which ONE of the following is NOT a characteristic of faithful representation?

- A Completeness
- B Neutrality
- C Free from error
- D Prudence

(2 marks)

118 An external auditor gives a modified audit report that is a "disclaimer of opinion".

This means that the auditor has:

A   been unable to access sufficient appropriate audit evidence

B   been unable to agree with the directors over an accounting treatment of a material item

C   found a few immaterial errors that have no impact on the auditor's opinion

D   found many errors causing material misstatements and has concluded that the financial statements do not present fairly the financial position and financial performance
(2 marks)

119 E, a trainee management accountant, prepares an annual analysis of the performance of all staff, including her own. The analysis is used by the financial director to calculate staff bonuses each year.

According to the CIMA code of ethics for professional accountants which ONE of the threats listed below would apply to E?

A   Advocacy threat

B   Intimidation threat

C   Familiarity threat

D   Self-interest threat
(2 marks)

120 Accounting and information disclosure practices are influenced by a variety of factors around the world.

Identify ONE of these factors and briefly explain how it influences accounting and information disclosure.
(2 marks)

121 Which ONE of the following is a function of the IFRS Foundation?

A   Complete responsibility for the preparation and publication of International Financial Reporting Standards (IFRSs)

B   Approving annually the budget and determining the funding of the International Accounting Standards Board (IASB)

C   To inform the IASB of the views of organisations and individuals on major standard setting projects

D   To review new financial reporting issues not yet covered by an IFRS
(2 marks)

122 An external auditor gives a modified audit report that is an "adverse opinion".

This means that the auditor:

- A has been unable to agree with the directors over an accounting treatment of a material but not pervasive item
- B has been unable to access important accounting records
- C was unable to attend the inventory count and is unable to agree the inventory value, which is material
- D has found many errors causing material misstatements in the financial statements

(2 marks)

123 R, a trainee management accountant is employed by JH. R has prepared the draft annual financial statements for JH and presented them to JH's Chief Executive prior to the executive board meeting. The Chief Executive has told R that the profit reported in the financial statements is too low and must be increased by $500,000 before the financial statements can be approved by the executive board.

Which ONE of the threats listed below would apply to R in this situation, according to the CIMA code of ethics for professional accountants?

- A Advocacy threat
- B Self-review threat
- C Intimidation threat
- D Self-interest threat

(2 marks)

124 List TWO functions of the IFRS Advisory Council. (2 marks)

125 The IASB's Conceptual Framework for Financial Reporting (2010) splits qualitative characteristics of useful information into two categories, fundamental and enhancing.

List the TWO fundamental qualitative characteristics. (2 marks)

126 An external audit report usually has the following 5 sections:

(i) Title and addressee

(ii) Introduction

(iii) Scope

(iv) ***

(v) Signature and name of audit firm

State the section marked (iv). (2 marks)

PAPER F1 : FINANCIAL OPERATIONS

127 The following are possible methods of measuring assets and liabilities other than historical cost:

(i) Current cost

(ii) Realisable value

(iii) Present value

(iv) Replacement cost

According to the IASB's *Conceptual Framework for Financial Reporting (Framework)* which of the measurement bases above can be used by an entity for measuring assets and liabilities shown in its statement of financial position?

A (i) and (ii)

B (i), (ii) and (iii)

C (ii) and (iii)

D (i), (ii) (iii) and (iv)   (2 marks)

128 Which ONE of the following bodies is responsible for the approval of interpretations of international financial reporting standards before they are issued?

A IASB

B IFRS Advisory Council

C IFRS Foundation

D IFRS Interpretations Committee   (2 marks)

129 The IASB's *Framework* identifies qualitative characteristics of financial statements.

Characteristics

(i) Relevance

(ii) Reliability

(iii) Faithful representation

(iv) Comparability

Which of the above characteristics are NOT fundamental qualitative characteristics according to the IASB's *Framework*?

A (i) and (ii)

B (i) and (iii)

C (iii) and (iv)

D (ii) and (iv)   (2 marks)

130 An external audit of XCD's financial statements has discovered that due to flooding of its administration offices a large proportion of XCD's financial records were destroyed. XCD's accountants have reconstructed the data to enable them to prepare the financial statements but there is insufficient evidence to enable the auditors to verify most of the sales and purchase transactions during the year.

State the appropriate type of audit report that the auditors should issue for XCD's financial statements.   (2 marks)

SECTION A-TYPE QUESTIONS : SECTION 1

SINGLE COMPANY FINANCIAL ACCOUNTS

131   In the statement of cash flow of BKS for the year to 31 December 20X5 the net cash flow from operating activities is to be arrived at by the 'indirect method'.

The following information is relevant:

	$000
Profit before tax	12,044
Depreciation	1,796
Loss on sale of tangible non-current assets	12
Increase in inventories	398
Increase in receivables	144
Increase in payables	468

State, in $000s, the cash generated from operations for the period. **(3 marks)**

132   At 30 September 20X5, BY had the following balances, with comparatives:

Statement of financial position extracts:

As at 30 September	20X5	20X4
	$000	$000
Non-current tangible assets		
Property, plant and equipment	260	180
Equity and reserves		
Property, plant and equipment revaluation reserve	30	10

The statement of profit or loss for the year ended 30 September 20X5 included:

Gain on disposal of an item of equipment	$10,000
Depreciation charge for the year	$40,000

Notes to the accounts:

Equipment disposed of had cost $90,000. The proceeds received on disposal were $15,000.

Calculate the property, plant and equipment purchases that BY would show in its statement of cash flow for the year ended 30 September 20X5, as required by IAS 7 *Statements of Cash Flows*. **(4 marks)**

133   At 1 October 20X4, BK had the following balance:

Accrued interest payable $12,000 credit

During the year ended 30 September 20X5, BK charged interest payable of $41,000 to its statement of profit or loss. The closing balance on accrued interest payable account at 30 September 20X5 was $15,000 credit.

How much interest paid should BK show on its cash flow statement for the year ended 30 September 20X5?

A $38,000
B $41,000
C $44,000
D $53,000

(2 marks)

31

134 There follows extracts from the financial statements of BET for the year to 31 March 20X5 (all figures are in $000).

Extract from the statement of profit or loss

	$000	$000
Profit on ordinary activities before taxation		1,600
Taxation		
Income taxes – current year	460	
– over provision in 20X4	(30)	
Deferred taxation	20	
		(450)
		1,150

Extracts from the statement of financial position as at 31 March

	20X4	20X3
Current liabilities – taxation	460	380
Non-current liabilities		
Deferred taxation	100	80

What amount (in $000) will appear in respect of income taxes in the cash flow statement for the year to 31 March 20X4? **(3 marks)**

135 The following balances were extracted from N's financial statements:

Extracts from the statement of financial position as at 31 December

	20X9 $000	20X8 $000
Non-current liabilities		
Deferred taxation	38	27
Current liabilities		
Current tax payable	119	106

Extract from statement of profit or loss and other comprehensive income for the year ended 31 December 20X9

	$000
Income tax expense	122

The amount of tax paid that should be included in N's statement of cash flows for the year ended 31 December 20X9 is:

A $98,000

B $109,000

C $122,000

D $241,000

(2 marks)

136 Which ONE of the following would be shown in a statement of cash flow using the direct method but not in a statement of cash flow using the indirect method of calculating cash generated from operations?

- A Cash payments to employees
- B Increase/(decrease) in receivables
- C Depreciation
- D Finance costs

(2 marks)

137 IAS 7 Statement of cash flows sets out the three main headings to be used in a statement of cash flows. Items that may appear on a statement of cash flows include:

- (i) Tax paid
- (ii) Purchase of investments
- (iii) Loss on disposal of machinery
- (iv) Purchase of equipment

Which of the above items would be included under the heading "Cash flows from operating activities" according to IAS 7?

- A (i) and (ii)
- B (i) and (iii)
- C (ii) and (iv)
- D (iii) and (iv)

(2 marks)

138 According to IFRS 8 *Operating Segments* which TWO of the following apply to reportable segments?

- (i) The results of the segment must be prepared using the same accounting policies as are used for the financial statements.
- (ii) A reportable segment is a component of the entity whose operating results are regularly reviewed by the entity's chief operating decision maker in order to make decisions about resource allocations.
- (iii) Information for reportable segments is required to be prepared based on products and geographical areas.
- (iv) A reportable segment is every segment that accounts for 10% or more of the sales revenue.

- A (i) and (ii)
- B (i) and (iii)
- C (ii) and (iii)
- D (ii) and (iv)

(2 marks)

PAPER F1 : FINANCIAL OPERATIONS

139 Which ONE of the following is NOT included in the definition of an operating segment in accordance with IFRS 8 *Operating Segments*?

- A A component of an entity that earns the majority of its revenue from sales to external customers
- B A component of an entity that engages in business activities from which it may earn revenues and incur expenses
- C A component of an entity whose operating results are regularly reviewed by the entity's chief operating decision maker, to make decisions about resource allocations and assess performance
- D A component of an entity for which discrete financial information is available

(2 marks)

140 IFRS 8 *Operating Segments* requires segment information to be disclosed by publicly quoted entities.

List THREE criteria identified by IFRS 8 to define a reportable business or geographical segment. **(3 marks)**

141 IFRS 8 *Operating Segments* requires information about operating segments to be disclosed in the financial statements.

According to IFRS 8 *Operating Segments* which ONE of the following defines an operating segment.

An operating segment is a component of an entity:

- A that is considered to be one of the entity's main products or services
- B whose operating results are regularly reviewed by the entity's chief operating decision maker
- C whose results contribute more than 10% of the entity's total sales revenue
- D whose assets are more than 10% of the entity's total assets **(2 marks)**

142 Briefly explain how operating segments disclosed in the financial statements are determined according to IFRS 8 *Operating Segments*. **(2 marks)**

143 According to IAS 8, how should a material error in the previous financial reporting period be accounted for in the current period?

- A By making an adjustment in the financial statements of the current period through the statement of profit or loss, and disclosing the nature of the error in a note
- B By making an adjustment in the financial statements of the current period as a movement on reserves, and disclosing the nature of the error in a note
- C By restating the comparative amounts for the previous period at their correct value, and disclosing the nature of the error in a note
- D By restating the comparative amounts for the previous period at their correct value, but without the requirement for a disclosure of the nature of the error in a note

(2 marks)

144 According to IAS 8 *Accounting Policies, Changes in Accounting Estimates and Errors,* which ONE of the following would require a prior period adjustment in JE's financial statements for the year ended 31 October 20X9?

- A Inventory at 31 October 20X8 had been materially over-valued due to an error in the year-end inventory count that caused inventory in one warehouse to be counted twice
- B The straight line method of depreciation used to depreciate vehicles up to 31 October 20X8 was changed by JE to reducing balance method from 1 November 20X8
- C JE acquired a business from a sole trader on 1 December 20X0. JE amortised the goodwill over 20 years. On 1 November 20X8 JE ceased amortization of goodwill as required by IFRS 3 *Business Combinations*
- D On 1 November 20X8, JE decided to change the method of calculating attributable profit recognized on uncompleted construction contracts from the percentage of cost method to the percentage of work completed method **(2 marks)**

145 According to IAS 8, under what TWO circumstances is a change in accounting policy permitted? **(4 marks)**

146 During its 20X6 accounting year, DL made the following changes.

Which ONE of these changes would be classified as 'a change in accounting policy' as determined by IAS 8 *Accounting Policies, Changes in Accounting Estimates and Errors*?

- A Increased the bad debt provision for 20X6 from 5% to 10% of outstanding debts
- B Changed the treatment of borrowing costs from expensing borrowing costs incurred on capital projects to capitalising all borrowing costs in the year incurred
- C Changed the depreciation of plant and equipment from straight line depreciation to reducing balance depreciation
- D Changed the useful economic life of its motor vehicles from six years to four years **(2 marks)**

147 According to IAS 8 *Accounting Policies, Changes in Accounting Estimates and Errors,* which ONE of the following is a change in accounting policy requiring a retrospective adjustment in financial statements for the year ended 31 December 20X0?

- A The depreciation of the production facility has been reclassified from administration to cost of sales in the current and future years
- B The depreciation method of vehicles was changed from straight line depreciation to reducing balance
- C The provision for warranty claims was changed from 10% of sales revenue to 5%
- D Based on information that became available in the current period a provision was made for an injury compensation claim relating to an incident in a previous year **(2 marks)**

148 Which ONE of the following would be regarded as a change of accounting estimate according to IAS *8 Accounting Policies, Changes in Accounting Estimates and Errors*?

- A An entity started capitalising borrowing costs for assets as required by IAS 23 *Borrowing Costs*. Borrowing costs had previously been charged to the statement of profit or loss
- B An entity started revaluing its properties, as allowed by IAS 16 *Property, Plant and Equipment*. Previously all property, plant and equipment had been carried at cost less accumulated depreciation
- C A material error in the inventory valuation methods caused the closing inventory at 31 March 20X8 to be overstated by $900,000
- D An entity created a provision for claims under its warranty of products sold during the year. 5% of sales revenue had previously been set as the required provision amount. After an analysis of three years sales and warranty claims the calculation of the provision amount has been changed to a more realistic 2% of sales **(2 marks)**

149 CI purchased equipment on 1 April 20X2 for $100,000. The equipment was depreciated using the reducing balance method at 25% per year. CI's reporting date is 31 March.

Depreciation was charged up to and including 31 March 20X6. At that date, the recoverable amount was $28,000.

Calculate the impairment loss on the equipment according to IAS 36 *Impairment of Assets*.

(3 marks)

Data for Questions 150 and 151

DOC purchased property for $320,000 exactly 10 years ago. The land included in the price was valued at $120,000. The property was estimated to have a useful economic life of 20 years.

DOC has now had the property revalued (for the first time) by a professional valuer. The total value had increased to $800,000, the land now being valued at $200,000. The useful economic life remained unchanged.

---

150 What is the amount that should be credited to DOC's revaluation reserve? **(2 marks)**

151 What should be the annual depreciation charge on the property in future years? **(2 marks)**

152 **Which of the following gives the best definition of *Property, Plant and Equipment*, based on the provisions of IAS 16?**

A   Any assets held by an enterprise for more than one accounting period for use in the production or supply of goods or services, for rental to others, or for administrative purposes

B   Tangible assets held by an enterprise for more than 12 months for use in the production or supply of goods or services, for rental to others, or for administrative purposes

C   Tangible assets held by an enterprise for more than one accounting period for use in the production or supply of goods or services, for rental to others, or for administrative purposes

D   Any assets held by an enterprise for more than 12 months for use in the production or supply of goods or services, for rental to others, or for administrative purposes

(2 marks)

153 **JT is registered with its local tax authority and can reclaim value added tax paid on items purchased.**

During the year JT purchased a large machine from another country. The supplier invoiced JT as follows:

	$
Cost of basic machine	100,000
Special modifications made to basic design	15,000
Supplier's engineer's time installing and initial testing of machine	2,000
Three years' maintenance and servicing	21,000
	138,000
Value added tax @ 20%	27,600
Total	165,600

Prior to delivery, JT spent $12,000 preparing a heavy duty concrete base for the machine. Calculate the amount that JT should debit to non-current assets for the cost of the machine.

(2 marks)

154 **Which of the following statements is correct?**

Statement 1: If the revaluation model is used for property, plant and equipment, revaluations must subsequently be made with sufficient regularity to ensure that the carrying amount does not differ materially from the fair value at each reporting date.

Statement 2: When an item of property, plant and equipment is revalued, there is no requirement that the entire class of assets to which the item belongs must be revalued.

A   Statement 1 only is correct

B   Statement 2 only is correct

C   Both statements are correct

D   Neither statement is correct

(2 marks)

PAPER F1 : FINANCIAL OPERATIONS

155 F's year-end is 30 June. F purchased a non-current asset for $50,000 on 1 July 20X2.

Depreciation was provided at the rate of 20% per annum on the straight-line basis. There was no forecast residual value.

On 1 July 20X4, the asset was revalued to $60,000 and then depreciated on a straight-line basis over its remaining useful economic life which was unchanged. On 1 July 20X5, the asset was sold for $35,000.

In addition to the entries in the non-current asset account and provision for depreciation account, which TWO of the following statements correctly record the entries required on disposal of the non-current asset?

(i) Debit statement of profit or loss with a loss on disposal of $5,000.

(ii) Credit statement of profit or loss with a gain on disposal of $25,000.

(iii) Transfer $60,000 from revaluation reserve to retained earnings as a movement on reserves.

(iv) Transfer $30,000 from revaluation reserve to retained earnings as a movement on reserves.

(v) Transfer $30,000 from revaluation reserve to statement of profit or loss.

(vi) Transfer $60,000 from revaluation reserve to statement of profit or loss.

A   (i) and (iv)

B   (ii) and (iii)

C   (i) and (v)

D   (ii) and (vi)

(2 marks)

156 Which ONE of the following items would CM recognise as subsequent expenditure on a non-current asset and capitalise it as required by IAS 16 *Property, Plant and Equipment*?

A   CM purchased a furnace five years ago, when the furnace lining was separately identified in the accounting records. The furnace now requires relining at a cost of $200,000. When the furnace is relined it will be able to be used in CM's business for a further five years

B   CM's office building has been badly damaged by a fire. CM intends to restore the building to its original condition at a cost of $250,000

C   CM's delivery vehicle broke down. When it was inspected by the repairers it was discovered that it needed a new engine. The engine and associated labour costs are estimated to be $5,000

D   CM closes its factory for two weeks every year. During this time, all plant and equipment has its routine annual maintenance check and any necessary repairs are carried out. The cost of the current year's maintenance check and repairs was $75,000

(2 marks)

157 DS purchased a machine on 1 October 20X2 at a cost of $21,000 with an expected useful economic life of six years, with no expected residual value. DS depreciates its machines using the straight line basis.

The machine has been used and depreciated for three years to 30 September 20X5. New technology was invented in December 20X5, which enabled a cheaper, more efficient machine to be produced; this technology makes DS's type of machine obsolete. The obsolete machine will generate no further economic benefit or have any residual value once the new machines become available. However, because of production delays, the new machines will not be available on the market until 1 October 20X7.

Calculate how much depreciation DS should charge to its statement of profit or loss for the year ended 30 September 20X6, as required by IAS 16 *Property, Plant and Equipment*.

(3 marks)

158 An item of plant and equipment was purchased on 1 April 20X1 for $100,000. At the date of acquisition its expected useful economic life was ten years. Depreciation was provided on a straight line basis, with no residual value.

On 1 April 20X3, the asset was revalued to $95,000. On 1 April 20X4, the useful life of the asset was reviewed and the remaining useful economic life was reduced to five years, a total useful life of eight years.

Calculate the amounts that would be included in the statement of financial position for the asset's cost/valuation and provision for accumulated depreciation at 31 March 20X5.

(4 marks)

159 IAS 16 *Property, Plant and Equipment* requires an asset to be measured at cost on its original recognition in the financial statements.

EW used its own staff, assisted by contractors when required, to construct a new warehouse for its own use.

Which ONE of the following costs would NOT be included in attributable costs of the non-current asset?

- A Clearance of the site prior to work commencing
- B Professional surveyors' fees for managing the construction work
- C EW's own staff wages for time spent working on the construction
- D An allocation of EW's administration costs, based on EW staff time spent on the construction as a percentage of the total staff time

(2 marks)

160 GK purchased a piece of development land on 31 October 20X0 for $500,000. GK revalued the land on 31 October 20X4 to $700,000. The latest valuation report, dated 31 October 20X8, values the land at $450,000.

GK has adjusted the land balance shown in non-current assets at 31 October 20X8.

Which ONE of the following shows the correct debit entry in GK's financial statements for the year ended 31 October 20X8?

A   DR   Revaluation reserve $50,000   and   DR   Statement of profit or loss $200,000

B   DR   Revaluation reserve $250,000

C   DR   Revaluation reserve $200,000   and   DR   Statement of profit or loss $50,000

D   DR   Statement of profit or loss $250,000

(2 marks)

161 On 1 July 20X4, Experimenter opened a chemical reprocessing plant. The plant was due to be active for five years until 30 June 20X9, when it would be decommissioned. At 1 July 20X4, the costs of decommissioning the plant were estimated to be $4 million. The company considers that a discount rate of 12% is appropriate for the calculation of a present value, and the discount factor at 12% for Year 5 is 0.567.

What is the total charge to the statement of profit or loss (depreciation and finance charge) in respect of the decommissioning for the year ended 30 June 20X5?

A $453,600

B $725,760

C $800,000

D $2,268,000

(3 marks)

162 An entity purchased an item of property for $6 million on 1 July 20X3. The value of the land was $1 million and the buildings $5 million. The expected life of the building was 50 years and its residual value nil. On 30 June 20X5 the property was revalued to $7 million (land $1.24 million, buildings $5.76 million). On 30 June 20X7, the property was sold for $6.8 million.

What is the gain on disposal of the property that would be reported in the statement of profit or loss for the year to 30 June 20X7?

A   Gain $40,000

B   Gain $240,000

C   Gain $1,000,000

D   Gain $1,240,000

(2 marks)

SECTION A-TYPE QUESTIONS : SECTION 1

163 Which ONE of the following CANNOT be recognised as an intangible non-current asset in GHK's statement of financial position at 30 September 20X1?

- A GHK spent $12,000 researching a new type of product. The research is expected to lead to a new product line in 3 years' time
- B GHK purchased another entity, BN on 1 October 20X0. Goodwill arising on the acquisition was $15,000
- C GHK purchased a brand name from a competitor on 1 November 20X0, for $65,000
- D GHK spent $21,000 during the year on the development of a new product. The product is being launched on the market on 1 December 20X1 and is expected to be profitable

(2 marks)

164 On 1 January Year 1, an entity purchased an item of equipment costing $76,000. The asset is depreciated using the reducing balance method, at a rate of 20% each year. After three years, an impairment review establishes that the asset has a value in use of $30,000 and a disposal value (less selling costs) of $27,000.

What is the amount of the impairment loss that should be written off in the statement of profit or loss for the year to 31 December Year 3? (3 marks)

165 The information below refers to three non-current assets of IDLE as at 31 March 20X5:

	A	B	C
	$000	$000	$000
Carrying value	200	300	240
Net selling price	220	250	200
Value in use	240	260	180

What is the total impairment loss? (3 marks)

Data for Questions 166 and 167

X acquired the business and assets from the owners of an unincorporated business: the purchase price was satisfied by the issue of 10,000 equity shares with a nominal value of $10 each and $20,000 cash. The market value of X shares at the date of acquisition was $20 each.

The assets acquired were:

- net tangible non-current assets with a book value of $20,000 and a current value of $25,000
- patents for a specialised process valued by a specialist valuer at $15,000
- brand name, valued by a specialist brand valuer on the basis of a multiple of earnings at $50,000
- publishing rights of the first text from an author that the management of X expects to become a best seller. The publishing rights were a gift from the author to the previous owners at no cost. The management of X has estimated the future value of the potential best seller at $100,000. However, there is no reliable evidence available to support the estimate of the management.

166 In no more than 30 words, explain the accounting treatment to be used for the publishing rights of the first text. (2 marks)

167 Calculate the value of goodwill to be included in the accounts of X for this purchase.

(4 marks)

41

168 IAS 38 *Intangible Assets* sets out six criteria that must be met before an internally generated intangible asset can be recognised.

List FOUR of IAS 38's criteria for recognition. **(4 marks)**

169 Which of the following statements does not comply with standard accounting practice in respect of the accounting treatment of purchased goodwill?

- A If there is an impairment in value of purchased goodwill, the amount of the impairment should be taken directly to the reserves and not through the statement of profit or loss
- B Purchased goodwill should not be revalued upwards
- C Purchased goodwill, insofar as it has not been written off, should be shown as a separate item under non-current assets in the statement of financial position
- D Purchased goodwill should not be amortised **(2 marks)**

170 A company has been carrying out work on the design and testing of a new product. The work began in May 20X1 and it is now the end of 20X3. From 31 December 20X1, the project to develop the new product met all the criteria in IAS 38 for the development costs to be recognised as an intangible asset.

The recoverable amount of the 'know-how' embodied in the development work has been estimated as follows:

At 31 December 20X1:	$400,000
At 31 December 20X2:	$1,500,000
At 31 December 20X3:	$2,000,000

The costs incurred on the project have been as follows:

Year to 31 December 20X1:	$500,000
Year to 31 December 20X2:	$1,000,000
Year to 31 December 20X3:	$1,200,000

For the year to 31 December 20X3, what expense should be charged in the statement of profit or loss for the costs of the development project? **(3 marks)**

171 Which ONE of the following could be classified as deferred development expenditure in M's statement of financial position as at 31 March 20Y0 according to IAS 38 *Intangible Assets*?

- A $120,000 spent on developing a prototype and testing a new type of propulsion system for trains. The project needs further work on it as the propulsion system is currently not viable
- B A payment of $50,000 to a local university's engineering faculty to research new environmentally friendly building techniques
- C $35,000 spent on consumer testing a new type of electric bicycle. The project is near completion and the product will probably be launched in the next twelve months. As this project is first of its kind for M it is expected to make a loss
- D $65,000 spent on developing a special type of new packaging for a new energy efficient light bulb. The packaging is expected to be used by M for many years and is expected to reduce M's distribution costs by $35,000 a year **(2 marks)**

SECTION A-TYPE QUESTIONS : **SECTION 1**

172 The following measures relate to a non-current asset:

(i) carrying value $20,000

(ii) net realisable value $18,000

(iii) value in use $22,000

(iv) replacement cost $50,000.

The recoverable amount of the asset is:

A $18,000

B $20,000

C $22,000

D $50,000 **(2 marks)**

173 IAS 2 *Inventories* states that when inventory is valued at cost, specific cost, FIFO and weighted average cost (calculated on a periodic basis or at each additional shipment) is required.

In no more than 30 words, state the rules in IAS 2 about the use of the following cost formulae for inventory:

(a) standard cost

(b) the retail method

(c) LIFO **(3 marks)**

174 Neville has only two items of inventory on hand at its reporting date.

Item 1 – Materials costing $24,000 bought for processing and assembly for a customer under a 'one off' order which is expected to produce a high profit margin. Since buying this material, the cost price has fallen to $20,000.

Item 2 – A machine constructed for another customer for a contracted price of $36,000. This has recently been completed at a cost of $33,600. It has now been discovered that, in order to meet certain health and safety regulations, modifications at an extra cost of $8,400 will be required. The customer has agreed to meet half the extra cost.

What should be the total value of these two items of inventory in the statement of financial position? **(3 marks)**

PAPER F1 : FINANCIAL OPERATIONS

175 IAS 2 *Inventories* specifies expenses that should be included in year-end inventory values. These could include:

(i) marketing and selling overhead

(ii) variable production overhead

(iii) general management overhead

(iv) accounting and finance overhead allocated to production

(v) cost of delivering raw materials to the factory

(vi) abnormal increase in overhead charges caused by unusually low production levels due to the exceptionally hot weather.

Which THREE of the above are allowable by IAS 2 as expenses that should be included in the cost of finished goods inventories?

A (i), (iii) and (v)

B (i), (ii) and (vi)

C (ii), (iv) and (v)

D (iii), (iv) and (vi)

(2 marks)

176 S announced a rights issue of 1 for every 5 shares currently held, at a price of $2 each. S currently has 2,000,000 $1 ordinary shares with a quoted market price of $2.50 each. Directly attributable issue costs amounted to $25,000.

Assuming all rights are taken up and all money paid in full, how much will be credited to the share premium account for the rights issue?

(2 marks)

177 At 1 January 20X5 CR had 2,000,000 ordinary shares of 25 cents each in issue. The company's only reserve at this date was retained profits amounting to $500,000.

On 1 May 20X5 the company made a one for two bonus issue.

On 1 September 20X5 the company made a one for three rights issue at a price of 40c. All shares in the issue were taken up.

What figures will appear in the capital and reserves section of the statement of financial position as at 31 December 20X5?

	Issued share capital	Share premium	Retained earnings
A	$1,150,000	Nil	$250,000
B	$1,000,000	Nil	$400,000
C	$1,000,000	$150,000	$250,000
D	$1,000,000	$250,000	$150,000

(2 marks)

SECTION A-TYPE QUESTIONS : SECTION 1

178 A company has issued share capital of 20 million shares of $1 each. The shares were all issued five years ago at a price of $2.25 per share. The company has now purchased 100,000 of its own shares in the stock market for $4 each, and has cancelled them.

Prior to the share repurchase, the retained earnings of the company were $10,000,000. The national law requires that when equity shares are purchased and cancelled, the company must create a capital reserve equal to the nominal value of the shares cancelled, to maintain the company's capital.

What is the balance on the retained earnings account after this share repurchase transaction? **(4 marks)**

179 Which ONE of the following gives the true meaning of "treasury shares"?

- A Shares owned by a country's Treasury
- B An entity's own shares purchased by the entity and still held at the period end
- C An entity's own shares purchased by the entity and resold before the period end at a gain
- D An entity's own shares purchased by the entity and cancelled **(2 marks)**

180 On 1 September 20X8 JS issued 200,000 $1 cumulative, redeemable 4% preference shares at nominal value. Issue expenses were $5,000. The preference shares are redeemable on 31 August 20Y3 (5 years time) at a premium of $13,000.

You may assume the effective interest rate is 5.75%

Calculate the total finance cost of issuing the preference shares and calculate the charge to each of the statement of profit or loss for the years ended 31 August 20X9 and 20Y0.
(4 marks)

181 BN is a listed entity and has the following balances included on its opening statement of financial position:

	$000
Equity and reserves:	
Equity shares, $1 shares, fully paid	750
Share premium	250
Retained earnings	500
	1,500

BN reacquired 100,000 of its shares and classified them as 'treasury shares'. BN still held the treasury shares at the year end.

How should BN classify the treasury shares on its closing statement of financial position in accordance with IAS 32 *Financial Instruments: Disclosure and Presentation?*

- A As a non-current asset investment
- B As a deduction from equity
- C As a current asset investment
- D As a non-current liability **(2 marks)**

45

182 Which ONE of the following would be regarded as a related party of Z in accordance with IAS 24 *Related Party Disclosures*?

- A   FG is Z's banker and has provided an extensive overdraft facility on favourable terms
- B   JK is Z's principal customer, accounting for 60% of its revenue
- C   MN is Z's marketing director who holds 20% of Z's equity shares
- D   QR is Z's main supplier, supplying nearly 50% of Z's purchases by value **(2 marks)**

183 Which ONE of the following would be regarded as a related party of BS?

- A   BX, a customer of BS
- B   The president of the BS Board, who is also the chief executive officer of another entity, BU, that supplies goods to BS
- C   BQ, a supplier of BS
- D   BY, BS's main banker **(2 marks)**

184 IAS 24 *Related Party Disclosures* deals with related parties of an organisation.

Which of the following would be presumed to be a related party of an enterprise?

- A   A major customer whose purchases account for 30% of the enterprise's annual sales
- B   A shareholder holding 25% of the enterprise's equity
- C   A manager of the bank providing a loan to the enterprise
- D   Employees of the enterprise **(2 marks)**

185 Which ONE of the following would NOT normally be treated as a related party of HJ in accordance with IAS 24 *Related Party Disclosures*?

- A   XX, HJ's largest customer, accounts for 75% of HJ's turnover
- B   HJ2, a subsidiary of HJ, that does not trade with HJ
- C   HJA, an associate of HJ
- D   A shareholder of HJ, holding 25% of HJ's equity shares **(2 marks)**

186 Which ONE of the following would be regarded as a related party of CXZ?

- A   The wife of CXZ's finance director
- B   CXZ's main supplier, supplying approximately 35% of CXZ's purchases
- C   CXZ's biggest customer, providing 60% of CXZ's annual revenue
- D   CXZ's banker providing CXZ with an overdraft facility and a short-term loan at market rates **(2 marks)**

187 Which ONE of the following would be regarded as a related party transaction of the entity NV?

    A   A close family member of the Chief Executive of NV purchased an asset from NV

    B   XYZ Bank lends NV $100,000 on commercial loan terms

    C   The government of Country X awarded NV a grant of $25,000 to help fund a new production facility

    D   YU supplies 60% of NV's raw materials   **(2 marks)**

Data for Questions 188 and 189

B entered into a three-year contract to build a leisure centre for an enterprise. The contract value was $6 million. B recognises profit on the basis of cost of work completed. At the end of the first year, the following figures were extracted from B's accounting records:

	$000
Certified value of work completed	2,000
Cost of work certified as complete	1,650
Cost of work-in-progress (not included in completed work)	550
Estimated cost of remaining work required to complete the contract	2,750
Amounts invoiced to customers	1,600
Cash paid to suppliers for work on the contract	1,300

188 How much profit should B recognise in its statement of profit or loss at the end of the first year?   **(2 marks)**

189 What values should B record for this contract as 'gross amounts due from customers' and 'current liabilities – trade and other payables'?

	Gross amounts due from customers	Current liabilities – trade and other payables
A	$950,000	$350,000
B	$950,000	$900,000
C	$1,250,000	$600,000
D	$2,550,000	$900,000

(2 marks)

Data for Questions 190 and 191

CN started a three-year contract to build a new university campus on 1 April 20X4. The contract had a fixed price of $90 million.

CN incurred costs to 31 March 20X6 of $77 million and estimated that a further $33 million would need to be spent to complete the contract.

CN uses the percentage of cost incurred to date to total cost method to calculate stage of completion of the contract.

190 Calculate revenue earned on the contract to 31 March 20X6, according to IAS 11 *Construction Contracts*. **(2 marks)**

191 State how much gross profit/loss CN should recognise in its statement of profit or loss for the year ended 31 March 20X6, according to IAS 11 *Construction Contracts*. **(2 marks)**

192 Details from DV's long-term contract, which commenced on 1 May 20X6, at 30 April 20X7 were:

	$000
Invoiced to client for work done	2,000
Costs incurred to date:	
Attributable to work completed	1,500
Inventory purchased, but not yet used	250
Progress payment received from client	900
Expected further costs to complete project	400
Total contract value	3,000

DV uses the percentage of costs incurred to total costs to calculate attributable profit.

Calculate the amount that DV should recognise in its statement of profit or loss for the year ended 30 April 2007 for revenue, cost of sales and attributable profits on this contract according to IAS 11 *Construction Contracts*. **(4 marks)**

193 BL started a contract on 1 November 20X4. The contract was scheduled to run for two years and has a sales value of $40 million.

At 31 October 20X5, the following details were obtained from BL's records:

	$m
Costs incurred to date	16
Estimated costs to completion	18
Percentage complete at 31 October 20X5	45%

Applying IAS 11 *Construction Contracts*, how much revenue and profit should BL recognise in its statement of profit or loss for the year ended 31 October 20X5? **(2 marks)**

194 Which ONE of the following would be treated as a non-adjusting event after the reporting date, as required by IAS 10 *Events after the Reporting Period*, in the financial statements of AN for the period ended 31 January 20X5? The financial statements were approved for publication on 15 May 20X5.

    A   Notice was received on 31 March 20X5 that a major customer of AN had ceased trading and was unlikely to make any further payments

    B   Inventory items at 31 January 20X5, original cost $30,000, were sold in April 20X5 for $20,000

    C   During 20X4, a customer commenced legal action against AN. At 31 January 20X5, legal advisers were of the opinion that AN would lose the case, so AN created a provision of $200,000 for the damages claimed by the customer. On 27 April 20X5, the court awarded damages of $250,000 to the customer

    D   There was a fire on 2 May 20X5 in AN's main warehouse which destroyed 50% of AN's total inventory

(2 marks)

195 Using the requirements set out in IAS 10 *Events after the Reporting Period*, which of the following would be classified as an adjusting event after the reporting period in financial statements ended 31 March 20X4 that were approved by the directors on 31 August 20X4?

    A   A reorganisation of the enterprise, proposed by a director on 31 January 20X4 and agreed by the Board on 10 July 20X4

    B   A strike by the workforce which started on 1 May 20X4 and stopped all production for 10 weeks before being settled

    C   A claim on an insurance policy for damage caused by a fire in a warehouse on 1 January 20X4. No provision had been made for the receipt of insurance money at 31 March 20X4 as it was uncertain that any money would be paid. The insurance enterprise settled with a payment of $1.5 million on 1 June 20X4

    D   The enterprise had made large export sales to the USA during the year. The year end receivables included $2 million for amounts outstanding that were due to be paid in US dollars between 1 April 20X4 and 1 July 20X4. By the time these amounts were received, the exchange rate had moved in favour of the enterprise and the equivalent of $2.5 million was actually received

(2 marks)

196 GD's financial reporting period is 1 September 20X7 to 31 August 20X8.

Which ONE of the following would be classified as a non-adjusting event according to IAS 10 *Events after the Reporting Period*?

Assume all amounts are material and that GD's financial statements have not yet been approved for publication.

- A On 30 October 20X8, GD received a communication stating that one of its customers had ceased trading and gone into liquidation. The balance outstanding at 31 August 20X8 was unlikely to be paid
- B At 31 August 20X8, GD had not provided for an outstanding legal action against the local government administration for losses suffered as a result of incorrect enforcement of local business regulations. On 5 November 20X8, the court awarded GD $50,000 damages
- C On 1 October 20X8, GD made a rights issue of 1 new share for every 3 shares held at a price of $1.75. The market price on that date was $2.00
- D At 31 August 20X8, GD had an outstanding insurance claim of $150,000. On 10 October 20X8, the insurance company informed GD that it would pay $140,000 as settlement

(2 marks)

197 Which ONE of the following material items would be classified as a non-adjusting event in HL's financial statements for the year ended 31 December 20X8 according to IAS *10 Events after the Reporting Period*?

HL's financial statements were approved for publication on 8 April 20X9.

- A On 1 March 20X9, HL's auditors discovered that, due to an error during the count, the closing inventory had been undervalued by $250,000
- B Lightning struck one of HL's production facilities on 31 January 20X9 and caused a serious fire. The fire destroyed half of the factory and its machinery. Output was severely reduced for six months
- C One of HL's customers commenced court action against HL on 1 December 20X8. At 31 December 20X8, HL did not know whether the case would go against it or not. On 1 March 20X9, the court found against HL and awarded damages of $150,000 to the customer
- D On 15 March 20X9, HL was advised by the liquidator of one of its customers that it was very unlikely to receive any payments for the balance of $300,000 that was outstanding at 31 December 20X8

(2 marks)

198 DT's final dividend for the year ended 31 October 20X5 of $150,000 was declared on 1 February 20X6 and paid in cash on 1 April 20X6. The financial statements were approved on 31 March 20X6.

The following statements refer to the treatment of the dividend in the accounts of DT:

(i) The payment clears an accrued liability set up in the statement of financial position as at 31 October 20X5.

(ii) The dividend is shown as a deduction in the statement of profit or loss for the year ended 31 October 20X6.

(iii) The dividend is shown as an accrued liability in the statement of financial position as at 31 October 20X6.

(iv) The $150,000 dividend was shown in the notes to the financial statements at 31 October 20X5.

(v) The dividend is shown as a deduction in the statement of changes in equity for the year ended 31 October 20X6.

Which of the above statements reflect the correct treatment of the dividend?

A (i) and (ii)
B (i) and (iv)
C (iii) and (v)
D (iv) and (v) (2 marks)

199 IAS 10 *Events after the Reporting Period* distinguishes between adjusting and non-adjusting events.

Which ONE of the following is an adjusting event in XS's financial statements?

A A dispute with workers caused all production to cease six weeks after the year end

B A month after the year end XS's directors decided to cease production of one of its three product lines and to close the production facility

C One month after the year end a court determined a case against XS and awarded damages of $50,000 to one of XS's customers. XS had expected to lose the case and had set up a provision of $30,000 at the year end

D Three weeks after the year end a fire destroyed XS's main warehouse facility and most of its inventory (2 marks)

200 List the THREE criteria set out in IAS 37 *Provisions, Contingent Liabilities and Contingent Assets* for the recognition of a provision. (3 marks)

201 AP has the following two legal claims outstanding:

- A legal action claiming compensation of $500,000 filed against AP in March 20X4.
- A legal action taken by AP against a third party, claiming damages of $200,000 was started in January 20X3 and is nearing completion.

In both cases, it is more likely than not that the amount claimed will have to be paid.

How should AP report these legal actions in its financial statements for the year ended 31 March 20X5?

	Legal action against AP	*Legal action by AP*
A	Disclose by a note	No disclosure
B	Make a provision	No disclosure
C	Make a provision	Disclosure as a note
D	Make a provision	Accrue the income

(2 marks)

202 Which ONE of the following would require a provision to be created by BW at its reporting date of 31 October 20X5?

A The government introduced new laws on data protection which come into force on 1 January 20X6. BW's directors have agreed that this will require a large number of staff to be retrained. At 31 October 20X5, the directors were waiting on a report they had commissioned that would identify the actual training requirements

B At the date, BW is negotiating with its insurance provider about the amount of an insurance claim that it had filed. On 20 November 20X5, the insurance provider agreed to pay $200,000

C BW makes refunds to customers for any goods returned within 30 days of sale, and has done so for many years

D A customer is suing BW for damages alleged to have been caused by BW's product. BW is contesting the claim and, at 31 October 20X5, the directors have been advised by BW's legal advisers it is very unlikely to lose the case **(2 marks)**

203 DH has the following two legal claims outstanding:

- A legal action against DH claiming compensation of $700,000, filed in February 20X7. DH has been advised that it is probable that the liability will materialise.
- A legal action taken by DH against another entity, claiming damages of $300,000, started in March 20X4. DH has been advised that it is probable that it will win the case.

How should DH report these legal actions in its financial statements for the year ended 30 April 20X7?

	Legal action against DH	*Legal action taken by DH*
A	Disclose by a note to the accounts	No disclosure
B	Make a provision	No disclosure
C	Make a provision	Disclose as a note
D	Make a provision	Accrue the income

(2 marks)

204 An item of machinery leased under a five-year finance lease on 1 October 20X3 had a fair value of $51,900 at date of purchase.

The lease payments were $12,000 per year, payable in arrears.

If the sum of digits method is used to apportion interest to accounting periods, calculate the finance cost for the year ended 30 September 20X5. **(3 marks)**

205 Z entered into a finance lease agreement on 1 November 20X2. The lease was for five years, the fair value of the asset acquired was $45,000 and the interest rate implicit in the lease was 7%. The annual payment was $10,975 in arrears.

The total amount owing under the lease at 31 October 20X4 was:

A $27,212

B $28,802

C $29,350

D $40,108 **(2 marks)**

206 A finance lease for 6 years has an annual payment in arrears of $24,000. The fair value of the lease at inception was $106,000. Using the sum of the digits method, the total liability for the lease at the end of year 2 is:

A $58,000

B $77,900

C $86,100

D $115,900 **(2 marks)**

Data for Questions 207 and 208

CS acquired a machine, using a finance lease, on 1 January 20X4. The machine had an expected useful life of 12,000 operating hours, after which it would have no residual value.

The finance lease was for a five-year term with rentals of $20,000 per year payable in arrears.

The cost price of the machine was $80,000 and the implied interest rate is 7.93% per year. CS used the machine for 2,600 hours in 20X4 and 2,350 hours in 20X5.

207 Using the actuarial method, calculate the non-current liability and current liability figures required by IAS 17 *Leases* to be shown in CS's statement of financial position at 31 December 20X5. **(3 marks)**

208 Calculate the non-current asset – property, plant and equipment carrying value that would be shown in CS's statement of financial position at 31 December 20X5. Calculate the depreciation charge using the machine hours method. **(2 marks)**

209 HP entered into an operating lease for a machine on 1 May 20X7 with the following terms:

- five years non-cancellable lease
- 12 months rent free period from commencement
- rent of $12,000 per annum payable at $1,000 a month from month 13 onwards
- machine useful life 15 years.

Calculate the amount that should be charged to HP's statement of profit or loss in respect of the lease, for each of the years ended 30 April 20X8 and 30 April 20X9. **(3 marks)**

210 N prepares financial statements to 31 December each year. On 30 November 20X4, N entered into a binding commitment to close a division on 31 January 20X5. The closure was completed on schedule and the following transactions occurred during January 20X5:

(i) N incurred closure costs of $4.2 million. $3 million of this figure was direct costs and $1.2 million was apportioned head office costs.

(ii) The division made a small operating profit of $300,000.

(iii) The division sold plant and made a loss on sale of $1,000,000. This fall in value had occurred before 31 December 20X4.

(iv) The division sold properties and made a profit on sale of $2,000,000.

The 20X4 financial statements were approved by the directors on 20 February 20X5.

What should be the amount reported in the statement of profit or loss of N for the year ended 31 December 20X4 in respect of the closure of the division, in compliance with IFRS 5 *Non-current Assets Held for Sale and Discontinued Operations*? **(4 marks)**

211 BN has an asset that was classified as held for sale at 31 March 20X2. The asset had a carrying value of $900 and a fair value of $800. The cost of disposal was estimated to be $50.

According to IFRS 5 *Non-current Assets Held for Sale and Discontinued Operations*, which ONE of the following values should be used for the asset in BN's statement of financial position as at 31 March 20X2?

A $750

B $800

C $850

D $900

(2 marks)

SECTION A-TYPE QUESTIONS : SECTION 1

212 IAS 1 (revised) *Presentation of Financial Statements* encourages an analysis of expenses to be presented on the face of the statement of profit or loss. The analysis of expenses must use a classification based on either the nature of expense, or its function, within the entity such as:

(i) raw materials and consumables used

(ii) distribution costs

(iii) employee benefit costs

(iv) cost of sales

(v) depreciation and amortisation expense.

Which of the above would be disclosed on the face of the statement of profit or loss if a manufacturing entity uses analysis based on function?

A   (i), (iii) and (iv)

B   (ii) and (iv)

C   (i) and (v)

D   (ii), (iii) and (v)   **(2 marks)**

213 IAS 1 (revised) states that either on the face of the statement of financial position or in notes to the financial statements, line items required in the statement of financial position should be disaggregated into sub-classifications. For example, property, plant and equipment should be shown in sub-classifications in accordance with IAS 16.

List THREE of the sub-classifications of the statement of financial position item 'receivables'.

(3 marks)

214 Which of the following must be presented on the face of the statement of profit or loss?

(i) Finance charges

(ii) Profits, gains and losses relating to discontinued operations

A   (i) only

B   (ii) only

C   Both (i) and (ii)

D   Neither   **(2 marks)**

215 Which of the following is NOT required by IAS 1 (revised) as an item to include in the notes to the accounts?

- A A statement that the entity is a going concern
- B A statement of compliance with International Financial Reporting Standards
- C The dividends declared or proposed before the publication of the financial statements but not included in the statements as a distribution to shareholders in the period
- D The key sources of estimation uncertainty in the financial statements **(2 marks)**

216 IAS 1 (revised) *Presentation of Financial Statements* requires some of the items to be disclosed on the face of the financial statements and others to be disclosed in the notes:

- (i) Depreciation
- (ii) Revenue
- (iii) Closing inventory
- (iv) Finance cost
- (v) Dividends

Which TWO of the above have to be shown on the face of the statement of profit or loss, rather than in the notes?

- A (i) and (iv)
- B (iii) and (v)
- C (ii) and (iii)
- D (ii) and (iv) **(2 marks)**

217 An enterprise undertakes a revaluation of its freehold property during the current period. The revaluation results in a significant surplus over carrying value.

In which of the components of the current period financial statements required by IAS 1 (revised) would the revaluation surplus appear?

- A Statement of financial position and statement of changes in equity
- B Statement of changes in equity and statement of cash flow
- C Statement of financial position and statement of profit or loss
- D Statement of financial position and statement of cash flow **(2 marks)**

218 IAS 18 *Revenue Recognition* defines when revenue may be recognised on the sale of goods.

List FOUR of the five conditions that IAS 18 requires to be met for income to be recognised.

(4 marks)

219 On 31 March 20X7, DT received an order from a new customer, XX, for products with a sales value of $900,000. XX enclosed a deposit with the order of $90,000.

On 31 March 20X7, DT had not completed credit referencing of XX and had not despatched any goods. DT is considering the following possible entries for this transaction in its financial statements for the year ended 31 March 20X7:

(i) include $900,000 in statement of profit or loss revenue for the year

(ii) include $90,000 in statement of profit or loss revenue for the year

(iii) do not include anything in statement of profit or loss revenue for the year

(iv) create a trade receivable for $810,000

(v) create a trade payable for $90,000.

According to IAS 18 *Revenue Recognition*, how should DT record this transaction in its financial statements for the year ended 31 March 20X7?

A (i) and (iv)

B (ii) and (v)

C (iii) and (iv)

D (iii) and (v) **(2 marks)**

220 On 28 September 20X1, GY received an order from a new customer, ZZ, for products with a sales value of $750,000. ZZ enclosed a deposit with the order of $75,000.

On 30 September 20X1, GY had not completed the credit referencing of ZZ and had not despatched any goods.

Which ONE of the following will correctly record this transaction in GY's financial statements for the year ended 30 September 20X1 according to IAS 18 *Revenue Recognition*:

A Debit Cash $75,000; Credit Revenue $75,000

B Debit Cash $75,000; Debit Trade Receivables $675,000; Credit Revenue $750,000

C Debit Cash $75,000; Credit Deferred Revenue $75,000

D Debit Trade Receivables $750,000; Credit Revenue $750,000 **(2 marks)**

221 LP received an order to supply 10,000 units of product A every month for 2 years. The customer had negotiated a low price of $200 per 1,000 units and agreed to pay $12,000 in advance every 6 months.

The customer made the first payment on 1 July 20X2 and LP supplied the goods each month from 1 July 20X2.

LP's year end is 30 September.

In addition to recording the cash received, how should LP record this order, in its financial statements for the year ended 30 September 20X2, in accordance with IAS 18 *Revenue*?

A Include $6,000 in revenue for the year and create a trade receivable for $36,000

B Include $6,000 in revenue for the year and create a current liability for $6,000

C Include $12,000 in revenue for the year and create a trade receivable for $36,000

D Include $12,000 in revenue for the year but do not create a trade receivable or current liability **(2 marks)**

222 IAS 18 *Revenue Recognition* sets out criteria for the recognition of revenue from the sale of goods.

Which ONE of the following is NOT a criterion specified by IAS 18 for recognising revenue from the sale of goods?

- A   The seller no longer retains any influence or control over the goods
- B   The cost to the seller can be measured reliably
- C   The buyer has paid for the goods
- D   The significant risks and rewards of ownership have been transferred to the buyer

(2 marks)

GROUP COMPANY FINANCIAL ACCOUNTS

223 At 1 January 20X4 Yogi acquired 100% of the share capital of Bear for $1,400,000. At that date the share capital of Bear consisted of 600,000 ordinary shares of 50c each and its reserves were $50,000.

Goodwill impairment at 31 December 20X8 is assumed to be 60% of the goodwill at the date of acquisition. In the consolidated statement of financial position of Yogi and its subsidiary Bear at 31 December 20X8, what amount should appear for goodwill?

- A $420,000
- B $630,000
- C $300,000
- D $450,000

(2 marks)

224 At 1 January 20X8 Tom acquired 100% of the share capital of Jerry for $100,000. At that date the share capital of Jerry consisted of 50,000 ordinary shares of $1 each and its reserves were $30,000.

At 31 December 20X9 the reserves of Tom and Jerry were as follows:

Tom $400,000

Jerry $ 50,000

Goodwill impairment at 31 December 20X9 is assumed to be 60% of the goodwill at the date of acquisition. In the consolidated statement of financial position of Tom and its subsidiary Jerry at 31 December 20X9, what amount should appear for reserves?

- A $450,000
- B $438,000
- C $408,000
- D $412,000

(2 marks)

SECTION A-TYPE QUESTIONS : SECTION 1

225 At 1 January 20X6 Fred acquired 100% of the share capital of Barney for $750,000. At that date the share capital of Barney consisted of 20,000 ordinary shares of $1 each and its reserves were $10,000.

Goodwill impairment at 31 December 20X9 is valued at 20% of the goodwill at the date of acquisition. In the consolidated statement of financial position of Fred and its subsidiary Barney at 31 December 20X9, what amount should appear for goodwill?

A $144,000

B $720,000

C $150,000

D $576,000   (2 marks)

226 At 1 January 20X6 Gary acquired 100% of the share capital of Barlow for $35,000. At that date the share capital of Barlow consisted of 20,000 ordinary shares of $1 each and its reserves were $10,000.

At 31 December 20X9 the reserves of Gary and Barlow were as follows:

Gary $40,000

Barlow $15,000

Goodwill impairment at 31 December 20X9 is valued at 20% of the goodwill at the date of acquisition. In the consolidated statement of financial position of Gary and its subsidiary Barlow at 31 December 20X9, what amount should appear for reserves?

A $44,000

B $55,000

C $50,000

D $54,000   (2 marks)

227 At 1 January 20X8 Williams acquired 100% of the share capital of Barlow for $300,000. At that date the share capital of Barlow consisted of 400,000 ordinary shares of 50c each and its reserves were $60,000.

At 31 December 20X9 the reserves of Williams and Barlow were as follows:

Williams $200,000

Barlow $ 75,000

Goodwill impairment at 31 December 20X9 is valued at 20% of the goodwill at the date of acquisition. In the consolidated statement of financial position of Williams and its subsidiary Barlow at 31 December 20X9, what amount should appear for goodwill?

A $32,000

B $40,000

C $ 8,000

D $20,000   (2 marks)

228 HA acquired 100% of SB's equity shares on 1 April 20X0 for $185,000. The values of SB's assets at that date were:

	Carrying value	Fair value
	$000	$000
Property	100	115
Plant and equipment	75	70

On 1 April 20X0 all other assets and liabilities had a fair value approximately equal to their book value.

SB's equity at 1 April 20X0 was:

	$000
$1 equity shares	150
Share premium	15
Retained earnings	(22)

Calculate the goodwill arising on the acquisition of SB. **(2 marks)**

229 The HC group acquired 30% of the equity share capital of AF on 1 April 20X8 paying $25,000.

At 1 April 20X8 the equity of AF comprised:

	$
$1 equity shares	50,000
Share premium	12,500
Retained earnings	10,000

AF made a profit for the year to 31 March 20X9 (prior to dividend distribution) of $6,500 and paid a dividend of $3,500 to its equity shareholders.

Calculate the value of HC's investment in AF for inclusion in HC's statement of financial position at 31 March 20X9. **(2 marks)**

230 HB sold goods to S2, its 100% owned subsidiary, on 1 November 20X8. The goods were sold to S2 for $33,000. HB made a profit of 25% on the original cost of the goods.

At the year-end, 31 March 20X9, 50% of the goods had been sold by S2. The remaining goods were included in inventory.

Calculate the amount of the adjustment required to inventory in the consolidated statement of financial position at 31 March 20X9. **(2 marks)**

SECTION A-TYPE QUESTIONS : SECTION 1

Data for Questions 231 and 232

Stress acquired 100% of the ordinary share capital of Full on 1 October 20X7 when Full's retained earnings stood at $300,000. Full's statement of financial position at 30 September 20X9 is as follows:

	$000
Non-current assets	
Property, plant and equipment	1,800
Current assets	1,000
	2,800
Equity and reserves	
Share capital	1,600
Retained earnings	500
Current liabilities	700
	2,800

On 1 October 20X7 the fair value of Full's non-current assets was $400,000 greater than the book value, this related to an asset with a remaining life of 10 years on 1 October 20X7. Stress had non-current assets at 30 September 20X9 at book value of $2.2m.

231 What is the total amount for non-current assets that will appear on the consolidated statement of financial position at 30 September 20X9?

 A $4,320,000
 B $4,400,000
 C $4,380,000
 D $4,000,000

(2 marks)

232 What is the net assets at the reporting date for Full for use in preparing the consolidated statement of financial position at 30 September 20X9?

 A $2,300,000
 B $2,220,000
 C $2,500,000
 D $2,420,000

(2 marks)

233 During the year Fluff sold $168,000 worth of goods to its 100% owned subsidiary Ball. These goods were sold at a mark-up of 50% on cost. On 31 December Ball still had $36,000 worth of these goods in inventory.

 What is the PUP adjustment in the group accounts?

 A $56,000
 B $12,000
 C $84,000
 D $18,000

(2 marks)

61

Data for Questions 234 to 235

Hard acquired 100% of the ordinary share capital of Work on 1 April 20X8. The summarised statement of profit or loss for the year-ended 31 March 20X9 is as follows:

	Hard $000	Work $000
Revenue	120,000	48,000
Cost of sales	84,000	40,000
Gross profit	36,000	8,000
Distribution costs	5,000	100
Administration expenses	7,000	300
Profit from operations	24,000	7,600
Investment income	150	–
Finance costs	–	400
Profit before tax	24,150	7200
Tax	6,000	1,200
Profit for the year	18,150	6,000

The fair values of Work's assets at the date of acquisition were mostly equal to their book values with the exception of plant, which had a fair value of $6.4m greater than book value. The remaining life of the plant was 4 years at acquisition. Depreciation is charged to cost of sales.

During the year Hard sold Work some goods for $24m, these had originally cost $18m. At the year-end Work had sold $20m (at cost to Work) of these goods to third parties for $26m.

Goodwill impairment of $600,000 needs to be recorded for the current year and treated as an administration expense.

234 What is the PUP adjustment for the year-ended 31 March 20X9?

  A $1,000,000

  B $6,000,000

  C $4,000,000

  D $7,000,000   (2 marks)

235 What is the fair value depreciation adjustment in the statement of profit or loss for the year-ended 31 March 20X9?

  A $1,600,000

  B $4,800,000

  C $8,000,000

  D $6,400,000   (2 marks)

SECTION A-TYPE QUESTIONS : SECTION 1

236 What is the total amount for revenue and cost of sales to be shown in the consolidated statement of profit or loss for the year-ended 31 March 20X9?

	Revenue	Cost of sales
A	$144,000,000	$100,000,000
B	$168,000,000	$ 97,400,000
C	$192,000,000	$100,600,000
D	$144,000,000	$102,600,000

(2 marks)

237 What is the total profit from operations to be shown in the consolidated statement of profit or loss?

- A $20,950,000
- B $28,150,000
- C $28,400,000
- D $27,850,000

(2 marks)

Data for Questions 238 to 239

Really acquired 100% of the ordinary share capital of Hard on 1 January 20X9 when Hard had retained losses of $112,000 and 30% of the ordinary share capital of Work on 1 January 20X9 when Work had retained earnings of $280,000. The summarised statement of financial position for the year-ended 31 December 20X9 is as follows:

	Really $000	Hard $000	Work $000
Non-current assets			
Property, plant and equipment	1,918	1,960	1,680
Investment in Hard	1,610		
Investment in Work	448		
	3,976	1,960	1,680
Current assets			
Inventory	760	1,280	380
Receivables	380	620	200
Cash	70	116	92
	5,186	3,976	2352
Equity and reserves			
$1 ordinary shares	2,240	1,680	1,120
Retained earnings	2,464	1,204	896
	4,704	2,884	2,016
Current liabilities			
Payables	300	960	272
Taxation	182	132	64
	5,186	3,976	2,352

An impairment test at year-end shows that goodwill for Hard remains unimpaired but the goodwill arising on the acquisition of Work has impaired by $5,600.

PAPER F1 : FINANCIAL OPERATIONS

238 What is the total non-current asset amount to be shown in the consolidated statement of financial position?

- A $3,878,000
- B $5,558,000
- C $5,552,400
- D $3,872,400

(2 marks)

239 What is the investment in associate amount to be shown in the consolidated statement of financial position?

- A $728,000
- B $632,800
- C $627,200
- D $722,400

(2 marks)

240 What is the goodwill amount to be shown in the consolidated statement of financial position?

- A $nil
- B $42,000
- C $(182,000)
- D $70,000

(2 marks)

241 What is the total assets amount to be shown in the consolidated statement of financial position?

- A $4,547,200
- B $7,773,200
- C $9,162,000
- D $6,899,200

(2 marks)

242 What is the total reserves amount to be shown in the consolidated statement of financial position?

- A $3,959,200
- B $3,968,800
- C $3,735,200
- D $3,740,800

(2 marks)

Section 2

SECTION B-TYPE QUESTIONS

PRINCIPLES OF BUSINESS TAXATION

243 ADJUSTED PROFITS (1) (MAY 07 EXAM)

Country Z has the following tax regulations in force for the years 20X5 and 20X6 (each year January to December):

- Corporate income is taxed at the following rates:
  - $1 to $10,000 at 0%
  - $10,001 to $25,000 at 15%
  - $25,001 and over at 25%.

- When calculating corporate income tax, Country Z does **not** allow the following types of expenses to be charged against taxable income:
  - entertaining expenses
  - taxes paid to other public bodies
  - accounting depreciation of non-current assets.

- Tax relief on capital expenditure is available at the following rates:
  - buildings at 4% per annum on straight line basis
  - all other non-current tangible assets are allowed tax depreciation at 27% per annum on reducing balance basis.

DB commenced business on 1 January 20X5 when all assets were purchased. No first year allowances were available for 20X5.

Non-current assets cost at 1 January 20X5

	$
Land	27,000
Buildings	70,000
Plant and equipment	80,000

On 1 January 20X6, DB purchased another machine for $20,000. This machine qualified for a first year tax allowance of 50%.

DB's Statement of profit or loss for the year to 31 December 20X6

	$
Gross profit	160,000
Administrative expenses	81,000
Entertaining	600
Tax paid to local government	950
Depreciation on buildings	1,600
Depreciation on plant and equipment	20,000
Distribution costs	20,000
	35,850
Finance cost	1,900
Profit before tax	33,950

Required:

Calculate DB's corporate income tax due for the year 20X6. **(5 marks)**

244 ADJUSTED PROFITS (2) (MAY 08 EXAM)

Country X has the following tax regulations in force:

- The tax year is 1 May to 30 April.
- All corporate profits are taxed at 20%.
- When calculating corporate taxable income, depreciation of non-current assets cannot be charged against taxable income.
- Tax depreciation is allowed at the following rates:
  - buildings at 5% per annum on straight line basis
  - all other non-current tangible assets are allowed tax depreciation at 25% per annum on a reducing balance basis.

No tax allowances are allowed on land or furniture and fittings.

FB commenced trading on 1 May 20X5 when it purchased all its non-current assets.

FB's non-current asset balances were:

	Cost 1 May 20X5 $	Carrying value 1 May 20X7 $	Tax written down value 1 May 20X7 $
Land	20,000	20,000	–
Buildings	80,000	73,600	72,000
Plant and equipment	21,000	1,000	11,812
Furniture and fittings	15,000	5,000	–

FB did not purchase any non-current assets between 1 May 20X5 and 30 April 20X7. On 2 May 20X7, FB disposed of all its plant and equipment for $5,000 and purchased new plant and equipment for $30,000. The new plant and equipment qualified for a first year tax allowance of 50%.

FB's Statement of profit or loss for the year ended 30 April 20X8

	$
Gross profit	210,000
Administrative expenses	(114,000)
Gain on disposal of plant and equipment	4,000
Depreciation – furniture and fittings	(5,000)
Depreciation – buildings	(3,200)
Depreciation – plant and equipment	(6,000)
Distribution costs	(49,000)
	36,800
Finance cost	(7,000)
Profit before tax	29,800

Required:

Calculate FB's corporate income tax due for the year ended 30 April 20X8. (5 marks)

245 TAX CHARGE (1) (MAY 10 EXAM)

Country Y has the following tax regulations in force:

- Corporate income is taxed at the rate of 25%.

- When calculating corporate income tax country Y does not allow entertaining or accounting depreciation on non-current assets to be charged against taxable income.

The following is an extract from JW's statement of profit or loss for the year to 31 December 20X8:

	$
Revenue	669,000
Cost of sales	(320,000)
Gross profit	349,000
Administration expenses	(124,000)
Distribution costs	(30,000)
	195,000
Finance cost	(45,000)
Profit before tax	150,000

Cost of sales includes depreciation charges of $27,000 for property, plant and equipment. Distribution costs include a depreciation charge for a new vehicle (see below). Included in administration expenses are entertainment costs of $2,200.

JW has been using third party delivery firms to get its products to customers. This has not proved very reliable, so on 1 January 20X8 purchased its first delivery vehicle for $12,000. The vehicle qualified for first year tax allowance of 40%. It had an estimated useful life of six years with no residual value.

The property, plant and equipment qualified for tax depreciation allowance of $40,000 in the year ended 31 December 20X8.

Required:

(a) Calculate the estimated amount of corporate income tax that JW is due to pay for the year ended 31 December 20X8.

(b) Prepare the note to the statement of profit or loss for "income tax expense" for the year ended 31 December 20X8. **(5 marks)**

246 TAX CHARGE (2) (NOV 11 EXAM)

The following is an extract from KM's statement of profit or loss for the year ended 31 March 20X1:

	$
Revenue	966,000
Cost of sales	(520,000)
Gross profit	446,000
Administrative expenses	(174,000)
Distribution costs	(40,000)
	232,000
Finance cost	(67,000)
Profit before tax	165,000

Cost of sales includes depreciation charges of $42,000 for property, plant and equipment. Distribution costs include a depreciation charge for a new vehicle (see below). Included in administrative expenses are entertainment costs of $9,800. These expenses are to be treated as disallowable for the year.

KM had been selling through retail outlets, but from 1 April 20X0 began selling on the internet and delivering to customers as well. KM purchased its first delivery vehicle on 1 April 20X0 for $18,000. The vehicle qualifies for a first year tax allowance of 50% and is depreciated on a straight line basis over six years.

The property, plant and equipment (excluding the delivery vehicle) qualified for tax depreciation allowance of $65,000 in the year ended 31 March 20X1.

Taxation is to be charged at 25%.

Required:

(i) Calculate the estimated amount of corporate income tax that KM is due to pay for the year ended 31 March 20X1.

(ii) Calculate the income tax expense charged to the statement of profit or loss and other comprehensive income for the year ended 31 March 20X1. **(5 marks)**

SECTION B-TYPE QUESTIONS : SECTION 2

247 HG (FEB 13)

HG is resident in Country X.

HG had a tax loss of $49,000 for the year ended 31 December 20X1.

HG made an accounting profit of $167,000 for the year ended 31 December 20X2. The profit was after charging $4,000 for entertaining and $5,000 for donations to a political party. HG's revenue includes a non-taxable government grant of $12,000 received during the year ended 31 December 20X2.

HG has plant and equipment that cost $50,000 on 1 January 20X1 and new equipment that cost $8,000 on 1 January 20X2. HG depreciates its plant and equipment on a straight line basis over 5 years with no residual value.

All expenses other than depreciation, amortisation, entertaining, taxes paid to other public bodies and donations to political parties are tax deductible.

Tax depreciation is deductible as follows:

- 50% of additions to property, plant and equipment in the accounting period in which they are recorded
- 25% per year of the written-down value (i.e. cost minus previous allowances) in subsequent accounting periods except that in which the asset is disposed of.

The corporate tax on profits is at a rate of 25%.

Required:

Calculate the tax payable by HG for the year ended 31 December 20X2. (5 marks)

248 MT (MAY 13 EXAM)

MT's summarised statement of profit or loss for the year ended 31 March 20X3 is as follows:

	$
Gross profit	187,000
Administrative expenses	(126,000)
Distribution costs	(22,000)
	39,000
Finance cost	(2,000)
Profit before tax	37,000

Administrative expenses include donations to the local ruling political party of $5,000 and depreciation of property, plant and equipment of $39,000 (inclusive of depreciation of new purchases).

MT an entity operating in Country X made a tax loss for the year ended 31 March 20X2. The loss carried forward at 31 March 20X2 was $12,000.

At 31 March 20X2 MT's tax written down value of its property, plant and equipment was $120,000. All of these assets qualified for the annual tax depreciation allowances. MT purchased property, plant and equipment during the year to 31 March 20X3 for $30,000.

All expenses other than depreciation, amortisation, entertaining, taxes paid to other public bodies and donations to political parties are tax deductible.

Tax depreciation is deductible as follows:

- 50% of additions to property, plant and equipment in the accounting period in which they are recorded
- 25% per year of the written-down value (i.e. cost minus previous allowances) in subsequent accounting periods except that in which the asset is disposed of
- The corporate tax on profits is at a rate of 25%.
- Tax losses can be carried forward to offset against future taxable profits from the same business.

Required:

Calculate the amount of tax that MT is due to pay for the year ended 31 March 20X3.

(5 marks)

249 DG (NOV 06 EXAM)

DG purchased its only non-current tangible asset on 1 October 20X2. The asset cost $200,000, all of which qualified for tax depreciation. DG's accounting depreciation policy is to depreciate the asset over its useful economic life of five years, assuming no residual value, charging a full year's depreciation in the year of acquisition and no depreciation in the year of disposal.

The asset qualified for tax depreciation at a rate of 30% per year on the reducing balance method. DG sold the asset on 30 September 20X6 for $60,000.

The rate of income tax to apply to DG's profit is 20%. DG's accounting period is 1 October to 30 September.

Required:

(i) Calculate DG's deferred tax balance at 30 September 20X5.

(ii) Calculate DG's accounting profit/loss that will be recognised in its statement of profit or loss on the disposal of the asset, in accordance with IAS 16 *Property, Plant and Equipment*.

(iii) Calculate DG's tax balancing allowance/charge arising on the disposal of the asset.

(5 marks)

SECTION B-TYPE QUESTIONS : SECTION 2

250 GJ (NOV 08 EXAM)

GJ commenced business on 1 October 20X5 and, on that date, it acquired property, plant and equipment for $220,000. GJ uses the straight line method of depreciation. The estimated useful life of the assets was five years and the residual value was estimated at $10,000. GJ's accounting year end is 30 September.

All the assets acquired qualified for a first year tax allowance of 50% and then an annual tax allowance of 25% of the reducing balance.

On 1 October 20X7, GJ revalued all of its assets; this led to an increase in asset values of $53,000.

GJ's applicable tax rate for the year is 25%.

Required:

Calculate the amount of the deferred tax provision that GJ should include in its statement of financial position at 30 September 20X8, in accordance with IAS 12 *Income Taxes*.

(5 marks)

251 DEFERRED TAX (SEP 11 EXAM)

Required:

(i) Explain the meaning of deferred tax as defined in IAS 12 *Income Taxes*. (2 marks)

(ii) Explain how a deferred tax debit balance can arise in an entity and the criteria for its recognition as an asset. (3 marks)

(Total: 5 marks)

252 FG (MAY 11 EXAM)

FG, an entity operating in Country X, purchased a machine costing $500,000 on 1 April 20X7, which qualified for tax depreciation allowances. All other non-current assets are leased.

FG's policy in respect of machines is to charge depreciation on a straight line basis over 5 years, with no residual value.

FG had profits of $192,000 for the year ended 31 March 20X9. These profits are after charging depreciation and before adjusting for tax allowances.

All expenses other than depreciation, amortisation, entertaining, taxes paid to other public bodies and donations to political parties are tax deductible

Tax depreciation is deductible as follows: 50% of additions to Property, Plant and Equipment in the accounting period in which they are recorded; 25% per year of the written-down value (i.e. cost minus previous allowances) in subsequent accounting periods except that in which the asset is disposed of. No tax depreciation is allowed on land.

The corporate tax on profits is at a rate of 25%.

Required:

(i) Calculate FG's corporate income tax due for the year-ended 31 March 20X9.

(2 marks)

(ii) Calculate the deferred tax charge to FG's statement of profit or loss for the year-ended 31 March 20X9 in accordance with IAS 12 *Income Taxes*. (3 marks)

(Total: 5 marks)

PAPER F1 : FINANCIAL OPERATIONS

253 TY (MAR 12 EXAM)

TY, an entity operating in Country X, purchased plant and equipment on 1 January 20X0 for $440,000. TY claimed a first year tax allowance of 50% and thereafter annual writing down allowances of 25% reducing balance.

TY is depreciating the plant and equipment over eight years using straight line depreciation, assuming no residual value.

On 1 January 20X1, TY revalued the plant and equipment and increased the carrying value by $70,000. The asset's useful life was not affected.

Assume there are no other temporary differences in the period.

Tax is charged at 25%.

Required:

Calculate the amount of deferred tax movement in the year ended 31 December 20X1 AND the deferred tax balance at 31 December 20X1, in accordance with IAS 12 *Income Taxes*. **(5 marks)**

254 TX (MAY 12 EXAM)

The draft financial statements for the year ended 31 March 20X2 for TX include the following:

	$000
Statement of profit or loss and other comprehensive income (extract)	
Income tax expense	850
Notes to the accounts:	
Over provision for the year to 31 March 20X1	(50)
Estimate of tax due for the year to 31 March 20X2	700
Increase in deferred tax provision for the year to 31 March 20X2	200
	850
Statement of cash flows (extract)	
Tax paid in the year to 31 March 20X2	600

Required:

(i) Explain how deferred tax arises.

Use the information given above to:

(ii) Identify the most likely reason for the increase of $200,000 in the deferred tax provision for the year to 31 March 20X2.

(iii) Explain what the over provision of $50,000 in the statement of profit or loss represents. **(5 marks)**

SECTION B-TYPE QUESTIONS : SECTION 2

255 KQ (NOV 12 EXAM)

For the year ended 30 September 20X2 KQ's income statement included a profit before tax of $147,000. KQ's expenses included political donations of $9,000 and entertaining expenses of $6,000.

KQ's statement of financial position at 30 September 20X2 included plant and machinery with a carrying value of $168,500. This is comprised of plant purchased on 1 October 20X0 at a cost of $180,000 and machinery purchased on 1 October 20X1 at a cost of $50,000.

KQ depreciates all plant and machinery on the straight line basis at 15% per year.

All expenses other than depreciation, amortisation, entertaining, taxes paid to other public bodies and donations to political parties are tax deductible.

Tax depreciation is deductible as follows:

- 50% of additions to property, plant and equipment in the accounting period in which they are recorded

- 25% per year of the written-down value (i.e. cost minus previous allowances) in subsequent accounting periods except that in which the asset is disposed of.

The corporate tax on profits is at a rate of 25%.

Required:

Calculate the tax payable by KQ for the year to 30 September 20X2. (5 marks)

256 GH (MAY 13 EXAM)

GH, an entity operating in Country X, purchased plant and equipment on 1 April 20X1 for $260,000. GH claimed first year allowances and thereafter annual writing down allowances.

Tax depreciation is deductible as follows:

- 50% of additions to property, plant and equipment in the accounting period in which they are recorded

- 25% per year of the written-down value (i.e. cost minus previous allowances) in subsequent accounting periods except that in which the asset is disposed of

- The corporate tax on profits is at a rate of 25%.

GH depreciates plant and equipment over 6 years, using the straight line method, assuming a 10% residual value.

Required:

(i) Define the meaning of the tax base of an asset and its significance for deferred tax. (2 marks)

(ii) Calculate the amount of the deferred tax provision that GH should include in its statement of financial position as at 31 March 20X3 in respect of this plant and equipment. (3 marks)

(Total: 5 marks)

257 PU (AUG 13 EXAM)

PU purchased machinery on 1 April 20X1 for $350,000.

PU depreciates machinery over 10 years, using the straight line method assuming no residual value.

Tax depreciation is deductible as follows:

- 50% of additions to property, plant and equipment in the accounting period in which they are recorded
- 25% per year of the written-down value (i.e. cost minus previous allowances) in subsequent accounting periods except that in which the asset is disposed of
- The corporate tax on profits is at a rate of 25%.

Required:

(i) Explain the meaning of "temporary difference" according to IAS 12 Income Taxes. Include an example to illustrate your answer. (2 marks)

(ii) Calculate the amount of deferred tax provision that PU should include in its statement of financial position as at 31 March 20X3. (3 marks)

(Total: 5 marks)

258 SALES TAX (1) (NOV 07 EXAM)

EF is an importer and imports perfumes and similar products in bulk. EF repackages the products and sells them to retailers. EF is registered for sales tax.

EF imports a consignment of perfume priced at $10,000 (excluding excise duty and sales tax) and pays excise duty of 20% and sales tax on the total (including duty) at 15%.

EF pays $6,900 repackaging costs, including sales tax at 15% and then sells all the perfume for $40,250 including sales tax at 15%.

EF has not paid or received any sales tax payments to/from the tax authorities for this consignment.

Required:

(i) Calculate EF's net profit on the perfume consignment.

(ii) Calculate the net sales tax due to be paid by EF on the perfume consignment.

(5 marks)

259 EXCISE DUTIES (1) (MAY 09 EXAM)

Governments use a range of specific excise duties as well as general sales taxes on goods.

Required:

(i) Explain the reasons why a government might apply a specific excise duty to a category of goods. (3 marks)

(ii) Explain the difference between a single stage and a multi-stage sales tax. (2 marks)

(Total: 5 marks)

260 SALES TAX (2) (MAY 10 EXAM)

W is a business in Country X, that uses locally grown fruit and vegetables to make country wines. During 20X9 W paid $30,000 plus VAT for the ingredients and other running costs.

When the wine is bottled W pays $1 tax per bottle to the tax authority. During 20X9 W produced 10,000 bottles.

W sold all the wine to retailers for an average of $8.05 per bottle, including VAT at standard rate of 15%.

Required:

(a) Explain the difference between unit taxes and ad valorem taxes, using the scenario above to illustrate your answer. (3 marks)

(b) Calculate the amounts of indirect tax payable by W for the year ended 31 December 20X9. (2 marks)

(Total: 5 marks)

261 SALES TAX (3) (SEP 11 EXAM)

SV is registered for value added tax (VAT) in country X. During the last VAT period, SV purchased materials and services costing $200,000, excluding VAT. All materials and services were at the standard rate of VAT.

SV converted the materials into two products Y and Z; product Y is zero rated and product Z is standard rated at 15% for VAT purposes.

During the same VAT period, SV made the following sales, inclusive of VAT:

	$
Y	90,000
Z	207,000

At the end of the period, SV pays the net VAT due to the tax authorities or claims a refund of the VAT paid.

Assume SV had no other VAT-related transactions in the period.

Required:

(i) Explain the difference between a single-stage sales tax and VAT. (2 marks)

(ii) Calculate the net amount of VAT due to be paid by SV or any refund to be claimed by SV at the end of the period. (3 marks)

(Total: 5 marks)

262 SALES TAX (4) (NOV 11 EXAM)

LM imports luxury goods in bulk. LM repackages the products and sells them to retailers. LM is registered for Value Added Tax (VAT) in Country X and pays at a rate of 15%.

LM imported a consignment of perfume costing $50,000, paying excise duty of 20% of cost. The consignment was subject to VAT on the total (including duty). LM paid $9,775 repackaging costs, including VAT and sold the perfume for $105,800 including VAT.

LM had not paid or received any VAT payments to or from the VAT authorities for this consignment.

Required:

(i) Calculate the net VAT due to be paid by LM on the perfume consignment.

(ii) Calculate LM's net profit on the perfume consignment. **(5 marks)**

263 SALES TAX (5) (MAR 12 EXAM)

UYT is an entity supplying goods and services to other businesses. UYT is registered for Value Added Tax (VAT) in Country X.

UYT is partially exempt for VAT purposes.

During the last VAT period UYT purchased materials and services costing $400,000 excluding VAT. UYT used these goods and services to produce both standard and exempt supplies. VAT was payable at standard rate 15% on all purchases.

UYT supplied goods and services to its customers, some of these were at standard rate VAT and some were exempt VAT.

Excluding VAT:	$
Standard rate goods and services	450,000
Exempt supplies	150,000

At the end of the period UYT prepared a VAT return. Assume UYT had no other VAT related transactions.

Required:

(i) Explain the difference between the treatment of items that are zero rated and items that are exempted from VAT. **(2 marks)**

(ii) Calculate the net VAT balance shown on UYT's VAT return. **(3 marks)**

(Total: 5 marks)

SECTION B-TYPE QUESTIONS : **SECTION 2**

264 SALES TAX (6) (NOV 12 EXAM)

A taxable person making a taxable supply of goods or services must register for VAT in most countries once their taxable turnover reaches a certain limit.

HJ is registered for VAT in Country X. HJ is partially exempt for VAT purposes.

During the latest VAT period HJ purchased materials and services costing $690,000 including VAT at standard rate. These goods and services were used to produce standard rated, zero rated and exempt goods.

Goods supplied to customers (excluding VAT) were:

	$
Goods at standard rate	720,000
Goods at zero rate	100,000
Exempt goods	205,000

Assume HJ had no other VAT related transactions.

VAT is charged at 15%.

Required:

(i) Once registered for VAT an entity must abide by the VAT regulations.

Identify FOUR typical requirements of VAT regulations. (2 marks)

(ii) Calculate the net VAT balance shown on HJ's VAT return for the period. (3 marks)

(Total: 5 marks)

265 EXCISE DUTIES (2) (FEB 13)

Excise duties are charged on certain types of specific goods by most governments. Excise duties are often charged in addition to VAT/sales tax.

Required:

Explain three reasons why an excise duty may be imposed on certain types of goods by a government. For each reason give an example to illustrate your answer. (5 marks)

266 SALES TAX (7) (MAY 13 EXAM)

During the last VAT period AV purchased materials and services costing $620,000 excluding VAT. $400,000 were standard rated of 15% for VAT and $220,000 were zero rated.

AV sold the following goods to its customers during the period, including VAT:

- At standard rate of 15% $828,000

- At zero rate $150,000

Assume that AV had no other VAT related transactions during the period.

Required:

(i) Explain the difference between a cascade sales tax and value added tax (VAT). (2 marks)

(ii) Calculate the net profit/loss that AV should recognise AND the VAT due for the period. (3 marks)

(Total: 5 marks)

267 SALES TAX (8) (AUG 13 EXAM)

YN is an importer and imports goods in bulk. YN repackages the products and sells them to retailers. YN is registered for Value Added Tax (VAT) in Country X.

YN imports a consignment of goods costing $90,000 and pays excise duty of 10% and VAT at standard rate of 15% on the total (including duty).

YN pays $19,435 repackaging costs, including VAT at standard rate of 15% and then sells all the goods to retailers for $218,500 including VAT at 15%.

Required:

(i) Calculate YN's net profit on the goods consignment.

(ii) Calculate the net VAT payable by YN on the goods consignment. (5 marks)

268 INDIRECT TAX (MAY 12 EXAM)

Required:

(i) Explain the difference between an excise duty and a single stage sales tax.

(3 marks)

(ii) Describe the characteristics of commodities that make them most suitable, from the revenue authority's point of view, for the application of excise duty. (2 marks)

(Total: 5 marks)

269 CAPITAL GAINS (MAY 11 EXAM)

JK, an entity operating in Country X, purchased land on 1 March 20X6 for $850,000. JK incurred purchase costs of surveyor's fees $5,000 and legal fees $8,000. JK spent $15,000 clearing the land and making it suitable for development. Local tax regulations classified all of JK's expenditure as capital expenditure.

JK sold the land for $1,000,000 on 1 February 20X9, incurring tax allowable costs of $6,000.

Assume JK had no temporary differences between taxable and accounting profits.

The corporate tax on profits is at a rate of 25%.

No indexation is allowable on the sale of land.

Required:

(i) Explain the meaning of a capital gain and capital gains tax. (2 marks)

(ii) Use the above information to calculate the capital gains tax due on the disposal of JK's land. (3 marks)

(Total: 5 marks)

SECTION B-TYPE QUESTIONS : SECTION 2

270 AVOIDANCE v EVASION (MAY 10 EXAM)

Cee has reduced her tax bill by taking advice from a tax expert and investing her surplus cash in government securities. The income from government securities is free of tax.

Gee works as a night security guard for a local entity and also has a job working in a supermarket during the day. Gee has reduced his tax bill by declaring only his day job income on his annual tax return.

Required:

Explain the difference between tax evasion and tax avoidance, using Cee and Gee to illustrate your answer. (5 marks)

271 TAX BASE (NOV 11 EXAM)

Required:

Explain the meaning of "tax base" and give THREE examples of the different tax bases regularly used by governments. (5 marks)

272 IMPUTATION SYSTEM (MAR 12 EXAM)

LKJ, an entity resident in Country X, reported a taxable profit for the year to 31 December 20X1 and declared a dividend for the year.

YT, a director and shareholder of LKJ, received a dividend payment from LKJ and is certain that the dividend he received will have been taxed twice.

Country X applies a full imputation system to corporate income taxes.

Tax is charged at 25%.

Required:

Explain to YT how the imputation system of corporate income tax works AND whether his dividend will have been taxed twice. (5 marks)

273 LOSSES (NOV 10 EXAM)

ZK is part of a group of entities and has traded profitably for a number of years. During the year to 31 August 20X7, ZK made a tax adjusted trading loss of $30,000 and a capital gain of $5,000. In the following year to 31 August 20X8, ZK made a taxable trading profit of $10,000. ZK expects to increase taxable trading profits to $50,000 for the year to 31 August 20X9. ZK does not expect any capital gains or losses in the year to 31 August 20X9.

Required:

Explain FOUR methods that a Country can allow to relieve trading losses of an entity and illustrate the effect of each method on ZK for the years ended 31 August 20X7 to 20X9.
(5 marks)

274 POWERS (NOV 12 EXAM)

Required:

Explain the powers that tax authorities may be given to enable them to enforce tax regulations. (5 marks)

275 BENEFITS IN KIND (AUG 13 EXAM)

BZ received a salary of $34,000 for the year ended 31 March 20X3. BZ also received a bonus of $1,700 and benefits in kind valued at $2,150.

BZ was entitled to a personal tax allowance of $5,750 for the year.

Personal taxation rates that apply to BZ are 20% for the first $20,000 of taxable earnings and 40% on the balance.

Required:

(i) Explain the meaning of "benefits in kind" for taxation purposes. (2 marks)

(ii) Prepare an income tax computation for BZ for the year ended 31 March 20X3. (3 marks)

(Total: 5 marks)

276 WITHHOLDING TAX (MAY 06 EXAM)

CW owns 40% of the equity shares in Z, an entity resident in a foreign country. CW receives a dividend of $45,000 from Z; the amount received is after deduction of withholding tax of 10%. Z had before tax profits for the year of $500,000 and paid corporate income tax of $100,000.

Required:

(a) Explain the meaning of 'withholding tax' and 'underlying tax.' (2 marks)

(b) Calculate the amount of withholding tax paid by CW. (1 mark)

(c) Calculate the amount of underlying tax that relates to CW's dividend. (2 marks)

(Total: 5 marks)

277 OVERSEAS (1) (MAY 10 EXAM)

H, an entity, carries out business in country X, buying and selling goods. The senior management of H meet regularly in the entity's offices in country X.

H owns 100% of S, an entity that buys and sells goods in Country Y. The senior management of S meet regularly in the entity's offices in country Y. S reported a profit of $500,000 for 20X9 and received an income tax bill from Country Y's tax authority for $100,000.

S declared a dividend of $200,000 and is required to deduct tax at 10% before remitting cash to overseas investors, such as H.

Assume country X and country Y have a double tax agreement based on the Organisation for Economic Co-Operation and Development (OECD) – Model Tax Convention.

Required:

Explain the terms "competent jurisdiction" and "withholding tax". Illustrate how each relates to the H group. (5 marks)

278 OVERSEAS (2) (NOV 10 EXAM)

HW, an entity resident in Country X, owns 40% of the equity shares in SV, an entity resident in a foreign country, Country Y. For the year to 31 March 20X0 SV had taxable profits of $12,500,000 and paid corporate income tax of $1,875,000. On 31 October 20X0 HW received a dividend of $3,375,000 from SV, the amount received is net of tax of 10%.

Country X has a double taxation treaty with Country Y. The treaty provides for a group of entities to only be taxed once on each entity's profits. Credit is given for withholding tax and underlying tax paid in other countries, but no refunds are available if a higher rate of tax has been paid. The corporate tax rate is 25%.

Required:

(i) Explain the meaning of "withholding tax" and provide an explanation as to why countries levy "withholding" taxes. **(2 marks)**

(ii) Calculate the amount due to be paid by HW on receipt of this dividend in Country X. Show all workings. **(3 marks)**

(Total: 5 marks)

279 UNDERLYING TAX (MAY 11 EXAM)

HC acquired a 75% holding in SU on 1 April 20X0.

HC received a dividend from SU of $156,000, the amount received is after deduction of withholding tax of 20%. SU profit before tax was $650,000 and it paid corporate income tax of $130,000 in respect of these profits.

Required:

(i) Explain the meaning of "underlying tax". **(2 marks)**

(ii) Calculate the amount of underlying tax that HC can claim for double tax relief. **(3 marks)**

(Total: 5 marks)

280 DOUBLE TAX RELIEF (1) (SEPT 11 EXAM)

Required:

(i) Explain the worldwide approach to taxing entities in a country. **(2 marks)**

(ii) Explain the problems caused by the worldwide approach and how they can be overcome. **(3 marks)**

(Total: 5 marks)

281 DOUBLE TAX RELIEF (2) (NOV 12 EXAM)

HC, resident in Country X for tax purposes, owns 100% of shares in a foreign entity, OC.

OC operates in a country that has a double taxation treaty with Country X that provides for the use of the tax credit method of double taxation relief.

OC reported profits before tax of $600,000 with corporate income tax of $126,000 for the year ended 31 March 2012.

OC paid HC a dividend for the year ended 31 March 2012 of $200,000 gross which was subject to withholding tax of 12%.

Required:

(i) Calculate the total foreign tax suffered on the dividend.

(ii) Calculate the amount of tax that HC will be liable to pay on receipt of the dividend in Country X, applying the tax credit method of double taxation relief. You should assume Country X charges tax at a rate of 25%. **(5 marks)**

PRINCIPLES OF REGULATION OF FINANCIAL REPORTING

282 DEVELOPMENT (MAY 06 EXAM)

C is a small developing country which passed legislation to create a recognised professional accounting body two years ago. At the same time as the accounting body was created, new regulations governing financial reporting requirements of entities were passed. However, there are currently no accounting standards in C.

C's government has asked the new professional accounting body to prepare a report setting out the country's options for developing and implementing a set of high quality local accounting standards. The government request also referred to the work of the IASB and its International Financial Reporting Standards.

Required:

As an advisor to the professional accounting body, outline THREE options open to C for the development of a set of high quality local accounting standards. Identify ONE advantage and ONE disadvantage of each option. **(5 marks)**

283 FRAMEWORK (1) (MAY 07 EXAM)

The *Conceptual Framework for Financial Reporting* was first published in 1989 and was adopted by The International Accounting Standards Board (IASB).

Required:

Explain the purposes of the *Framework*. **(5 marks)**

284 FRAMEWORK (2) (NOV 09 EXAM)

Required:

Identify FIVE of the purposes of *The Conceptual Framework for Financial Reporting*, as set out by the International Accounting Standards Board. **(5 marks)**

285 EXTERNAL AUDIT (MAY 10 EXAM)

AB's profits have suffered due to a slow-down in the economy of the country in which it operates. AB's draft financial statements show revenue of $35 million and profit before tax of $4 million for the year ended 31 December 20X9.

AB's external auditors have identified a significant quantity of inventory that is either obsolete or seriously impaired in value. The auditor senior has calculated the inventory write down of $1 million. AB's directors have been asked by the audit senior to record this in the financial statements for the year ended 31 December 20X9.

AB's directors are refusing to write-down the inventory at 31 December 20X9, claiming that they were not aware of any problems at that date and furthermore do not agree with the auditor that there may be a problem now. The directors are proposing to carry out a stock-take at 31 May 20Y0 and to calculate their own inventory adjustment, if required. If necessary the newly calculated figure will be used to adjust inventory values in the year to 31 December 20Y0.

Required:

(a) Explain the objective of an external audit.

(b) Assuming that AB's directors continue to refuse to amend the financial statements, explain the type of audit report that would be appropriate for the auditor to issue.

(5 marks)

286 PRINCIPLE-BASED STANDARDS (MAY 11 EXAM)

Generally accepted accounting practice (GAAP) in a country can be based on legislation and accounting standards that are either:

- Very prescriptive in nature; or
- Principle-based.

Required:

Explain the possible advantages of having principle-based accounting standards as opposed to prescriptive standards. (5 marks)

287 ELEMENTS OF FINANCIAL STATEMENTS (MAY 05 EXAM)

List the FIVE elements of financial statements defined in the IASB's *Framework* and explain the meaning of each. (5 marks)

288 ASSETS AND LIABILITIES (SEP 11 EXAM)

The International Accounting Standards Board's (IASB) *Conceptual Framework for the Financial Reporting* (*Framework*) identifies assets and liabilities as two key elements.

Required:

(i) Define assets and liabilities in accordance with the *Framework*. (2 marks)

(ii) Explain the criteria that must be met for assets and liabilities to be recognised in an entity's financial statements. (3 marks)

(Total: 5 marks)

289 OBJECTIVES AND UNDERLYING ASSUMPTIONS (MAY 11 EXAM)

Required:

(i) Explain the objective of financial statements according to the IASB's *Conceptual Framework for the Financial Reporting* (*Framework*). **(2 marks)**

(ii) Explain the underlying assumptions outlined in the *Framework*. **(3 marks)**

(Total: 5 marks)

290 INFLUENCES ON REGULATION (SEP 11 EXAM)

Accounting and disclosure practices are subject to a number of influences that vary from country to country. This leads to a variety of different accounting regulations around the world.

Required:

Explain the factors that may influence accounting regulations in a country. **(5 marks)**

291 ETHICS (MAY 11 EXAM)

CX, a professional accountant is facing a dilemma. She is working on the preparation of a long term profit forecast required by the local stock market listing regulations prior to a new share issue of equity shares.

At a previous management board meeting, her projections had been criticised by board members as being too pessimistic. She was asked to review her assumptions and increase the profit projections.

She revised her assumptions, but this had only marginally increased the forecast profits.

At yesterday's board meeting the board members had discussed her assumptions and specified new values to be used to prepare a revised forecast. In her view the new values grossly overestimate the forecast profits.

The management board intends to publish the revised forecasts.

Required:

Explain the ethical problems that CX faces and identify her possible options. You should refer to CIMA's Code of ethics for professional accountants. **(5 marks)**

292 CAPITAL MAINTENANCE (NOV 11 EXAM)

Required:

Explain the concepts of capital and capital maintenance as defined in the International Accounting Standards Board's (IASB) *Conceptual Framework for the Financial Reporting* (*Framework*). **(5 marks)**

SECTION B-TYPE QUESTIONS : SECTION 2

293 AUDIT (NOV 11 EXAM)

You are the partner in charge of the audit of LMN. The following matter has been brought to your attention in the audit working papers.

During the year LMN spent $500,000 on applied research, trying to find an application for a new process it had developed. LMN's management has capitalised this expenditure. LMN management is refusing to change its accounting treatment as it does not want to reduce the year's profit. The draft financial statements show revenue of $40 million and net profit of $4.5 million.

Required:

(i) Explain what is meant by "materiality" AND whether the matter highlighted above is material.

(ii) Identify the type of audit report that would be appropriate to the above statements, assuming that LMN's management continue to refuse to change the financial statements. **(5 marks)**

294 ETHICAL PROBLEMS (1) (NOV 11 EXAM)

RS, an employee, prepares monthly management accounting information for XYZ which includes detailed performance data that is used to calculate staff bonuses. Based on information prepared by RS this year's bonuses will be lower than expected.

RS has had approaches from other staff offering various incentives to make accruals for additional revenue and other reversible adjustments, to enable all staff (including RS) to receive increased or higher bonuses.

Required:

Explain the requirements of the CIMA Code of Ethics for Professional Accountants in relation to the preparation and reporting of information AND the ethical problems that RS faces. **(5 marks)**

295 ROLES (1) (MAR 12 EXAM)

Required:

Identify the four main entities that are involved in developing and implementing International Accounting Standards. Briefly describe the role of each entity. **(5 marks)**

296 AUDIT OBJECTIVE AND REPORT (MAR 12 EXAM)

Countries differ quite widely in their audit requirements, but most agree that large corporate entities should have an annual external audit.

Required:

(i) Explain the objective of an external audit of the financial statements of an entity. **(2 marks)**

(ii) Briefly explain THREE key areas of content of the audit report as required by ISA 700 *The Auditor's Report on Financial Statements*. **(3 marks)**

(Total: 5 marks)

297 ETHICAL PROBLEMS (2) (MAR 12 EXAM)

XQ, an employee of ABC, prepares monthly management accounting information for ABC. This information includes detailed performance data that is used to evaluate managers' performance. The directors are considering the closure of some facilities and XQ's management information will be included in the review.

XQ has had approaches from a number of concerned managers offering various incentives to make adjustments to the management accounting information to improve their performance statistics.

Required:

Briefly explain the ethical problem that XQ faces AND what XQ should do in this situation. Your answer should refer to the appropriate fundamental principles of the CIMA Code of Ethics. (5 marks)

298 BENEFITS OF EXTERNAL AUDIT (MAY 12 EXAM)

You are a trainee accountant working for ABC, which is listed on the local stock exchange. new chief executive has recently been appointed and has queried the benefits to ABC of having an external audit carried out each year.

Required:

Prepare a short briefing note that highlights the benefits of an external audit to ABC.

(5 marks)

299 ROLES (2) (NOV 12 EXAM)

Required:

Explain the roles of the following in relation to International Financial Reporting Standards.

- The IFRS Interpretations Committee
- The IFRS Advisory Council (5 marks)

300 PURPOSE OF THE FRAMEWORK (FEB 13)

Required:

The IASB has developed a conceptual framework called The Conceptual Framework for Financial Reporting (Framework).

Identify FIVE purposes of the Framework. (5 marks)

SECTION B-TYPE QUESTIONS : SECTION 2

301 ETHICAL DILEMA (MAY 13 EXAM)

Ace is a management accountant working as part of a small team that has been set up by ZY, his employer, to evaluate tenders submitted for contracts being awarded by ZY.

He has just discovered that one of the other team members accepted large payments in exchange for information, from an entity at the time it was considering tendering. Ace suspects that this may have influenced the winning tender submitted by the entity.

Required:

Explain the steps that Ace could follow to ensure that he adheres to CIMA's code of ethics for professional accountants. (5 marks)

302 ETHICAL ISSUES (AUG 13 EXAM)

XY has recently begun to lease an expensive machine. The lease agreement effectively means that XY takes on substantially the risk and rewards associated with owning the asset.

The managing director has instructed XY's finance director to treat the lease as an operating lease in order to show a better financial position.

Required:

Explain any ethical issues that this may cause for the finance director. (5 marks)

SINGLE COMPANY FINANCIAL ACCOUNTS

303 DF (NOV 06 EXAM)

You are in charge of the preparation of the financial statements for DF. You are nearing completion of the preparation of the accounts for the year ended 30 September 20X6 and two items have come to your attention.

(1) Shortly after a senior employee left DF in April 20X6, a number of accounting discrepancies were discovered. With further investigation, it became clear that fraudulent activity had been going on. DF has calculated that, because of the fraud, the profit for the year ended 30 September 20X5 had been overstated by $45,000.

(2) On 1 September 20X6, DF received an order from a new customer enclosing full payment for the goods ordered; the order value was $90,000. DF scheduled the manufacture of the goods to commence on 28 November 20X6. The cost of manufacture was expected to be $70,000. DF's management wants to recognise the $20,000 profit in the statement of profit or loss for the year ended 30 September 20X6. It has been suggested that the $90,000 should be recognised as revenue and a provision of $70,000 created for the cost of manufacture.

DF's statement of profit or loss for the year ended 30 September 20X5 showed a profit of $600,000. The draft statement of profit or loss for the year ended 30 September 20X6 showed a profit of $700,000. The 30 September 20X5 accounts were approved by the directors on 1 March 20X6.

Required:

Explain how the events described above should be reported in the financial statements of DF for the years ended 30 September 20X5 and 20X6. (5 marks)

PAPER F1 : FINANCIAL OPERATIONS

304 STATEMENT OF PROFIT OR LOSS (MAY 06 EXAM)

The following is an extract from the trial balance of CE at 31 March 20X6:

	$000	$000
Administration expenses	260	
Cost of sales	480	
Interest paid	190	
Interest bearing borrowings		2,200
Inventory at 31 March 20X6	220	
Property, plant and equipment at cost	1,500	
Property, plant and equipment, depreciation to 31 March 20X5		540
Distribution costs	200	
Revenue		2,000

Notes:

(i) Included in the closing inventory at the reporting date was inventory at a cost of $35,000, which was sold during April 20X6 for $19,000.

(ii) Depreciation is provided for on property, plant and equipment at 20% per year using the reducing balance method. Depreciation is regarded as cost of sales.

(iii) A member of the public was seriously injured while using one of CE's products on 4 October 20X5. Professional legal advice is that CE will probably have to pay $500,000 compensation.

Required:

Prepare CE's statement of profit or loss for the year ended 31 March 20X6 down to the line 'profit before tax'. (5 marks)

305 BJ (NOV 05 EXAM)

BJ is an entity that provides a range of facilities for holidaymakers and travellers. At 1 October 20X4 these included:

- a short-haul airline operating within Europe, and
- a travel agency specialising in arranging holidays to more exotic destinations, such as Hawaii and Fiji.

BJ's airline operation has made significant losses for the last two years. On 31 January 20X5, the directors of BJ decided that, due to a significant increase in competition on short haul flights within Europe, BJ would close all of its airline operations and dispose of its fleet of aircraft. All flights for holiday-makers and travellers who had already booked seats would be provided by third party airlines. All operations ceased on 31 May 20X5.

On 31 July 20X5, BJ sold its fleet of aircraft and associated non-current assets for $500 million; the carrying value at that date was $750 million.

At the reporting date, BJ was still in negotiation with some employees regarding severance payments. BJ has estimated that, in the financial period October 20X5 to September 20X6, it will agree a settlement of $20 million compensation.

The closure of the airline operation caused BJ to carry out a major restructuring of the entire entity. The restructuring has been agreed by the directors and active steps have been taken to implement it. The cost of restructuring to be incurred in year 20X5/20X6 is estimated at $10 million.

Required:

Explain how BJ should report the events described above and quantify any amounts required to be included in its financial statements for the year ended 30 September 20X5. (Detailed disclosure notes are not required.) **(5 marks)**

306 TANGIBLE NON-CURRENT ASSETS

Diva has tangible non-current assets in its statement of financial position at 31 December 20X4 and 31 December 20X5 as follows:

	At 31 December 20X5 $000	At 31 December 20X4 $000
Property, plant and equipment at carrying amount	8,417	6,228

The following information is also available:

(1)

	31 December 20X5 Cost or valuation $000	31 December 20X4 Cost or valuation $000	Accumulated depreciation/ amortisation $000
Land	3,520	2,743	0
Buildings	3,703	3,177	612
Plant, machinery and equipment	2,653	1,538	671
Assets under construction	0	53	0

(2) The land was revalued by $375,000 on 31 December 20X5.

(3) During the year, machines were disposed of for net sales proceeds of $20,000. The machines originally cost $125,000 and accumulated depreciation on the assets at the date of disposal was $111,000.

(4) *Depreciation charge:*

Depreciation charges for the year are as follows:

Buildings: $75,000

Plant and machinery: $212,000

(5) Assets under construction refer to a contract, started in November 20X4, to build and supply C with new machinery. The machinery was installed and testing was completed by 31 September 20X5. Production began early October 20X5. The balance on the assets under construction account was transferred to the plant and machinery account on 31 December 20X5. The amount transferred was $350,000.

Required:

Prepare the disclosure note for property, plant and equipment for the year ended 31 December 20X5, in the form prescribed by International Accounting Standards.

(5 marks)

PAPER F1 : FINANCIAL OPERATIONS

307 DW

The following problems and issues have arisen during the preparation of the draft financial statements of DW for the year to 30 September 20X5:

The following schedule of the movement of plant has been drafted:

	Cost $m	Depreciation $m
At 1 October 20X4	97.20	32.50
Additions at cost excluding Leased assets (see (1) and (2) below)	22.50	–
Depreciation charge for year	–	19.84
Disposal (see (2) below)	(5.00)	
Balance 30 September 20X5	114.70	52.34

Notes:

(1) The addition to plant is made up of:

	$m
Basic cost from supplier	20.00
Installation costs	1.00
Pre-production testing	0.50
Annual insurance and maintenance contract	1.00
	22.50

(2) The disposal figure of $5 million is the proceeds from the sale of an item of plant during the year which had cost $15 million on 1 October 20X1 and had been correctly depreciated prior to disposal. Dawes charges depreciation of 20% per annum on the cost of plant held at the year end.

Required:

Prepare a corrected schedule of the movements of the cost and depreciation of plant.

(5 marks)

308 BI (NOV 05 EXAM)

BI owns a building which it uses as its offices, warehouse and garage. The land is carried as a separate non-current tangible asset at the reporting date.

BI has a policy of regularly revaluing its non-current tangible assets. The original cost of the building in October 20X2 was $1,000,000; it was assumed to have a remaining useful life of 20 years at that date, with no residual value. The building was revalued on 30 September 20X4 by a professional valuer at $1,800,000.

BI also owns a brand name which it acquired 1 October 20X0 for $500,000. The brand name is being amortised over 10 years.

The economic climate had deteriorated during 20X5, causing BI to carry out an impairment review of its assets at 30 September 20X5. BI's building was valued at a market value of $1,500,000 on 30 September 20X5 by an independent valuer. A brand specialist valued BI's brand name at market value of $200,000 on the same date.

BI's management accountant calculated that the brand name's value in use at 30 September 20X5 was $150,000.

Required:

Explain how BI should report the events described above and quantify any amounts required to be included in its financial statements for the year ended 30 September 20X5.

(5 marks)

309 REVALUATION (NOV 06 EXAM)

DV purchased two buildings on 1 September 20W6. Building A cost $200,000 and had a useful economic life of 20 years. Building B cost $120,000 and had a useful economic life of 15 years. DV's accounting policies are to revalue buildings every five years and depreciate them over their useful economic lives on the straight line basis. DV does not make an annual transfer from revaluation reserve to retained profits for excess depreciation.

DV received the following valuations from its professionally qualified external valuer:

31 August 20X1	Building A	$180,000
	Building B	$75,000
31 August 20X6	Building A	$100,000
	Building B	$30,000

Required:

Calculate the gains or impairments arising on the revaluation of Buildings A and B at 31 August 20X6 and identify where they should be recognised in the financial statements of DV.

(5 marks)

310 USEFUL ECONOMIC LIFE

A new type of delivery vehicle, when purchased on 1 April 20X0 for $20,000, was expected to have a useful economic life of four years. It now appears that the original estimate of the useful economic life was too short, and the vehicle is now expected to have a useful economic life of six years from the date of purchase. All delivery vehicles are depreciated using the straight-line method and are assumed to have zero residual value.

Required:

As the trainee management accountant, draft a memo to the transport manager explaining whether it is possible to change the useful economic life of the new delivery vehicle. Using appropriate International Accounting Standards, explain how the accounting entries relating to the delivery vehicle should be recorded in the statement of profit or loss for the year ended 31 March 20X3 and the statement of financial position at that date.

(5 marks)

311 DECOMMISSIONING

NDL drilled a new oil well, which started production on 1 March 20X3. The licence granting permission to drill the new oil well included a clause that requires NDL to 'return the land to the state it was in before drilling commenced'.

NDL estimates that the oil well will have a 20-year production life. At the end of that time, the oil well will be decommissioned and work carried out to reinstate the land. The cost of this decommissioning work is estimated to be $20 million.

Required:

As the trainee management accountant, draft a memo to the production manager explaining how NDL must treat the decommissioning costs in its financial statements for the year to 31 March 20X3. Your memo should refer to appropriate International Accounting Standards. (5 marks)

312 HOTELS

AH owns three hotels. It has employed a firm of surveyors to revalue some of its properties during the past year. The directors have decided that the valuations should be incorporated into the entity's financial statements.

This is the first time that such a revaluation has taken place and the accountant responsible for the preparation of the non-current asset note in the statement of financial position is unsure of the correct treatment of the amounts involved. The entity's year end is 30 September 20X4.

The accountant has extracted the following table from the report prepared by the surveyors:

	Original cost $000	Depreciation to 30 September 20X3 $000	Market value at 1 January 20X4 $000	Estimated useful life from 1 January 20X4 Years
Hotel G	400	96	650	50
Hotel H	750	56	820	30
Hotel K	500	70	320	40

Depreciation for the first three months of the year is to be based on the entity's original valuation of its hotels. Depreciation for the remaining nine months of the year to 30 September 20X4 is to be based on the new valuations and the estimated useful remaining lives in the surveyor's report.

Required:

Prepare a memo giving an answer to the following questions from the accountant. You should explain the principles of the accounting treatments, and you are not required to provide calculations or figures for the actual valuations.

(a) The carrying value of Hotel K has fallen as a result of the revaluation. How should this decrease be reflected in the financial statements?

(b) Does *all* of the depreciation based on the revalued amounts for Hotels G and H have to be charged to the statement of profit or loss for the year to 30 September 20X4, or can a proportion be offset against the revaluation reserve instead?

(c) What should be the carrying value for the hotels in the statement of financial position as at 30 September 20X4? (5 marks)

SECTION B-TYPE QUESTIONS : SECTION 2

313 DEVELOPMENT COSTS (1) (MAY 06 EXAM)

CD is a manufacturing entity that runs a number of operations including a bottling plant that bottles carbonated soft drinks. CD has been developing a new bottling process that will allow the bottles to be filled and sealed more efficiently. The new process took a year to develop. At the start of development, CD estimated that the new process would increase output by 15% with no additional cost (other than the extra bottles and their contents). Development work commenced on 1 May 20X5 and was completed on 20 April 20X6. Testing at the end of the development confirmed CD's original estimates.

CD incurred expenditure of $180,000 on the above development in 20X5/X6.

CD plans to install the new process in its bottling plant and start operating the new process from 1 May 20X6.

CD's statement of financial position date is 30 April.

Required:

(a) Explain the requirements of IAS 38 *Intangible Assets* for the treatment of development costs. (3 marks)

(b) Explain how CD should treat its development costs in its financial statements for the year ended 30 April 20X6. (2 marks)

(Total: 5 marks)

314 DEVELOPMENT COSTS (2) (MAY 08 EXAM)

EK publishes various types of book and occasionally produces films which it sells to major film distributors.

(i) On 31 March 2007, EK acquired book publishing and film rights to the next book to be written by an internationally acclaimed author, for $1 million. The author has not yet started writing the book, but expects to complete it in 2009.

(ii) Between 1 June and 31 July 2007, EK spent $500,000 exhibiting its range of products at a major international trade fair. This was the first time EK had attended this type of event. No new orders were taken as a direct result of the event, although EK directors claim to have made valuable contacts that should generate additional sales or additional funding for films in the future. No estimate can be made of additional revenue at present.

(iii) During the year, EK employed an external consultant to redesign EK's corporate logo and to create advertising material to improve EK's corporate image. The total cost of the consultancy was $800,000.

EK's directors want to treat all of the above items of expenditure as assets.

Required:

Explain how EK should treat these items of expenditure in its financial statements for the year ended 31 October 20X7 with reference to the International Accounting Standards Board's (IASB) *Conceptual Framework for the Financial Reporting* (*Framework*) and relevant International Financial Reporting Standards. (5 marks)

315 HF ERRORS (MAY 09 EXAM)

Selected balances in HF's financial records at 30 April 2009 were as follows:

	$000
Revenue	15,000
Profit	1,500
Property, plant and equipment – carrying value	23,000
Inventory	1,500

After completing the required audit work the external auditors of HF had the following observations:

(a) Inventory with a book value of $500 is obsolete and should be written off.

(b) Development expenditure carrying value $600,000, relating to the development of a new product line, had been capitalised and amortised in previous years but the project has now been abandoned.

(c) Decommissioning costs relating to HF's production facilities, estimated to be $5,000,000 in 17 years' time is being provided for, over 20 years, at $250,000 a year.

Assume there are no other material matters outstanding.

An external auditor you have just completed a meeting with HF management. At the meeting HF management decided the following:

- Item (1) is not material, so it is not necessary to write off the obsolete inventory.

- Item (2) the development expenditure should be written off against current year profits.

- Item (3) the decommissioning cost will continue to be provided for over 20 years.

Required:

(i) Explain whether or not the management's decisions taken in the meeting are correct for items (1) and (2). **(2 marks)**

(ii) Explain whether you agree with the management's treatment of the decommissioning costs in item (3) and explain the type of audit report that should be issued, giving your reasons. **(3 marks)**

(Total: 5 marks)

316 REDEEMABLE SHARES (1) (MAY 06 EXAM)

CR issued 200,000 $10 redeemable 5% preference shares at par on 1 April 20X5. The shares were redeemable on 31 March 20Y0 (5 years time) at a premium of 15%. Issue costs amounted to $192,800.

Required:

(a) Calculate the total *finance* cost over the life of the preference shares. **(2 marks)**

(b) Calculate the annual charge to the statement of profit or loss for finance expense, as required by IAS 32 *Financial Instruments: Recognition and Measurement*, for each of the five years 20X6 to 20Y0. Assume the constant annual rate of interest as 10%. **(3 marks)**

(Total: 5 marks)

317 REDEEMABLE SHARES (2) (MAY 08 EXAM)

FG issued 10,000,000 $1, 5% preferred shares at par on 1 May 20X6. The shares are redeemable at a 10% premium four years after issue on 30 April 20Y0. Issue costs were $601,500.

Required:

(i) Calculate the finance charge for EACH of the four years 1 May 20X6 to 30 April 20Y0 using the sum of digits method. (3 marks)

(ii) Prepare extracts from FG's statement of profit or loss for the year ended 30 April 20X8 and its statement of financial position as at that date, to show the accounting entries required for the preferred shares. (2 marks)

(Total: 5 marks)

318 REDEEMABLE SHARES (3) (MAY 13 EXAM)

On 1 January 20X2 PS issued at par, 500,000 $1 5% cumulative preferred shares, redeemable at par in four years. The issue costs were $20,000.

PS has not issued preferred shares before and the managing director has asked you to explain how the preferred shares should be treated in the financial statements of PS.

Required:

Explain with reasons, how PS should:

(i) Classify the preferred shares in its financial statements for the year ended 31 December 20X2, in accordance with IAS 32 *Financial Instruments: Recognition and Measurement.*

(ii) Account for the related costs in accordance with IAS 32 *Financial Instruments: Recognition and Measurement.*

(5 marks)

319 SHARE ISSUES (AUG 13 EXAM)

CD had 5,000,000 $1 ordinary shares in issue.

Subsequently, CD made a rights issue of 1 new ordinary share at $3.50 per share for every 5 ordinary shares currently held. At the same date CD's ordinary shares were trading at $4.75.

Required:

(i) Explain the difference between a bonus issue and a rights issue of shares.

(ii) Prepare the journal entries required to record CD's rights issue in its financial records, assuming that all rights were taken up.

(5 marks)

PAPER F1 : FINANCIAL OPERATIONS

320 CB IMPORTERS (MAY 06 EXAM)

CB is an entity specialising in importing a wide range of non-food items and selling them to retailers. George is CB's president and founder and owns 40% of CB's equity shares:

- CB's largest customer, XC, accounts for 35% of CB's revenue. XC has just completed negotiations with CB for a special 5% discount on all sales.
- During the accounting period, George purchased a property from CB for $500,000. CB had previously declared the property surplus to its requirements and had valued it at $750,000.
- George's son, Arnold, is a director in a financial institution, FC. During the accounting period, FC advanced $2 million to CB as an unsecured loan at a favourable rate of interest.

Required:

Explain, with reasons, the extent to which each of the above transactions should be classified and disclosed in accordance with IAS 24 *Related Party Disclosures* in CB's financial statements for the period. (5 marks)

321 RELATED PARTIES (NOV 07 EXAM)

The objective of IAS 24 *Related Party Disclosures* is to ensure that financial statements disclose the effect of the existence of related parties.

Required:

With reference to IAS 24, explain the meaning of the terms 'related party' and 'related party transaction'. (5 marks)

322 AE (MAY 05 EXAM)

AE has a three-year contract which commenced on 1 April 20X4. At 31 March 20X5, AE had the following balances in its ledger relating to the contract:

	$000	$000
Total contract value		60,000
Cost incurred up to 31 March 20X5:		
Attributable to work completed	21,000	
Inventory purchased for use in 20X5/6	3,000	24,000
Progress payments received		25,000
Other information:		
Expected further costs to completion		19,000

At 31 March 20X5, the contract was certified as 50% complete.

Required:

Prepare the statement of profit or loss and statement of financial position extracts showing the balances relating to this contract, as required by IAS 11 *Construction Contracts*. (5 marks)

SECTION B-TYPE QUESTIONS : SECTION 2

323 HS (MAY 09 EXAM)

HS, a contractor, signed a two year fixed price contract on 31 March 20X8 for $300,000 to build a bridge. Total costs were originally estimated at $240,000.

At 31 March 20X9, HS extracted the following figures from its financial records:

	$000
Contract value	300
Costs incurred to date	170
Estimated costs to complete	100
Progress payments received	130
Value of work completed	165

HS calculates the stage of completion of contracts using the value of work completed as a proportion of total contract value.

Required:

Calculate the following amounts for the contract that should be shown in HS's financial statements:

- **Statement of profit or loss:**
    - **Revenue recognised for the year ended 31 March 20X9**
    - **Profit recognised for the year ended 31 March 20X9.**
- **Statement of financial position:**
    - **Gross amounts due to/from customer at 31 March 20X9, stating whether it is an asset or liability.** (5 marks)

324 CC (MAY 10 EXAM)

On 1 April 20X8 CC started work on a three year construction contract. The fixed vale of the contract is $63 million.

During the year ended 31 March 20X9 CC's contract costs escalated.

The value of work done and the cash received for the two years to 31 March 20Y0 are summarised below:

	Year to 31 March 20Y0	Year to 31 March 20X9
Percentage of work completed in the year	40%	35%
Cost incurred in the year	$26 million	$18 million
Estimated further costs after the year end to complete	$20 million	$36 million
Progress payments received in the year	$22 million	$15 million
Amounts recognised by CC in SOCI for YE 31/03/X9		
Revenue		$22 million
Cost of sales		$18 million

Required:

Calculate the amounts to be recorded for the above contract in CC's statement of profit or loss and other comprehensive income for the year ended 31 March 20Y0 and in the statement of financial position at that date.

Show all calculated figures to the nearest $ million. (5 marks)

325 INTANGIBLES (NOV 09 EXAM)

JX acquired the business and assets of a sole trader for $700,000 on 1 November 20X8.

The fair value of the identifiable assets acquired were:

	$000
Non-current intangible assets	
Brand Z – brand name	200
Deferred development expenditure	90
Non-current tangible assets	
Plant and equipment	350
Current assets	
Inventory	10
	650

The deferred development expenditure related to expenditure incurred on development of a new product. After the acquisition JX continued developing this new product and spent a further $500,000 completing the development and getting the product ready for market. The product was launched on 1 November 20X9. The new product is expected to generate significant profits for JX over the next five years.

On 31 October 20X9 brand Z was independently valued at $250,000.

Required:

Explain how JX should treat the following items relating to the acquisition in its financial statements for the year ended 31 October 20X9.

(i) Goodwill

(ii) The development expenditure

(iii) Brand Z (5 marks)

326 EARTHQUAKE (NOV 10 EXAM)

MN obtained a licence free of charge from the government to dig and operate a gold mine.

MN spent $6 million digging and preparing the mine for operation and erecting buildings on site. The mine commenced operations on 1 September 20X8.

The licence requires that at the end of the mine's useful life of 20 years, the site must be reinstated, all buildings and equipment must be removed and the site landscaped. At 31 August 20X9 MN estimated that the cost in 19 years' time of the removal and landscaping will be $5 million and its present value is $3 million.

On the 31 October 20X9 there was a massive earthquake in the area and MN's mine shaft was badly damaged. It is estimated that the mine will be closed for at least six months and will cost $1 million to repair.

Required:

(i) Explain how MN should record the cost of the site reinstatement as at 31 August 2010 in accordance with IAS 37 *Provisions, Contingent Liabilities and Contingent Assets*. (2 marks)

(ii) Explain how MN should treat the effects of the earthquake in its financial statements for the year ended 31 August 20X9 in accordance with IAS 10 *Events after the Reporting Period*. (3 marks)

(Total: 5 marks)

327 SHOE FACTORY (MAY 10 EXAM)

AD operates five factories in different locations in a country. Each factor produces a different product line and each product line is treated as a separate segment under IFRS 8 *Operating Segments*.

One factory, producing a range of shoes, had an increased annual loss of an estimated $2,000,000 for the year to 31 March 20X0. On 1 March 20X0 AD's management decided to close the factory and cease the sale of its range of shoes. Closure costs, net of any gains on disposal of the assets, are estimated at $150,000.

On 31 March 20X0 AD's management is still negotiating payment terms with the shoe factory workforce and has not agreed an actual closure date. AD has not yet attempted to find a buyer for the factory or its assets.

AD's management wants to completely exclude the shoe factory results from AD's financial statements for the year ended 31 March 20X0. They argue that as the shoe factory is about to be closed or sold, it would mislead investors to include the results of the shoe factory in the results of the year.

Required:

Assume you are a trainee accountant with AD.

AD's finance director has asked you to draft a note that she can use to prepare a response to AD's management.

Your note should explain how AD should treat the shoe factory in its financial statements for the year ended 31 March 20X0.

You should make reference to any relevant International Financial Reporting Standards and to CIMA's Code of Ethics for Professional Accountants. (5 marks)

328 OPERATING SEGMENTS (NOV 12 EXAM)

Required:

Define an operating segment according to IFRS 8 *Operating segments* and explain when a segment is classified as a reportable segment. (5 marks)

329 FINANCE LEASE (1)

A lessee leases a non-current asset on a non-cancellable lease contract of five years, the details of which are:

The asset has a useful economic life of five years.

The rental is $21,000 per annum payable at the end of each year.

The lessee also has to pay all insurance and maintenance costs.

The fair value of the asset was $88,300.

The lessee uses the sum of digits method to calculate finance charges on the lease.

Required:

Prepare statement of profit or loss and statement of financial position extracts for years one and two of the lease. (5 marks)

330 FINANCE LEASE (2) (MAY 05 EXAM)

A five-year finance lease commenced on 1 April 20X3. The annual payments are $30,000 in arrears. The fair value of the asset at 1 April 20X3 was $116,000. Use the sum of digits method for interest allocations and assume that the asset has no residual value at the end of the lease term.

Required:

In accordance with IAS 17 *Leases*:

(a) Calculate the amount of finance cost that would be charged to the statement of profit or loss for the year ended 31 March 20X5

(b) Prepare statement of financial position extracts for the lease at 31 March 20X5.
(5 marks)

331 FINANCE LEASE (3) (MAY 07 EXAM)

On 1 April 20X5, DX acquired plant and machinery with a fair value of $900,000 on a finance lease. The lease is for five years with the annual lease payments of $228,000 being paid in advance on 1 April each year. The interest rate implicit in the lease is 13.44%. The first payment was made on 1 April 20X5.

Required:

(i) Calculate the finance charge in respect of the lease that will be shown in DX's statement of profit or loss for the year ended 31 March 20X7.

(ii) Calculate the amount to be shown as a current liability and a non-current liability in DX's statement of financial position at 31 March 20X7.

(All workings should be to the nearest $000.) (5 marks)

332 CLOSURE (1) (MAY 07 EXAM)

On 1 June 20X6, the directors of DP commissioned a report to determine possible actions they could take to reduce DP's losses. The report, which was presented to the directors on 1 December 20X6, proposed that DP cease all of its manufacturing activities and concentrate on its retail activities.

The directors formally approved the plan to close DP's factory. The factory was gradually shut down, commencing on 5 December 20X6, with production finally ceasing on 15 March 20X7. All employees had ceased working or had been transferred to other facilities in the company by 29 March 20X7. The plant and equipment was removed and sold for $25,000 (carrying value $95,000) on 30 March 20X7.

The factory land and building was being advertised for sale, but had not been sold by 31 March 20X7. The carrying value of the land and building at 31 March 20X7, based on original cost, was $750,000. The estimated net realisable value of the land and building at 31 March 20X7 was $1,125,000.

Closure costs incurred (and paid) up to 31 March 20X7 were $620,000.

The cash flows, revenues and expenses relating to the factory were clearly distinguishable from DP's other operations. The output from the factory was sold directly to third parties and to DP's retail outlets. The manufacturing facility was shown as a separate segment in DP's segmental information.

Required:

With reference to relevant International Accounting Standards, explain how DP should treat the factory closure in its financial statements for the year ended 31 March 20X7.

(5 marks)

333 CLOSURE (2) (NOV 07 EXAM)

On 1 September 20X7, the Directors of EK decided to sell EK's retailing division and concentrate activities entirely on its manufacturing division.

The retailing division was available for immediate sale, but EK had not succeeded in disposing of the operation by 31 October 20X7. EK identified a potential buyer for the retailing division, but negotiations were at an early stage. The Directors of EK are certain that the sale will be completed by 31 August 20X8.

The retailing division's carrying value at 31 August 20X7 was:

	$000
Non-current tangible assets – property, plant and equipment	300
Non-current tangible assets – goodwill	100
Net current assets	43
Total carrying value	443

The retailing division has been valued at $423,000, comprising:

	$000
Non-current tangible assets – property, plant and equipment	320
Non-current tangible assets – goodwill	60
Net current assets	43
Total carrying value	423

EK's directors have estimated that EK will incur consultancy and legal fees for the disposal of $25,000.

Required:

(i) Explain whether EK can treat the sale of its retailing division as a 'discontinued operation', as defined by IFRS 5 *Non-current Assets Held for Sale and Discontinued Operations*, in its financial statements for the year ended 31 October 20X7.

(3 marks)

(ii) Explain how EK should treat the retailing division in its financial statements for the year ended 31 October 20X7, assuming the sale of its retailing division meets the classification requirements for a disposal group (IFRS 5). (2 marks)

(Total: 5 marks)

334 WZ (SEP 11 EXAM)

WZ is an assistant accountant with ABC. On 31 March 20X1 ABC decided to sell a property. This property was correctly classified as held for sale in accordance with IFRS5 *Non-current Assets Held For Sale and Discontinued Operations*.

In its draft financial statements ABC has written down the property by $3.4 million. The write down was charged to the statement of profit or loss for the year ended 31 August 20X1. The draft financial statements showed a loss of $1.3 million for the year to 31 August 20X1.

When the management board of ABC reviewed the draft financial statements the board members were unhappy that the draft statements showed a loss and decided that the property should continue to be shown under non-current assets at its previous carrying value.

Required:

Explain the ethical problems that WZ faces AND identify his possible options. Your answer should refer to CIMA's Code of ethics for professional accountants. (5 marks)

335 LP (FEB 13)

LP is an entity that up until 30 June 20X2 operated 3 divisions; division A, B and C. LP closed division C on 30 June 20X2.

Division C had the following results for the period 1 January 20X2 to 30 June 20X2:

	$000
Revenue	95
Operating expenses	(110)
Operating loss	(15)
Tax refund	3
Loss	(12)

(excluding disposal of assets and restructuring)

The disposal of the assets of division C incurred a loss of $30,000.

LP incurred an expense of $75,000 for restructuring the remaining divisions after the closure of division C. LP regards $75,000 as material in the context of its financial statements.

Required:

Explain how the closure of division C and restructuring of the other divisions will be reported in LP's Statement of profit or loss and other comprehensive income for the year ended 31 December 20X2, according to IFRS 5 *Non-current assets held for sale and discontinued operations.* **(5 marks)**

336 REVENUE RECOGNITION (1) (NOV 07 EXAM)

EJ publishes trade magazines and sells them to retailers. EJ has just concluded negotiations with a large supermarket chain for the supply of a large quantity of several of its trade magazines on a regular basis.

EJ has agreed a substantial discount on the following terms:

- the same quantity of each trade magazine will be supplied each month
- quantities can only be changed at the end of each six-month period
- payment must be made six monthly in advance.

The supermarket paid $150,000 on 1 September 20X7 for six months supply of trade magazines to 29 February 20X8. At 31 October 20X7, EJ had supplied two months of trade magazines. EJ estimates that the cost of supplying the supermarket each month is $20,000.

Required:

(i) State the criteria in IAS 18 *Revenue Recognition* for income recognition. (2 marks)

(ii) Explain, with reasons, how EJ should treat the above in its financial statements for the year ended 31 October 20X7. (3 marks)

(Total: 5 marks)

337 REVENUE RECOGNITION (2) (NOV 09 EXAM)

JG sells large scale computer systems hardware. The price charged to its customers includes an amount for two years' repair and maintenance.

JG sold computer hardware to a customer on 1 April 20X9 and invoiced the customer as follows:

	$
Supply of computer hardware	1,500,000
Two years' repair and maintenance	400,000
	1,900,000
Value added tax at 20%	380,000
	2,280,000

Required:

(i) Identify the conditions that are required to be met before income from the sale of services can be recognised according to IAS 18 *Revenue Recognition*.

(ii) Explain how the repair and maintenance contract will be treated in the financial statements of JG for the year ended 30 September 20X9. **(5 marks)**

338 DIRECT METHOD (MAY 08 EXAM)

The following financial information relates to FC for the year ended 31 March 20X8.

Statement of profit or loss for the year ended 31 March 20X8

	$000
Revenue	445
Cost of sales	(220)
Gross profit	225
Other income	105
	330
Administrative expense	(177)
	153
Finance costs	(20)
Profit before tax	133
Income tax expense	(43)
Profit	90

The following administrative expenses were incurred in the year:

	$000
Wages	70
Other general expenses	15
Depreciation	92
	177

Other income:

	$000
Rentals received	45
Gain on disposal of non-current assets	60
	105

Statements of financial position extracts at:

	31 March 20X8 $000	31 March 20X7 $000
Inventories	40	25
Trade receivables	50	45
Trade payables	(30)	(20)

Required:

Prepare FC's statement of cash flows for the year ended 31 March 20X8, down to the line 'Cash generated from operations', using the direct method. (5 marks)

339 GK (NOV 08 EXAM)

The following data are to be used to answer parts (a) and (b)

The financial statements of GK for the year to 31 October 20X8 were as follows:

Statement of financial positions at	31 October 20X8 $000	$000	31 October 20X7 $000	$000
Assets				
Non-current tangible assets				
Property	10,000		10,500	
Plant and equipment	5,000		4,550	
		15,000		15,050
Current assets				
Inventory	1,750		1,500	
Trade receivables	1,050		900	
Cash and cash equivalents	310		150	
		3,110		2,550
Total assets		18,110		17,600

Equity and liabilities

Ordinary shares @ $0.50 each	6,000	3,000
Share premium	2,500	1,000
Revaluation reserve	3,000	3,000
Retained earnings	1,701	1,000
	13,201	8,000

Non-current liabilities

Interest bearing borrowings	2,400	7,000
Deferred tax	540	450
	2,940	7,450

Current liabilities

Trade and other payables	1,060	1,400
Tax payable	909	750
	1,969	2,150
	18,110	17,600

Statement of profit or loss for the year to 31 October 20X8

	$000	$000
Revenue		16,000
Cost of sales		10,000
Gross profit		6,000
Administrative expenses	(2,000)	
Distribution costs	(1,200)	(3,200)
		2,800
Finance cost		(600)
Profit before tax		2,200
Income tax expense		(999)
Profit for the period		1,201

Additional information:

1 Trade and other payables comprise:

	31 October 20X8	31 October 20X7
	$000	$000
Trade payables	730	800
Interest payable	330	600
	1,060	1,400

2   Plant disposed of in the year had a carrying value of $35,000; cash received on disposal was $60,000.

3   GK's statement of profit or loss includes depreciation for the year of $1,110,000 for properties and $882,000 for plant and equipment.

4   Dividends paid during the year were $500,000.

Required:

(a) Using the data relating to GK above, calculate the cash generated from operations that would appear in GK's Statement of cash flows, using the indirect method, for the year ended 31 October 20X8, in accordance with IAS 7 *Statement of Cash Flows.*
(5 marks)

(b) Using the data relating to GK above, calculate the cash flow from investing activities and cash flows from financing activities sections of GK's Statement of cash flows for the year ended 31 October 20X8, in accordance with IAS 7 *Statement of Cash Flows.*
(5 marks)

(Total: 10 marks)

340 BENEFITS OF CASH FLOW (MAY 12 EXAM)

Required:

Explain the main benefits, to users of the accounts, of including a statement of cash flows in published financial statements. (5 marks)

341 INVESTING ACTIVITIES (MAY 13 EXAM)

Extracts from CFQ's Statement of financial position at 31 March 20X3, with comparatives appear below:

	31 March 20X3	31 March 20X2
	$million	$million
Property, plant and equipment	635	645
Non-current asset investments at fair value	93	107
Deferred development expenditure	29	24

During the year to 31 March 20X3, CFQ sold property, plant and equipment for $45m. It had originally cost $322m and had a carrying value of $60m at the date of disposal.

CFQ's statement of profit or loss for the year ended 31 March 20X3 included:

- depreciation of property, plant and equipment of $120m
- amortisation of deferred development expenditure of $8m
- revaluation loss on investments of $21m.

Required:

Prepare the cash flows from the investing activities section of CFQ's statement of cash flows for the year ended 31 March 20X3. (5 marks)

342 FINANCING ACTIVITES (AUG 13 EXAM)

Extracts from SF's statement of financial position at 31 March 20X3, with comparatives, are shown below:

	20X3	20X2
	$000	$000
Equity		
Ordinary shares	460	400
Share premium	82	70
Revaluation reserve	44	24
Retained earnings	273	246
Non-current liabilities		
Finance lease payables	98	60
Long term borrowings	129	105
Current liabilities		
Finance lease payables	10	6

Extracts from SF's statement of changes in equity for the year ended 31 March 20X3:

	$000
Retained earnings:	
Retained earnings at 31 March 20X2	246
Profit for the year	46
Dividends paid	(19)
Retained earnings at 31 March 20X3	273

During the year ended 31 March 20X3 SF's transactions included the following:

(i) Acquired property plant and equipment on a finance lease, debiting $55,000 to property, plant and equipment.

(ii) Repaid $25,000 of its long term borrowings during the year.

(iii) Issued some ordinary shares at a 20% premium.

(iv) Charged finance costs for the finance lease of $16,000 for the year.

Required:

Prepare the "cash flows from financing activities" section of SF's statement of cash flows for the year ended 31 March 20X3. (5 marks)

SECTION B-TYPE QUESTIONS : SECTION 2

GROUP COMPANY FINANCIAL ACCOUNTS

343 GOODWILL (NOV 10 EXAM)

HB paid $2.50 per share to acquire 100% of PN's equity shares on 1 September 20X8. At that date PN's statement of financial position showed the following balances with equity:

	$000
Equity shares of $1 each	180
Share premium	60
Retained earnings	40

PN's net asset values were the same as carrying values, except for land which was valued at $70,000 more than its carrying value.

HB directors estimate that any goodwill arising on the acquisition will have a useful life of 10 years.

Required:

(i) Calculate goodwill arising on the acquisition of PN. **(2 marks)**

(ii) Explain how HB should record the goodwill in its group financial statements for the year ended 31 August 20X9, in accordance with IFRS 3 *Business Combinations*.

(3 marks)

(Total: 5 marks)

344 INVESTMENTS (NOV 10 EXAM)

HI, a parent entity, is planning to acquire a shareholding in ABC. The following alternative investment strategies are being considered:

(i) HI can purchase 80,000 preferred shares in ABC

(ii) HI can purchase 40,000 equity shares and 50,000 preferred shares in ABC

(iii) HI can purchase 70,000 equity shares in ABC and no preferred shares.

ABC has the following issued share capital:

	$
$1 Equity shares	100,000
$1 10% Preferred Shares	100,000

Holders of preferred shares do not have any votes at annual general meetings.

Required:

Identify with reasons how HI would classify its investment in ABC in its consolidated financial Statements for each of the alternative investment strategies. **(5 marks)**

Section 3

SECTION C-TYPE QUESTIONS

SINGLE COMPANY FINANCIAL ACCOUNTS

345 AF (MAY 05 EXAM)

AF is a furniture manufacturing entity. The trial balance for AF at 31 March 20X5 was as follows:

	$000	$000
6% loan notes (redeemable 20Y0)		1,500
Retained earnings at 31 March 20X4		388
Administrative expenses	1,540	
Available for sale investments at market value 31 March 20X4	1,640	
Cash and cash equivalents	822	
Cost of sales	3,463	
Distribution costs	1,590	
Dividend paid 1 December 20X4	275	
Interest paid on loan notes – half year to 30 September 20X4	45	
Inventory at 31 March 20X5	1,320	
Investment income received		68
Land and buildings at cost	5,190	
Ordinary shares of $1 each, fully paid		4,500
Plant and equipment at cost	3,400	
Provision for deferred tax		710
Provisions for depreciation at 31 March 20X4: Buildings		1,500
Provisions for depreciation at 31 March 20X4: Plant and equipment		1,659
Revaluation reserve		330
Revenue		8,210
Share premium		1,380
Trade payables		520
Trade receivables	1,480	
	20,765	20,765

PAPER F1 : FINANCIAL OPERATIONS

Additional information provided:

(i) Available for sale investments are carried in the financial statements at market value. The market value of the available for sale investments at 31 March 20X5 was $1,750,000.

(ii) There were no sales or purchases of non-current assets or available for sale investments during the year ended 31 March 20X5.

(iii) Income tax due for the year ended 31 March 20X5 is estimated at $250,000. There is no balance outstanding in relation to previous years' corporate income tax. The deferred tax provision needs to be increased by $100,000.

(iv) Depreciation is charged on buildings using the straight-line basis at 3% each year. The cost of land included in land and buildings is $2,000,000. Plant and equipment is depreciated using the reducing balance method at 20%. Depreciation is regarded as a cost of sales.

(v) AF entered into a non-cancellable five year operating lease on 1 April 20X4 to acquire machinery to manufacture a new range of kitchen units. Under the terms of the lease, AF will receive the first year rent free, then $62,500 is payable for four years commencing in year two of the lease. The machine is estimated to have a useful economic life of 20 years.

(vi) The 6% loan notes are 10 year loans due for repayment March 20Y0. AF incurred no other finance costs in the year to 31 March 20X5.

Required:

Prepare the statement of profit or loss and other comprehensive income for AF for the year to 31 March 20X5 and a statement of financial position at that date, in a form suitable for presentation to the shareholders and in accordance with the requirements of International Financial Reporting Standards.

Notes to the financial statements are NOT required, but all workings must be clearly shown. Do NOT prepare a statement of accounting policies or a statement of changes in equity.

(20 marks)

SECTION C-TYPE QUESTIONS : SECTION 3

346 DZ (MAY 07 EXAM)

DZ is a manufacturing entity and produces one group of products, known as product Y.

DZ's trial balance at 31 March 20X7 is shown below:

	$000	$000
8% loan 20Y0 (see note (xiv))		2,000
Administration expenses	891	
Cash and cash equivalents	103	
Cash received on disposal of land		1,500
Cash received on disposal of plant		5
Cost of raw materials purchased in year	2,020	
Direct production labour costs	912	
Distribution costs	462	
Equity shares $1 each, fully paid		1,000
Income tax (see note (xi))	25	
Inventory of finished goods at 31 March 20X6	240	
Inventory of raw materials at 31 March 20X6	132	
Land at valuation at 31 March 20X6	1,250	
Loan interest paid – half year	80	
Plant and equipment at cost at 31 March 20X6	4,180	
Production overheads (excluding depreciation)	633	
Property at cost at 31 March 20X6	11,200	
Provision for deferred tax at 31 March 20X6 (see note (xii))		773
Provision for depreciation at 31 March 20X6: (see notes (iv) and (v))		
Property		1,900
Plant and equipment		2,840
Research and development (see note (vi))	500	
Retained earnings at 31 March 20X6		2,024
Revaluation reserve at 31 March 20X6		2,100
Revenue		8,772
Trade payables		773
Trade receivables	1,059	
	23,687	23,687

Further information:

(i) The property cost of $11,200,000 consisted of land $3,500,000 and buildings $7,700,000.

(ii) During the year, DZ disposed of non-current assets as follows:

- A piece of surplus land was sold on 1 March 20X7 for $1,500,000.
- Obsolete plant was sold for $5,000 scrap value on the same date.
- All the cash received is included in the trial balance.

Details of the assets sold were:

Asset type	Cost	Revalued amount	Accumulated depreciation
Land	$500,000	$1,250,000	$0
Plant and equipment	$620,000		$600,000

113

(iii) On 1 April 20X6, DZ revalued its properties to $9,800,000 (land $4,100,000 and buildings $5,700,000).

(iv) Buildings are depreciated at 5% per annum on the straight line basis. Buildings, depreciation is treated as 80% production overhead and 20% administration.

(v) Plant and equipment is depreciated at 25% per annum using the reducing balance method, the depreciation being treated as a production overhead.

(vi) Product Y was developed in-house. Research and development is carried out on a continuous basis to ensure that the product range continues to meet customer demands. The research and development figure in the trial balance is made up as follows:

	$000
Development costs capitalised in previous years	867
Less: Amortisation to 31 March 20X6	534
	333
Research costs incurred in the year to 31 March 20X7	119
Development costs (all meet IAS 38 *Intangible Assets* criteria) incurred in the year to 31 March 20X7	48
Total	500

(vii) Development costs are amortised on a straight line basis at 20% per annum.

(viii) Research and development costs are treated as cost of sales when charged to the statement of profit or loss.

(ix) DZ charges a full year's amortisation and depreciation in the year of acquisition and none in the year of disposal.

(x) Inventory of raw materials at 31 March 20X7 was $165,000. Inventory of finished goods at 31 March 20X7 was $270,000.

(xi) The directors estimate the income tax charge on the year's profits at $811,000. The balance on the income tax account represents the under-provision for the previous year's tax charge.

(xii) The deferred tax provision is to be reduced to $665,000.

(xiii) No interim dividend was paid during the year.

(xiv) The 8% loan is a 20-year loan issued in 20X0.

Required:

(a) Prepare DZ's property, plant and equipment note to the accounts for the year ended 31 March 20X7. (6 marks)

(b) Prepare the statement of profit or loss and other comprehensive income and a statement of changes in equity for the year to 31 March 20X7 and a statement of financial position at that date, in a form suitable for presentation to the shareholders and in accordance with the requirements of International Financial Reporting Standards.

(All workings should be to the nearest $000.) (24 marks)

Notes to the financial statements are NOT required (except as specified in part (a) of the question), but ALL workings must be clearly shown. Do NOT prepare a statement of accounting policies.
(Total: 30 marks)

347 EY (NOV 07 EXAM)

EY is an office and industrial furniture manufacturing entity that specialises in developing and using new materials and manufacturing processes in the production of its furniture.

The statement of financial position below relates to the previous year, 31 October 20X6, which is followed by a summary of EY's cash book for the year to 31 October 20X7.

EY Statement of financial position at 31 October 20X6

		$000	$000	$000
Non-current assets				
Development costs	– cost	1,000		
	– amortisation	200		
			800	
Property, plant and equipment	– cost	7,300		
	– depreciation	1,110		
			6,190	
				6,990
Current assets				
Inventory		1,200		
Trade receivables		753		
Cash and cash equivalents		82		
			2,035	
				9,025
Equity				
Share capital			3,000	
Revaluation reserve			600	
Retained earnings			1,625	
				5,225
Non-current liabilities				
Loan notes		2,260		
Deferred tax		180		
				2,440
Current liabilities				
Trade and other payables		573		
Tax payable		670		
Interest payable		117		
				1,360
				9,025

PAPER F1 : FINANCIAL OPERATIONS

EY's summarised cash book for the year ended 31 October 20X7

	Note	Receipts/Payment $000
Cash book balance at 1 November 20X6		82
Expenditure incurred on government contract	(i)	(600)
Interest paid during the year	(ii)	(160)
Administration expenses paid		(500)
Research and development costs	(iii)	(1,600)
Income tax	(iv)	(690)
Purchase cost of property, plant and equipment	(v)	(3,460)
Final dividend of 25c per share for year ended 31 October 20X6		(750)
Receipt for disposal of land	(vi)	1,200
Cash received from customers		7,500
Payments to suppliers of production materials, wages and other production costs		(3,000)
Distribution and selling costs		(730)
Cash received from increase in loan notes		2,500
Cash book balance at 31 October 20X7		(208)

Notes:

(i) The government contract is a long-term project for the supply of a new type of seating for government offices involving the development of new materials. The total contract value is $1,400,000. The expenditure includes all costs incurred during the first year of the contract. The project leader is confident that the remainder of the work will cost no more than $400,000. The contract provides that EY can charge for the proportion of work completed by 31 October each year. The percentage of cost incurred to total cost should be used to apportion profit/losses on the contract.

(ii) Interest outstanding at 31 October 20X7 was $130,000.

(iii) During the year EY spent $1,600,000 on research and development. This comprised three projects:

- cost in the year $300,000 – funded research projects carried out at the local university

- cost in the year $500,000 – development of a new type of laminate expected to be a very profitable product line. The final development phase has just finished, and production of the laminate is expected from January 20X8

- cost in the year $800,000 – development of a new type of artificial wood, to replace real wood in some furniture and help reduce EY's use of wood. The development produced a good substitute for wood, but was five times more expensive and hence not viable.

Capitalised development expenditure is amortised on the straight line basis over five years and treated as a cost of sale.

(iv) Income tax due for the year was estimated by EY at $420,000.

(v) The property, plant and equipment balance at 31 October 20X6 was made up as follows:

	Land	Premises	Plant & equipment	Total
	$000	$000	$000	$000
Cost/valuation	2,000	1,500	3,800	7,300
Depreciation	0	350	760	1,110
Carrying value	2,000	1,150	3,040	6,190

During the year EY purchased new premises at a cost of $1,600,000, and new plant and equipment for $1,860,000. Premises are depreciated on the straight line basis at 6% per year, and plant and machinery are depreciated on the reducing balance at 15% per year and are treated as a cost of sale. EY charges a full year's depreciation in the year of acquisition. No assets were fully depreciated at 31 October 20X6.

(vi) Land originally costing $600,000, which had previously been revalued to $1,000,000, was sold during the year for $1,200,000.

(vii) A bonus issue of shares was made on the basis of one new share for every six shares held.

(viii) Deferred tax is to be increased by $42,000.

(ix) Balances at 31 October 20X7:

Trade receivables	$620,000
Outstanding trade payables	$670,000
Inventory	$985,000

Required:

Prepare the statement of profit or loss and other comprehensive income and a statement of changes in equity for the year to 31 October 20X7 and a statement of financial position at that date, in a form suitable for presentation to the shareholders and in accordance with the requirements of International Financial Reporting Standards. (All workings should be to the nearest $000.)

Notes to the financial statements are NOT required, but all workings must be clearly shown. Do NOT prepare a statement of accounting policies. (30 marks)

PAPER F1 : FINANCIAL OPERATIONS

348 FZ (MAY 08 EXAM)

FZ is an entity which owns a number of factories that specialise in packaging and selling fresh dairy products in bulk to wholesale entities and large supermarkets. FZ also owns a chain of small newsagents' shops.

At its meeting on 1 January 20X8, the Board of FZ decided that, to maximise its strategic opportunities, it would sell the newsagents' shops and concentrate on its dairy product business.

FZ's trial balance at 31 March 20X8 is shown below:

	Notes	$000	$000
5% Loan notes (redeemable 2020)			1,000
Administrative expenses		440	
Cash and cash equivalents		853	
Cash received on disposal of vehicles			15
Cost of goods sold		4,120	
Distribution costs		432	
Equity dividend paid		500	
Factory buildings at valuation		12,000	
Goodwill		300	
Inventory at 31 March 20X8		900	
Newsagents shops at cost		6,200	
Ordinary shares $1 each, fully paid at 31 March 20X8			5,000
Plant and equipment		2,313	
Provision for deferred tax at 31 March 20X7			197
Provision for property, plant and equipment depreciation at 31 March 20X7	(iii)		3,337
Retained earnings at 31 March 20X7			5,808
Revaluation reserve			190
Revenue			10,170
Share premium at 31 March 20X8			3,000
Trade payables			417
Trade receivables		929	
Vehicles at cost		147	
		29,134	29,134

Notes:

(i) The newsagents' shops were valued at $5,000,000 by a qualified external valuer on 1 January 20X8. On the same date, a prospective buyer expressed an interest at that price. At 31 March 20X8, detailed negotiations were continuing, with the sale expected to be concluded by 31 July 20X8, for the full valuation of $5,000,000.

The carrying values (all included in the relevant figures in the trial balance) of the assets relating to the newsagents' shops at 1 January 20X8, before revaluation, were:

	$000
Goodwill	300
Newsagents' shops	4,960
	5,260

The newsagents' shops are regarded as a cash generating unit. The cost of selling the shops is estimated at $200,000.

The revenue and expenses of the newsagents' shops for the year ended 31 March 20X8, all included in the trial balance figures, were as follows:

	$000
Revenue	772
Cost of sales	580
Administrative expenses	96
Distribution costs	57

The sale agreement provides for all employee contracts to be transferred to the new owners of the shops.

Loan note interest does not relate to newsagents shops.

(ii) At their meeting on 1 February 20X8, the directors of FZ agreed a $2,000,000 reorganisation package for all of FZ, excluding the newsagents' shops. The restructuring was announced to the staff on 16 February 20X8. It was scheduled to begin implementation on 1 June 20X8 and to be completed by 31 December 20X8. The reorganisation package covered staff retraining, staff relocation and development of new computer systems.

(iii) Property, plant and equipment depreciation at 31 March 20X7 comprised:

	$000
Factory buildings	720
Plant and equipment	1,310
Vehicles	67
Newsagents shops	1,240

(iv) On 1 May 20X8, FZ was informed that one of its customers, X, had ceased trading. The liquidators advised FZ that it was very unlikely to receive payment of any of the $62,000 due from X at 31 March 20X8.

(v) The taxation due for the year ended 31 March 20X8 is estimated at $920,000 (net of tax credit for newsagents' shops of $120,000) and the deferred tax provision needs to be increased to $237,000, (all relating to continuing activities).

(vi) Depreciation is to be charged on non-current assets as follows:

- Factory buildings, straight line basis at 3%.
- Plant and equipment, straight line basis at 20%.
- Newsagents' shops, straight line basis at 10%.

These items of depreciation are regarded as a cost of sales.

- Vehicles, reducing balance at 25%.

This depreciation is regarded as a distribution cost.

FZ provides a full year's depreciation in the year of purchase and no depreciation in the year of sale.

(vii) During the year, FZ disposed of old vehicles for $15,000. The original cost of these vehicles was $57,000 and accumulated depreciation at 31 March 20X7 was $52,000.

(viii) The revaluation reserve arose when the factory buildings were revalued in 20X5.

(ix) During the year, FZ raised new capital by making a rights issue of 1,000,000 $1 equity shares at $1.50 each. All rights were taken up and all amounts are included in the trial balance.

(x) The 5% loan notes were issued in 20X0.

(xi) FZ wants to disclose the minimum information allowed by IFRS in its primary financial statements.

Required:

(a) Explain, with reasons, how items (i) and (ii) above should be treated in FZ's financial statements for the year ended 31 March 20X8. (5 marks)

(b) Prepare FZ's statement of profit or loss and a statement of changes in equity for the year to 31 March 20X8 and a statement of financial position at that date, in a form suitable for presentation to the shareholders and in accordance with the requirements of International Financial Reporting Standards. (25 marks)

Notes to the financial statements are NOT required, but ALL workings must be clearly shown. Do NOT prepare a statement of accounting policies. (Total: 30 marks)

SECTION C-TYPE QUESTIONS : SECTION 3

349 GZ (NOV 08 EXAM) — Walk in the footsteps of a top tutor

GZ is a small mining entity which operated a single gold mine for many years. The gold mine ceased operations on 31 October 20X7 and was closed on 1 January 20X8.

On 1 November 20X7, GZ commenced operating a new silver mine.

The trial balance for GZ at 31 October 20X8 was as follows:

	$000	$000
4% Loan notes (redeemable 1 April 20X9)		1,900
Administrative expenses	1,131	
Available for sale investments at market value 31 October 20X7	2,177	
Cash and cash equivalents	2,025	
Decommissioning and landscaping expenses of gold mine (see note (iii))	1,008	
Direct operating expenses (excluding depreciation)	5,245	
Distribution costs	719	
Dividend paid 1 March 20X8	550	
Equity shares $1 each, fully paid		5,000
Finance lease payable (see note (ix))		900
Government operating licence, silver mine at cost (see note (ii))	100	
Income tax	13	
Interest paid on loan notes – half year to 30 April 20X8	38	
Inventory at 31 October 20X8	2,410	
Investment income received		218
Mine properties at cost (see note (iv))	6,719	
Plant (finance lease) (see note (ix))	900	
Plant and equipment at 31 October 20X7 (excluding finance lease)	3,025	
Plant lease rentals paid in year	160	
Provision for decommissioning gold mine at 31 October 20X7		950
Provision for deferred tax at 31 October 20X7		731
Provision for depreciation at 31 October 20X7:		
Mine properties (see note (iv))		2,123
Plant and equipment		370
Receipt from sale of plant (see note (iii))		2
Retained earnings at 31 October 20X7		2,810
Revaluation reserve at 31 October 20X7		80
Revenue		9,600
Suspense account (see note (xii))		1,820
Trade payables		2,431
Trade receivables	2,715	
	28,935	28,935

PAPER F1 : FINANCIAL OPERATIONS

Additional information provided:

(i) Each mine requires a government operating licence for 20 years and is expected to be productive for that time. After 20 years, the mine will be closed and decommissioned.

(ii) On 1 November 20X7, GZ received a government operating licence to operate the new silver mine. The licence cost $100,000 and is for 20 years. Included in the licence is a condition that, on closure of the mine, all above-ground structures must be removed and the ground landscaped. GZ has estimated this cost and discounted it to a present value of $3,230,000 at 31 October 20X8. The trial balance excludes this decommissioning provision.

(iii) On 1 January 20X8, GZ closed its gold mine. The $950,000 shown in the trial balance provision as "provision for decommissioning gold mine" has been charged against profits in the previous year. The removal of buildings and other above ground structures, landscaping and other decommissioning costs was complete at 31 October 20X8; the actual cost incurred was $1,008,000.

GZ sold old plant and equipment from the gold mine for $2,000 (original cost $200,000, carrying value $5,000). The gold mine property is now surplus to GZ's requirements. At 31 October 20X8, the gold mine property had a market value of $520,000 with estimated selling and legal costs of $27,000.

(iv) The mine property balances in the trial balance comprised:

Mine property	Gold Mine	Silver Mine	Total
	$000	$000	$000
Cost	2,623	4,096	6,719
Provision for depreciation	2,123	0	2,123
	500	4,096	4,596

(v) The market value of the available for sale investments at 31 October 20X8 was $2,311,000.

(vi) There were no sales or purchases of available for sale investments during the year ended 31 October 20X8 and no acquisitions of other non-current assets, except for those in note (ix) below.

(vii) Income tax due for the year ended 31 October 20X8 is estimated at $375,000. The deferred tax provision needs to be reduced by $60,000.

(viii) Depreciation is charged on mining property using the straight-line basis at 5% per annum. Plant and equipment is depreciated using the reducing balance method at 25%. The depreciation policy is to charge a full year's depreciation in the year of acquisition and no depreciation in the year of disposal. Depreciation is regarded as a cost of production.

(ix) GZ entered into a non-cancellable seven-year finance lease on 1 November 20X7 to acquire mining machinery. Under the terms of the lease, GZ will make annual payments of $160,000 in arrears, the first payment being made on 31 October 20X8. The machinery is estimated to have a useful economic life of seven years. The fair value of the machinery at 1 November 20X7 was $900,000. GZ allocates finance charges using the sum of digits method.

(x) The 4% loan notes are ten-year loans due for repayment 1 April 20X9. GZ incurred no other interest charges in the year to 31 October 20X8.

(xi) The final dividend for the year to 31 October 20X7 was paid on 1 March 20X8.

(xii) GZ made a new issue of 1,400 equity shares on 31 October 20X8 at a premium of 30%. The cash received was debited to the bank account and credited to the suspense account.

Required:

(a) Prepare GZ's Property, Plant and Equipment note to the financial statements for the year to 31 October 20X8. **(6 marks)**

(b) Prepare GZ's Statement of profit or loss and other comprehensive income and a statement of changes in equity for the year to 31 October 20X8 and a statement of financial position at that date, in a form suitable for presentation to the shareholders and in accordance with the requirements of International Financial Reporting Standards. (All workings should be to the nearest $000). **(24 marks)**

Notes to the financial statements, except as indicated in part (a) above, are NOT required, but all workings must be clearly shown. Do NOT prepare a statement of accounting policies. **(Total: 30 marks)**

350 JZ (NOV 09 EXAM)

JZ is a manufacturing and construction entity. JZ produces pre-fabricated building sections and undertakes construction contracts for clients.

JZ's trial balance at 30 September 20X9 is shown below:

	$000	$000
5% bond (note i)		1,800
Administrative expenses	784	
Cash and cash equivalents	87	
Cash received on account from construction contract client (note ii)		95
Contract work in progress (note ii)	74	
Cost of goods sold (excluding depreciation and construction contract)	2,561	
Distribution costs	405	
Equity shares $1 each, fully paid		1,500
Inventory at 30 September 20X9 (excluding construction contract)	212	
Lease payment (note iii)	60	
Loan interest paid	45	
Plant and equipment at 30 September 20X8 (note iv)	3,680	
Property at cost at 30 September 20X8 (notes v & vi))	10,960	
Provision for deferred tax at 30 September 20X8 (note vii))		620
Provision for depreciation at 30 September 20X8 (notes viii, ix & x)		
Property		1,930
Plant and equipment		1,720
Provision for legal claim (note xi)		45
Retained earnings at 30 September 20X8		2,064
Revenue		7,720
Share premium at 30 September 20X9 (note xii)		250
Suspense account (note vi)		1,320
Trade payables		741
Trade receivables	937	
	19,805	19,805

Further Information:

(i) The 5% bond, was issued on the 1 October 20X8 for 20 years, and has interest paid twice a year.

(ii) JZ signed a construction contract on 1 November 20X8. The contract was for 3 years and had a fixed price of $300,000. JZ uses the value of work completed method to recognise attributable profit on construction contracts. At 30 September 20X9 a quantity surveyor certified that JZ had completed 35% of the contract. JZ estimates that the additional cost to complete the contract is $124,000. All costs incurred to date are included under contract work in progress in the trial balance.

(iii) JZ acquired new equipment on 1 October 20X8 using a finance lease. The fair value of the equipment was $300,000, which is approximately equal to the present value of the minimum lease payment. JZ agreed to make 6 annual payments of $60,000 in advance, commencing on 1 October 20X8. Only the rental payment has so far been recorded in the accounts. The interest rate implicit in the lease is 7.93%.

(iv) Obsolete plant was disposed of during the year. The plant had cost $720,000, was fully depreciated and had no scrap value.

(v) The property cost of $10,960,000 consisted of land $3,500,000 and buildings $7,460,000.

(vi) On 1 March 20X9 JZ disposed of a piece of surplus land for $1,320,000, which had originally cost $600,000. Cash received has been correctly posted to the bank account and the credit entry posted to suspense. Under local tax legislation no tax charge arises from this sale.

(vii) The deferred tax provision is to be reduced to $600,000.

(viii) Plant and equipment is depreciated at 25% per annum using the reducing balance method and is treated as cost of sales.

(ix) Buildings are depreciated at 5% per annum on the straight line basis. No buildings were fully depreciated at 30 September 20X8. Buildings depreciation is treated as an administrative expense.

(x) JZ charges a full years depreciation in the year of acquisition and none in the year of disposal.

(xi) On 15th October 20X9 the court reached a verdict on a long running legal case brought against JZ. The court awarded damages and costs to a customer of JZ, totalling $40,000. JZ had created a provision of $45,000 at 30 September 20X8, this was charged to cost of sales. Legal advice at that time was that JZ would probably lose the case.

(xii) During the year JZ issued 300,000 equity shares at a 50% premium. The issue is included in the trial balance.

(xiii) The directors estimate the income tax charge on the year's profits at $795,000.

(xiv) No dividends were paid during the year.

Required:

(a) Prepare JZ's Property, Plant and Equipment note to the financial statements for the year to 30 September 20X9. **(5 marks)**

(b) Prepare JZ's Statement of profit or loss and other comprehensive income and a statement of changes in equity for the year to 30 September 20X9 and a statement of financial position at that date, in a form suitable for presentation to the shareholders and in accordance with the requirements of International Financial Reporting Standards. (All workings should be to the nearest $000). **(24 marks)**

Notes to the financial statements, except as indicated in part (a) above, are NOT required, but all workings must be clearly shown. Do NOT prepare a statement of accounting policies.

(Total: 30 marks)

351 EZ (MAY 10 EXAM)

EZ trial balance at 31 March 20Y0 was as follows:

	$000	$000
Administrative expenses	86	
Cash and cash equivalents	22	
Cost of goods sold	418	
Distribution costs	69	
Equity dividend paid	92	
Inventory at 31 March 20Y0	112	
Land market value – 31 March 20X9	700	
Lease	15	
Long term borrowings		250
Equity shares of $1 each, fully paid at 31 March 20Y0		600
Plant and equipment at cost 31 March 20X9	480	
Provision for deferred tax at 31 March 20X9		30
Provision for property, plant and equipment depreciation at 31 March 20X9		144
Retained earnings at 31 March 20X9		181
Revaluation reserve 31 March 20X9		10
Revenue		720
Share premium at 31 March 20Y0		300
Suspense		2
Trade payables		32
Trade receivables	275	
	2,269	2,269

PAPER F1 : FINANCIAL OPERATIONS

Additional information provided:

(i) Land is carried in the financial statements at market value. The market value of the land at 31 March 20Y0 was $675,000. There were no purchases or sales of land during the year.

(ii) The tax due for the year ended 31 March 20Y0 is estimated at $18,000. Deferred tax is estimated to decrease by $10,000.

(iii) During the year EZ disposed of old equipment for $2,000. No entry has been made in the accounts for this transaction except to record the cash received in the cash book and in the suspense account. The original cost of the equipment sold was $37,000 and its carrying value at 31 March 20X9 was $7,000.

(iv) Property, plant and equipment is depreciated at 10% per year straight line. Depreciation of property, plant and equipment is considered to be part of cost of sales. EZ's policy is to charge a full year's depreciation in the year of acquisition and no depreciation in the year of disposal.

(v) During the year EZ paid a final dividend of $92,000 for the year ended 31 March 20X9.

(vi) EZ issued 200,000 equity shares on 30 September 20X9 at a premium of 50%.

(vii) Long term borrowings consist of a loan taken out on 1 April 20X9 at 4% interest per year. No loan interest has been paid at 31 March 20Y0.

(viii) On 22 April 20Y0 EZ discovered that ZZZ, its largest customer, had gone into liquidation. EZ has been informed that is very unlikely to receive any of the $125,000 balance outstanding at 31 March 20Y0.

(ix) On 1 April 20X9 EZ acquired additional vehicles on a 2.5 year (30 months) operating lease. The lease included an initial 6 months rent-free period as an incentive to sign the lease. The lease payments were $2,500 per month commencing on 1 October 20X9.

Required:

Prepare EZ's statement of profit or loss and other comprehensive income and statement of changes in equity for the year to 31 March 20Y0 and a statement of financial position at that date, in a form suitable for presentation to the shareholders and in accordance with the requirements of International Financial Reporting Standards.

Notes to the financial statements are NOT required, but all workings must be clearly shown. Do NOT prepare a statement of accounting policies. (25 marks)

SECTION C-TYPE QUESTIONS : SECTION 3

352 XB (NOV 10 EXAM) *Walk in the footsteps of a top tutor*

XB trial balance at 31 October 20X9 is shown below:

	Notes	$000	$000
Administrative expenses		185	
Cash and cash equivalents		216	
Cost of sales		237	
Distribution costs		62	
Donations to political party		5	
Entertaining expenses		12	
Equity dividend paid	(i)	50	
Interest paid	(ii)	3	
Inventory at 31 October 20X9		18	
Land at cost – 31 October 20X8	(iii)	730	
Long-term borrowings	(ii)		200
Ordinary Shares $1 each, fully paid at 31 October 20X9	(iv)		630
Property, plant and equipment – at cost 31 October 20X8	(iii)	320	
Provision for deferred tax at 31 October 20X8			10
Provision for property, plant and equipment depreciation at 31 October 20X8	(v)		192
Purchase of property, plant and equipment during the year	(v)	110	
Retained earnings at 31 October 20X8			168
Revenue			690
Share premium at 31 October 20X9	(iv)		99
Suspense	(vi)	3	
Taxation	(vii)	6	
Trade payables			77
Trade receivables		109	
		2,066	2,066

Additional information provided:

(i) The final dividend for the year to 31 October 20X8 of $50,000 was paid on 31 March 20X9.

(ii) Long-term borrowings consist of a loan taken out on 1 May 20X8 at 3% interest per year. Six months loan interest has been paid in the year to 31 October 20X9.

(iii) At 31 October 20X8 the tax written down value of XB's assets was $90,000. None of these assets were fully depreciated at this date.

(iv) XB issued 330,000 equity shares on 30 June 20X9 at a premium of 30%.

PAPER F1 : FINANCIAL OPERATIONS

(v) Property, plant and equipment is depreciated at 20% per annum using the straight line method. Depreciation of property, plant and equipment is considered to be part of cost of sales. XB's policy is to charge a full year's depreciation in the year of acquisition and no depreciation in the year of disposal.

(vi) Purchased goods, invoiced at $3,000 received in September 20X9 were returned to the supplier in October. At 31 October 20X9 the supplier had not issued a credit note. XB had correctly deducted the amount from purchases with the corresponding double entry posted to the suspense account.

(vii) The balance on the taxation account is the income tax underestimated in the previous year's financial statements.

Required:

(a) Prepare XB's statement of profit or loss and other comprehensive income for the year to 31 October 20X9, including a calculation of income tax expense. **(14 marks)**

All expenses other than depreciation, amortisation, entertaining, taxes paid to other public bodies and donations to political parties are tax deductible.

Tax depreciation is deductible as follows: 50% of additions to Property, Plant and Equipment in the accounting period in which they are recorded; 25% per year of the written-down value (i.e. cost minus previous allowances) in subsequent accounting periods except that in which the asset is disposed of.

The corporate tax on profits is at a rate of 25%.

(Note there are up to 8 marks available for the taxation computation)

(b) Prepare XB's statement of changes in equity for the year to 31 October 20X9 and a statement of financial position at that date. **(11 marks)**

All statements should be in a form suitable for presentation to the shareholders and in accordance with the requirements of International Financial Reporting Standards.

Notes to the financial statements are not required, but all workings must be clearly shown. Do NOT prepare a statement of accounting policies.

Note: Your answer should be to the nearest $000. **(Total: 25 marks)**

SECTION C-TYPE QUESTIONS : SECTION 3

353 MN (MAY 11 EXAM)

MN operates a number of retail outlets around the country. One retail outlet was closed on 31 March 20X9 when trading ceased and the outlet was put up for sale. All income and expenses of the outlet are included in the trial balance. The retail outlet is regarded as a cash generating unit, all its assets are being sold in one unit. At 31 March 20X9 the directors are certain that the outlet meets the requirements of IFRS 5 *Non-current Assets Held for Sale and Discontinued Operations* for treatment as non-current assets held for sale.

MN's trial balance at 31 March 20X9 is shown below:

	Notes	$000	$000
Administrative expenses	(ii)	160	
Cash and cash equivalents			14
Cost of goods sold	(ii)	622	
Distribution costs	(ii)	170	
Equity dividend paid	(ix)	30	
Inventory at 31 March 20X9		65	
Long term borrowings	(vii)		300
Equity Shares $1 each, fully paid			600
Property, plant and equipment – carrying value 31 March 20X8	(i) to (iii)	2,073	
Provision for deferred tax at 31 March 20X8	(vi)		83
Provision for repairs under warranty at 31 March 20X8	(iv)		76
Retained earnings at 31 March 20X8			777
Revenue			1,120
Share premium at 31 March 20X8			200
Trade payables			51
Trade receivables		101	
		3,221	3,221

Additional information provided:

(i) The carrying values of the property, plant and equipment at 31 March 20X8 were as follows:

Asset type	Cost – continuing activities	Cost – discontinued operations	Accumulated depreciation – continuing activities	Accumulated depreciation – discontinued operations	Carrying value
	$000	$000	$000	$000	$000
Land	1,220	150	0	0	1,370
Buildings	700	40	140	20	580
Plant & equipment	240	60	142	35	123
	2,160	250	282	55	2,073

(ii) The fair value less cost to sell of the assets of the closed retail outlet at 31 March 20X9 was $176,000.

The results of the closed outlet for the period 1 April 20X8 to 31 March 20X9 were as follows:

	$
Revenue	80,000
Cost of sales	(130,000)
Administration expenses	(40,000)
Distribution costs	(90,000)

(iii) MN depreciates buildings at 5% per annum on the straight-line basis and plant and equipment at 20% per annum using the reducing balance basis method. Depreciation is included in cost of sales.

(iv) MN sells electronic goods with a one year warranty. At 31 March 20X8 MN created a provision of $76,000 for the cost of honouring the warranties at that date. On 31 March 20X9 the outstanding warranties were reviewed and the following estimates prepared:

	Probability	Anticipated cost
Worse case	10%	$190,000
Best case	15%	$20,000
Most likely	75%	$80,000

All warranties relate to continuing activities. Actual repair costs incurred during the year were charged to cost of sales.

(v) The directors estimate the income tax charge on the year's profits at $67,000, of this a tax reduction of $10,000 relates to discontinued operations.

(vi) The deferred tax provision is to be reduced to $78,000.

(vii) The long term borrowings incur annual interest at 4% per year paid annually in arrears.

Required:

Prepare MN's statement of profit or loss and other comprehensive income and statement of changes in equity for the year to 31 March 20X9 and a statement of financial position at that date, in a form suitable for presentation to the shareholders and in accordance with the requirements of International Financial Reporting Standards.

Notes to the financial statements are not required, but all workings must be clearly shown. Do NOT prepare a statement of accounting policies. (25 marks)

354 ZY (SEP 11 EXAM)

ZY's trial balance at 30 June 20X1 is shown below:

	Notes	$000	$000
Administrative expenses		338	
Cash and cash equivalents		229	
Cash received on disposal of vehicles	(ii)		10
Distribution costs		221	
Equity dividend paid	(v)	90	
Equity Shares $1 each, fully paid at 30 June 20X1			500
Finance lease rental paid	(iii)	30	
Income tax	(viii)	15	
Interest paid – half year to 31 December 20W0		8	
Inventory at 30 June 20W0	(vii)	358	
Long term borrowings (repayable 20Y0)	(iv)		320
Plant and equipment at 30 June 20W0		864	
Preferred shares, 4% cumulative redeemable 20Y1	(vi)		150
Property at valuation 30 June 20W0	(i)	844	
Provision for deferred tax at 30 June 20W0	(ix)		45
Provision for plant and equipment depreciation at 30 June 20W0	(i)		249
Provision for property depreciation at 30 June 20W0	(i)		8
Purchase of goods for resale		987	
Retained earnings at 30 June 20W0			288
Revaluation reserve at 30 June 20W0	(i)		220
Sales revenue			2,084
Share premium at 30 June 20X1			270
Trade payables			120
Trade receivables	(x)	280	
		4,264	4,264

Additional information provided:

(i) Property is depreciated at 1% per year and plant and equipment is depreciated at 20% per year straight line. Depreciation is charged to cost of sales. ZY's policy is to charge a full year's depreciation in the year of acquisition and no depreciation in the year of disposal. Property is revalued every three years.

(ii) ZY disposed of its old vehicles on 1 October 20W0 for $10,000. The original cost was $95,000 and the carrying value at the date of disposal was zero. Vehicles are included in plant and equipment. No adjusting entries have yet been made to ZY's plant and equipment for this disposal.

PAPER F1 : FINANCIAL OPERATIONS

(iii) ZY purchased new vehicles using a finance lease on 1 July 20W0. The finance lease terms are:

- Lease for a five year period
- Rentals paid annually in arrears on 30 June
- Each annual rental is $30,000
- The fair value of the vehicles was $120,000
- The interest rate implicit in the lease is 7.93% per year

(iv) The long term borrowings incur annual interest at 5% per year, and is paid six monthly in arrears.

(v) During the current accounting period ZY paid a final dividend for the year ended 30 June 20W0 of $50,000 and an interim dividend for the year ended 30 June 20X1 of $40,000.

(vi) On 1 January 20X1 ZY issued $150,000 4% cumulative redeemable preferred shares. At 30 June 20X1 no dividend had been paid.

(vii) Inventory at 30 June 20X1 amounted to $390,000 at cost. A review of inventory items revealed the need for some adjustments for two inventory lines.

- Items which had cost $100,000 and which would normally sell for $220,000 were found to have deteriorated. Remedial work costing $30,000 would be needed to enable the items to be sold for $110,000.
- Some items sent to customers on sale or return terms had been omitted from inventory and included as sales in June 20X1. The cost of these items was $15,000 and they were included in sales at $30,000. On 30 June 20X1, the items were returned in good condition by the customers but no entries have been made to record this.

(viii) The income tax balance in the trial balance is a result of the under provision of tax for the year ended 30 June 20W0. The directors estimate the income tax charge on the profits of the year ended 30 June 20X1 at $56,000.

(ix) The deferred tax provision is to be reduced to $38,000.

(x) On 1 August 20X1, ZY was informed that one of its customers, X, had ceased trading. The liquidators advised ZY that it was very unlikely to receive payment of any of the $48,000 due from X at 30 June 20X1.

Required:

Prepare ZY's statement of profit or loss and other comprehensive income and statement of changes in equity for the year to 30 June 2011 AND a statement of financial position at that date, in accordance with the requirements of International Financial Reporting Standards.

Notes to the financial statements are not required, but all workings must be clearly shown. Do NOT prepare a statement of accounting policies. **(25 marks)**

355 ABC (NOV 11) — Walk in the footsteps of a top tutor

ABC sells goods to the building industry and carries out construction contracts for clients. ABC's trial balance at 30 September 20X1 is shown below:

	Notes	$000	$000
Administrative expenses		1,020	
Cash and cash equivalents		440	
Cash received on account from construction contract clients during year to 30 September 20X1 – contract 1	(i)		4,000
Cash received on account from construction contract clients during year to 30 September 20X1 – contract 2	(i)		1,800
Cash received on disposal of plant and equipment	(iii)		15
Construction contract 1 – work in progress for year to 30 September 20X1	(i)	3,750	
Construction contract 2 – work in progress for year to 30 September 20X1	(i)	2,250	
Distribution costs		590	
Equity dividend paid	(viii)	250	
Equity Shares $1 each, fully paid at 30 September 20X1			2,500
Income tax	(v)	15	
Interest paid – half year to 31 March 20X1		58	
Inventory at 30 September 20X1 (excluding construction contracts)		310	
Long term borrowings (redeemable 20Y1)	(iv)		2,300
Plant and equipment at cost 30 September 20X1	(iii)	4,930	
Property at valuation 30 September 20X0	(ii)	11,000	
Provision for deferred tax at 30 September 20X0	(vi)		250
Provision for plant and equipment depreciation at 30 September 20X0	(iii)		2,156
Provision for property depreciation at 30 September 20X0	(ii)		3,750
Cost of goods sold (excluding construction contracts)		3,210	
Retained earnings at 30 September 20X0			627
Sales revenue			9,500
Share premium at 30 September 20X1			1,500
Trade payables			235
Trade receivables	(vii)	810	
		28,633	28,633

Additional information provided:

(i) At 30 September 20X1 ABC had two construction contracts in progress.

	Contract 1	Contract 2
Contract length	3 years	2 years
Date commenced	1 October 20X0	1 April 20X1
Fixed contract value	$11,000,000	$8,000,000

Contract detail for year ended 30 September 20X1

	Contract 1	Contract 2
Proportion of work certified as completed	40%	25%
	$000	$000
Construction contract work in progress	3,750	2,250
Estimated cost to complete contract	5,400	6,750
Cash received on account from construction contract clients during year	4,000	1,800

Both contracts use the value of work completed method to recognise attributable profit for the year.

(ii) Property consists of land $3,500,000 and buildings $7,500,000. Buildings are depreciated at 5% per year on the straight line basis. No buildings were fully depreciated at 30 September 20X1.

(iii) Plant and equipment is depreciated at 25% per year using the reducing balance method. During the year to 30 September 20X1 ABC sold obsolete plant for $15,000. The plant had cost $75,000 and had been depreciated by $65,000. All depreciation is considered to be part of cost of sales. ABC's policy is to charge a full year's depreciation in the year of acquisition and no depreciation in the year of disposal.

(iv) The long term borrowings incur annual interest at 5% paid six monthly in arrears.

(v) The income tax balance in the trial balance is a result of the under provision of tax for the year ended 30 September 20X0. The directors estimate the income tax charge on the profit of the year to 30 September 20X1 at $910,000.

(vi) The deferred tax provision is to be increased by $19,000.

(vii) On 1 August 20X1, ABC was informed that one of its customers, EF, had ceased trading. The liquidators advised ABC that it was very unlikely to receive payment of any of the $25,000 due from EF at 30 September 20X1.

(viii) ABC made no new share issues during the year. ABC paid a final dividend for the year to 30 September 20X0.

Required:

Prepare ABC's statement of profit or loss and other comprehensive income and statement of changes in equity for the year to 30 September 20X1 AND a statement of financial position at that date in accordance with the requirements of International Financial Reporting Standards.

Notes to the financial statements are not required, but all workings must be clearly shown. Do NOT prepare a statement of accounting policies. (25 marks)

SECTION C-TYPE QUESTIONS : SECTION 3

356 RTY (MAR 12)

RTY's trial balance at 31 January 20X2 is shown below:

	Notes	$000	$000
Administrative expenses		1,225	
Cash and cash equivalents		142	
Cash received on disposal of non-current assets	(i)		2,068
Cost of goods sold		4,939	
Distribution costs		679	
Equity dividend paid	(iii)	138	
Equity Shares $1 each, fully paid at 31 January 20X1			1,375
Income tax	(vi)	35	
Interest paid – half year to 31 July 20X1		69	
Inventory at 31 January 20X2		330	
Long term borrowings (redeemable 20Y5)	(v)		2,740
Plant and equipment at cost 31 January 20X1	(i)	5,750	
Property at valuation 31 January 20X1	(i)	17,120	
Provision for deferred tax at 31 January 20X1	(vii)		1,064
Provision for plant and equipment depreciation at 31 January 20X1	(i)		3,900
Provision for property depreciation at 31 January 20X1	(i)		2,610
Research and development	(ii)	689	
Retained earnings at 31 January 20X1			2,785
Revaluation reserve at 31 January 20X1			2,900
Sales revenue			9,320
Share premium at 31 January 20X1			2,750
Trade payables			1,080
Trade receivables	(iv)	1,476	
		32,592	32,592

Additional information provided:

(i) **Property, plant and equipment**

The property valuation at 31 January 20X1 of $17,120,000 consisted of land $6,220,000 and buildings $10,900,000. On 1 February 20X1 RTY revalued its properties to $15,750,000 (land $6,850,000 and buildings $8,900,000).

During the year RTY disposed of non-current assets as follows:

- A piece of surplus land was sold on 1 March 20X1 for $2,060,000.
- Obsolete plant was sold for $8,000 scrap value on the same date.
- All the cash received is included in the trial balance.
- Details of the assets sold were:

Asset type	Cost	Revalued amount	Accumulated depreciation
Land	$1,000,000	$1,800,000	$0
Plant and equipment	$820,000		$800,000

135

Buildings are depreciated at 5% per annum on the straight line basis. No buildings were fully depreciated at 31 January 20X1. Plant and equipment is depreciated at 25% per annum using the reducing balance method. All depreciation is treated as a cost of sales. RTY charges a full year's depreciation in the year of acquisition and none in the year of disposal.

(ii) **Research and development**

RTY carries out research and development on a continuous basis to ensure that its product range continues to meet customer demands. The research and development figure in the trial balance is made up as follows:

	$000
Development costs capitalised in previous years	1,199
Less amortisation to 31 January 20X1	744
	455
Research costs incurred in the year to 31 January 20X2	163
Development costs (all meet IAS 38 *Intangible Assets* criteria) incurred in the year to 31 January 20X2	71
Total	689

Development costs are amortised on a straight line basis at 20% per year. No development costs were fully amortised at 31 January 20X1. Research and development costs are treated as cost of sales when charged to statement of profit or loss. RTY charges a full year's amortisation in the year of acquisition.

(iii) During the year RTY paid a final dividend for the year to 31 January 20X2.

(iv) On 1 March 20X2, RTY was informed that one of its customers, BVC, had ceased trading. The liquidators advised RTY that it was very unlikely to receive payment of any of the $48,000 due from BVC at 31 January 20X2.

(v) The long term borrowings incur annual interest at 5% per year paid six monthly in arrears.

(vi) The income tax balance in the trial balance is a result of the under provision of tax for the year ended 31 January 20X1. The directors estimate the income tax charge on the year's profits to 31 January 20X2 at $765,000.

(vii) The deferred tax provision is to be decreased by $45,000.

Required:

Prepare RTY's statement of profit or loss and other comprehensive income and statement of changes in equity for the year to 31 January 20X2 AND a statement of financial position at that date in accordance with the requirements of International Financial Reporting Standards.

Notes to the financial statements are not required, but all workings must be clearly shown. Do NOT prepare a statement of accounting policies. (25 marks)

357 DFG (MAY 12)

DFG's trial balance at 31 March 20X2 is shown below:

	Notes	$000	$000
5% Loan notes (issued 20X0, redeemable 20Y0)			280
Administrative expenses		180	
Amortisation of patent at 1 April 20X1			27
Cash and cash equivalents			56
Cost of sales		554	
Distribution costs		90	
Equity dividend paid 1 September 20X1		55	
Income tax	(i)	10	
Inventory at 31 March 20X2		186	
Land and buildings at cost	(ii)	960	
Loan interest paid		7	
Ordinary Shares $1 each, fully paid at 1 April 20X1			550
Patent	(vii)	90	
Plant and equipment at cost	(ii)	480	
Provision for deferred tax at 1 April 20X1	(iii)		75
Provision for buildings depreciation at 1 April 20X1	(iv)		33
Provision for plant and equipment depreciation at 1 April 20X1	(v)		234
Retained earnings at 1 April 20X1			121
Sales revenue	(vi)		1,200
Share premium			110
Trade payables			61
Trade receivables		135	
		2,747	2,747

Additional information:

(i) The income tax balance in the trial balance is a result of the under provision of tax for the year ended 31 March 20X1.

(ii) There were no sales of non-current assets during the year ended 31 March 20X2.

(iii) The tax due for the year ended 31 March 20X2 is estimated at $52,000 and the deferred tax provision should be increased by $15,000.

(iv) Depreciation is charged on buildings using the straight line method at 3% per annum. The cost of land included in land and buildings is $260,000. Buildings depreciation is treated as an administrative expense.

(v) Up to 31 March 20X1 all plant and equipment was depreciated using the straight line method at 12.5%. However some plant and equipment has been wearing out and needing to be replaced on average after six years. DFG management have therefore decided that from 1 April 20X1 the expected useful life of this type of plant and equipment should be changed to a total of six years from acquisition. The plant and equipment affected was purchased on 1 April 20W7 and had an original cost of $120,000. This plant and equipment is estimated to have no residual value. All plant and equipment depreciation should be charged to cost of sales.

(vi) The sales revenue for the year to 31 March 20X2 includes $15,000 received from a new overseas customer. The $15,000 was a 10% deposit for an order of $150,000 worth of goods. DFG is still waiting for the results of the new customer's credit reference and at 31 March 20X2 has not despatched any goods.

(vii) On 1 April 20W8 DFG purchased a patent for the secret recipe and manufacturing process for one of its products. Due to recent world economic difficulties DFG has carried out an impairment review of its patent. At 31 March 20X2 the patent was found to have the following values:

Value in use $50,000

Fair value less cost to sell $47,000

On 1 July 20X1 one of DFG's customers started litigation against DFG, claiming damages caused by an allegedly faulty product. DFG has been advised that it will probably lose the case and that the claim for $35,000 will probably succeed.

Required:

(a) Briefly explain how items (vi) and (vii) should be treated by DFG in its financial statements for the year ended 31 March 20X2. **(6 marks)**

(b) Prepare DFG's statement of profit or loss and other comprehensive income and statement of changes in equity for the year to 31 March 20X2 AND a statement of financial position at that date in accordance with the requirements of International Financial Reporting Standards. **(19 marks)**

Notes to the financial statements are NOT required, but all workings must be clearly shown. Do NOT prepare a statement of accounting policies. **(Total: 25 marks)**

358 QWE (AUG 12)

QWE's trial balance at 31 March 20X2 is shown below:

	Notes	$000	$000
4% Loan notes (redeemable 20Y0)			500
Administrative expenses		190	
Amortisation of deferred development expenditure			30
Cash and cash equivalents		42	
Deferred development expenditure	(i)	150	
Distribution costs		72	
Equity dividend paid 1 September 20X1		62	
Income tax	(ii)	8	
Inventory at 31 March 20X2		214	
Cost of sales		1,605	
Land and buildings at cost at 1 April 20X1		2,410	
Loan interest paid		10	
Ordinary Shares $1 each, fully paid at 1 April 20X1			930
Plant and equipment at cost at 1 April 20X1		560	
Provision for deferred tax at 1 April 20X1	(iii)		86
Provision for buildings depreciation at 1 April 20X1	(v)		386
Provision for plant and equipment depreciation at 1 April 20X1	(v)		185
Retained earnings at 1 April 20X1			621
Sales revenue			2,220
Share premium at 1 April 20X1			310
Trade payables			190
Trade receivables		130	
Suspense account	(iv)	5	
		5,458	5,458

Additional information:

(i) Deferred development expenditure is being amortised at 10% pa on the straight line basis.

(ii) The income tax balance in the trial balance is a result of the under provision of tax for the year ended 31 March 20X1.

(iii) The tax due for the year ended 31 March 20X2 is estimated at $83,000 and the deferred tax provision needs to be increased by $25,000.

PAPER F1 : FINANCIAL OPERATIONS

(iv) The suspense account is comprised of two items:

- Expenditure of $20,000 incurred during the year on original research aimed at possibly finding a new material for QWE to use in manufacturing its products.

- $15,000 cash received from disposal of some plant and equipment that had an original cost of $82,000 and a carrying value of $3,000.

The only entries made in QWE's ledgers for these items were in cash and cash equivalents and the suspense account.

(v) Depreciation is charged on buildings using the straight line method at 3% per annum. The cost of land included in land and buildings is $800,000. Buildings depreciation should be included in administrative expenses. Depreciation of plant and equipment is at 12.5% on the reducing balance basis and is treated as part of the cost of sales.

QWE's policy is to charge a full year's depreciation in the year of acquisition and no depreciation in the year of disposal.

(vi) On 1 July 20X1 one of QWE's customers started litigation against QWE, claiming damages caused by an allegedly faulty product. QWE has been advised that it will probably lose the case and the claim for $25,000 will probably succeed.

(vii) On 1 August 20X2 QWE was advised that one of its customers, that had been in some financial difficulties at 31 March 20X2, had gone into liquidation and that the $32,000 balance outstanding at 31 March 20X2 was very unlikely to be paid.

(viii) QWE has not previously made any provisions for legal claims or irrecoverable debts.

Required:

(a) Prepare journal entries, with a short narrative, to eliminate the balance on QWE's suspense account. (3 marks)

(b) Prepare the statement of profit or loss and other comprehensive income and a statement of changes in equity for QWE for the year to 31 March 2012 and a statement of financial position at that date, in accordance with the requirements of International Financial Reporting Standards. (22 marks)

Notes to the financial statements are not required, but all workings must be clearly shown. Do NOT prepare a statement of accounting policies.

(Total: 25 marks)

SECTION C-TYPE QUESTIONS : SECTION 3

359 YZ (NOV 12)

YZ is a manufacturing entity which produces and sells a range of products.

YZ's trial balance at 30 September 20X2 is shown below:

	Notes	$000	$000
Administrative expenses		910	
Borrowings @ 7% per year			3,000
Buildings at cost at 30 September 20X1		3,400	
Cash and cash equivalents		130	
Cash received on disposal of machinery	(i)		8
Cost of raw materials purchased in year to 30 September 20X2		2,220	
Direct production labour costs		670	
Distribution costs		515	
Equity dividend paid		170	
Equity shares $1 each, fully paid at 30 September 20X2	(xi)		1,700
Income tax	(viii)	30	
Inventory of finished goods at 30 September 20X1	(vii)	190	
Inventory of raw materials at 30 September 20X1	(vii)	275	
Land at valuation at 30 September 20X1	(ii)	9,000	
Loan interest paid		210	
Plant and equipment at cost at 30 September 20X1	(i)	3,900	
Production overheads (excluding depreciation)		710	
Provision for deferred tax at 30 September 20X1	(ix)		430
Accumulated depreciation at 30 September 20X1:			
Buildings	(iii)		816
Plant and equipment	(iv)		2,255
Patent	(v)	526	
Retained earnings at 30 September 20X1			3,117
Revaluation reserve at 30 September 20X1			1,800
Sales revenue			9,820
Share premium	(xi)		100
Trade payables			940
Trade receivables		1,130	
		23,986	23,986

Additional information:

(i) During the year YZ disposed of obsolete machinery for $8,000. The cash received is included in the trial balance. The obsolete machinery had originally cost $35,000 and had accumulated depreciation of $32,000.

(ii) On 30 September 20X2 YZ revalued its land to $9,500,000.

(iii) Buildings are depreciated at 2% per annum on the straight line basis. Buildings depreciation should be treated as an administrative expense. No buildings were fully depreciated at 30 September 20X1.

PAPER F1 : FINANCIAL OPERATIONS

(iv) Plant and equipment is depreciated at 25% per annum using the reducing balance method and is treated as a production overhead.

(v) The patent for one of YZ's products was purchased on 1 October 20W9. The patent had a useful life of 10 years when it was purchased and is being amortised on a straight line basis with no residual value anticipated. Amortisation of the patent is treated as cost of sales when charged to the income statement. Research is carried out on a continuous basis to develop the patented process and ensure that the product range continues to meet customer demands. The patent figure in the trial balance is made up as follows:

	$000
Original cost of patent	420
less amortisation to 30 September 20X1	(84)
	336
Research costs incurred in the year to 30 September 20X2	190
Total	526

(vi) YZ's accounting policy for amortisation and depreciation is to charge a full year in the year of acquisition and none in the year of disposal.

(vii) Inventory of raw materials at 30 September 20X2 was $242,000. Inventory of finished goods at 30 September 20X2 was $180,000.

(viii) The directors estimate the income tax charge on the year's profits at $715,000. The balance on the income tax account represents the under-provision for the previous year's tax charge.

(ix) The deferred tax provision is to be reduced by $47,000.

(x) YZ entered into a non-cancellable 4 year operating lease on 1 October 20X1, to acquire machinery to replace the old machinery sold. Under the terms of the lease YZ will pay no rent for the first year. $8,000 is payable for each of 3 years commencing on 1 October 20X2. The machine is estimated to have a useful economic life of 10 years.

(xi) During the year YZ issued 200,000 $1 equity shares at a premium of 50%. The total proceeds were received before 30 September 20X2 and are reflected in the trial balance figures.

Required:

Prepare YZ's statement of profit or loss and other comprehensive income and a statement of changes in equity for the year to 30 September 2012 and a statement of financial position at that date, in accordance with the requirements of International Financial Reporting Standards. (All workings should be to the nearest $000).

Notes to the financial statements are not required, but all workings must be clearly shown. Do not prepare a statement of accounting policies. **(25 marks)**

SECTION C-TYPE QUESTIONS : SECTION 3

360 CQ (FEB 13)

CQ's trial balance at 31 December 20X2 is shown below:

	Notes	$000	$000
Bank loan	(i)		375
Administrative expenses		395	
Cash and cash equivalents		192	
Distribution costs		140	
Equity dividend paid		30	
Finance lease payment	(iii)	12	
Income tax	(iv)	32	
Inventory at 31 December 20X1	(v)	196	
Land and buildings at cost at 1 January 20X2	(vi)	1,415	
Bank loan interest paid	(i)	30	
Equity shares $1 each, fully paid at 1 January 20X2			500
Patent	(ii)	180	
Amortisation of patent at 1 January 20X2	(ii)		90
Plant and equipment at cost at 1 January 20X2	(vii)	482	
Provision for deferred tax at 1 January 20X2	(viii)		210
Accumulated depreciation - buildings at 1 January 20X2	(vi)		120
Accumulated depreciation - plant and equipment at 1 January 20X2	(vii)		279
Purchase of goods for resale		996	
Retained earnings at 1 January 20X2			168
Sales revenue			1,992
Share premium			150
Trade payables			140
Trade receivables		249	
Proceeds of issue of equity shares	(ix)		325
		4,349	4,349

Additional information:

(i) The bank loan is a 10 year 8% loan received in 20W7 and repayable in 20X7. Interest is paid annually in December.

(ii) The patent was purchased on 1 January 20W7, it was estimated to have a useful life of 10 years with no residual value. At 31 December 20X2 the fair value of the patent was $65,000. Amortisation should be included in cost of sales.

(iii) CQ acquired a motor vehicle on a finance lease on 1 January 20X2. The present value of the minimum lease payments are $46,260 and legal title will not pass to CQ at the end of the lease. The lease terms are 5 annual payments of $12,000 due on 1 January commencing 1 January 20X2. The rate of interest implicit in the lease is 15%. Depreciation on vehicles should be included in cost of sales. The only entry made for this transaction was to record the first rental payment.

(iv) The income tax balance in the trial balance is a result of the under provision of tax for the year ended 31 December 20X1.

(v) An inventory count at 31 December 20X2 valued inventory at $183,000. This value includes inventory that had originally cost $15,000 but it is now obsolete and its estimated scrap value is $2,000.

(vi) Depreciation is charged on buildings using the straight line method at 3% per annum. The cost of land included in land and buildings is $1,015,000. Buildings depreciation is treated as an administrative expense. There were no sales of non-current assets during the year ended 31 December 20X2.

(vii) Depreciation is charged on owned plant and equipment using the reducing balance method at 25% per year. Plant and equipment depreciation should be included as a cost of sales.

(viii) The tax due for the year ended 31 December 20X2 is estimated at $77,000 and the deferred tax provision should be decreased by $42,000.

(ix) On 30 September 20X2 CQ issued 250,000 $1 equity shares at a premium of 30%. The proceeds were received before 31 December 20X2.

Required:

Prepare the statement of profit or loss and other comprehensive income and a statement of changes in equity for CQ for the year to 31 December 20X2 and a statement of financial position at that date, in accordance with the requirements of International Financial Reporting Standards.

Notes to the financial statements are not required, but all workings must be clearly shown. Do not prepare a statement of accounting policies. **(25 marks)**

SECTION C-TYPE QUESTIONS : SECTION 3

361 SA (MAY 13 EXAM)

SA has two divisions, division A and division B. On 31 March 20X3, SA's management board agreed to dispose of its loss-making division B. In previous accounting periods the two divisions had been classified as separate operating segments in accordance with IFRS 8 *Operating Segments*.

On 31 March 20X3 division B was classified as "held for sale" in accordance with IFRS 5 *Non-current assets held for sale and discontinued operations*. All net assets, income and expenditure of division B are included in the trial balance.

SA trial balance at 31 March 20X3 is shown below:

	Notes	$000	$000
Long term borrowings	(vii)		450
Administrative expenses	(vi)	263	
Cash and cash equivalents		202	
Distribution costs	(vi)	145	
Equity dividend paid		55	
Inventory at 31 March 20X3		68	
Buildings at valuation	(i); (iv)	995	
Loan interest paid		13	
Ordinary shares $1 each			800
Plant and equipment at cost	(i); (iv)	1,010	
Provision for deferred tax at 31 March 20X2	(ii)		72
Provision for plant & equipment depreciation at 31 March 20X2	(iii); (iv)		360
Provision for buildings depreciation at 31 March 20X2	(iii); (iv)		50
Retained earnings at 31 March 20X2			183
Revaluation reserve at 31 March 20X2			80
Sales revenue – division B			185
Sales revenue – division A			2,784
Cost of goods sold – division B		230	
Cost of goods sold – division A		1900	
Trade payables			51
Division B disposal costs		78	
Trade receivables		56	
		5,015	5,015

Additional information:

(i) There were no sales of non-current assets during the year ended 31 March 20X3.

(ii) The tax due for the year ended 31 March 20X3 is estimated to be $50,000. This includes a tax reduction of $40,000 that relates to discontinued operations. The deferred tax provision relates to division A and should be reduced to $69,000.

PAPER F1 : FINANCIAL OPERATIONS

(iii) Plant and equipment depreciation is provided at 20% per year on the reducing balance basis. Buildings are depreciated at 2.5% per year on a straight line basis. All depreciation is charged to administrative expenses. SA's policy is to charge a full year's depreciation in the year of acquisition and no depreciation in the year of disposal.

(iv) Division B's assets included in the trial balance at 31 March 20X3 are:

The plant and equipment cost and related provision for depreciation include the following amounts for division B:

plant and equipment cost $180,000

plant and equipment, provision for depreciation $140,000

The buildings balances in the trial balance include:

	Cost	Depreciation
	$000	$000
Factory – division B	460	23

Division B has no further assets at 31 March 20X3.

(v) The fair value of division B's net assets at 31 March 20X3 was $431,000.

(vi) The running costs of division B for the period 1 April 20X2 to 31 March 20X3 (included in the trial balance) are:

Administrative expenses $30,000

Distribution costs $125,000

(vii) The long term borrowings incur an annual interest rate of 6%.

Required:

(a) Explain the criteria that have to be met in order to classify division B as "held for sale" in accordance with IFRS 5 *Non-current assets held for sale and discontinued operations*. **(3 marks)**

(b) Prepare the statement of profit or loss and a statement of changes in equity for SA for the year to 31 March 20X3 and a statement of financial position at that date, in accordance with the requirements of International Financial Reporting Standards.
(22 marks)

Notes to the financial statements are not required, but all workings must be clearly shown. Do not prepare a statement of accounting policies. **(Total: 25 marks)**

362 BVQ (AUG 13 EXAM)

BVQ's trial balance at 31 March 20X3 is shown below:

	Notes	$000	$000
6% Loan notes (issued 20X0, redeemable at par 20Y0)			600
Administrative expenses		357	
Leased delivery vehicles	(vi)	324	
Cash and cash equivalents		118	
Cost of sales		1,873	
Distribution costs		226	
Equity dividend paid 1 December 20X2		70	
Income tax	(i), (iii)	27	
Inventory at 31 March 20X3		198	
Land and buildings at cost	(vii)	2,553	
Loan interest paid		18	
Ordinary Shares $1 each, fully paid at 31 March 20X3			1,400
Finance lease liability at 31 March 20X2			268
Finance lease payment on 1 April 20X2		74	
Plant and machinery at cost	(iv)	3,888	
Provision for deferred tax at 31 March 20X2	(iii)		362
Provision for buildings depreciation at 31 March 20X2	(v)		190
Provision for delivery vehicle depreciation at 31 March 20X2	(v)		65
Provision for plant and machinery depreciation at 31 March 20X2	(v)		2,489
Retained earnings at 31 March 20X2			728
Sales revenue			4,364
Trade payables			176
Trade receivables		916	
		10,642	10,642

Additional information:

(i) The income tax balance in the trial balance is a result of the under provision of tax for the year ended 31 March 20X2.

(ii) There were no sales of non-current assets during the year ended 31 March 20X3.

(iii) The tax due for the year ended 31 March 20X3 is estimated at $180,000 and the deferred tax provision should be increased by $31,000

(iv) Due to a general downturn in the economic environment property prices in Country X reduced during the year to 31 March 20X3. BVQ also suffered a reduction in sales demand and decided to sell one of its specialist machines on 31 March 20X3. The machine had cost $180,000 on 1 April 20X1. The market value of the machine at 31 March 20X3 was $73,000. BVQ's management was confident that they have a buyer ready to buy the machine at that price, but at 31 March 20X3 the sale had not been agreed. It will cost BVQ $800 to get the machine ready to sell.

(v) Depreciation is charged on buildings using the straight line method at 3% per annum. The cost of land included in land and buildings is $1,653,000. Plant and equipment is depreciated using the reducing balance method at a rate of 30% per year. All property, plant and equipment depreciation is treated as an administrative expense. Vehicles are depreciated using the straight line method.

(vi) BVQ leased its fleet of delivery vehicles through a finance lease on 1 April 20X1. The fair value of the vehicles at that date was $324,000. The lease is for 5 years and payments of $74,000 are made every April in advance. The interest rate implicit in the lease is 7.12%.

(vii) BVQ carried out an impairment review of its land and buildings on 31 March 20X3 and calculated that they had suffered impairment of $103,000.

Required:

(a) Explain why BVQ might have carried out an impairment review of its land and buildings on 31 March 20X3. **(3 marks)**

(b) Prepare the statement of profit or loss and a statement of changes in equity for BVQ for the year to 31 March 20X3 and a statement of financial position at that date, in accordance with the requirements of International Financial Reporting Standards. **(22 marks)**

Notes to the financial statements are not required, but all workings must be clearly shown. Do not prepare a statement of accounting policies. **(Total: 25 marks)**

363 CJ (MAY 06 EXAM)

The financial statements of CJ for the year to 31 March 20X6 were as follows:

Statements of financial position at:

	31 March 20X6		31 March 20X5	
	$000	$000	$000	$000
Non-current tangible assets				
Property	19,160		18,000	
Plant and equipment	8,500		10,000	
Available for sale investments	1,500		2,100	
		29,160		30,100
Current assets				
Inventory	2,714		2,500	
Trade receivables	2,106		1,800	
Cash at bank	6,553		0	
Cash in hand	409		320	
		11,782		4,620
Total assets		40,942		34,720

Equity and liabilities

Ordinary shares $0.50 each	12,000		7,000	
Share premium	10,000		5,000	
Revaluation reserve	4,200		2,700	
Retained profit	3,009		1,510	
		29,209		16,210

Non-current liabilities

Interest-bearing borrowings	7,000		13,000	
Provision for deferred tax	999	7,999	800	13,800

Current liabilities

Bank overdraft	0		1,200	
Trade and other payables	1,820		1,700	
Corporate income tax payable	1,914		1,810	
		3,734		4,710
		40,942		34,720

Statement of profit or loss and other comprehensive income for the Year to 31 March 20X6

	$000
Revenue	31,000
Cost of sales	(19,000)
Gross profit	12,000
Other income	200
Administrative expenses	(3,900)
Distribution costs	(2,600)
	5,700
Finance cost	(1,302)
Profit before tax	4,398
Income tax expense	(2,099)
Profit for the period	2,299
Comprehensive income:	
Revaluation gain	1,500
Total comprehensive income	3,799

PAPER F1 : FINANCIAL OPERATIONS

Additional information:

(1) On 1 April 20X5, CJ issued 10,000,000 $0.50 ordinary shares at a premium of 100%.

(2) No additional available for sale investments were acquired during the year.

(3) On 1 July 20X5, CJ repaid $6,000,000 of its interest-bearing borrowings.

(4) Properties were revalued by $1,500,000 during the year.

(5) Plant disposed of in the year had a carrying value of $95,000; cash received on disposal was $118,000.

(6) Depreciation charged for the year was properties $2,070,000 and plant and equipment $1,985,000.

(7) The trade and other payables balance includes interest payable of $650,000 at 31 March 20X5 and $350,000 at 31 March 20X6.

(8) Dividends paid during the year, $800,000, comprised last year's final dividend plus the current year's interim dividend. CJ's accounting policy is not to accrue proposed dividends.

(9) Other income comprises:

Dividends received	180,000
Gain on disposal of available for sale investments	20,000
	200,000

Dividends receivable are not accrued

(10) Income tax expense comprises:

	$
Corporate income tax	1,900,000
Deferred tax	199,000
	2,099,000

Required:

Prepare CJ's statement of cash flows for the year ended 31 March 20X6, in accordance with IAS 7 *Statement of Cash Flows*. **(20 marks)**

SECTION C-TYPE QUESTIONS : SECTION 3

364 DN (NOV 06 EXAM)

DN's draft financial statements for the year ended 31 October 20X6 are as follows:

DN Statement of profit or loss and other comprehensive income for the Year to 31 October 20X6

	$000	$000
Revenue		2,600
Cost of sales		
Parts and sub-assemblies	(500)	
Labour	(400)	
Overheads	(400)	(1,300)
Gross profit		1,300
Administrative expenses	(300)	
Distribution costs	(100)	(400)
Profit from operations		900
Finance cost		(110)
Profit before tax		790
Income tax expense		(140)
Profit for the period		650
Comprehensive income:		
Revaluation gain		400
Total comprehensive income		1,050

DN Statement of financial position at

	31 October 20X6		31 October 20X5	
	$000	$000	$000	$000
Assets				
Non-current assets				
Property, plant and equipment		4,942		4,205
Current assets				
Inventories	190		140	
Trade receivables	340		230	
Cash and cash equivalents	0	530	45	415
Total assets		5,472		4,620
Equity and liabilities				
Equity				
Equity shares of $0.50 each	1,300		1,000	
Share premium	300		0	
Revaluation reserve	400		0	
Retained earnings	1,660		1,410	
Total equity		3,660		2,410

PAPER F1 : FINANCIAL OPERATIONS

Non-current liabilities

Bank loans (various rates)	1,500	2,000
	5,160	4,410
Current liabilities	312	210
Total equity and liabilities	5,472	4,620

Additional information:

(i) Property, plant and equipment comprises:

	20X6	20X5
	$000	$000
Property	3,100	2,800
Plant and equipment	1,842	1,405

(ii) Plant and equipment sold during the year for $15,000 had originally cost $60,000 five years ago. The plant and equipment were depreciated on the straight line basis over six years. Any gain/loss on disposal has been included in overheads.

(iii) Properties were revalued on 31 October 20X6.

(iv) DN made an equity share issue on 31 October 20X6. The new shares do not rank for dividend until the following accounting period.

(v) DN's funding includes two bank loans:

- $1,500,000 6% loan commenced 30 June 20X6, due for repayment 29 June 20X9
- $2,000,000 7% loan repaid early on 1 July 20X6.

(vi) Current liabilities:

	20X6	20X5
	$000	$000
Trade payables	105	85
Interest payable	55	75
Tax payable	70	50
Bank overdraft	82	0
Total current liabilities	312	210

(vii) A dividend of $0.20 per share was paid on 1 May 20X6.

(viii) Overheads include the annual depreciation charge of $100,000 for property and $230,000 for plant and equipment.

Required:

Prepare DN's statement of cash flows for the year ended 31 October 20X6, using the indirect method, in accordance with IAS 7 *Statement of Cash Flows*. (20 marks)

SECTION C-TYPE QUESTIONS : SECTION 3

365 HZ (MAY 09 EXAM) — Walk in the footsteps of a top tutor

The accountant of HZ started preparing the financial statements for the year ended 31 March 20X9, but was suddenly taken ill. The draft financial statements for HZ for the year ended 31 March 20X9 are given below:

HZ Statement of financial positions at

	31 March 20X9 (draft) $000	$000	31 March 20X8 (final) $000	$000
Assets				
Non-current assets				
Property, plant and equipment	5,854		6,250	
Goodwill	217		350	
Other intangible assets	198		170	
		6,269		6,770
Current assets				
Inventories	890		750	
Trade receivables	924		545	
Cash and cash equivalents	717		300	
		2,531		1,595
Total assets		8,800		8,365
Equity and liabilities				
Equity share capital	2,873		2,470	
Share premium account	732		530	
Revaluation reserve	562		400	
Retained earnings	1,623		1,840	
Total equity		5,790		5,240
Non-current liabilities				
10% loan notes	–		1,250	
5% loan notes	700		700	
Deferred tax	312		250	
Total non-current liabilities		1,012		2,200
Current liabilities				
Trade payables	744		565	
Income tax	117		247	
Suspense account	1,000		–	
Provision	120		–	
Accrued interest	17		113	
Total current liabilities		1,998		925
Total equity and liabilities		8,800		8,365

Statement of profit or loss and other comprehensive income for the year ended 31 March 20X9 (draft)

	$000
Revenue	9,750
Cost of sales	(5,200)
Gross profit	4,550
Distribution costs	(1,195)
Administrative expenses	(2,990)
Profit from operations	365
Finance costs	(60)
Profit before tax	305
Income tax expense	(182)
Profit for the period	123
Other comprehensive income:	
Revaluation gain	162
Total comprehensive income	285

Additional information:

(i) Non-current tangible assets include properties which were revalued upwards during the year.

(ii) Non-current tangible assets disposed of in the year had a carrying value of $98,000; cash received on their disposal was $128,000. Any gain or loss on disposal has been included under cost of sales.

(iii) During the year goodwill became impaired. The impairment was charged to cost of sales.

(iv) Depreciation charged for the year was $940,000, included in cost of sales.

(v) On 1 April 20X8, HZ issued 806,000 $0.50 equity shares at a premium of 50%.

(vi) On 1 April 20X8, HZ issued 1,000,000 5% cumulative $1 preference shares at par, redeemable at 10% premium on 1 April 20Y8. Issue costs of $70,000 have been paid and included in administration expenses. The constant annual rate of interest is 6.72%. The cash received for the issue of the preference shares has been debited to cash and credited to suspense.

(vii) The other intangible assets relate to research and development expenditure. Development expenditure of $170,000 was incurred and paid in the year ended 31 March 20X7; the remaining expenditure met the IAS 38 *Intangible Assets* criteria for deferral. When development expenditure was assessed at 31 March 20X9, it was clear that the expenditure incurred in 20X6/X7 no longer met the IAS 38 criteria, but the expenditure incurred in 20X8/X9 did still meet the requirements. No action has yet been taken to write off any development expenditure.

(viii) On 1 May 20X8, HZ purchased and cancelled all of its 10% loan notes at par plus accrued interest (included in finance costs).

(ix) Ordinary dividends paid during the year were $290,000 and preferred share dividends paid were $50,000.

(x) HZ has been advised that it is probably going to lose a court case and has provided $120,000 for the estimated cost of this case. This is included in administration expenses.

Required:

(a) Explain the accounting adjustments required by HZ to clear the balance on the suspense account at 31 March 20X9 and calculate a revised profit before tax for the year ended 31 March 20X9. (*Note:* A detailed statement of profit or loss and other comprehensive income is NOT required) (5 marks)

(b) Prepare a statement of cash flows, using the indirect method, for HZ for the year ended 31 March 20X9, in accordance with IAS 7 *Statement of Cash Flows*.

(20 marks)

(c) Prepare HZ's statement of changes in equity for the year to 31 March 20X9, in a form suitable for presentation to the shareholders and in accordance with the requirements of International Accounting Standards. (5 marks)

Notes to the financial statements are not required, but all workings must be clearly shown. Do NOT prepare a statement of accounting policies.

(Total: 30 marks)

366 YG (NOV 10 EXAM)

The financial statements of YG are given below:

Statement of financial position as at

	31 Oct 20X9 $000	31 Oct 20X9 $000	31 Oct 20X8 $000	31 Oct 20X8 $000
Non-current assets				
Property, plant and equipment	4,676		4,248	
Development expenditure	417		494	
		5,093		4,742
Current assets				
Inventory	606		509	
Trade receivables	456		372	
Cash and cash equivalents	1,989	3,051	205	1,086
Total assets		8,144		5,828
Equity and liabilities				
Equity shares of $1 each	3,780		2,180	
Share premium	1,420		620	
Revaluation reserve	560		260	
Retained earnings	1,314	7,074	1,250	4,310
Non-current liabilities				
Long term borrowings	360		715	
Deferred tax	210	570	170	885
Current liabilities				
Trade payables	425		310	
Current tax	70		170	
Accrued interest	5		3	
Provision for redundancy costs	0	500	150	633
Total equity and liabilities		8,144		5,828

Statement of profit or loss and other comprehensive income for the year ended 31 October 20X9

	$000	$000
Revenue		6,640
Cost of sales		(3,530)
		3,110
Administrative expenses	(2,040)	
Distribution costs	(788)	(2,828)
		282
Finance cost		(16)
		266
Taxation		(120)
Profit for the year		146
Other comprehensive income		
Gain on revaluation of property, plant and equipment		300
		446

Additional information:

(i) On 1 November 20X8, YG issued 1,600,000 $1 ordinary shares at a premium of 50%. No other finance was raised during the year.

(ii) YG paid a dividend during the year.

(iii) Plant and equipment disposed of in the year had a carrying value of $70,000; cash received on disposal was $66,000. Any gain or loss on disposal has been included under cost of sales.

(iv) Cost of sales includes $145,000 for development expenditure amortised during the year.

(v) Depreciation charged for the year was $250,000.

(vi) The income tax expense for the year to 31 October 20X9 is made up as follows:

	$000
Corporate income tax	80
Deferred tax	40
	120

(vii) During the year to 31 October 20X8 YG set up a provision for redundancy costs arising from the closure of one of its activities. During the year to 31 October 20X9, YG spent $177,000 on redundancy costs, the additional cost being charged to administrative expenses.

PAPER F1 : FINANCIAL OPERATIONS

Required:

(a) Prepare a statement of cash flows, using the indirect method, for YG for the year ended 31 October 20X9, in accordance with IAS 7 *Statement of Cash Flows*.

(20 marks)

(b) Someone you have known for many years has heard that you work for YG, a well known international entity. There are rumours in the press that YG's latest share issue was to raise cash to enable it to launch a takeover bid for another entity. Your friend wants to treat you to dinner at an expensive local restaurant, so that you can give him details of the proposed takeover before it is made public.

Explain how you would respond to your friend. Your answer should include reference to CIMA's Code of Ethics for Professional Accountants.

(5 marks)

(Total: 25 marks)

367 OP (MAY 11 EXAM) — Walk in the footsteps of a top tutor

Extracts of OP's financial statements for the year ended 31 March 20X9 are as follows:

OP Statements of financial position as at

	31 March 20X9		31 March 20X8	
	$000	$000	$000	$000
Non-current assets:				
Plant, property and equipment	977		663	
Development expenditure	60		65	
Brand	30	1,067	40	768
Current assets:				
Inventories	446		450	
Trade receivables	380		310	
Cash and cash equivalents	69	895	35	795
Total assets		1,962		1,563
Equity and liabilities equity:				
Equity shares of $1 each	400		200	
Share premium account	200		100	
Revaluation reserve	30		95	
Retained earnings	652		423	
Total equity		1,282		818
Non-current liabilities:				
Long term borrowings	100		250	
Deferred tax	130		120	
Total non-current liabilities		230		370

SECTION C-TYPE QUESTIONS : SECTION 3

	31 March 20X9		31 March 20X8	
	$000	$000	$000	$000
Current liabilities:				
Trade payables	150		95	
Current tax	250		260	
Accrued interest	10		20	
Other provisions	40		0	
Total current liabilities:		450		375
Total equity and liabilities		1,962		1,563

OP Statement of profit or loss and other comprehensive income for the year ended 31 March 20X9

	$000	$000
Revenue		10,400
Cost of sales		(4,896)
Gross profit		5,504
Distribution costs	(1,890)	
Administrative expenses	(2,510)	(4,400)
Profit from operations		1,104
Finance costs		(15)
Profit before tax		1,089
Income tax expense		(280)
Profit for the period		809
Other comprehensive income:		
Revaluation loss		(65)
Total comprehensive income		744

Additional information:

(i) Property plant and equipment comprises:

Asset type	Cost at 31 March 20X9	Cost at 31 March 20X8	Depreciation to 31 March 20X8
	$000	$000	$000
Land	426	320	0
Buildings	840	610	366
Plant & equipment	166	180	81
	1,432	1,110	447

PAPER F1 : FINANCIAL OPERATIONS

(ii) Depreciation for the year-ended 31 March 20X9 was:

	$000
Buildings	17
Plant & equipment	25

(iii) Plant and equipment disposed of during the year had a carrying value of $11,000 (cost $45,000). The loss on disposal of $6,000 is included in cost of sales.

(iv) All land was revalued on 31 March 20X9, the decrease in value of $65,000 was deducted from the revaluation reserve.

(v) Cost of sales includes $15,000 for development expenditure amortised during the year and $10,000 for impairment of the purchased brand name.

(vi) On 1 November 20X8, OP issued $1 equity shares at a premium. No other finance was raised during the year.

(vii) OP paid a dividend during the year.

(viii) Other provisions relate to legal claims made against OP during the year ended 31 March 20X9. The amount provided is based on legal opinion at 31 March 20X9 and is included in cost of sales.

Required:

(a) Prepare a statement of cash flows, using the indirect method, for OP for the year ended 31 March 20X9 in accordance with IAS 7 *Statement of Cash Flows*.

(19 marks)

The following information should not be included in your answer to part (a). It is only required to answer part (b) of the question.

OP's directors acquired equipment on 1 April 20X1 on a finance lease.

The finance lease terms are:

- Lease for a ten year period
- Rentals paid annually in arrears on 31 March
- Each annual rental is $44,000
- Original cost of the equipment was $248,610
- The interest rate implicit in the lease is 12% per year

Required:

(b) Calculate the amounts in respect of this finance lease that would be included in OP's:

(i) Statement of profit or loss and other comprehensive income for the year ended 31 March 20X2

(ii) Statement of financial position as at 31 March 20X2

(iii) Statement of cash flows for the year ended 31 March 20X2 (6 marks)

(Total: 25 marks)

368 UV (SEP 11 EXAM)

UV's draft financial statements for the year ended 30 June 20X1 and financial statements for the year ended 30 June 20W0 are as follows:

Statement of financial position as at 30 June

	Other Information	20X1 $000	20X1 $000	20W0 $000	20W0 $000
Non-current assets					
Property, plant & equipment	(i) to (v)	5,675		4,785	
Deferred development expenditure	(vi)	170		69	
			5,845		4,854
Current assets					
Inventory		95		80	
Trade receivables		190		145	
Cash and cash equivalents		95		160	
			380		385
			6,225		5,239
Equity and liabilities					
Equity					
Share capital	(vii)	910		760	
Share premium	(vii)	665		400	
Revaluation reserve		600		0	
Retained earnings		2,899		1,982	
			5,074		3,142
Non-current liabilities					
Deferred tax		410		0	
Long-term loans		250		1,500	
			660		1,500
Current liabilities					
Trade payables		60		85	
Income tax		321		305	
Interest payable		5		32	
Provision for restructuring costs	(ix)	0		100	
Provision for legal claim	(viii)	105		75	
			491		597
			6,225		5,239

Statement of profit or loss and other comprehensive income for the year ended 30 June 20X1

	$000
Revenue	2,300
Cost of sales	(450)
Gross profit	1,850
Administration expenses and distribution costs	(200)
Loss on disposal of plant	(15)
Profit from operations	1,635
Interest payable	(95)
Profit before tax	1,540
Income tax	(455)
Profit for the year	1,085
Other comprehensive Income:	
Revaluation of property, net of deferred tax at 25%	600
Total comprehensive income	1,685

Other information:

(i) Non-current assets – property, plant and equipment, balances at 30 June 20W0 were:

	$000	$000
Cost or valuation:		
Property	4,150	
Plant	2,350	
Equipment	985	
		7,485
Depreciation:		
Property	450	
Plant	1,350	
Equipment	900	
		2,700
Carrying value		4,785

SECTION C-TYPE QUESTIONS : **SECTION 3**

(ii) Equipment was purchased during the year at a cost of $275,000 and plant was purchased for $215,000.

(iii) During the year UV disposed of plant with a carrying value of $30,000 and accumulated depreciation of $60,000.

(iv) On 1 July 20W0 property was revalued to $4,500,000. At that time the average remaining life of property was 90 years. Property is depreciated on a straight line basis.

(v) Depreciation for the year was $280,000 and $40,000 for plant and equipment respectively.

(vi) Development expenditure incurred during the year to 30 June 20X1 was $114,000. Deferred development expenditure is amortised over its useful economic life.

(vii) UV issued equity shares during the year at a premium.

(viii) Provision was made by UV for outstanding legal claims against the entity at the year end.

(ix) The restructuring costs relate to a comprehensive restructuring and reorganisation of the entity that began in 20W9. UV's financial statements for the year ended 30 June 20W0 included a provision for restructuring costs of $100,000. Restructuring costs incurred in the year to 30 June 20X1 were $160,000. No further restructuring and reorganisation costs are expected to occur. UV treats restructuring costs as a cost of sales.

Required:

(a) Prepare a property plant and equipment note for UV for the year ended 30 June 20X1, in accordance with the requirements of IAS 16 *Property Plant and Equipment*.
(6 marks)

(b) Prepare a statement of cash flows, for UV for the year ended 30 June 20X1 using the indirect method, in accordance with the requirements of IAS 7 *Statement of Cash Flows*. (19 marks)

(Total: 25 marks)

GROUP COMPANY FINANCIAL ACCOUNTS

369 JASPER — *Walk in the footsteps of a top tutor*

The statements of financial position of Jasper and its investee companies Carrot and Swede at 31 December 20X4 are given below:

Statements of financial position at 31 December 20X4

	Jasper $000	Jasper $000	Carrot $000	Carrot $000	Swede $000	Swede $000
Non-current assets						
Property, plant and equipment		2,960		1,720		810
Investments		2,300		–		–
		5,260				
Current assets						
Inventories	625		320		275	
Receivables	350		300		375	
Cash	55		120		30	
		1,030		740		680
		6,290		2,460		1,490
Equity						
Share capital ($1 ordinary shares)		2,200		800		800
Reserves		2,530		1,260		410
		4,730		2,060		1,210
Non-current liabilities						
Loans		500		200		–
Current liabilities						
Bank overdraft	560		–		–	
Trade payables	500		200		280	
		1,060		200		280
		6,290		2,460		1,490

SECTION C-TYPE QUESTIONS : SECTION 3

Additional information

(i) Jasper acquired 800,000 ordinary shares in Carrot on 1 January 20W9 for $1,800,000 when the reserves of Carrot were $500,000. On the same date they made a long term loan of $200,000 to Carrot that is still outstanding at 31 December 20X4.

(ii) At the date of acquisition of Carrot, the fair value of its net assets was the same as their book value with the exception of some land, whose market value was $300,000 more than its book value. This land is still held by Carrot at 31 December 20X4

(iii) J acquired 240,000 ordinary shares in Swede on 1 January 20X3 for $300,000 when the reserves of Swede were $150,000.

(iv) Jasper manufactures a component used by both Carrot and Swede. Jasper consistently earns a gross profit margin of 25% on these transfers. Carrot held $200,000 inventories of these components at 31 December 20X4 and Swede held $160,000 at the same date.

(v) The receivables of Jasper include $100,000 in respect of amounts owing by Carrot and $80,000 in respect of amounts owing by Swede. Both Carrot and Swede sent a cheque to Jasper in full settlement of the amounts owed on 30 December 20X4. Jasper received and recorded these payments on 2 January 20X5

Required:

Prepare the consolidated statement of financial position of the Jasper group at 31 December 20X4. **(20 marks)**

370 HOT

The statement of profit or loss and extracts from the statement of changes in equity of Hot, Warm and Tepid for the year ended 31 December 20X4 are given below:

	Hot $000	Warm $000	Tepid $000
Statement of profit or loss			
Revenue	60,000	45,000	42,000
Cost of sales	(30,000)	(22,500)	(21,000)
Gross profit	30,000	22,500	21,000
Other operating expenses	(9,000)	(4,500)	(4,200)
Profit from operations	21,000	18,000	16,800
Investment income (Note 1)	9,300	2,250	
Interest payable (Note 1)	(3,000)	(2,250)	(2,100)
Profit before tax	27,300	18,000	14,700
Taxation	(7,600)	(5,500)	(4,800)
Profit for the year	19,700	12,500	9,900

PAPER F1 : FINANCIAL OPERATIONS

	Hot $000	Warm $000	Tepid $000
Extracts from statements of changes in equity			
Retained earnings b/d	20,000	18,000	16,000
Profit for the year	19,700	12,500	9,900
Dividends	(7,000)	(6,000)	(5,000)
Retained earnings c/d	32,700	24,500	20,900

Notes to the financial statements:

(1) Hot owns all the shares in Warm and 40% of the shares in Tepid. Hot has provided each company with a loan of $8 million at an interest rate of 10% to Warm and 12% to Tepid. Both loans have been outstanding throughout the period.

(2) When Hot acquired Warm the fair value of its net assets were approximately the same as their book values.

(3) Hot supplies a component which is used as a raw material by Warm and Tepid. During the year ended 31 March 20X5, sales of such components by Hot to Warm were $2 million and by Hot to Tepid $1.6 million. The inventories of the above-mentioned raw material were included in the accounts of Warm at 31 December 20X4 at cost to Warm of $600,000. Tepid held no inventory purchased from Hot at the year end. Hot marks up all sales to Warm and Tepid by one-third

Required:

Prepare the consolidated statement of profit or loss of the Hot group for the year ended 31 December 20X4. **(10 marks)**

371 AX GROUP (MAY 10 EXAM) — *Walk in the footsteps of a top tutor*

AX holds shares in two other entities, AS and AA.

AX purchased 100% of AS shares on 1 April 20X9 for $740,000, when the fair value was $75,000 more than book value. The excess of fair value over book value was attributed to land held by AS.

At 1 April 20X9 the retained earnings of AS showed a debit balance of $72,000.

AX purchased 120,000 ordinary shares in AA on 1 April 20X9 for $145,000 when AA's retained earnings were $49,000. AX is able to exercise significant influence over all aspects of AA's strategic and operational decisions. At 1 April 20X9 the fair values of AA's assets were the same as their carrying value.

The draft summarised financial statements for the three entities as at 31 March 20Y0 are given on the next page.

SECTION C-TYPE QUESTIONS : SECTION 3

Draft Summarised Statement of financial position at 31 March 20Y0

	AX $000	AX $000	AS $000	AS $000	AA $000	AA $000
Non-current assets						
Property, plant and equipment	1,120		700		740	
Investments:						
600,000 ord shares in AS	740		–		–	
120,000 ord shares in AA	145		–		–	
		2,005		700		740
Current assets						
Inventories	205		30		14	
Receivables	350		46		30	
Cash	30		–		11	
		585		76		55
		2,590		776		795
Equity						
Equity shares ($1 each)		1,500		600		550
Retained earnings		518		15		100
		2,018		615		650
Non-current liabilities						
Borrowings	360		80		109	
Deferred tax	120		16		10	
		480		96		119
Current liabilities						
Trade payables	92		29		15	
Tax (see note i)	–		16		11	
Bank overdraft	–		20		–	
		92		65		26
		2,590		776		795

PAPER F1 : FINANCIAL OPERATIONS

Summarised statement of profit or loss and other comprehensive income for the year ended 31 March 20Y0

	AX $000	AS $000	AA $000
Revenue	820	285	147
Cost of sales	(406)	(119)	(52)
Gross profit	414	166	95
Administration expenses	(84)	(36)	(14)
Distribution costs	(48)	(22)	(11)
Finance cost	(18)	(5)	(8)
Profit before tax	264	103	62
Taxation (note i)	–	(16)	(11)
Profit for the year		87	51

Additional information:

(i) AX has not yet calculated its tax charge for the year to 31 March 20Y0. AX is deemed resident in country X for tax purposes which means all expenses other than depreciation, amortisation, entertaining, taxes paid to other public bodies and donations to political parties are tax deductable.

Tax depreciation is deductable as follows: 50% of additions on property, plant and equipment in the accounting period in which they are recorded; 25% per year of the written-down value (i.e. cost minus previous allowances) in subsequent accounting periods except that in which the asset is disposed of. No tax depreciation is given on land.

Corporate tax on profits is at a rate of 25%.

AX's cost of sales includes a depreciation charge of $31,000 for property, plant and equipment. Included in administration expenses are entertaining expenses of $4,000. AX's property, plant and equipment qualified for tax depreciation allowances of $49,000 for the year ended 31 March 20Y0.

(ii) In the year since acquisition AS sold goods for $55,000 to AX of which $25,000 remained in AX's closing inventory at 31 March 20Y0. AS uses a mark up of 25% on cost. All invoices from AS for goods had been paid by the year end.

(iii) No dividends are proposed by any of the entities.

Required:

(a) Calculate the estimated amount of corporate income tax that AX will be due to pay for the year ended 31 March 20Y0 and any required adjustment to the provision for deferred tax at that date. **(5 marks)**

(b) Prepare a Consolidated Statement of profit or loss and other comprehensive income for the AX Group of entities for the year ended 31 March 20Y0 and a Consolidated Statement of Financial Position as at that date. **(20 marks)**

Notes to the financial statements are not required, but all workings must be clearly shown.

(Total: 25 marks)

372 PH GROUP (NOV 11)

The Draft summarised Statement of financial position at 30 September 20X1 for three entities, PH, SU and AJ are given below:

	PH $000	SU $000	AJ $000
Non-current assets			
Property, plant and equipment	50,390	57,590	41,270
Investments:			
48,000,000 Ordinary shares in SU at cost	75,590		
Loan to SU	12,600		
8,000,000 Ordinary shares in AJ at cost	16,400		
	154,980	57,590	41,270
Current assets			
Inventory	10,160	14,410	10,260
Current account with SU	10,000		
Trade receivables	21,400	13,200	11,940
Cash and cash equivalents	1,260	3,600	3,580
	42,820	31,210	25,780
Total Assets	197,800	88,800	67,050
Equity and liabilities			
Equity shares of $1 each	126,000	48,000	24,000
Retained earnings	26,500	15,600	28,800
	152,500	63,600	52,800
Non-current liabilities			
Long term borrowings	32,700	12,600	11,800
Current liabilities			
Trade payables	12,600	5,400	2,450
Current account with PH	0	7,200	0
	12,600	12,600	2,450
Total equity and liabilities	197,800	88,800	67,050

PAPER F1 : FINANCIAL OPERATIONS

Additional information:

(i) PH acquired all of SU's equity shares on 1 October 20X0 for $75,590,000 when SU's retained earnings were $7,680,000. PH also advanced SU a ten year loan of $12,600,000 on 1 October 20X0.

(ii) The fair value of SU's property, plant and equipment on 1 October 20X0 exceeded its book value by $1,300,000. The excess of fair value over book value was attributed to buildings owned by SU. At the date of acquisition these buildings had a remaining useful life of 20 years. PH's accounting policy is to depreciate buildings using the straight line basis.

(iii) At 30 September 20X1 $90,000 loan interest was due on the loan made by PH to SU and had not been paid. Both PH and SU had accrued this amount at the year end.

(iv) PH purchased 8,000,000 of AJ's equity shares on 1 October 20X0 for $16,400,000 when AJ's retained earnings were $24,990,000. PH exercises significant influence over all aspects of AJ's strategic and operational decisions.

(v) SU posted a cheque to PH for $2,800,000 on 29 September 20X1 which did not arrive until 7 October 20X1.

(vi) No dividends are proposed by any of the entities.

(vii) PH occasionally trades with SU. In September 20X1 PH sold SU goods for $4,800,000. PH uses a mark-up of one third on cost. On 30 September 20X1 all the goods were included in SU's closing inventory.

Required:

(a) Define what is meant by control and explain how this is determined according to IFRS 10 *Consolidated Statements*. **(5 marks)**

(b) Prepare the consolidated statement of financial position for the PH group of entities as at 30 September 20X1, in accordance with the requirements of International Financial Reporting Standards. **(20 marks)**

Notes to the financial statements are NOT required but all workings must be shown.

(Total: 25 marks)

373 TREE GROUP (MAR 12)

The draft statements of financial position at 31 January 20X2 and statements of comprehensive income for the year ended 31 January 20X2 for three entities, Tree, Branch and Leaf are given below:

Statements of financial position at 31 January 20X2

	Notes	Tree $000	Branch $000	Leaf $000
Non-current assets				
Property, plant and equipment		1,535	1,155	1,025
Investments:				
790,000 Ordinary shares in Branch at cost	(ii); (iii)	1,500		
Loan to Branch	(ii)	600		
332,000 Ordinary shares in Leaf at cost	(iv)	550		
		4,185	1,155	1,025
Current assets				
Inventory	(v)	1,360	411	123
Current account with Branch	(vii)	123	0	0
Trade receivables		1,540	734	142
Cash and cash equivalents		47	75	55
		3,070	1,220	320
Total assets		7,255	2,375	1,345
Equity and liabilities				
Equity shares of $1 each		3,900	790	830
Retained earnings		665	495	220
		4,565	1,285	1,050
Non-current liabilities				
Long term borrowings		0	600	0
Current liabilities				
Trade payables		2,690	365	295
Loan interest payable	(vi)	0	30	0
Current account with Tree	(vii)	0	95	0
		2,690	490	295
Total equity and liabilities		7,255	2,375	1,345

Statements of profit or loss for the year ended 31 January 20X2

	Tree $000	Branch $000	Leaf $000
Revenue	2,200	777	411
Cost of sales	(1,112)	(456)	(146)
Gross profit	1,088	321	265
Expenses	(221)	(115)	(62)
	867	206	203
Finance cost	(102)	(59)	(34)
	765	147	169
Taxation	(145)	(32)	(19)
Profit for the year	620	115	150

Additional information:

(i) Tree holds shares in two other entities, Branch and Leaf.

(ii) Tree acquired all of Branch's equity shares on 1 February 20X1 for $1,500,000 when Branch's retained earnings were $380,000. Tree also advanced Branch a ten year loan of $600,000 on 1 February 20X1.

(iii) The fair value of Branch's property, plant and equipment on 1 February 20X1 exceeded its book value by $240,000. The excess of fair value over book value was attributed to buildings owned by Branch. At the date of acquisition these buildings had a remaining useful life of 10 years. Tree's accounting policy is to depreciate buildings using the straight line basis.

(iv) Tree purchased its shareholding in Leaf on 1 February 20X1 for $550,000 when Leaf's retained earnings were $70,000. The fair value of Leaf's net assets was the same as its net book value at that date. Tree exercises significant influence over all aspects of Leaf's strategic and operational decisions.

(v) Tree occasionally trades with Branch. During September 20X1 Tree sold Branch goods for $180,000. Tree uses a mark up of fifty percent on cost. By 31 January 20X2 Branch had sold one third of the goods, $120,000 being included in Branch's closing inventory.

(vi) At 31 January 20X2 $30,000 loan interest was due and had not been paid. Branch had accrued this amount at the year end but Tree had not accrued any interest income.

(vii) Branch posted a cheque to Tree for $28,000 on 29 January 20X2 which did not arrive until 7 February 20X2.

(viii) No dividends are proposed by any of the entities.

Required:

Prepare a consolidated statement of profit or loss and other comprehensive income for the Tree group of entities for the year ended 31 January 20X2 AND a consolidated statement of financial position for the Tree group of entities as at 31 January 20X2, in accordance with the requirements of International Financial Reporting Standards.

Notes to the financial statements are NOT required but all workings must be shown.

(25 marks)

SECTION C-TYPE QUESTIONS : SECTION 3

374 LOCH GROUP (MAY 12)

The draft statements of financial position at 31 March 20X2 and statements of comprehensive income for the year ended 31 March 20X2 for three entities, Loch, River and Stream are given below:

Statements of financial position as at 31 March 20X2:

	Notes	Loch $000	River $000	Stream $000
Non-current assets				
Property, plant and equipment	(iv)	1,193	767	670
Investments:				
Loan to River	(iii)	300	0	0
156,000 Ordinary shares in Stream at cost	(vi)	223	0	0
		1,716	767	670
Current assets				
Inventory	(vii)	1,107	320	87
Trade receivables		1,320	570	90
Current a/c with River	(viii)	101	0	0
Cash and cash equivalents		62	58	14
		2,590	948	191
Total assets		4,306	1,715	861
Equity and liabilities				
Equity shares of $1 each		3,500	600	520
Retained earnings		413	385	125
		3,913	985	645
Non-current liabilities				
Loan from Loch	(iii)	0	300	0
Current liabilities				
Trade payables		393	340	216
Loan interest payable	(ix)	0	15	0
Current a/c with Loch	(viii)	0	75	0
		393	430	216
Total Equity and liabilities		4,306	1,715	861

173

Statements of profit or loss for the year ended 31 March 20X2

	Loch $000	River $000	Stream $000
Revenue	1,500	693	227
Cost of sales	(865)	(308)	(84)
Gross profit	635	385	143
Expenses	(124)	(70)	(35)
	511	315	108
Finance cost	(80)	(40)	(12)
	431	275	96
Income tax expense	(118)	(20)	(16)
Profit for the year	313	255	80

Additional information:

(i) Loch holds shares in two other entities, River and Stream.

(ii) Loch acquired all of River's equity shares on 1 April 20X1 in a share for share exchange. The agreed purchase consideration was $950,000, however Loch has not yet recorded the acquisition in its accounting records. On the 1 April 20X1 Loch's shares had a market value of $2.00 each. River's retained earnings were $130,000 on 1 April 20X1.

(iii) On 1 April 20X1 Loch advanced River a 10 year loan of $300,000.

(iv) The fair value of River's property, plant and equipment on 1 April 20X1 exceeded its carrying value by $144,000. The excess of fair value over carrying value was attributed to buildings owned by River. At the date of acquisition these buildings had a remaining useful life of 12 years. Loch's accounting policy is to depreciate buildings using the straight line basis with no residual value.

(v) Loch carried out an impairment review of the goodwill arising on acquisition of River and found that as at 31 March 20X2 the goodwill had been impaired by $20,000.

(vi) Loch purchased its shareholding in Stream on 1 April 20X1 for $223,000 when Stream's retained earnings were $45,000. The fair value of Stream's net assets was the same as its carrying value at that date. Loch exercises significant influence over all aspects of Stream's financial and operating policies.

(vii) Loch occasionally trades with River. During September 20X1 Loch sold River goods for $220,000. Loch uses a mark-up of 50% on cost. At 31 March 20X2 all the goods remained in River's closing inventory.

(viii) River posted a cheque to Loch for $26,000 on 29 March 20X2 which did not arrive until 7 April 20X2.

(ix) At 31 March 20X2 $15,000 loan interest was due and had not been paid. River had accrued the loan interest due at the year end but Loch had not accrued any interest income.

Required:

(a) Prepare the journal entry to record the purchase of River in Loch's accounting records. **(3 marks)**

(b) Prepare the consolidated statement of profit or loss and other comprehensive income for Loch for the year ended 31 March 20X2 AND a consolidated statement of financial position for Loch as at 31 March 20X2, in accordance with the requirements of International Financial Reporting Standards. **(22 marks)**

Notes to the financial statements are NOT required, but all workings must be clearly shown.

(Total: 25 marks)

375 WOOD GROUP (AUG 12) — Walk in the footsteps of a top tutor

The draft statements of financial position at 31 March 20X2 and statements of comprehensive income for the year ended 31 March 20X2 for three entities, Wood, Plank and Bush are given below:

Statements of financial position at 31 March 20X2

	Notes	Wood $000	Plank $000	Bush $000
Non-current assets				
Property, plant and equipment	(iii)/(vii)	11,820	7,240	6,730
Investments:				
6,000,000 Ordinary shares in Plank at cost	(ii)	9,200		
Loan to Plank	(ii)	3,100		
1,540,000 Ordinary shares in Bush at cost	(v)	2,420		
		26,540	7,240	6,730
Current assets				
Inventory	(vi)	12,060	3,215	890
Trade receivables		13,400	5,710	920
Cash and cash equivalents	(ix)	1,730	510	110
		27,190	9,435	1,920
Total assets		53,730	16,675	8,650

	Notes	Wood $000	Plank $000	Bush $000
Equity and liabilities				
Equity shares of $1 each		38,900	6,000	5,500
Share premium		5,520	0	0
Retained earnings		5,400	3,680	1,240
		49,820	9,680	6,740
Non-current liabilities				
Loan from Wood		0	3,100	0
Current liabilities				
Trade payables		3,910	3,740	1,910
Loan interest payable		0	155	0
		3,910	3,895	1,910
Total equity and liabilities		53,730	16,675	8,650

Statements of profit or loss for the year ended 31 March 20X2

	Wood $000	Plank $000	Bush $000
Revenue	15,500	6,900	2,300
Cost of sales	(8,700)	(3,080)	(840)
Gross profit	6,800	3,820	1,460
Expenses	(1,250)	(750)	(340)
	5,550	3,070	1,120
Finance cost	(810)	(440)	(120)
	4,740	2,630	1,000
Tax	(1,250)	(230)	(170)
Profit for the year	3,490	2,400	830

Additional information:

(i) Wood holds shares in two other entities, Plank and Bush.

(ii) Wood acquired all of Plank's equity shares on 1 April 20X1 for $9,200,000 when Plank's retained earnings were $1,280,000. Wood also advanced Plank a 10 year loan of $3,100,000 on 1 April 20X1.

(iii) The fair value of Plank's property, plant and equipment on 1 April 20X1 exceeded its carrying value by $1,350,000. The excess of fair value over carrying value was attributed to buildings owned by Plank. At the date of acquisition these buildings had a remaining useful life of 15 years. Wood's accounting policy is to depreciate buildings using the straight line basis with no residual value.

(iv) Wood carried out an impairment review of the goodwill arising on acquisition of Plank and found that as at 31 March 20X2 the goodwill had been impaired by $80,000.

(v) Wood purchased its shareholding in Bush on 1 April 20X1 for $2,420,000 when Bush's retained earnings were $410,000. The fair value of Bush's net assets was the same as its carrying value at that date. Wood exercises significant influence over all aspects of Bush's financial and operating policies.

(vi) Wood occasionally trades with Plank. During February 20X2 Wood sold Plank goods for $520,000. Wood uses a mark up of 100% on cost. At 31 March 20X2 all the goods remained in Plank's closing inventory and Plank had not paid for the goods.

(vii) Wood sold a piece of machinery to Plank on 30 September 20X1 for $95,000. The machinery had previously been used in Wood's business and had been included in Wood's property, plant and equipment at a carrying value of $75,000. The machinery had a remaining useful life of ten years at 30 September 20X1.

(viii) At 31 March 20X2 $155,000 loan interest was due and had not been paid. Plank had accrued the loan interest due at the year-end but Wood had not accrued any interest income.

(ix) Plank posted a cheque to Wood for $210,000 on 31 March 20X2 which did not arrive until 5 April 20X2.

Required:

(a) Explain how item (vii) above should be treated in Wood's consolidated financial statements for the year ended 31 March 20X2. **(3 marks)**

(b) Prepare the consolidated statement of profit or loss and other comprehensive income for Wood for the year ended 31 March 20X2 AND the consolidated statement of financial position for Wood as at 31 March 20X2, in accordance with the requirements of International Financial Reporting Standards. **(22 marks)**

Notes to the financial statements are not required but all workings must be shown.

(Total: 25 marks)

PAPER F1 : FINANCIAL OPERATIONS

376 AZ GROUP (NOV 12)

The draft statements of financial position at 30 September 2012 for three entities, AZ, PQ and SY are given below:

Statements of financial position at 30 September 20X2:

	Notes	AZ $000	PQ $000	SY $000
Non-current assets				
Property, plant and equipment	(vii)	400	297	380
Investments:				
100,000 Equity shares in PQ at cost	(i) to (iii)	500	–	–
80,000 Equity shares in SY at cost	(iv)	125	–	–
		1,025	297	380
Current assets				
Inventory	(vi)	190	60	160
Trade receivables		144	63	88
Cash and cash equivalents	(viii)	48	21	73
		382	144	321
Total assets		1,407	441	701
Equity and liabilities				
Equity shares of $1 each		900	100	400
Share premium		300	50	100
Retained earnings	(v)	111	112	95
Revaluation reserve		-	60	-
		1,311	322	595
Current liabilities				
Trade payables		96	119	106
Total equity and liabilities		1,407	441	701

Additional information:

(i) AZ acquired all of PQ's equity shares on 1 October 20X0 for $500,000. PQ's retained earnings at 1 October 20X0 were $38,000.

(ii) AZ commissioned a professional valuer to value PQ's net assets at 1 October 20X0. The results were as follows:

	Original cost $000	Carrying value $000	Valuation $000
Property	100	200	300
Plant and equipment	200	97	117
All other assets and liabilities			Equal to carrying value

Plant and equipment had an average remaining useful life of 5 years at 1 October 2010.

AZ's accounting policy is to depreciate plant and equipment using the straight line basis with no residual value.

(iii) AZ carried out an impairment review of the goodwill arising on acquisition of PQ and found that as at 30 September 20X2 the goodwill had been impaired by $20,000.

(iv) AZ purchased its shareholding in SY on 1 October 20X1 for $125,000. The fair value of all SY's net assets was the same as their carrying value at that date. AZ exercises significant influence over all aspects of SY's financial and operating policies.

(v) The statements of profit or loss and other comprehensive income for the year ended 30 September 20X2 showed the following amounts for the profit for the year for each entity:

	$000
AZ	67
PQ	49
SY	55

(vi) During August 2012 PQ sold goods to AZ for $52,000 at a mark up of 33 1/3% on cost. At 30 September 20X2 all of the goods remained in AZ's closing inventory and AZ had not paid for the goods.

(vii) AZ sold a piece of machinery to PQ on 1 October 20X1 for $74,000. The machinery had previously been used in AZ's business and had been included in AZ's property, plant and equipment at a carrying value of $50,000. The machinery had a remaining useful life of 4 years at that date. Profit on disposal was included in revenue.

(viii) AZ made a payment to PQ for $60,000 on 30 September 20X2 which was not recorded by PQ until 5 October 20X2.

Required:

(a) Explain the meaning of fair value according to IFRS 10 *Consolidated financial statements*.

Calculate the fair value of PQ's net assets acquired by AZ on 1 October 20X0.

(4 marks)

(b) Prepare the consolidated statement of financial position for AZ as at 30 September 20X2, in accordance with the requirements of International Financial Reporting Standards. **(21 marks)**

Notes to the financial statements are not required, but all workings must be clearly shown.

(Total: 25 marks)

377 TX GROUP (FEB 13)

The draft statements of financial position at 31 December 2012 for three entities, TX, SX and LW are given below:

Statements of financial position as at 31 December 20X2:

	Notes	TX $000	SX $000	LW $000
Non-current assets				
Property, plant and equipment		545	480	468
Investments at cost:				
SX	(i),(ii)	530	0	0
LW (150,000 equity shares)	(iii)	190	0	0
		1,265	480	468
Current assets				
Inventory	(iv)	221	55	170
Trade receivables		98	75	124
Cash and cash equivalents	(v)	72	0	110
		391	130	404
Total assets		1,656	610	872
Equity and liabilities				
Equity shares of $1 each		800	360	500
Share premium		400	0	100
Retained earnings		300	140	120
		1,500	500	720
Current liabilities				
Trade payables		156	47	152
Bank overdraft		0	63	0
		156	110	152
Total equity and liabilities		1,656	610	872

SECTION C-TYPE QUESTIONS : SECTION 3

Additional information:

(i) TX acquired all of SX's equity shares on 1 January 20X2 for an agreed purchase consideration of $530,000. SX's retained earnings were $110,000 on 1 January 20X2.

(ii) The fair value of SX's property on 1 January 20X2 exceeded its carrying value by $72,000. The excess of fair value over carrying value was attributed to buildings with a remaining useful life of 18 years. TX's accounting policy is to depreciate buildings using the straight line basis with no residual value.

(iii) TX purchased its shareholding in LW on 1 January 20X2 for $190,000 when LW's retained earnings were $70,000. The fair value of all LW's net assets was the same as their carrying value at that date. TX exercises significant influence over all aspects of LW's financial and operating policies.

(iv) During September 20X2 TX sold SX goods for $44,000 at a mark up of 331/3% on cost. At 31 December 20X2 all the goods remained in SX's closing inventory. At 31 December 2012 TX had not recorded any payment for the goods.

(v) SX made a part payment to TX for $15,000 on 29 December 20X2 which was not recorded by TX until 4 January 20X3.

Required:

(a) If an entity, TX, owns more than half the equity (voting) shares of another entity, SX, then SX will be deemed to be the subsidiary of TX. However a parent/subsidiary relationship can exist even when the parent owns less than 50% of the equity shares.

Explain the circumstances that can give rise to a parent/subsidiary relationship other than a majority shareholding. **(5 marks)**

(b) Prepare the consolidated statement of financial position for TX as at 31 December 20X2, in accordance with the requirements of International Financial Reporting Standards. **(20 marks)**

Notes to the financial statements are NOT required, but all workings must be clearly shown.

(Total: 25 marks)

378 CLUB GROUP (MAY 13)

The draft statements of financial position at 31 March 20X3 and statements of profit or loss for the year ended 31 March 20X3 for three entities, are given below:

Statements of financial position as at 31 March 20X3

	Notes	Club $000	Green $000	Tee $000
Non-current assets				
Property, plant and equipment	(vi)	50,050	30,450	28,942
Investments:				
17,370,000 Ordinary shares in Green at cost	(i);(ii);(iii)	35,610	0	0
3,980,000 Ordinary shares in Tee at cost	(iv)	8,000	0	0
		93,660	30,450	28,942
Current assets				
Inventory	(v)	34,910	9,310	2,580
Trade receivables		38,790	16,530	2,660
Cash and cash equivalents	(vii)	5,010	1,480	318
		78,710	27,320	5,558
Total assets		172,370	57,770	34,500
Equity and liabilities				
Equity shares of $1 each		112,620	17,370	15,920
Share premium		0	3,470	0
Retained earnings		15,630	10,650	3,590
		128,250	31,490	19,510
Non-current liabilities				
Long term borrowings		32,000	15,000	9,140
Current liabilities				
Trade payables		11,320	10,830	5,530
Loan interest payable		800	450	320
		12,120	11,280	5,850
Total equity and liabilities		172,370	57,770	34,500

SECTION C-TYPE QUESTIONS : SECTION 3

Summarised statements of profit or loss for the year ended 31 March 20X3

	Club $000	Green $000	Tee $000
Revenue	130,000	67,410	31,890
Cost of sales	(75,470)	(40,470)	(18,920)
Gross profit	54,530	26,940	12,970
Expenses	(37,660)	(20,230)	(9,460)
	16,870	6,710	3,510
Finance cost	(1,600)	(900)	(640)
	15,270	5,810	2,870
Income tax expense	(3,050)	(1,160)	(580)
Profit for the year	12,220	4,650	2,290

Additional information:

(i) Club acquired all of Green's equity shares on 1 April 20X1 in a share for share exchange. The agreed purchase consideration was $35,610,000. Green's retained earnings were $3,000,000 on 1 April 20X1.

(ii) The fair value of Green's property, plant and equipment on 1 April 20X1 exceeded its carrying value by $1,200,000. The excess of fair value over carrying value was attributed to buildings owned by Green. At the date of acquisition these buildings had a remaining useful life of 12 years. Club's accounting policy is to depreciate all property, plant and equipment using the straight line basis with no residual value.

(iii) Club carried out an impairment review of the goodwill arising on acquisition of Green and found that as at 31 March 20X3 the goodwill had NOT been impaired but had actually increased in value by $50,000.

(iv) Club purchased its shareholding in Tee on 1 April 20X2 for $8,000,000. The fair value of Tee's net assets was the same as its carrying value at that date. Club exercises significant influence over all aspects of Tee's financial and operating policies.

(v) Club occasionally trades with Green. During February 20X3 Club sold Green goods for $960,000. Green had not paid for the goods by 31 March 20X3. Club uses a mark-up of 33 1/3% on cost. 20% of the goods had been sold by Green at 31 March 20X3.

(vi) Club sold a piece of machinery to Green on 1 April 20X2 for $115,000. The machinery had previously been used in Club's business and had been included in Club's property, plant and equipment at a carrying value of $90,000. Club had recognised the profit on disposal in revenue. The machinery had a remaining useful life of 5 years on 1 April 20X2.

(vii) Green transferred $115,000 to Club on 31 March 20X3 which was not recorded by Club until April 20X3.

PAPER F1 : FINANCIAL OPERATIONS

Required:

(a) Explain how a post acquisition increase in goodwill, for example in note (iii) above, should be treated in consolidated financial statements. **(2 marks)**

(b) Prepare the consolidated statement of financial position for Club as at 31 March 20X3, in accordance with the requirements of International Financial Reporting Standards. **(23 marks)**

Notes to the financial statements are not required, but all workings must be clearly shown.

(Total: 25 marks)

379 ROAD GROUP (AUG 13)

The draft statements of financial position at 31 March 20X3 and statements of comprehensive income for the year ended 31 March 20X3 for three entities, are given below:

Statements of financial position as at 31 March 20X3:

	Notes	Road $000	Street $000	Drive $000
Non-current assets				
Property, plant and equipment	(ii); (vi)	1,840	1,060	930
Investments	(i)	1,923	0	0
		3,763	1,060	930
Current assets				
Inventory	(v)	310	236	287
Trade receivables		140	119	215
Cash and cash equivalents	(vii)	71	27	63
		521	382	565
Total assets		4,284	1,442	1,495
Equity and liabilities				
Equity shares of $1 each		2,000	550	700
Share premium		500	150	200
Retained earnings		814	339	458
		3,314	1,039	1,358
Non-current liabilities				
Borrowings		700	250	0

Current liabilities

Trade payables		270	128	137
Loan interest payable	(viii)	0	25	0
		270	153	137
Total equity and liabilities		4,284	1,442	1,495

Additional information:

(i) Road's investments comprise the following:

- Road acquired 100% of Street's equity shares on 1 April 20X0 paying $1,350,000. At this date Street's retained earnings were $122,000.

- On 1 April 20X1 Road advanced Street a 10 year loan of $250,000.

- Road purchased its shareholding of 175,000 shares in Drive on 1 April 20X2 for $323,000 when Drive's retained earnings were $350,000. Road exercises significant influence over all aspects of Drive's financial and operating policies.

(ii) The fair value of Street's property, plant and equipment on 1 April 20X0 exceeded its carrying value by $320,000. The excess of fair value over carrying value was attributed to buildings owned by Street. At the date of acquisition these buildings had a remaining useful life of 20 years. Road's accounting policy is to depreciate buildings using the straight line basis with no residual value.

(iii) Road carried out an impairment review of the goodwill arising on the acquisition of Street and found that as at 31 March 20X3 the goodwill had been impaired by $38,000.

(iv) Road carried out an impairment review of its investment in Drive and found that as at 31 March 20X3 its investment in Drive had been impaired by $20,000.

(v) Road occasionally trades with Street. During February 20X3 Street sold Road goods for $220,000. Street uses a mark-up of 25% on cost. At 31 March 20X3 Road had sold 40% of the goods.

(vi) Road sold a piece of machinery to Street on 1 April 20X2 for $95,000. The machinery had previously been used in Road's business and had been included in Road's property, plant and equipment at a carrying value of $65,000. The machinery had a remaining useful life of 5 years at that date.

(vii) Road had previously paid Street for half of the goods purchased and on 30 March 20X3 Road transferred the balance of the amount due to Street for the goods purchased, $110,000. This was not recorded by Street until 3 April 20X3.

(viii) At 31 March 20X3 $25,000 loan interest due to Road in respect of its loan to Street was due and had not been paid. Street had accrued the loan interest due at the year end but Road had not accrued any interest income.

Required:

(a) Define what is meant by control and explain how this is determined according to IFRS 10 *Consolidated Financial Statements*. **(5 marks)**

(b) Prepare the consolidated statement of financial position for Road as at 31 March 20X3, in accordance with the requirements of International Financial Reporting Standards. **(20 marks)**

Notes to the financial statements are not required, but all workings must be clearly shown.

(Total: 25 marks)

Section 4

ANSWERS TO SECTION A-TYPE QUESTIONS

PRINCIPLES OF BUSINESS TAXATION

1   The competent jurisdiction is the country whose tax laws apply to the entity.

2   A taxable person is an individual, company or other organisation who is liable to pay direct taxes.

3   Tax evasion is an illegal way of avoiding paying taxes, i.e. Not declaring income or claiming false expenses.

4   Two from:

   Exemption

   Tax credit

   Deduction

5   D

6   C

7   A direct tax is one that is levied directly on the person who is intended to pay the tax.

8   1   Domestic legislation and judicial rulings.

   2   Tax authority statements of practice.

   3   Directives from a supranational body.

   4   International treaties (for example, double taxation treaties).

PAPER F1 : FINANCIAL OPERATIONS

9 B

The question says "a dividend of $350,000 was paid" which implies this is the gross amount. Grossing up the $350 was not required as it was meant to be assumed that this was the gross figure. The answer was therefore calculated on the gross figure of $350,000 as follows:

	$
Tax on profits (25% × 750,000)	187,500
Shareholder:	
Dividend received	
Net – (350,000 × 75%)	262,500
Tax credit (262,500/75 × 25)	87,500
Gross dividend	350,000
Tax @ 30%	105,000
Less tax credit	(87,500)
Tax on dividend	17,500
Total (187,500 + 17,500)	205,000

10 C

11 D

12 A

A tax authority is unlikely to have the power of arrest. This power will usually be restricted to the police or other law enforcement officers.

13 B

The OECD's list of permanent establishments includes a place of management, a workshop and a quarry. A building site is only included if it lasts more than 12 months. Specifically excluded from the definition of permanent establishment are facilities used only for the purpose of storage, display or delivery of goods.

14 C

A = 17/75 = 22.7% tax paid on profits

B = 4.8/44 = 10.9% tax paid on profits

Therefore, the greater the profits, the greater the tax percentage, hence this is a progressive tax.

15 Government sets deadlines for filing returns and paying tax so that:
- taxpayers know when payment is required
- the tax authorities can forecast their cash flows
- they can impose penalties for late payment/late filing.

ANSWERS TO SECTION A-TYPE QUESTIONS : SECTION 4

16 **C**

Equity

17 From the perspective of the government, three advantages of the PAYE system are:
- Tax is collected regularly throughout the year, giving rise to a cash flow advantage
- There is less risk of default as individuals do not need to budget for their tax payments
- The administrative costs are largely passed to the employers.

18 From the revenue authority's point of view, a commodity is suitable for an excise duty to be imposed if:
- there are few large producers/suppliers
- demand is inelastic with no close substitutes
- sales volumes are large
- it is easy to define the products to be covered by the tax.

19 **B**

20 **A**

Hypothecation is the means of devoting certain types of expenditure for certain things, e.g. Road tax is used for maintaining roads.

21 **C**

22 The answer is capital and consumption.

23 **C**

24 **A**

25 **A**

HD has the responsibility to pay the sales tax to the tax authorities and will have direct contact with them, therefore this is known as formal incidence.

26 **B**

27 **B**

28 **C**

29 **D**

	$000
Accounting profit	860
Add depreciation	42
Add amortisation	15
	917
Less tax depreciation	(51)
Taxable profit	866
Tax @ 25%	216.5

30 **D**

31 **D**

32 Under the OECD model tax convention an entity will generally have residence for tax purposes in the country of its effective management.

33 **B**

34 Any two from:
- Power to review and query filed returns
- Power to request special reports or returns
- Power to examine records
- Powers of entry and search
- Power to exchange information with tax authorities in other jurisdictions
- Power to impose penalties

35 **C**

36 **A**

37 **D**

38 Tax avoidance is tax planning to arrange affairs, within the scope of the law, to minimise the tax liability.

39 To ensure that for similar investments all entities are allowed the same rates of depreciation for tax purposes.

Entities can use any rate for accounting depreciation, so to ensure that all entities are taxed equally the tax authority sets rates for tax depreciation for all entities. The tax depreciation rates then replace accounting depreciation in the tax computations.

ANSWERS TO SECTION A-TYPE QUESTIONS : SECTION 4

40 **D**

41 **A**

200 items × $50 × 15% = $1,500 VAT payable (output tax).

200 items × ($30 + $5) × 15% = $1,050 VAT reclaimable (input tax).

The net amount payable is therefore $450 ($1,500 − $1,050).

42 The answer is $300

Output VAT on standard sales ($18,400 × 15/115)		2,400
Input VAT on standard purchases ($10,000 × 15%)	1,500	
Input VAT on zero purchases ($4,000 × 15%)	600	
		2,100
VAT due		300

VAT can be claimed back from standard and zero rated supplies where standard rate has been charged.

43 The answer is profit ($70,000 + $150,000 − $120,000) = $100,000 and VAT paid is ($33,000 − $18,000) = $15,000

	Net	VAT	Gross
Sales			
Product A	70	0	70
Product B	150	(183 × 22/122) = 33	183
Cost of goods	(120)	(138 × 15/115) = 18	(138)

The profit is always calculated on the net amount.

44 **C**

The excise duty must be added to the cost before the VAT is calculated, i.e. $14 + $3 = $17 × 15% = $2.55. Total tax = ($3 + $2.55) × 1000 units = $5,550

45 **D**

	$
Cost	15
Excise duty	3
	18
VAT at 15% × $18	2.7
Excise duty	3
Total tax per item	5.7
2,000 items × 5.7	11,400 tax

PAPER F1 : FINANCIAL OPERATIONS

46 The answer is UF pays VAT of $225 and ZF pays VAT of $525

UF	Output tax	2,875 × 15/115 =	375
	Input tax	1,000 × 15% =	(150)
	VAT payable		225
ZF	Output tax	6,900 × 15/115 =	900
	Input tax	2,875 × 15/115 =	(375)
	VAT payable		525

47 CU (250,000 – 100,000) × 15%= $22,500

CZ (600,000 – 250,000) × 15%= $52,500

48 Sales tax payable:

DA   (500 – 200) @ 15% = 45

DB   (1,000 – 500) @ 15% = 75

49 The answer is $119

	$
Sales tax on manufacturing costs 200 @ 7%	14
Sales tax to DB 500 @ 7%	35
Sales tax to customer 1,000 @ 7%	70
	119

> *Tutorial note*
>
> *CIMA's official answer ignores the initial sale of the goods from the manufacture to DA and instead shows the answer as $105 (35 + 70).*

50 The answer is $450.

Outputs: 15,000 × 15% =	2,250
Inputs: (9,000 + 3,000) × 15% =	1,800
Net payment due from DE	450

Sales tax relating to exempt items cannot be reclaimed and is ignored.

ANSWERS TO SECTION A-TYPE QUESTIONS : SECTION 4

51 **Year 1: No taxable trading profits and taxable capital gains of $6,000.** $50,000 of the trading losses in Year 2 can be carried back and set off against the profit in Year 1, reducing the taxable trading profit to 0. The capital loss in Year 2 cannot be carried back to Year 1.

Year 2: No taxable trading profits or gains. Trading loss and capital loss in the year. Unrelieved trading losses of $40,000 and the unrelieved capital losses of $8,000 are carried forward to Year 3.

Year 3: No taxable trading profits or gains. Unrelieved trading losses of $40,000 are set against the trading profits of $30,000. The unrelieved trading loss is now $10,000 and is carried forward to Year 4. The unrelieved capital loss brought forward is set off against the capital gain in Year 3, leaving $3,000 of unrelieved capital losses to carry forward to Year 4.

Year 4: Taxable trading profits of $60,000 and taxable capital gains of $3,000. Taxable trading profits = $70,000 – $10,000 unrelieved losses brought forward. Taxable capital gains = $6,000 – $3,000 unrelieved losses brought forward.

52 C

Group loss relief allows members of the group to surrender their losses to any other member of the group. Consolidation of profits and losses does not apply to tax computations and so answer A is incorrect. Group loss relief is an option that can be taken by the group, and is not compulsory. Therefore answers B and D are incorrect.

53 *30/9/X3* Trading profit $200 × 20% = **$40,000**

Capital loss c/f $100,000

30/9/X4 Trading loss c/f $120,000

Capital loss of $100,000 b/f is c/f

30/9/X5 Trading profit $150,000 – $120,000 = $30,000

Capital gain $130,000 – $100,000 = $30,000

Total $30,000 + $30,000 = $60,000 × 20% = **$12,000**

54 A group may want to claim relief of losses so that:

(a) Relief can be claimed as early as possible.

(b) The group company may pay tax at a higher rate, therefore more tax can be saved.

55 A

	$000
Selling price	1,200
Selling costs	(9)
Net proceeds	1,191
Cost	(600)
Additional costs	(5)
	586
Indexation (605 × 60%)	(363)
Taxable gain	223
Tax @ 25%	55.75

56 The answer is $41,400.

	$
Disposal proceeds	1,250,000
Less: Costs of disposal	(2,000)
	1,248,000
Acquisition costs:	
Purchase cost	630,000
Costs arising on purchase ($3,500 + $6,500)	10,000
Renovation costs	100,000
	(740,000)
Indexation – 50% × $740,000	(370,000)
	138,000
Tax @ 30%	41,400

57 The answer is $42,625

	$
Selling price	1,200,000
Costs to sell	(17,000)
Net proceeds	1,183,000
Cost	(650,000)
Duties	(25,000)
	508,000
Indexation (675,000 × 50%)	(337,500)
Taxable gain	170,500
Tax @ 25%	42,625

ANSWERS TO SECTION A-TYPE QUESTIONS : SECTION 4

58 The answer is $12,000

	$
Selling price	450,000
Costs to sell	(15,000)
Net proceeds	435,000
Cost	(375,000)
Duties	(12,000)
Taxable gain	48,000
Tax @ 25%	12,000

59 D

The site of the 11 month construction contract is not a permanent establishment according to the OECD model because it is less 12 months.

60 B

An overseas branch is an extension of the main business activity and not treated as a separate entity for taxation purposes.

61 C

Withholding tax is a tax deducted at source before payment of interest or dividends.

62 B

	$
Gross dividend taken into DP's taxable income	50,000
Tax @ 12%	6,000
Less tax credit	(5,000)
Remaining tax liability	1,000

63 The answer is $360,000.

$3,000,000 × 80% × 15% = $360,000.

64 Under the OECD model an entity will have residence in the country of its **effective management**.

PAPER F1 : FINANCIAL OPERATIONS

65 D

Each of the other three factors can be taken into account in determining tax residence

66 C

Effective management and control is the over-riding test under the OECD model tax convention.

67 The answer is $20,000.

	$
Gross dividend = 90,000/0.9	100,000

Underlying tax paid in respect of dividend:

$$\frac{200,000}{1,200,000 - 200,000} \times 100,000 = \$20,000$$

EB will be able to claim double taxation relief of $20,000, provided that its actual tax liability on the dividend income is of at least that amount.

68 B

Double tax relief does not prevent you from paying tax twice. For example, suppose that your company is based in Country A and has a subsidiary operating in Country B, and there is a double taxation agreement between the countries. If tax on profits in Country B is 10% and in Country A is 15%, your company would pay tax at 10% in Country B and tax at 15% in Country A on the subsidiary's profits. Double tax relief therefore mitigates tax – you don't have to pay 35% in tax (10% + 25%) – but you might still have to pay tax on the profits twice, once in each country.

69 C

The country of control overrides the others for residency.

70 D

71 Two from:
- Exemption
- Tax credit
- Deduction

72 D

ANSWERS TO SECTION A-TYPE QUESTIONS : SECTION 4

73 The answer is a $34,000 liability at 31/3/X7 and a $2,000 asset at 31/3/X8 (to the nearest $000).

Year		Accounting base $		Tax base $	Diff	X 25%
31/3/X6	Cost	600,000	Cost	600,000		
	Depreciation	(120,000)	FYA 50%	(300,000)		
	CV	480,000	TWDV	300,000		
31/3/X7	Depreciation	(120,000)	WDA25%	(75,000)		
	CV	360,000	TWDV	225,000	135,000	33,750
	Impairment	(120,000)				
		240,000		225,000		
31/3/X8	Depreciation	(80,000)	WDA 25%	(56,000)		
	CV	160,000	TWDV	169,000	(9,000)	(2,250)

74 The answer is a $21,120 reduction in the total tax charge due to a release of the deferred tax provision. This occurs when the accounting base is greater than the tax base.

	Accounting CV		Tax base
Y/e 30/6/X3	$	Y/e 30/6/X3	$
Cost	600,000	Cost	600,000
Depn	(80,000)	CA's 20%	(120,000)
C/f	520,000	C/f	480,000
Y/e 30/6/X4		Y/e 30/6/X4	
Depreciation	(80,000)	CA's × 20%	(96,000)
C/f	440,000	C/f	384,000
Y/e 30/6/X5		Y/e 30/6/X5	
Depreciation	(80,000)	CA's × 20%	(76,800)
C/f	360,000		307,200

Deferred tax provision at 30/6/X5

	$
Accounting carrying value	360,000
Tax base	307,200
Difference	52,800
Tax at 40% = Release provision	21,120

Alternative calculation:

	$
Tax base of asset after 3 years	307,200
Selling price	300,000
Loss on disposal for tax purposes	7,200
Accounting carrying value after 3 years	360,000
Selling price	300,000
Loss on disposal for accounting purposes	60,000
Difference = 60,000 – 7,200 × 40%	21,120

75 The answer is $2,013.

	Accounting depreciation $	Tax depreciation $	Difference $
Cost	20,000	20,000	
Less: Depreciation b/fwd	5,000	12,500	
	15,000	7,500	
20X3	1,630	2,120	
20X4	1,590	1,860	
20X5	1,530	1,320	
Written down value at 31 December 20X5	10,250	2,200	8,050
Tax at 25%			2,013

76

Year		Accounting base $		Tax base $	Diff	X 25%
31/3/X8	Cost	220,000	Cost	220,000		
	Depreciation	(27,500)	FYA 30%	(66,000)		
	CV	192,500	TWDV	154,000	38,500	9,625
	Revalued	50,000				
		242,500		154,000		
31/3/X9	Depreciation	(34,643)	WDA 20%	30,800		
	CV	207,857	TWDV	123,200	84,657	21,164

At 31/03/X9 the statement of financial position deferred tax provision will be $21,164 and the statement of profit or loss will be $11,539 (movement $21,164 – $9,625).

77 The answer is $294,120.

	$
Deferred tax increase (759,000 – 642,000) =	117,000
Charge for year (946,000 × 22%) =	208,120
Overprovision from previous year	(31,000)
Income tax expense	294,120

78 A

	$
Current year charge	320,000
Over-provision for prior year (290,000 – 280,000)	(10,000)
Charge	310,000

79 B

	Accounting CV		Tax base
Y/e 31/3/X8	$	Y/e 31/3/X8	$
Cost	60,000	Cost	60,000
Depn 20%	(12,000)	CA's (60,000 × 50%)	(30,000)
C/f	48,000	C/f	30,000
Y/e 31/3/X9		Y/e 31/3/X9	
Depreciation 20% × $48,000	(9,600)	CA's (30,000 × 25%)	(7,500)
C/f	38,400	C/f	22,500
Y/e 31/3/Y0		Y/e 31/3/Y0	
Depreciation 20% × $38,400	(7,680)	CA's (22,500 × 25%)	(5,625)
C/f	30,720		16,875

Deferred tax provision at 31 March 20Y0

	$
Accounting carrying value	30,720
Tax base	16,875
Difference	13,845
Tax at 25% =	3,461

80 The answer is $17,500.

(4/12 × $75,000 × 20%) + (8/12 × $75,000 × 25%)

81 The answer is $90,625.

	Accounting CV		Tax base
Y/e 01/10/X8	$	Y/e 01/10/X8	$
Cost	900,000	Cost	900,000
Depn (900,000 – 100,000)/8 years	(100,000)	CA's 50%	(450,000)
C/f	800,000	C/f	450,000
Y/e 01/10/X9		Y/e 01/10/X9	
Depreciation	(100,000)	CA's 25%	(112,500)
C/f	700,000	C/f	337,500

Deferred tax provision at 30/09/X9

	$
Accounting carrying value	700,000
Tax base	337,500
Difference	362,500
Tax at 25% =	90,625

ANSWERS TO SECTION A-TYPE QUESTIONS : SECTION 4

82 The answer is $22,500.

	$
Accounting profit	95,000
Adjustments:	
Non-taxable income	(15,000)
Non-tax allowable expenditure	10,000
Taxable profits	90,000
Tax at 25%	22,500

83 B

	$
Purchase cost	200,000
Tax allowance in year to 31 March 20X2	(50,000)
	150,000
Tax allowance in year to 31 March 20X3	(37,500)
	112,500
Tax allowance in year to 31 March 20X4	(28,125)
Tax written down value at 31 March Year X4	84,375
Carrying value in the accounts	140,000
($200,000 minus (3 × 10% × $200,000))	
Temporary difference	55,625
Tax rate	30%
Deferred tax balance	$16,688

84 The answer is $66,750.

	Accounting CV		Tax base
Y/e 30/9/X4	$	Y/e 30/9/X4	$
Cost	900,000	Cost	900,000
Depn (900,000 – 50,000)/5 years	(170,000)	CA's (900,000 × 50%)	(450,000)
C/f	730,000	C/f	450,000
Y/e 30/9/X5		Y/e 30/9/X5	
Depreciation	(170,000)	CA's (450,000 × 25%)	(112,500)
C/f	560,000	C/f	337,500

Deferred tax provision at 30 September 20X5

	$
Accounting carrying value	560,000
Tax base	337,500
Difference	222,500
Tax at 30% =	66,750

85 The answer's are $36,000 SOFP and $6,000 IS

	Accounting CV $		Tax base $
Cost	500,000	Cost	500,000
31/3/X5 Depn	(100,000)	31/3/X5 FYA 50%	(250,000)
	400,000		250,000
31/3/X6 Depn	(100,000)	31/3/X6 20%	(50,000)
	300,000		200,000
Revaluation	120,000		
	420,000		
31/3/X7 Depn (420,000/3)	(140,000)	31/3/X7 20%	(40,000)
	280,000		160,000

	31/3/X6 $	31/3/X7 $
Accounting carrying value	300,000	280,000
Tax base	200,000	160,000
Temporary difference	100,000	120,000
Deferred tax at 30%	30,000	36,000

Statement of profit or loss, increase (36,000 − 30,000) = 6,000

Statement of financial position − deferred tax provision 20X7   36,000

ANSWERS TO SECTION A-TYPE QUESTIONS : SECTION 4

86 The answer is $200,250.

The accounting profit should be reported before recognising any dividends paid and, under a classical tax system, it is irrelevant whether or not profits are distributed.

	$
Accounting profit	822,000
Add: Entertaining expenses	32,000
Donation to political party	50,000
Less: Government grant income	(103,000)
	801,000
Tax @ 25%	200,250

87 The answer is $49,500.

ED has depreciated the asset more quickly for tax than it has done for accounts purposes, such that it should recognise a deferred tax liability, calculated as follows:

	$
Cost	400,000
Depreciation 30/9/X6	(100,000)
	300,000
Depreciation 30/9/X7	(75,000)
Carrying value	225,000
Tax base	0
Difference	225,000
Deferred tax liability @ 22%	49,500

88 B

Year		Accounting Base $		Tax Base $	Diff	X 25%
1/10/X1	CV	132,000	TWDV	82,500		
	Depreciation	(44,000)	25%	(20,625)		
	CV	88,000	TWDV	61,875	26,125	6,531

Accounting depreciation = $220,000/5 = $44,000 pa

PRINCIPLES OF REGULATION OF FINANCIAL REPORTING

89 An asset is a resource controlled by the enterprise as a result of past events and from which future economic benefits are expected to flow to the enterprise.

90 B

The auditor expresses an *opinion* on the truth and fairness of the financial statements; the auditor does *not certify* that the financial statements give a true and fair view – statement (i) is therefore false. All the other statements are correct.

91 C

The disagreement is material and it affects the auditor's opinion. However, as the financial statements are not seriously misleading, the auditor should issue an 'except for' qualification. (If the financial statements were seriously misleading, he would issue an adverse opinion.)

92 The *Framework* states that 'the objective of financial statements is to provide information about the financial position, performance and changes in financial position of an enterprise that is useful to a wide range of users in making economic decisions'.

93 D

The two assumptions underlying the conceptual framework are the accruals basis and the going concern basis.

94 D

The IFRS Interpretations Committee interprets International Financial Reporting Standards and, after public consultation and reporting to the IASB, it issues an interpretation.

95 A

The IFRS Foundation is the supervisory body, and consists of trustees whose main responsibilities are governance issues and ensuring that sufficient funding is available.

96 B

When there is a material misstatement in the external auditor's opinion (as distinct from a pervasive qualification) the audit report should give a qualified opinion. The auditors will state that, in their opinion, the financial statements give a true and fair view, except for ....

97 B

The auditor has been prevented from obtaining sufficient appropriate audit evidence.

98 B

ANSWERS TO SECTION A-TYPE QUESTIONS : SECTION 4

99 Auditors usually have the power to:
- access the books, records, documents and accounts
- attend and speak at meetings of equity holders
- require officers of the entity to provide them with information and explanations.

100 C

101 Expenses and equity.

102 C

An auditor will give their opinion of whether the financial statements show a true and fair view and can suggest to the directors to change the statements but cannot correct the statements themselves.

103 A

104 D

105 A

106 The answer is financial and physical concept.

107 The answer is any two of the following:
- Lenders.
- General public.
- Customers.
- Suppliers.
- Competitors

108 Going Concern and Accruals Concept

109 To enable the auditor to see if the accounts show a true and fair view and have been prepared in accordance with appropriate accounting standards.

110 D

The objectives of financial statements are set out in the IASB *Framework*. Note that providing information about 'changes in the financial position', as well as information about financial position and financial performance, is included in these objectives.

111 B

You should learn the IASB definitions of both assets and liabilities. The definition in the question is in two parts: (1) a liability is a present obligation that has arisen out of a past event, and (2) it is certain or probable that settlement of this obligation will result in an outflow of economic benefits, such as a payment of money. It is also necessary for the amount of the liability to be measured reliably.

PAPER F1 : FINANCIAL OPERATIONS

112 C

The IASB *Framework* states that materiality is a threshold or cut-off point for reporting information, but is not a qualitative characteristic that financial information must have to be useful.

113

Decreases in economic benefits during the accounting period in the form of outflows or depletions of assets that result in decreases in equity, other than those relating to distributions to equity participants.

114 A

115 A

116 C

The IASB *Framework* defines equity as the residual interest in the assets of the enterprise after all the liabilities have been deducted from total assets. It is important to recognise this idea that equity is a balancing figure: Assets – Liabilities. Statements of financial position should be prepared with a view to measuring assets and liabilities in the best manner, and equity is the amount left over when liabilities are subtracted from assets.

117 D

118 A

119 D

120 Any one of the following:

Sources of finance and capital markets – more demand for information and disclosure where there is a higher proportion of capital raised from shareholders.

The ownership of entities – more accountability and disclosure expected where the majority of capital provided through a stock market instead of government or family shareholdings.

The political system in a country – nature of regulation and control of accounting will be influenced by the political party in control at the time.

Cultural differences – the culture within a country will influence societal and national values which can influence accounting.

121 B

122 D

123 C

124 Any two from:
- To give advice to the IASB on agenda decisions;
- To give advice to the IASB on the priorities in its work;
- In relation to major standard setting projects to inform the IASB of the views of organisations and individuals on the Council;
- To give any other advice to the IASB or the Trustees.

125 The answer is "relevance" and "faithful representation"```.

126 The answer is "Opinion".

127 D

128 A

129 D

130 A modified report, based on insufficient appropriate evidence, with a disclaimer of opinion.

SINGLE COMPANY FINANCIAL ACCOUNTS

131 The answer is (in $000) $13,778.

The calculation is as follows:

	$000
Profit before tax	12,044
Add Depreciation	1,796
Loss on sale of tangible non-current assets	12
	13,852
Increase in inventories	(398)
Increase in receivables	(144)
Increase in payables	468
Cash generated from operations	13,778

PAPER F1 : FINANCIAL OPERATIONS

132 The answer is $105,000.

	$000
Balance at 30 September 20X4	180
Revaluation (30 – 10)	20
Disposal at CV (90 – 85)	(5)
Depreciation	(40)
	155
Balance at 30 September 20X5	(260)
Purchases	105

Disposal

	$000		$000
Cost	90	Bank	15
Profit	10	Dep'n (balance)	85
	100		100

133 A

	$
Accrued interest b/f	12,000
Interest payable per statement of profit or loss	41,000
Accrued interest c/f	(15,000)
Paid	38,000

134 The answer (in $000) is 350.

	$000
Total opening balances (380 + 80)	460
Add: Tax charge for the year	450
	910
Less: Total closing balances (460 + 100)	(560)
Tax paid during the period	350

208

ANSWERS TO SECTION A-TYPE QUESTIONS : SECTION 4

135 A

Tax creditor

Paid	98	B/f (27 + 106)	133
		Statement of profit or loss	122
C/f (38 + 119)	157		
	255		255

136 A

137 B

138 D

139 A

140
- It must be a distinguishable component of the entity.
- The risks and returns are different from those for other parts of the business.
- It contributes at least 10% of total sales revenue, profits or assets.

141 B

142 An operating segment is defined by IFRS 8 as a component of an entity whose operating results are regularly reviewed by the entity's chief operating decision maker to make decisions about resources to be allocated to the segment and assess its performance.

143 C

The prior period error is corrected by restating the comparative amounts for the previous period at their correct value. A note to the accounts should disclose the nature of the error, together with other details.

144 A

B and D are examples of changes in estimates and C is an example of a change in policy.

145 (1) When a change in accounting policy is required by a new or revised accounting standard.

(2) If the change in policy results in financial statements providing reliable and more relevant information.

146 B

A change from capitalising a cost to treating it as a revenue expense would be classified as a change in accounting policy under IAS 8.

PAPER F1 : FINANCIAL OPERATIONS

147 A

Items B and C are examples of changes in estimates and item D is an example of an error.

148 D

Items A and B are a change in policy and item C is an error.

149 The answer is $3,640.

	$
Cost	100,000
Depreciation 31/3/X3	(25,000)
	75,000
Depreciation 31/3/X4	(18,750)
	56,250
Depreciation 31/3/X5	(14,063)
	42,187
Depreciation 31/3/X6	(10,547)
	31,640
Recoverable amount	(28,000)
Impairment loss	3,640

150 The answer is $580,000.

	Land $000	Buildings $000	Total $000
Cost	120	200	
Accumulated depreciation to the revaluation date	–	(100)	
Carrying value at the revaluation date	120	100	220
Revalued amount	200	600	800
Credit to revaluation reserve			580

151 The answer is $60,000.

The building will be depreciated over its remaining expected useful economic life, which is 10 years. The annual depreciation charge for the building will therefore be $600,000/10 years = $60,000 each year.

152 C

The four definitions might all seem similar, but property, plant and equipment are **tangible** assets, not any assets. IAS 16 states that a tangible asset should be held for **more than one accounting period** (rather than for more than 12 months) to qualify as property, plant and equipment.

ANSWERS TO SECTION A-TYPE QUESTIONS : SECTION 4

153 The answer is $129,000

	$
Cost of basic machine	100,000
Special modifications made to basic design	15,000
Supplier's engineer's time installing and initial testing of machine	2,000
Concrete base	12,000
	129,000

We do not include the three year maintenance cost as this is not a one off cost and would be expensed to the statement of profit or loss.

JT can reclaim back VAT hence would not form part of the cost of non-current assets.

154 A

IAS 16 states that when the revaluation model is used, revaluations should be made with sufficient regularity to ensure that the carrying value of the assets remain close to fair value. IAS 16 also states that, if one item in a class of assets is revalued, all the assets in that class must be revalued.

155 A

			$
1 July 20X2	Cost		50,000
30 June 20X3	Carrying amount	80% × 50,000	40,000
30 June 20X4	Carrying amount	60% × 50,000	30,000

On 1 July 20X4 the asset is revalued from a carrying amount of $30,000 to a fair value of $60,000, establishing a revaluation reserve of $30,000. There are three years of useful life remaining.

		$
30 June 20X5	Carrying amount = ⅔ × 60,000	40,000
1 July 20X5	Disposal proceeds	35,000
Loss on disposal		(5,000)

There is a loss on disposal of $5,000, and the $30,000 revaluation reserve is transferred to retained earnings as a movement on reserves.

156 A

As the lining of the furnace was identified as a separate item in the accounting records, its replacement will be viewed as capital expenditure. The other three options all involve either replacing part of an asset or restoring it to its original condition.

157 The answer is $5,250 pa.

	$
1.10.X2 purchase	21,000
Depreciation to 30.9.X5	
21,000/6 × 3	(10,500)
Balance 30.9.X5	10,500

The machine will be used for two more years, at which point it will be worthless. Assuming that production is still profitable with the increased depreciation charge, it should be written off over its remaining useful life, such that the charge recognised in the year to 30 September 20X6 should be $5,250 ($10,500 × ½).

158 Valuation $95,000.

Provision for accumulated depreciation at 31 March 20X5 $28,500 (11,875 + 1,625).

Workings:	$
Cost (1/4/X1)	100,000
$100,000/10 × 2 years	20,000
CV 31/03/X3	80,000
To revaluation reserve	15,000
Revaluation (1/4/X3)	95,000
Depreciation $95,000/8 years	11,875
B/f 1/4/X4	83,125
Depreciation $83,125/5 years	16,625
Carrying value at 31/3/X5	66,500

159 D

The allocation of EW's administration costs would not be included as these costs are not directly incurred as a result of carrying out the construction.

160 C

The asset was previously revalued by $200,000, therefore when it is devalued by $250,000 the reserve is removed and the balance charged to the statement of profit or loss.

161 B

The cost of the decommissioning is assumed to be an obligation for the company. If so, an amount should be included in the cost of the asset when it is first recognised (on 1 July 20X4).

The amount to include in the cost of the asset for decommissioning costs is the present value of the expected future decommissioning costs. The present value is calculated by multiplying the expected future cost by a discount factor, which in this case is the discount factor for Year 5 (20X9) at 12%. $4,000,000 × 0.567 = $2.268 million.

ANSWERS TO SECTION A-TYPE QUESTIONS : SECTION 4

Therefore:

| Debit: | Cost of asset | $2.268 million |
| Credit: | Provision for decommissioning costs | $2.268 million |

The asset is depreciated in the normal way, which in this example is on a straight-line basis over five years.

In addition, the decommissioning cost should be increased to $4 million by the end of Year 5. This is done by making a finance charge each year. This is charged at the cost of capital (12%) and applied to the balance on the provision account. The finance charge for the year to 30 June 20X5 is 12% × $2.268 million = $272,160.

| Debit: | Finance charge (expense) | $272,160 |
| Credit: | Provision for decommissioning costs | $272,160 |

	$
Depreciation charge ($2.268 million/5 years)	453,600
Finance charge	272,160
Impairment loss	725,760

162 A

	Land $ million	Buildings $ million	Total $ million
At 30 June 20X5			
Carrying amount	1.00	4.80	5.80
Building depreciation = $5 million/50 years = $100,000 per year			
Revalued amount	1.24	5.76	7.00
Transfer to revaluation reserve			1.20
At 30 June 20X7			
Carrying amount	1.24	5.52	6.76
Building depreciation = $5.76 million/48 years = $120,000 per year			
Disposal value			6.80
Gain on disposal			0.04

The gain on disposal is $40,000. The $1.2 million balance on the revaluation reserve is transferred from the revaluation reserve to another reserve account (probably retained earnings) but is not reported through the statement of profit or loss for the year.

163 A

Research costs are expensed to the statement of profit or loss as per IAS 38.

PAPER F1 : FINANCIAL OPERATIONS

164 The answer is $8,912.

	$
Carrying amount at the time of the impairment review ($76,000 × 80% × 80% × 80%)	38,912
Revised carrying amount after impairment review	30,000
Impairment (charge in the statement of profit or loss)	8,912

Note: The revised carrying amount (recoverable amount), is the higher of value in use $30,000 or fair value less costs to sell $27,000.

165 The answer is $80,000.

An asset should be valued at the lower of carrying amount and recoverable amount. Recoverable amount is the higher of (a) fair value less costs to sell and (b) value in use.

	A	B	C
Carrying amount	200	300	240
Recoverable amount	240	260	200
Impairment loss	nil	40	40

Total: 80

166 The rights do not meet the definition of an asset. As a gift they do not have a cost and there is no reliable measurement of probable future benefit.

167 The answer is $130,000.

Goodwill is the remaining balance after the fair value of the net tangible assets acquired and the other intangible assets acquired have been subtracted from the total purchase consideration.

	$	$
Purchase price		
Shares (10,000 × $20)		200,000
Cash		20,000
		220,000
Assets acquired		
Net tangible non-current assets	25,000	
Patents	15,000	
Brand name	50,000	
		90,000
Value of goodwill		130,000

ANSWERS TO SECTION A-TYPE QUESTIONS : SECTION 4

168 Any FOUR of the following:
- the technical feasibility of completing the project
- the intention to complete the project and use or sell the developed item
- an ability to use or sell the item
- the generation of probable future economic benefits from the developed item
- availability of adequate technical, financial and other resources to complete the project
- ability to measure the expenditure reliably.

169 A

When purchased goodwill is reduced in value due to impairment, the impairment loss should be reported through the statement of profit or loss as a loss for the period, and should not be taken directly to reserves.

170 The answer is $200,000.

Expenditures on the project during the year to 31 December 20X1 are research costs, which are charged as an expense in the statement of profit or loss for the year.

Expenditure in the year to 31 December 20X2 ($1,000,000) should be capitalised and reported in the statement of financial position at the year end. All the expenditure should be capitalised, because the recoverable amount of the expected future benefits exceeds the costs incurred.

In the year to 31 December 20X3, the expenditures should again be included in development costs as a non-tangible asset. However, at the end of the year, the accumulated expenditures capitalised are $2,200,000 ($1,000,000 + $1,200,000). This exceeds the recoverable amount of $2,000,000.

For the year to 31 December 20X3, an impairment cost of $200,000 should therefore be charged in the statement of profit or loss.

The value of the development costs in the statement of financial position at 31 December 20X3 is $2,000,000.

171 D

Item A cannot be capitalised because it does not meet all the criteria, i.e. it is not viable.

Item B is research and cannot be capitalised.

Item C cannot be capitalised because it does not meet all the criteria, i.e. making a loss.

172 C

The recoverable amount of an asset is the higher of (a) fair value less costs to sell ($18,000) and (b) value in use ($22,000).

173 Standard cost or the retail method of inventory costing may be used for convenience if the results approximate to cost. LIFO cannot be used.

PAPER F1 : FINANCIAL OPERATIONS

174 The answer is $55,800.

	Cost	Recoverable amount (Net Realisable Value)	Lower of cost and recoverable amount
Item 1	$24,000	See note 1	$24,000
Item 2	$33,600	$31,800 (note 2)	$31,800
			$55,800

Notes:

(1) The recoverable amount is not known, but it must be above cost because the contract is expected to produce a high profit margin. The subsequent fall in the cost price to $20,000 is irrelevant for the inventory valuation.

(2) The recoverable amount is $36,000 minus 50% of $8,400.

175 C

IAS 2 states that:

(a) selling costs cannot be included in inventory cost, therefore item (i) cannot be included

(b) general overheads cannot be included (item (iii))

(c) overhead costs should be added to inventory cost on the basis of normal capacity of the production facilities, therefore item (vi) cannot be included in cost

(d) the cost of **factory** management and administration can be included, so that item (iv) can be included in inventory values.

176 The answer is $375,000.

Number of shares before rights issue	2,000,000
Number of shares issued in rights issue $\frac{1}{5}$ × 2,000,000	400,000
	$
Premium on new shares issued 400,000 × $(2 – 1)	400,000
Less: Issue costs	25,000
Net credit to share premium account	375,000

ANSWERS TO SECTION A-TYPE QUESTIONS : SECTION 4

177 C

	Issued share capital $	Share premium $	Retained profits $
Opening	500,000	nil	500,000
Bonus issue			
(2,000,000/2 × 25c)	250,000		(250,000)
	750,000		
Rights issue			
(3,000,000/3 × 25c)	250,000		
(3,000,000/3 × 15c)		150,000	
	1,000,000	150,000	250,000

When a company makes a bonus issue of shares, the nominal value of the new shares issued can be deducted from the share premium reserve. However, in May when the bonus issue was made, the share premium was zero; therefore the nominal value of the new shares issued must be deducted from retained earnings. A share premium is created in September when the rights issue occurs, but it cannot be used for the bonus issue.

178 The answer is $9,725,000.

The share premium can be reduced, but in this example the maximum reduction permitted is the amount of the share premium created when the shares were issued. This is 100,000 shares × $1.25 = $125,000.

The effect of the share purchase transaction is therefore as follows:

Credit	Bank (100,000 shares × $4)	$400,000
Credit	Capital reserve (100,000 shares × $1)	$100,000
Debit	Share capital (100,000 shares × $1)	$100,000
Debit	Share premium	$125,000
Debit	Retained earnings (balance)	$275,000

The retained earnings reserve falls from $10,000,000 by $275,000 to $9,725,000.

179 B

PAPER F1 : FINANCIAL OPERATIONS

180 The answer is $11,212 for YE 31/08/X9 and $11,397 for YE 31/08/Y0.

	$
The total finance cost is:	
Issue costs	5,000
Annual dividend (200,000 × 4%) × 5	40,000
Redemption cost	13,000
	58,000

	Balance b/fwd $	Finance cost 5.75% $	Paid $	Balance c/fwd $
31/08/X9	*195,000	11,212	(8,000)	198,212
31/08/Y0	198,212	11,397	(8,000)	201,609
31/08/Y1	201,609	11,592	(8,000)	205,201
31/08/Y2	205,201	11,799	(8,000)	209,000
31/08/Y3	209,000	**12,000	***(221,000)	0

Note: The opening balance represents the net proceeds, i.e. $200,000 less $5,000 issue costs.

**Note:* The final year interest cost includes a rounding difference of 17.

***Note:* In the final year we repay the nominal loan of $200,000 plus $13,000 premium plus the annual dividend of $8,000.

181 B

IAS 32 *Financial Instruments: Disclosure and Presentation* states that treasury shares should be shown as a deduction from equity, either on the face of statement of financial position or in the notes.

182 C

183 B

Under IAS 24 a party is related to an entity if the party is controlled or significantly influenced by an individual who is a member of the key management personnel of the entity. Customers, suppliers and providers of finance are not normally related parties.

ANSWERS TO SECTION A-TYPE QUESTIONS : SECTION 4

184 B

IAS 24 states that the following are not necessarily related parties:

- providers of finance (such as a bank) simply by virtue of their normal business dealings with the entity
- a customer or supplier or general agent with whom the entity transacts a considerable volume of business, merely by virtue of the resulting economic dependence.

A shareholder holding 25% of the shares can presumably exercise significant influence, and so is a related party. IAS 24 states that 'significant influence is the power to participate in the financial and operating policy decisions of an entity, but is not control over those policies. Significant influence may be gained by share ownership, statute or agreement.'

185 A

186 A

187 A

188 The answer is $350,000.

	$000
Cost of work certified as complete	1,650
Cost of WIP not included in completed work	550
Estimated cost to complete the contract	2,750
Total expected costs	4,950
Contract value	6,000
Expected profit	1,050

Profit to recognise in the first year = (1,650/4,950) × $1,050,000 = $350,000.

189 B

	$000
Costs incurred to date (1,650 + 550)	2,200
Plus: Recognised profits	350
	2,550
Amounts invoiced	(1,600)
Gross amount due from customers	950
Costs incurred to date (1,650 + 550)	2,200
Less: Cash paid to suppliers	(1,300)
Current liability still due to suppliers	900

PAPER F1 : FINANCIAL OPERATIONS

190 The answer is $63m.

	$m
Revenue	90
Total cost – incurred to date	(77)
– estimated future	(33)
Overall loss	(20)

Total cost = cost incurred 77 + future cost 33 = 110

Stage of completion = cost incurred 77/total cost 110 = 70%

Recognise 70% of revenue of 90 = $63m

191 The answer is $(20)m.

	$m
Cost of sales = 110 × 70%	(77)
Loss	(14)
Provision for future loss	(6)
Total loss	(20)

We must recognise all of the loss, not a percentage, if we are to be prudent.

192

	$000
Total cost	
Cost incurred on attributable work	1,500
Inventory not yet used	250
Expected further costs	400
	2,150
Cost incurred on attributable work	1,500

% complete 1,500/2,150 = 69.76% (round to 70%)

Total contract revenue	3,000
Total cost	2,150
Total profit	**850**

Statement of profit or loss figures for contract	
Revenue (3,000 × 70%)	2,100
Cost of sales	1,500
Profit	600

ANSWERS TO SECTION A-TYPE QUESTIONS : SECTION 4

193

	$m
Total cost incurred to date	16
Estimated further costs to completion	18
	34
Contract value	40
Expected profit	6
Percentage of work completed	45%
Profit recognised in year to 31 October 20X5 (6 × 45%)	2.7
Revenue recognised in year to 31 October 20X5 (40 × 45%)	18

194 D

The fire is an example of a non-adjusting event as it arose after the reporting date and does not provide evidence of a condition that existed at the reporting date.

195 C

The warehouse fire is an adjusting event as it occurred before the reporting date. Settlement of the insurance claim should therefore be included in the financial statements. The other events are non-adjusting as they occurred after the reporting date and do not provide evidence of conditions existing at the reporting date.

196 C

The share issue takes place after the reporting date is not an adjusting event.

197 B

198 D

Dividends declared after the reporting date but before the accounts are signed are not provided for but should be disclosed by way of note.

The dividend is shown as a deduction in the statement of changes in equity for the year in which it is actually paid.

199 C

200 The three conditions set out in IAS 37 *Provisions, Contingent Liabilities and Contingent Assets* for the recognition of a provision are:

There must be a present obligation (legal or constructive) arising from a past event.

It must be probable that an outflow of resources embodying economic benefits will be required to settle the obligation.

There should be a reliable estimate of the amount of the obligation.

PAPER F1 : FINANCIAL OPERATIONS

201 C

The legal action against AP is a contingent liability. As it is probable, AP should make a provision. The legal action taken by AP is a contingent asset. As it is probable, it should be disclosed in a note.

202 C

A provision is only required when (i) there is a present obligation arising as a result of a past event, (ii) it is probable that an outflow of resources embodying economic benefits will be required to settle the obligation, and (iii) a reliable estimate can be made of the amount. Only answer C meets all these criteria. Answer A is incorrect because the obligation does not exist at the reporting date and also cannot be reliably measured at present. Answer B is an example of an adjusting event after the reporting date as it provides evidence of conditions existing at the reporting. Answer D is a contingent liability. However, as it is remote, no provision is necessary.

203 C

The legal action against DH gives rise to a probable liability and a provision is therefore required. The legal action taken by DH gives rise to a probable asset and therefore should be disclosed as a note.

204 The answer is $2,160.

	$
Total lease payments (5 × $12,000)	60,000
Less: Fair value at beginning of lease	51,900
Total finance charge	8,100

Sum of the digits from 1 to 5 = 1 + 2 + 3 + 4 + 5 = 15

The year ended 30 September 20X5 is the second year of the lease, therefore:

Finance charge in year 2 = 4/15 × $8,100 = $2,160

205 B

	Balance	Interest at 7.00%	Instalment	Balance
	$	$	$	$
31/10/X3	45,000	3,150	10,975	37,175
31/10/X4	37,175	2,602	10,975	28,802

ANSWERS TO SECTION A-TYPE QUESTIONS : SECTION 4

206 B

	Balance $	Interest $	Instalment $	Balance $
Year 1	106,000	10,857	(24,000)	92,857
Year 2	92,857	9,048	(24,000)	77,905

	$
Total lease payments (6 × $24,000)	144,000
Less: Fair value at beginning of lease	144,000
Total finance charge	38,000

Sum of the digits from 1 to 6 = 1 + 2 + 3 + 4 + 5 + 6 = 21

Finance charge in year 1 = 6/21 × $38,000 = $10,857

Finance charge in year 2 = 5/21 × $38,000 = $9,048

207 Non-current liability = $35,697

Current liability (51,605 − 35,697) = $15,908

Interest rate 7.93%

	Bal b/fwd	Interest	Payment	Balance c/fwd
20X4	80,000	6,344	(20,000)	66,344
20X5	66,344	5,261	(20,000)	51,605
20X6	51,605	4,092	(20,000)	35,697

208 The answer is $47,000.

Depreciation $\frac{(2,600+2,350) \times 80,000}{12,000} = \$33,000$

Cost $80,000 − $33,000 = $47,000

209 The answer is $9,600 for both years

The total payments = $12,000 × 4 = $48,000

Operating leases divide the total payments by the number of years the lease is for, i.e. $48,000/5 = $9,600 pa

The charge to the Statement of profit or loss is the same each year regardless of the payments made through the bank. Depreciation is not charged on an operating lease.

PAPER F1 : FINANCIAL OPERATIONS

210 The answer is $3,700,000.

The division is presumably a cash-generating unit that will be classified as a discontinued operation within the meaning of IFRS 5. A discontinued operation is one that has been disposed of or is classified as 'held for sale'.

IFRS 5 requires that assets (or a group of assets) classified as held for sale should be measured at the lower of carrying amount and fair value less costs to sell. This means that any future profits on disposal cannot be recognised (since carrying amount is lower).

IFRS 5 also requires that on the face of the statement of profit or loss there should be a total figure for:

(a) the post-tax profit or loss of the discontinued operation, and

(b) the post-tax gain or loss recognised on the measurement to fair value less costs to sell of the assets constituting the discontinued operation.

This total figure should also be analysed into its component elements (either in a note to the accounts or on the face of the statement of profit or loss).

The total figure to be shown for the year is therefore:

	$
Profit from discontinued operation	300,000
Item (i): Provision for closure costs	(3,000,000)
Item (iii): Impairment of plant	(1,000,000)
Amount to disclose for the discontinued operation	(3,700,000)

Notes:

(1) The closure costs should not include any apportionment of head office costs.

(2) It is assumed that the loss on the sale of the plant in January gives evidence of an impairment in value, which is therefore included as an adjusting event after the reporting date.

(3) We could also argue the gain of $2,000,000 could also be included as it is certain to happen, however, has been excluded from the answer under prudence. We do not normally recognise income until it is virtually certain.

211 A

212 B

Expenses are analysed into cost of sales, distribution costs and administrative expenses.

213 The following items are mentioned in IAS 1 as the sub-classifications of receivables:

(a) amounts receivable from trade customers

(b) amounts receivable from related parties

(c) prepayments

(d) other items.

ANSWERS TO SECTION A-TYPE QUESTIONS : SECTION 4

214 C

Both items must be shown on the face of the statement of profit or loss. Other items to include in the statement of profit or loss include revenue, the tax expense and the profit or loss for the period (IAS 1).

215 A

IAS 1 states that the financial statements must be prepared on a going concern basis, unless management intends to liquidate the entity or to cease trading, or has no realistic alternative but to do so. When the financial statements are not prepared on a going concern basis, this fact must be disclosed. It is not therefore a requirement of IAS 1 that a note should state that the accounts are prepared on a going concern basis. (However, there might be a similar requirement, for example in a corporate governance code, that the directors should state in the annual report and accounts that the entity is a going concern.)

216 D

Revenue and finance costs must be shown on the face of the statement of profit or loss.

217 A

A revaluation of a non-current asset is not reported through the statement of profit or loss, but as an adjustment to the equity reserves (revaluation reserve account). The revaluation will therefore affect the statement of financial position and the statement of changes in equity, but not the statement of profit or loss. A revaluation is not a cash flow transaction, and so would not appear in the statement of cash flows.

218 IAS 18 states that revenue from the sale of goods should be recognised when the following five conditions have been met:
- The significant risks and rewards of ownership have been transferred to the buyer.
- The seller does not retain any continuing influence or control over the goods.
- Revenue can be measured reliably.
- It is reasonably certain that the buyer will pay for the goods.
- The seller's costs can be measured reliably.

Note: Only FOUR of the above were required.

219 D

DT should not record any revenue as it has not yet transferred the risks and rewards of ownership of the goods to XX. However, as it has received a deposit, it should create a trade payable for $90,000.

220 C

221 B

Only three months of the contract has been delivered between July and September, therefore, we can only recognise three months of the sales as revenue. The revenue would be $2,000 per month × 3 = $6,000. This means that the remainder of the $12,000 received in advance must treated as deferred income as a current liability.

222 C

GROUP COMPANY FINANCIAL ACCOUNTS

223 A

	$
Cost of investment	1,400,000
Reserves at acquisition –	
(600,000 × 0.50) + $50,000	350,000
	1,050,000
Impairment 60%	(630,000)
Goodwill at 31 December 20X8	420,000

224 C

	$
Cost of investment	100,000
Reserves at acquisition –	
$30,000 + $50,000	80,000
	20,000
Impairment 60%	(12,000)
Goodwill at 31 December 20X9	8,000

	$
Reserves of Tom	400,000
Post acquisition reserves of Jerry –	
($50,000 + $50,000) – ($50,000 + $30,000)	20,000
Impairment (above working)	(12,000)
Goodwill at 31 December 20X9	408,000

225 D

	$
Cost of investment	750,000
Reserves at acquisition –	
$20,000 + $10,000	30,000
	720,000
Impairment 20%	(144,000)
Goodwill at 31 December 20X9	576,000

226 A

	$
Cost of investment	35,000
Reserves at acquisition –	
$20,000 + $10,000	30,000
	5,000
Impairment 20%	(1,000)
Goodwill at 31 December 20X9	4,000

	$
Reserves of Gary	40,000
Post acquisition reserves of Barlow –	
($20,000 + $15,000) – ($20,000 + $10,000)	5,000
Impairment (above working)	(1,000)
Goodwill at 31 December 20X9	44,000

227 A

	$
Cost of investment	300,000
Reserves at acquisition –	
$200,000 + $60,000	260,000
	40,000
Impairment 20%	(8,000)
Goodwill at 31 December 20X9	32,000

228 The answer is $32,000

Net assets of SB

	Date of acquisition $000
$1 equity shares	150
Share premium	15
Retained earnings	(22)
Fair value adjustment – property (115 – 100)	15
Fair value adjustment –plant and equipment (70 – 75)	(5)
	153

Goodwill

	$000
Cost of investment	185
Net assets of SB at acquisition (as above)	153
Goodwill	32

229 The answer is $25,900

Investment in associate

	$
Cost of investment	25,000
Profits after dividends (6,500 – 3,500) × 30%	900
Investment in associate	25,900

230 The answer is $3,300

Total PUP = $33,000/125 × 25 = $6,600 × 50% still in inventory = $3,300

231 A

Non-current assets = $1,800,000 + $2,200,000 + fair value adj 400,000 – depn 80,000 = $4,320,000

Workings:

Depreciation = $400,000/10 × 2 = $80,000

It has been 2 years since the fair value adjustment was made

232 D

Reserves as acquisition = 1,600 + 300 + 400 = 2,300

Reserves at reporting date = 1,600 + 500 + 400 – 80 = 2,420

233 B

	$	
Sales value	168	150%
Cost value	112	100%
Profit	56	50%

Workings:

Mark up means profit is based on cost, therefore cost represents 100%. If profit is 50%, the sales value must be worth 150%. $36,000 of goods are still in stock. This represents 150%.

The profit element = $36,000/150 × 50 = $12,000

234 A

	$m	
Sales value	24	100%
Cost value	18	75%
Profit	6	25%

Workings:

Profit is $6m and represents 25% of the selling price.

$4m of goods are still in stock (24–20). The profit element = $4m × 25% = $1m

235 A

The depreciation adjustment = fair value adjustment of $6.4m/4 × 1 year = $1.6m

236 D

Revenue = 120 + 48 – 24 (inter-company) = $144m

Cost of sales = 84 + 40 – 24 + 1 (PUP) + 1.6 (depn) = $102.6m

237 C

		$000
Revenue (above Qu 194)		144,000
Cost of sales (above Qu 194)		(102,600)
Gross profit		41,400
Distribution cost	5000 + 100	(5,100)
Administration expense	7,000 + 300 + 600	(7,900)
Profit from operations		28,400

238 A

Non-current assets = 1,918,000 + 1,960,000 = 3,878,000

Note: We do not include the associates assets and liabilities in the consolidated statement of financial position.

239 C

Cost of investment	448,000
Post acquisition reserves – ($896,000 – $280,000) × 30%	184,800
Impairment	(5,600)
Investment in associate	627,200

240 B

Cost of investment	1,610,000
Reserves at acquisition – $1,680,000 – $112,000	1,568,000
	42,000

Note: The subsidiary has losses at the date of acquisition, hence are deducted from the ordinary share capital.

241 B

		$
Non-current assets		
Property, plant and equipment	1,918 + 1,960	3,878,000
Goodwill	(above Qu 198)	42,000
Investment in associate	(above Qu 197)	627,200
		4,547,200
Current assets		
Inventory	760 + 1,280	2,040,000
Receivables	380 + 620	1,000,000
Cash	70 + 116	186,000
		7,773,200

242 A

Reserves of Really	2,464,000
Post acquisition reserves –	
($1,204,000 + $112,000)	1,316,000
($896,000 – $280,000) × 30%	184,800
Impairment	(5,600)
	3,959,200

Section 5

ANSWERS TO SECTION B-TYPE QUESTIONS

PRINCIPLES OF BUSINESS TAXATION

243 ADJUSTED PROFITS (1) (MAY 07 EXAM)

DB – Corporate income tax

			20X6 $
Profit before tax per accounts			33,950
Add back:			
Entertaining			600
Local government tax			950
Depreciation on buildings			1,600
Depreciation on plant and equipment			20,000
			57,100
Less tax depreciation			
Building (70,000 × 4%)			2,800
Plant and equipment (W1)			25,768
Taxable profit			28,532

			Tax $
Taxable at 15%	(25,000 – 10,000) =	15,000	2,250
Taxable at 25%	(28,532 – 25,000) =	3,532	883
Corporate income tax 20X6			3,133

(W1)

	Plant and equipment $	New plant $	Total $
Cost	80,000		
20X5 tax depreciation @ 27%	21,600		
	58,400		
20X6 tax depreciation @ 27%	15,768		15,768
Cost		20,000	
20X6 first year allowance @ 50%		10,000	10,000
	42,632	10,000	25,768

244 ADJUSTED PROFITS (2) (MAY 08 EXAM)

FB – Corporate income tax

	$	$	$
Profit for the year			29,800
Add back:			
Depreciation building		3,200	
Depreciation plant and equipment		6,000	
Depreciation furniture and fittings		5,000	
			14,200
Less: gain on disposal			(4,000)
			40,000
Less: tax writing down allowances			
FYA – plant and equipment		(15,000)	
Disposal balancing allowance	(11,812)		
Cash received	5,000	(6,812)	
Buildings (80,000 × 5%)		(4,000)	(25,812)
Taxable profit			14,188
Tax at 20%			2,838

245 TAX CHARGE (1) (MAY 10 EXAM)

(a) **JW – Corporate income tax**

	20X8 $
Profit before tax per accounts	150,000
Add back:	
Entertaining	2,200
Depreciation on vehicle ($12,000/6)	2,000
Depreciation on plant and equipment	27,000
	181,200
Less tax depreciation	
Plant and equipment	(40,000)
Vehicle ($12,000 × 40%)	(4,800)
Taxable profit	136,400
Tax at 25%	34,100

(b) **JW – Income tax expense**

	$
*Deferred tax increase (29,000 – 44,800 × 25%)	3,950
Current tax charge (part a)	34,100
Income tax expense	38,050

Tutorial note

The deferred tax movement is calculated by comparing the accounting depreciation of $29,000 ($27,000 + $2,000) and the tax depreciation ($40,000 + $4,800). The tax depreciation is greater than the accounting depreciation, hence income is deferred for tax purposes and the provision must increase.

246 TAX CHARGE (2) (NOV 11 EXAM)

(i) **KM – Corporate income tax**

	$
Profit before tax	165,000
Add back:	
Entertaining	9,800
PP&E and Vehicle depreciation (note 1)	45,000
	219,800
Less tax allowances – PPE and Vehicle (note 1)	(74,000)
Taxable amount	145,800
Tax at 25%	36,450

(ii) **KM – Income tax expense**

	$
Estimated tax for year to 31 March 2011	36,450
Deferred tax increase (note 1)	7,250
	43,700

Note 1:

Vehicle – Cost $18,000

Depreciation 18000/6 = $3,000

Tax allowance – first year 50% = $9,000

Depreciation	– PPE	42,000	
	– Vehicle	3,000	45,000
Tax allowances	– PPE	65,000	
	– Vehicle	9,000	74,000

Deferred tax increase in year   29,000 × 25% = $7,250

Tutorial note

The tax allowance for the year is greater than the accounting depreciation; therefore we are deferring income and increasing the deferred tax provision by $7,250.

247 HG (FEB 13)

	$
Profit before tax	167,000
Add back:	
Disallowable expenses (4,000 + 5,000)	9,000
Accounting depreciation (W1)	11,600
Less: non-taxable income	(12,000)
Less tax depreciation (W1)	(10,250)
Taxable amount	165,350
Less: losses b/fwd	(49,000)
	116,350
Tax at 25%	29,088

(W1)

Accounting depreciation = 50,000 + 8,000 = 58,000 × 1/5 = 11,600

Tax depreciation:	Plant and equipment	New plant	Total
	$	$	$
Cost	50,000		
20X1 tax depreciation @ 50%	25,000		
	25,000		
20X2 tax depreciation @ 25%	6,250		6,250
Cost		8,000	
20X2 first year allowance @ 50%		4,000	4,000
	18,750	4,000	10,250

248 MT (MAY 13 EXAM)

	$
Profit before tax	37,000
Add back:	
Donations	5,000
PPE depreciation	39,000
	81,000
Less tax depreciation – PPE	(45,000)
Taxable amount	36,000
Loss B/fwd	(12,000)
	24,000
Tax at 25%	6,000

*Note: Tax depreciation = (120,000 × 25%) + (30,000 × 50%) = $45,000

249 DG (NOV 06 EXAM)

	Accounts $	Tax $
Purchase 1.10.X2	200,000	200,000
UEL	5	
30.9.X3 – depreciation	(40,000)	(60,000)
	160,000	140,000
30.9.X4 – depreciation	(40,000)	(42,000)
	120,000	98,000
30.9.X5 – depreciation	(40,000)	(29,400)
	80,000	68,600

(i) Deferred tax balance 30.9.X5

	$
Carrying value	80,000
Tax base	(68,600)
Difference	11,400
@ 20%	2,280

(ii) Accounts profit or loss on disposal

	$
Carrying value	80,000
Proceeds	(60,000)
Loss	20,000

(iii) Balancing allowance

	$
Tax written down value	68,600
Proceeds	(60,000)
Balancing allowance	8,600

ANSWERS TO SECTION B-TYPE QUESTIONS : **SECTION 5**

250 GJ (NOV 08 EXAM)

Year		Tax Base		Accounting Base	Diff	X 25%
30/9/X6	Cost	220,000	Cost	220,000		
	FYA 50%	110,000	Depreciation *	42,000		
	TWDV	110,000	CV	178,000		
30/9/X7	WDA25%	27,500	Depreciation	42,000		
	TWDV	82,500	CV	136,000		
			Revaluation	53,000		
				189,000		
30/9/X8	WDA25%	20,625	Depreciation *	63,000		
	TWDV	61,875	CV	126,000	64,125	16,031

*Note: The depreciation has been calculated in the first year based on ($220,000 – $10,000)/5 years. In year 3 the depreciation has been calculated as $189,000/remaining life of 3 years assuming no residual value. The question does not make it clear that this is the case and it would've been reasonable to calculate depreciation using the residual value of $10,000.

251 DEFERRED TAX (SEP 11 EXAM)

(i) A temporary difference arises when an expense is allowed for both accounting and tax purposes, but there is a difference in the timing of the allowance.

A temporary difference is the difference between the carrying amount of an asset in the statement of financial position and its tax base. The temporary difference times the tax rate is the amount of deferred tax required to be recognised by IAS 12 *Income Taxes*.

(ii) A deferred tax debit balance can arise from the following:
- deductible temporary difference,
- unused tax losses,
- unused tax credits.

A deductible temporary difference is a temporary difference that will result in a deduction from future taxable profits when sold or realised.

Some tax authorities may permit the tax effect of losses to be carried forward and offset against future taxable profits. IAS 12 requires that these unused tax losses be recognised as assets, where it is probable that the entity will make future profits against which these losses can be offset.

Deferred tax debit balances should be recognised in the financial statements provided that it is probable that future taxable profits will be available for the asset to be utilised, that is future tax payable can be reduced.

PAPER F1 : FINANCIAL OPERATIONS

252 FG (MAY 11 EXAM)

(i) **FG – Corporate income tax**

	$
Accounting profit	192,000
Adjustments:	
Add back: accounting depreciation	100,000
Deduct: tax depreciation	(62,500)
Taxable profits	229,500
Tax at 25%	57,375

(ii) The answer is to credit the statement of profit or loss with $9,375

	Accounting carrying value	Tax base	Difference	X 25%
	$	$	$	
Cost 1 April 20X7	500,000	500,000		
Depreciation	(100,000)	(250,000)		
31 March 20X8	400,000	250,000	150,000	37,500
Depreciation	(100,000)	(62,500)		
31 March 20X9	300,000	187,500	112,500	28,125

The cumulative provision at 31 March 20X9 is $28,125. This would be shown as a non-current liability on the SOFP.

The amount shown on the IS will be the movement in the provision, i.e. $37,500 – $28,125 = $9,375. The provision is reducing, hence will credit the statement of profit or loss and reduce this year's tax expense.

253 TY (MAR 12 EXAM)

Deferred tax balance at 31 December 20X1:

	Carrying value $000	Tax base $000
Cost 1 January 20X0	440	440
Year to 31 December 20X0	(55)	(220)
	385	220
Revaluation 1 Jan 20X1	70	0
	455	220
Year to 31 December 20X1	(65)	(55)
	390	165

At 31 December 20X0: $385,000 – $220,000 = $165,000

At 31 December 20X1: $390,000 – $165,000 = $225,000

Change (Increase) = $60,000

Tax at 25% = $15,000

Deferred tax movement in year to 31 December 20X1:

Debit (charge) to statement of profit or loss of $15,000

Deferred tax balance at 31 December 20X1:

Credit balance (NLC) $225,000 × 25% = $56,250

254 TX (MAY 12 EXAM)

(i) Deferred tax is the estimated future tax consequences of transactions and events that have been recognised in the financial statements of the current and previous periods. Deferred tax arises due to the temporary differences between the accounting profit and the taxable profit. The temporary differences cause the carrying value of some items in the statement of financial position to be different from their tax base (the amount recognised for tax calculation).

(ii) TX's statement of profit or loss and other comprehensive income shows an increase in deferred tax, this suggests that temporary differences increased by $800,000 in the year to 31/3/20X2. The main reason was probably an increase in non-current assets causing the tax depreciation to be $800,000 more than the accounting depreciation for the year to 31/3/20X2, thus causing the increase of $200,000 in deferred tax provision (25% × $800,000).

(iii) Current tax is the estimated amount of corporate income tax payable on the taxable profits of the entity for the period. The amount of current tax is accrued in the financial statements and carried forward as a current liability to the next accounting period when it will be paid. When the tax is paid there will usually be a difference between the amount paid and the amount accrued. If the amount paid is less than the amount accrued there will be an over provision of income tax. The amount over provided will be an adjustment to the income tax expense in the following period. In TX the current tax estimate for year to 31 March 20X1 was $650,000, the statement of cash flows shows that $600,000 was paid in the following period leaving a balance of $50,000 over provided.

255 KQ (NOV 12 EXAM)

	$
Accounting profit	147,000
Adjustments:	
Add back: disallowed expenses (9 + 6)	15,000
Add back: accounting depreciation	34,500
Deduct: tax depreciation	(47,500)
Taxable profits	149,000
Tax at 25%	37,250

Accounting depreciation:

Cost (180,000 + 50,000) × 15% = 34,500

Tax depreciation:	$
First year allowance 50,000 × 50% =	25,000
Annual allowance (180,000 – 90,000 FYA 50% for 30/9/X1) × 25% =	22,500
Total tax depreciation =	47,500

256 GH (MAY 13 EXAM)

(i) The tax base of an asset is the tax written down value of the asset. i.e. its cost less accumulated tax depreciation.

Deferred tax arises as a result of temporary differences caused by a difference between an asset's tax base and its accounting carrying value.

(ii) The answer is $21,125

	Accounts $	Tax $
Purchase 1.4.X1	260,000	260,000
UEL	6	
Residual value 10%	26,000	
31.03.X2 – depreciation	(39,000)	(130,000)
	221,000	130,000
31.03.X3 – depreciation	(39,000)	(32,500)
	182,000	97,500

Note: The depreciation has been calculated in the first year based on ($260,000 – $26,000)/6 years.

Deferred tax balance 31.03.X3

	$
Carrying value	182,000
Tax base	(97,500)
Difference	84,500
@ 25%	21,125

257 PU (AUG 13 EXAM)

(i) Temporary differences are differences between the carrying amount of an asset or liability in the statement of financial position and the balance calculated according to the tax regulations, its tax base. This is caused by the timing difference in treatment between the accounting rules and the tax rules.

An asset is charged against the statement of profit or loss by way of a depreciation policy which is adjusted at the end of its useful life by a gain or loss on its sale. This depreciation policy may not agree with the tax rules and although over the life of the asset the total allowance will be the same there may be differences in timing. The difference will be greater where a country has a high level of first year allowances that reduce the tax bill in the first year of an asset's life.

(ii) The answer is $37,188

	$ Accounting	$ Tax base
Cost 1 April 20X1	350,000	350,000
Depreciation	(35,000)	(175,000)
Balance 31 March 20X2	315,000	175,000
Depreciation	(35,000)	(43,750)
Balance 31 March 20X3	280,000	131,250

*Note:** The depreciation has been calculated in the first year based on $350,000/ 10 years.

Deferred tax balance 31.03.X3

	$
Carrying value	280,000
Tax base	(131,250)
Difference	148,750
@ 25%	37,188

258 SALES TAX (1) (NOV 07 EXAM)

	(i) Profit $	(ii) Sales tax $
Sale price	40,250	
Less: Sales tax @ 15%	(5,250)	(5,250)
	35,000	
Cost of goods	(10,000)	
Excise duty @ 20%	(2,000)	
Sales tax on purchase @ 15%		(1,800)
Repackaging	(6,900)	
Sales tax @ 15%	900	(900)
	17,000	2,550

259 EXCISE DUTIES (1) (MAY 09 EXAM)

The government might apply a specific excise duty to a category of goods because:

- It may want to raise extra revenue from luxury products that are inelastic and people will buy regardless of cost
- To discourage use of harmful substances by making them expensive to buy, i.e. Tobacco and alcohol
- To pay for the healthcare that harmful substances cause, i.e. Medical treatment from smokers.

A single stage tax is a tax at one level of production, e.g. Manufacturer

A multi stage tax is a tax at each level of production, e.g. Manufacturer, wholesaler, retailer, consumer. This could be cascade tax (tax not refundable from inputs) or VAT (tax refunded from inputs).

260 SALES TAX (2) (MAY 10 EXAM)

(a) A unit tax is a tax charged on each unit sold, i.e. an amount per sale. This could be measured on weight or size. This can be seen in the scenario when W pays $1 per bottle sold.

An ad valorem tax is a tax charged on the value of the unit sold, i.e. selling price. The more the goods are sold for, the greater the tax charge. This can be seen in the scenario when W sells the goods for $8.05 including VAT at 15%. This would give a net price of $7 per bottle and VAT of $1.05 per bottle ($8.05/115 × 15).

(b) The total indirect tax is $16,000.

VAT 10,000 units × $1.05 =	10,500
Unit tax 10,000 units × $1 =	10,000
VAT on purchases $30,000 × 15% =	(4,500)
	16,000

ANSWERS TO SECTION B-TYPE QUESTIONS : SECTION 5

261 SALES TAX (3) (SEP 11 EXAM)

(i) Single stage sales tax is payable on sales at a specific part of the trade cycle, e.g. retail sales. There will be no credit given to an entity for sales tax paid on purchases.

VAT is a multi-stage tax, taxing sales at every stage of the transaction cycle. However most VAT paid by an entity is reimbursed by the tax authorities, usually by deducting from VAT collected.

(ii) Tax reimbursable by tax authorities is $3,000

Output tax product Z = $207,000 × 15/115 =	$27,000
Input tax on purchases = $200,000 × 15% =	$30,000
Tax reimbursable by tax authorities	$3,000

262 SALES TAX (4) (NOV 11 EXAM)

Perfume consignment income, expenditure and VAT are as follows:

	Totals (incl VAT) $	VAT $	Net of VAT $
Expenditure:			
Cost	50,000		
Excise duty 20%	10,000		
	60,000		
Input VAT @ 15%	9,000		
	69,000	9,000	60,000
Repackaging costs (note 2)	9,775	1,275	8,500
Total costs	78,775	10,275	68,500
Sales revenue (note 1)	105,800	13,800	92,000
Net	27,025	3,525	23,500

Note 1: VAT = $105,800/115 × 15 = $13,800

Note 2: VAT = $9,775/115 × 15 = $1,275

(i) Net profit is $23,500

(ii) Net Vat due to be paid is $3,525

Deferred tax increase in year = 29,000 × 25% = $7,250

Tutorial note

Net profit is always based on net sales less net expenses. You must extract the VAT element from the gross amounts before calculating profit.

263 SALES TAX (5) (MAR 12 EXAM)

(i) An item that is Zero rated means that no VAT is charged on sales but UYT can reclaim VAT paid on its inputs.

An item exempted from VAT means that the revenue earned is exempt VAT, so no VAT is charged but UYT cannot reclaim the portion of input VAT that relates to the exempted goods. If an actual figure cannot be calculated it will be on a proportional basis.

	Excl VAT $	VAT 15% $
Inputs:		
Cost	400,000	60,000
Input VAT claim limited to 450/600		45,000
Outputs:		
Standard rate	450,000	67,500
Exempt	150,000	0
	600,000	67,500
Net (67,500 – 45,000)		22,500

(ii) Net VAT due to be paid is $22,500

> *Tutorial note*
>
> *The input VAT to reclaim is restricted to $45,000, i.e. the ratio of standard rated sales to total sales made. Remember we cannot reclaim input VAT from exempt sales, hence the pro-rata calculation.*

264 SALES TAX (6) (NOV 12 EXAM)

(i) Once registered for VAT the regulations will normally require an entity to:
- Issue VAT invoices.
- Keep appropriate VAT records.
- Charge VAT on taxable supplies to customers.
- Complete a quarterly VAT return.
- Make payments to VAT authority and be able to claim back VAT when due.

(ii) Exempt outputs as percentage of total outputs: 205,000/1,025,000 x 100 = 20%

Therefore, we can claim back 80% of the VAT charged on inputs.

Total VAT on inputs = $690,000/115 × 15 = $90,000 × 80% to claim back = $72,000

	Net of VAT	VAT	Totals (incl VAT)
Outputs:	$	$	$
Standard rate	720,000	108,000	828,000
Zero rate	100,000	0	100,000
Exempt	205,000	0	205,000
Inputs:	(618,000)	(72,000)	(690,000)
Net	407,000	36,000	443,000

The VAT due to the authority = $36,000

265 EXCISE DUTIES (2) (FEB 13)

An excise duty may be imposed on certain types of goods by a government:

- to discourage over-consumption of products which may harm the consumer or others for example alcohol
- to alter the distribution of income by taxing 'luxuries', for example, in the USA there are excise duties on fishing equipment, firearms and airplane tickets
- to seek to allow for externalities and to place the burden of paying the tax on the consumer of the product/service. For example the social and environmental cost of consuming the product is paid for by the consumer of products such as tobacco to help pay for the increased cost of healthcare of smokers.
- to improve infrastructure and other facilities. For example excise duty on petrol and diesel is used by some governments to build and maintain roads, bridges and mass transit systems.
- to protect or promote growth of home industries by increasing the price of imports with taxes, for example car manufacturing.
- to raise revenue for government by taxing goods with inelastic demand, thus enabling revenue to be raised without distorting consumption, for example luxury goods.

266 SALES TAX (7) (MAY 13 EXAM)

(i) Cascade tax – tax is taken at each stage of production and is treated as a business cost. No refunds are provided by local government.

VAT – charged each time a component or product is sold but government allows businesses to claim back all the tax they have paid. The entire tax burden is passed to the final consumer.

(ii) Profit for period $250,000 and VAT due for period $48,000

	Net of VAT $	VAT $	Totals (incl VAT) $
Sales revenue :			
Standard rate (W1)	720,000	108,000	828,000
Zero rate	150,000	0	150,000
Purchases:			
Standard rate	(400,000)	(60,000)	(460,000)
Zero rate	(220,000)	0	(220,000)
Net	250,000	48,000	298,000

(W1) VAT = $828,000/115 × 15 = $108,000

267 SALES TAX (8) (AUG 13 EXAM)

(i) The answer is profit will be $74,100

(ii) The answer is VAT due to be paid will be $11,115

	$ Net of VAT	$ VAT	$ Totals (incl VAT)
Sales revenue :	190,000	28,500	218,500
Cost of goods:	90,000		
Excise duty @ 10%	9,000		
	(99,000)	(14,850)	(113,850)
Repackaging cost	(16,900)	(2,535)	(19,435)
	74,100	11,115	85,215

ANSWERS TO SECTION B-TYPE QUESTIONS : SECTION 5

268 INDIRECT TAX (MAY 12 EXAM)

(i) Excise Duty is a selective commodity tax, levied on certain types of goods. It is a unit tax based on the weight or size of the tax base. E.g. Petroleum products, tobacco products alcoholic drinks and motor vehicles.

Single stage sales tax is a more general consumption tax. It is applied at one level of the production/distribution chain only. It can be applied to any level but when it is used in practice it is most often applied at the retail sales level. Single stage sales taxes are levied as a percentage of value, e.g. retail sales value.

(ii) From the revenue authority's point of view, the characteristics of commodities that make them most suitable for excise duty to be applied are:

- Few large producers
- Inelastic demand with no close substitutes
- Large sales volumes
- Easy to define products covered by the duty

269 CAPITAL GAINS (MAY 11 EXAM)

(i) A capital gain is a gain made when an asset not covered by income tax rules, is disposed of. E.g. gains on disposal of investments or non-current assets.

The gain is calculated by taking the selling price and deducting any tax allowable expenses. These can vary from country but usually include original costs, buying and selling costs and costs for enhancements to the asset. Some tax authorities allow a reduction for inflation, often referred to as indexation allowance.

Capital gains tax is charged on the profits on the disposal of the asset, i.e. the capital gain.

(ii) **JK – Capital gains tax**

		$
Disposal proceeds		1,000,000
Less: Costs of disposal		(6,000)
		994,000
Acquisition costs:		
Purchase cost	850,000	
Costs arising on purchase ($5,000 + $8,000)	13,000	
Clearing land costs	15,000	
		(878,000)
Taxable gain		116,000
Tax @ 25%		29,000

270 AVOIDANCE v EVASION (MAY 10 EXAM)

Tax evasion is an illegal way of reducing your tax bill, for example, not telling the truth about your income or expenditure. This can be seen in the scenario when Gee does not declare his income from his night security job.

Tax avoidance is a legal way of reducing your tax bill, i.e. using tax loopholes. This can be seen in scenario when Cee invests in the tax-free securities to avoid paying tax on her interest. This is within the law but it is often not in the spirit of the law, hence the government will often try to close loopholes as soon as it is identified.

271 TAX BASE (NOV 11 EXAM)

A tax base is something that is liable to tax, e.g. income or consumption of goods.

Tax bases regularly used by governments are:

- income – for example, income taxes and taxes on an entity's profits
- capital or wealth – for example, taxes on capital gains and taxes on inherited wealth
- consumption – for example, excise duties and sales taxes/VAT.

272 IMPUTATION SYSTEM (MAR 12 EXAM)

YT is incorrect in thinking that his dividend has been taxed twice.

With an imputation system of corporate income tax the entity pays corporate income tax on all the profits before paying a dividend but then all or part of the underlying corporate income tax that relates to the distribution is imputed to the shareholders as a tax credit. Therefore avoiding the problem of double taxation of dividends.

If the personal income tax rate of the shareholder is higher than the rate of tax credit the shareholder may have to pay additional tax on the dividend, however it will still only have been taxed once.

With systems using the full imputation system all of the underlying corporate income tax is passed to the shareholder as a tax credit if a partial imputation system is used only part of the tax paid by the entity will be passed to the shareholder.

YT has received a dividend from LKJ and will have received a tax credit for the proportion of tax paid by LKJ on the underlying profit. As LKJ is an entity resident in Country X it will have paid corporate income tax at 25% on its taxable profit for the year. This will be passed on to its shareholders as a tax credit as Country X uses the full imputation system.

YT will receive a tax credit and will be able to set this tax credit against any tax due on the dividend leaving additional tax to be paid if YT's personal tax rate is higher than 25%.

Under the classical system of corporate income tax the entity's profit for the year is taxed and then when a dividend is paid the shareholder is taxed on the full amount received. In this case the dividends have been taxed twice.

273 LOSSES (NOV 10 EXAM)

The four methods that a Country can choose from when relieving trading losses of an entity are:

(i) Carry forward against future trading profits

The effect on ZK would be:

Year ended 31 August 20X7 taxable profits, chargeable gains of $5,000

Year ended 31 August 20X8 no tax payable ($10,000 – $10,000)

Year ended 31 August 20X9 taxable profits $30,000 ($50,000 – ($30,000 – $10,000))

(ii) Offset against other income and chargeable gains of the same period and carry any balance forward.

The effect on ZK would be:

Year ended 31 August 20X7 no tax payable ($5,000 – $5,000)

Year ended 31 August 20X8 no tax payable ($10,000 – $10,000)

Year ended 31 August 20X9 taxable profits $35,000 ($50,000 – ($30,000 – $10,000 – $5,000))

(iii) Offset against other income and chargeable gains of the previous period

As ZK has traded profitably for a number of years it should be possible to offset at least some of the $30,000 loss against last year's taxable profits this could result in a refund of tax previously paid.

(iv) Group relief

As ZK is part of a group, group relief may be available. ZK would transfer its loss to another group entity so that entity could offset it against taxable profits. As a result the total group tax payable would be reduced for the year.

274 POWERS (NOV 12 EXAM)

Tax authorities may be given various powers to enable them to enforce the tax regulations. These powers may include:

- Power to impose penalties and charge interest on late payments of tax.
- Power to query tax returns filed by entities.
- Power to request special reports from an entity if they believe the entity has given incorrect information.
- Power to enter an entity's premises and to search for and seize documents
- Power to examine documents of previous years
- Power to give information to foreign tax authorities

275 BENEFITS IN KIND (AUG 13 EXAM)

(i) "Benefits in kind" are non-cash benefits given to an employee as part of the remuneration package often in lieu of further cash payments.

A benefit in kind can include any of the following:
- Company cars
- Private medical insurance
- Free loans or loans at very low rates of interest
- Living accommodation

(ii) The answer is $8,840

BZ income tax for the year ended 31 March 20X3

	$
Salary	34,000
Bonus	1,700
Benefits in kind	2,150
	37,850
Personal tax allowance	(5,750)
Taxable amount	32,100
Tax due:	
20,000 × 20%	4,000
12,100 × 40%	4,840
	8,840

276 WITHHOLDING TAX (MAY 06 EXAM)

(a) **Withholding tax**

A withholding tax is a tax deducted at source before a payment is made to the recipient.

Underlying tax

Underlying tax is the tax on the profits out of which a dividend is paid.

(b) The gross amount received by CW is $45,000 × 100/90 = $50,000. The withholding tax is therefore $5,000 ($50,000 × 10%).

(c) After-tax profits of Z are $500,000 – $100,000 = $400,000

Underlying tax is $50,000/$400,000 × $100,000 = $12,500

277 OVERSEAS (1) (MAY 10 EXAM)

Competent jurisdiction is the tax authority that has the legal powers to assess and collect the taxes. In simple terms this is usually the country whose tax laws apply to the entity.

This is decided by looking at an entities country of residence. This is deemed to be either the place of incorporation or place of control/central management. Generally, an entity will be resident in the country of control, i.e. the place where head office is located or board meetings are held.

In the scenario H meet regularly in Country X, hence Country X is their competent jurisdiction and S meet regularly in Country Y, hence Country Y is their competent jurisdiction.

Withholding tax is the tax deducted at source from the income generated in the country of residency. In this scenario, S pays a dividend of $200,000 to H and S must deduct withholding tax of 10% ($20,000). Therefore, H will only receive the net dividend amount of $180,000.

H is resident in country X, hence will be required to pay tax in Country X on the dividend received from S. However, because this dividend has already been taxed in Country Y and both countries have a double tax agreement; H will receive double tax relief in Country X.

278 OVERSEAS (2) (NOV 10 EXAM)

(i) A withholding tax is a tax deducted from a payment at source, before it is made to the recipient abroad.

As a tax authority cannot tax individuals in foreign countries, a withholding tax ensures that the tax authority gains some tax revenues from the payment before it is sent out of the country.

(ii) The answer is $0

Withholding Tax

Receipt $3,375,000 = 90%

Tax deducted at 10% = $3,375,000 × 10/90 = $375,000

Gross amount $3,375,000 × 100/90 = $3,750,000

Underlying Tax

$1,875,000 × 3,750,000/(12,500,000-1,875,000) = $661,765

Total

$375,000 + $661,765 = $1,036,765

Tax due in Country X

$3,375,000 dividend received + total foreign tax $1,036,765 = $4,411,765 × 25% = $1,102,941

Tax to pay in Country X = $1,102,941 − DTR (lower of $1,102,941 and $1,036,765) $1,036,765 = $66,176 to pay

Alternative acceptable answer:

$3,750,000 × 25% = $937,500

Tax to pay in Country X = $937,500 − $1,036,765 = $0

279 UNDERLYING TAX (MAY 11 EXAM)

(i) Underlying tax is tax on the profits out of which an overseas entity has paid a dividend to its holding company, e.g. a subsidiary or associated entity pays a dividend out of taxed profits. The underlying tax is the tax on the profits.

(ii) The answer is $48,750

	$000
Profit before tax	650
Tax	(130)
Profit after tax	520

Gross dividend = 156/0.8 = 195

$$\frac{130,000}{520,000} \times 195,000 = \$48,750$$

280 DOUBLE TAX RELIEF (1) (SEP 11 EXAM)

(i) The worldwide approach is where a country claims the right to tax income earned outside its border if that income is received by an entity deemed resident for tax purposes within the country.

(ii) The problem with the worldwide approach is that it leads to double taxation as income will usually be taxed in the country where it is earned and again in the country where the holding entity is resident.

Double tax relief exists to reduce the total amount of tax payable on tax income earned in other countries. The effect of double tax relief is to reduce the total tax payable to the higher of the two, the home country or overseas tax rate.

Most countries applying the worldwide approach grant some form of relief from double taxation. Double tax relief is given according to double tax agreements that a country has entered into.

281 DOUBLE TAX RELIEF (2) (NOV 12 EXAM)

Withholding tax = $200,000 × 12% = $24,000

Underlying tax = 126,000/(600,000 − 126,000) × 200,000 = $53,165

Total foreign tax = $24,000 + $53,165 = $77,165

The tax credit method means that in the country where the dividend is received the recipient with be given credit for the tax already paid in the foreign country. Relief will usually be restricted to the lower of the foreign tax paid and the amount due in the country of residence.

Tax due in Country X

Tax will be due on the dividend received of $176,000 + total foreign tax $77,165 = $253,165

Country X tax due @ 25% = $63,291

Relief will be given on the lower of the County X tax of $63,291 or foreign tax of $77,165. In this case the relief will be $63,291 resulting in no more tax to pay in Country X.

PRINCIPLES OF REGULATION OF FINANCIAL REPORTING

282 DEVELOPMENT (MAY 06 EXAM)

The options available include:

(1) Adopting International Financial Reporting Standards (IFRS) as its local standards.

The advantage of this approach is that it is quick to implement.

The disadvantage is that it may not take into account any specific local traditions or variations.

(2) Modelling its local accounting standards on the IASB's IFRSs, but amending them to reflect local needs and conditions.

The advantage is that the standards should be more relevant to local needs and compliant with International Standards.

The disadvantage is that it will take longer to implement and requires an adequate level of expertise to exist within the country.

(3) C could develop its own accounting standards with little or no reference to IFRSs.

The advantage is that any standards developed will be specific to C's requirements.

The disadvantage is that, as C does not yet have any accounting standards, it will be a long time before the project is completed as it is a very slow process. Standards may not be compliant with International Standards. This approach requires expertise, which may not be available in C at present.

283 FRAMEWORK (1) (MAY 07 EXAM)

The purposes of the *Framework* are to:

- assist the Board in the development of future IFRSs and in its review of existing IFRSs
- assist the Board in promoting harmonisation of regulations, accounting standards and procedures relating to the presentation of financial statements by providing a basis for reducing the number of alternative treatments permitted by IFRSs
- assist national standard-setting bodies in developing national standards
- assist preparers of financial statements in applying IFRSs and in dealing with topics that have yet to be covered in an IFRS
- assist auditors in forming an opinion as to whether financial statements conform with IFRSs
- assist users of financial statements that are prepared using IFRSs
- provide information about how the IASB has formulated its approach to the development of IFRSs.

284 FRAMEWORK (2) (NOV 09 EXAM)

Any five of the following:

- Assist he IASB in the development of future IASs and in its review of existing IASs.
- Assist the IASB in promoting harmonisation of regulations, accounting standards and procedures by reducing the number of alternative treatments permitted by IASs.
- Assist national standard-setting bodies in developing national standards.
- Assist preparers of financial statements in applying IASs and in dealing with topics that are not subject to an IAS.
- Assist auditors in forming an opinion as to whether financial statements comply with IASs.
- Assist users of financial statements in interpreting the information contained in a set of financial statements.
- Provide those who are interested in the work of the IASC information about its approach to the formulation of IASs.

285 EXTERNAL AUDIT (MAY 10 EXAM)

(a) **Objective of an external audit:**

To make an independent report to the shareholders as to whether the financial statements give a true and fair view and whether they have been prepared in accordance with legal regulations (e.g. Companies Act) and accounting standards. There may be additional objectives, depending upon the requirements of local law.

(b) As the directors refuse to amend the valuation of inventory and inventory amount is material ($1m = 25% of profit) but not pervasive (only inventory is a problem – not the whole accounts) a modified audit report should be issued.

The modified report should have a qualified opinion because we have a material misstatement in the accounts. This means the auditors would say something like...." the accounts show a true and fair view, except on the valuation of inventory......".

286 PRINCIPLE-BASED STANDARDS (MAY 11 EXAM)

The possible advantages of having principle-based accounting standards include:

It will be harder to construct ways to avoid the detailed requirements of individual standards. For example, a prescriptive standard may set out specific values that should be used when applying a standard. If an actual value is specified it may be possible for some entries to construct various means of avoiding the application of that requirement. Whereas if the standard sets out general principles it is much harder to avoid the standard's requirements as a principle will apply no matter what the value is put on it.

A prescriptive standard would require a certain treatment to be used, regardless of the situation, which could lead to similar items being treated the same way even if the circumstances are very different. Principle based standards will require a standard to be applied using professional judgement, which can help ensure the correct application is used, hence more flexible.

Principle based standards should ensure the spirit of the regulations are adhered to, whereas the prescriptive system is more likely to lead to the letter of the law being followed rather than the spirit.

Principle based standards are easier to apply to local legislation for use in different countries.

ANSWERS TO SECTION B-TYPE QUESTIONS : SECTION 5

287 ELEMENTS OF FINANCIAL STATEMENTS (MAY 05 EXAM)

The IASB's *Framework* defines the five elements of financial statements as follows:

Assets – an asset is a resource controlled by the entity as a result of past events and from which future economic benefits are expected to flow to the entity.

Liabilities – a liability is a present obligation of the entity arising from past events, the settlement of which is expected to result in an outflow of resources from the entity.

Equity – the residual interest in the assets of the entity after deducting all its liabilities.

Income – increases in economic benefits during the accounting period in the form of inflows or enhancements of assets; or decreases of liabilities that result in increases in equity, other than those relating to combinations from equity participants.

Expenses – decreases in economic benefits during the accounting period in the form of outflows or depletions of assets that result in decreases in equity, other than those relating to distributions to equity participants.

288 ASSETS AND LIABILITIES (SEP 11 EXAM)

(i) **Asset** – An asset is a resource controlled by the entity as a result of past events and from which future economic benefits are expected to flow to the entity.

Liability – A liability is a present obligation of the entity arising from past events, the settlement of which is expected to result in an outflow of resources from the entity.

(ii) To be recognised the item must meet the definition of an element and the two criteria set by the *Framework*.

The criteria are:

- it is probable that any future economic benefit associated with the item will flow to or from the entity; and
- the item has a cost or value that can be measured with reliability.

289 OBJECTIVES AND UNDERLYING ASSUMPTIONS (MAY 11 EXAM)

(i) The *Framework* states that the objective of financial statements is to provide information about the financial position, performance and changes in financial position of an entity that is useful to a wide range of users in making economic decisions.

(ii) The two underlying assumptions in the *Framework* are going concern and accruals basis of accounting.

Going concern

Financial statements are normally prepared on the assumption that an entity is a going concern and will continue in operation for the foreseeable future. Any intention to liquidate or significantly reduce the scale of its operations would require the accounts to be prepared on a different basis and this basis would have to be disclosed.

Accruals basis of accounting

Financial statements are prepared on the accruals basis of accounting where the effects of the transactions are recognised when they occur and are recorded and reported in the accounting periods to which they relate, irrespective of cash flows arising from these transactions.

290 INFLUENCES ON REGULATION (SEP 11 EXAM)

The main factors that may influence accounting regulations in a country are:

The legal system and tax legislation

Taxable profits are based on accounting profit but the number and type of adjustments required to compute taxable profits varies from country to country. Part of this variation is due to the differences in the tax regulations but part of them is due to the different approaches to the calculation of accounting profit. In some countries taxable income is closely linked to the accounting profit and accounting rules are largely driven by taxation laws. These countries are usually known as code law countries; countries where the legal system originated in Roman law. Accounting regulation in these countries is usually in the hands of the government and financial reporting is a matter of complying with a set of legal rules.

In other countries the common law system is used. Common law is based on case law and tends to have less detailed regulations. In countries with common law systems the accounting regulation within the legal system is usually kept to a minimum; with detailed accounting regulations produced by professional organisations or other private sector accounting standard setting bodies.

Sources of finance and capital markets

There is more demand for financial information and disclosure where a higher proportion of capital is raised from external shareholders rather than from banks or family members. Banks and family members are usually in a position to be able to demand information directly from the entity, whereas stock market and shareholders have to rely on published financial information.

The political system

The nature of regulation and control exerted on accounting will reflect political philosophies and objectives of the ruling party.

Entity ownership

The need for public accountability and disclosure will be greater where there is a broad ownership of shares as opposed to family or government ownership.

Cultural differences

The culture within a country can influence societal and national values which can influence accounting regulations.

ANSWERS TO SECTION B-TYPE QUESTIONS : SECTION 5

291 ETHICS (MAY 11 EXAM)

According to CIMA's Code of ethics for professional accountants CX is in a position where she may be compromising her integrity and objectivity.

Integrity – This principle imposes an obligation to be truthful and honest on the accountant. A professional accountant should not be associated with reports or other information where she/he believes that the information contains misleading statements. This seems to be the case with the revised forecasts; CX believes that the revised forecasts are "grossly overstated".

Objectivity – A professional accountant should not allow conflict of interest or undue influence of others to override professional or business judgements or to compromise their professional judgements. The management board are overriding CX's professional and business judgement as they are imposing their assumptions on the forecast profits.

The possible options for CX in this situation would be:

(i) To refuse to remain associated with the forecasts and disassociate herself from them as much as possible.

(ii) To consider reporting the situation to appropriate authorities, possibly after taking legal advice.

(iii) To consider resignation of her post as a professional accountant.

292 CAPITAL MAINTENANCE (NOV 11 EXAM)

The International Accounting Standards Board's (IASB) *Conceptual Framework for the Financial Reporting* (*Framework*) section on concepts of capital and capital maintenance discusses concepts of capital, determining profit under each concept and capital maintenance.

Concepts of capital

The *Framework* refers to two concepts of capital: financial concept of capital and physical concept of capital.

Most entities adopt the financial concept of capital which deals with the net assets or equity of the entity.

If, instead of being primarily concerned with the invested capital of the entity, the users are concerned with, for example, the operating capability of the entity, then the physical concept of capital should be used.

Capital maintenance

In general terms, an entity has maintained its capital if it has as much capital at the end of the period as it had at the beginning of the period. The key in capital maintenance is deciding which concept is being adopted, because this then defines the basis on which profit is calculated.

Financial capital maintenance is measured in either nominal monetary units or units of constant purchasing power.

Physical capital maintenance requires the adoption of the current cost basis of measurement – an appreciation of what it would cost to replace assets at current prices.

The main difference between the two is how they treat the effects of increases in prices of assets and liabilities.

293 AUDIT (NOV 11 EXAM)

(i) By definition, a matter is material 'if its omission or misstatement could influence the economic decisions of users taken on the basis of the financial statements' (IASB *Framework*).

Materiality cannot always be measured in terms of any objective criteria. Some items are material due to their size but some matters are material by their very nature.

If size is used in the case of LMN $500,000 is 11% of profit and 1.25% of turnover. Both would be regarded as material due to the size.

(ii) International Standard on Auditing 701 (revised) Modifications to the independent Auditors Report deals with qualified audit reports. ISA 701 classifies qualified audit reports into categories.

The report category required for LMN would be "Matters that Do Affect the Auditor's Opinion – A qualified opinion".

A qualified opinion is expressed when the auditor concludes that an unqualified opinion cannot be expressed but that the effect of any disagreement with management is not so material and pervasive as to require an adverse opinion or a disclaimer of opinion. The qualified opinion will be expressed as being 'except for' the effects of the misclassification of the research expenditure.

> *Tutorial note*
>
> *The research cost should be expensed to the statement of profit or loss and NOT capitalised as per IAS 38. The mistake is material but not material and pervasive, hence a qualified opinion.*

294 ETHICAL PROBLEMS (1) (NOV 11 EXAM)

Section 220 of the CIMA Code of Ethics deals with preparation and reporting of information.

A professional accountant in business should prepare or present such information fairly, honestly and in accordance with relevant professional standards so that the information will be understood in its context.

Section 220 requires a professional accountant in business to maintain information for which they are responsible in a manner that:

(a) Describes clearly the true nature of business transactions, assets or liabilities

(b) Classifies and records information in a timely and proper manner; and

(c) Represents the facts accurately and completely in all material respects.

The approaches from other staff are threats to compliance with the fundamental principles. If RS altered the figures they would not describe clearly the true nature of the business transactions nor would they represent the facts accurately.

RS may be tempted out of self-interest as he will benefit from the increased bonus.

RS must also comply with the CIMA codes fundamental principles of integrity and objectivity. Changing the management information would breach both of these principles.

Safeguards should be applied to eliminate the threats or reduce them to an acceptable level. As other staff are offering incentives RS will need to decline these and refuse to alter the accounting information.

295 ROLES (1) (MAR 12 EXAM)

The four main entities involved in developing and implementing IFRS are:

IFRS Foundation (formerly known as the International Accounting Standards Committee Foundation (IASCF).

Role – governance and fund raising

International Accounting Standards Board (IASB)

Role – responsibility for all technical matters including the preparation and publication of international financial reporting standards

IFRS Advisory Council (formerly known as the Standards Advisory Council)

Role – to provide a forum for wider participation. Provides strategic advice to the IASB and informs the IASB of public views on major standard setting projects.

IFRS Interpretations Committee (formerly known as the International Financial Reporting Interpretations Committee IFRIC)

Role – provides timely guidance on the application and interpretation of IFRSs

296 AUDIT OBJECTIVE AND REPORT (MAR 12 EXAM)

(i) According to the International Standard on Auditing (ISA) 200 "Objective and General Principles Governing an Audit of Financial Statements" the objective of an audit is to enable auditors to express an opinion as to whether the financial statements give a true and fair view ... of the affairs of the entity at the period end and of its profit or loss ... for the period then ended and have been properly prepared in accordance with the applicable reporting framework (e.g. relevant legislation and applicable accounting standards).

(ii) Three key areas of content of the audit report as required by ISA 700 The Auditor's Report on Financial Statements include:

- *Management's responsibility for the financial statements*

    Report should state that management is responsible for the preparation and fair presentation of the financial statements.

- *Auditor's responsibility*

    Report should state that the responsibility of the auditor is to express an opinion on the financial statements based on the audit.

- *Description of the audit work done*

  Report should give an overview of the type of work done during the audit, such as obtaining audit evidence, risk assessment, procedures selected and the evaluation of the accounting policies used.

- *Auditor's opinion*

  Report should give the auditor's opinion on whether the financial statements give a true and fair view or are presented fairly in all material respects, in accordance with the applicable financial reporting framework.

297 ETHICAL PROBLEMS (2) (MAR 12 EXAM)

The ethical problem that XQ faces is that a professional accountant in business should prepare or present information fairly, honestly and in accordance with relevant professional standards so that the information will be understood in its context. A professional accountant is expected to act with integrity and objectivity and not allow any undue influence from others to override his professional judgement.

XQ is facing pressure from others to change the results and therefore break the CIMA Code.

XQ is being asked to misrepresent the facts of the actual situation which would be contrary to the CIMA Code's fundamental principles of integrity and objectivity. XQ would also be breaking the due care requirement of the CIMA Code.

XQ should apply safeguards to eliminate the threats or reduce them to an acceptable level. As other staff are offering incentives XQ will need to decline these and refuse to alter the accounting information.

XQ should also consult with his line manager. XQ may also wish to get advice from the CIMA helpline.

The situation is unlikely to require XQ to seek legal advice or resign.

298 BENEFITS OF EXTERNAL AUDIT (MAY 12 EXAM)

Briefing note

To: Chief Executive

The benefits of having an external audit carried out each year:

- The external audit should give an independent opinion on the truth and fairness of the accounts and therefore the shareholders should have comfort that there is no material error or misrepresentation of the financial position of the entity in the statements presented
- Whilst the auditors are conducting the audit they will consider the controls in place and may be able to give constructive advice to management
- Whilst the purpose of the audit is not to find fraud, the fact that an external review is taking place is likely to act as a fraud deterrent
- Applications to third parties for finance may be enhanced
- Avoids breaking the law, for some entities an audit is not an option. Local legislation relating to entities may require an annual independent audit to be carried out. Local stock exchange regulations will usually require an annual audit.

299 ROLES (2) (NOV 12 EXAM)

The role of the IFRS Interpretations Committee in relation to International Financial Reporting Standards is:

- Reviews new financial reporting issues not specifically addressed in an IFRS.
- Examines existing accounting standards and other financial reporting issues where unsatisfactory or conflicting interpretations have developed with the objective of reaching a consensus on the most appropriate treatment. The consensus is then published in support of IFRS.

The role of the IFRS Advisory Council in relation to International Financial Reporting Standards is:

- To gives advice to the IASB on its agenda and priorities in its work.
- To informs the IASB on the views of organisations and individuals on the Council on the major accounting standard setting projects being considered/developed.

300 PURPOSE OF THE FRAMEWORK (FEB 13)

According to the Framework, its purpose is to:

- assist the IASB in the development of future IFRSs and in its review of existing IFRSs
- assist the IASB in promoting harmonisation of regulations, accounting standards and procedures by providing a basis for reducing the number of alternative treatments permitted by IFRSs
- assist national standard-setting bodies in developing national standards
- assist preparers of financial statements in applying IFRSs and in dealing with topics that have yet to be covered in an IFRS
- assist auditors in forming an opinion as to whether financial statements comply with IFRSs
- assist users in interpreting the information contained in a set of financial statements that are prepared using IFRSs
- provide information about how the IASB has formulated its approach to the development of IFRSs.

(Any 5 of the above)

301 ETHICAL DILEMA (MAY 13 EXAM)

He should start by gathering all relevant information so that he can be sure of the facts and decide if there really is an ethical problem. All steps taken should be fully documented.

Initially he should raise his concern internally, possibly with the team's manager or a trusted colleague.

If this is not a realistic option, for example because of the relationship of the manager and the team member that Ace is concerned about, he may have to consider escalating the issue and speak to the manager's boss, a board member or a non-executive director. If there is an internal whistle blowing procedure or internal grievance procedure he should use that.

If after raising the matter internally nothing is done and he still has concerns he should take it further, for example if the other team member is an accountant Ace could consider reporting the team member to his professional body.

Ace could also distance himself from the problem and ask to be moved to a different department or to a different team.

302 ETHICAL ISSUES (AUG 13 EXAM)

As XY takes on substantially the risk and rewards associated with owning the machine, the lease should be treated as a finance lease.

The ethical issues that may arise as a result of the managing director's instruction include:

- Objectivity – the finance director would be allowing other people to influence his professional judgement if the lease was treated incorrectly in the financial statements.
- Professional behaviour – the finance director should follow relevant laws and regulations. That would include following the requirements of IFRSs including IAS 17 *Leases*, not to do so could cause a negative impact on his reputation.
- Integrity – he should not be associated with any information that contains materially false or misleading information. Incorrectly classifying the lease could be misleading to users of the financial statements.
- Professional competence and due care – the finance director needs to ensure that he keeps up to date and follows relevant professional and technical standards. He will therefore need to follow IAS 17 *Leases* and treat the lease appropriately.

SINGLE COMPANY FINANCIAL ACCOUNTS

303 DF (NOV 06 EXAM)

(1) **Over-statement due to fraud**

As the error is material in terms of the profit previously reported for the prior year, a prior year adjustment should be made in accordance with IAS 8 *Accounting Policies, Changes in Accounting Estimates and Errors*. This will reduce the prior year profit and retained reserves brought forward by $45,000. The comparative figures in the financial statements would also be restated and the $45,000 would be excluded from the current year's figures. The nature of the error and the amount of the correction must be disclosed in the notes.

(2) **Sale in respect of order received before the year end**

In accordance with IAS 18 *Revenue*, the sale cannot be recognised until significant risks and rewards of ownership have passed to the customer. In this case, whilst the revenue arises from the ordinary course of the company's activities, the costs and revenues can be estimated reliably and it can be anticipated that economic benefit will flow to the company, the risks and rewards of ownership have not been passed to the customer at the year end. Accordingly, the revenue and costs should be excluded from the financial statements for the year ended 30 September 20X6.

304 STATEMENT OF PROFIT OR LOSS (MAY 06 EXAM)

CE – Statement of profit or loss for the year ended 31 March 20X6

	$000
Revenue	2,000
Cost of sales	(688)
Gross profit	1,312
Distribution costs	(200)
Administrative expenses	(760)
Profit	352
Finance costs	(190)
Profit before tax	162

Workings:

Cost of sales		Administration	
Trial balance	480	Trial balance	260
Depreciation	192	Provision	500
Inventory adjustment *	16		
	688		760

*__Note:__ The inventory is valued at lower of cost or NRV, hence must be reduced by $16. By reducing the closing inventory value it will have the impact of increasing cost of sales.

305 BJ (NOV 05 EXAM)

IFRS 5 *Non-current Assets Held for Sale and Discontinued Operations* defines a discontinued operation as a component of an entity that has either been disposed of or is classified as held for sale.

The airline operation appears to be a major and separate line of business that is clearly distinguishable from the other business activities of BJ. Its sale therefore requires separate disclosure in the financial statements, as a discontinued operation. The following disclosures are required by IFRS 5 *Non-current Assets Held for Sale and Discontinued Operations*:

(a) a single amount on the face of the statement of profit or loss comprising the total of the post-tax profit or loss of the operation and the post-tax gain or loss on the disposal of the assets constituting the discontinued operation

(b) an analysis of this amount into the revenue, expenses and pre-tax profit or loss; the related income tax expense; the gain or loss on the disposal of the assets of the operation (loss $250 million ($750 – $500)); and the related income tax expense

(c) the net cash flows attributable to the operating, investing and financing activities of the discontinued operation in the current year

(d) a description of the operation (airline)

(e) a description of the facts and circumstances of the sale (sale of fleet on 31 July 20X5)

(f) the industry and geographical segment in which it is reported (airline operating within Europe).

A provision of $20 million must be made in respect of the severance payments to employees as these constitute a present obligation arising as a result of a past event. The $20 million therefore appears in both the statement of profit or loss and the statement of financial position.

The costs of restructuring the remaining business should be classified as 'restructuring' within continuing activities. A provision of $10 million is required in the financial statements for the year ended 30 September 20X5 as at that date the entity is committed to the restructuring.

ANSWERS TO SECTION B-TYPE QUESTIONS : **SECTION 5**

306 TANGIBLE NON-CURRENT ASSETS

Property, plant and equipment

	Land	Buildings	Plant and machinery	Under construction	Total
Cost/valuation	$000	$000	$000	$000	$000
Balance at 1 January 20X5	2,743	3,177	1,538	53	7,511
Revaluation of assets	375				375
Disposal of assets			(125)		(125)
Transfers			350	(350)	0
New purchases (balancing figure)	402	526	890	297	2,115
Balance at 31 December 20X5	3,520	3,703	2,653	0	9,876
Depreciation					
Balance at 1 January 20X5	–	612	671	–	1,283
Disposal of assets	–	–	(111)	–	(111)
Depreciation for the year	–	75	212	–	287
Balance at 31 December 20X5	0	687	772	0	1,459
Carrying amount 31 December 20X5	3,520	3,016	1,881	0	8,417
Carrying amount 31 December 20X4	2,743	2,565	867	53	6,228

307 DW

Corrected schedule of the movements on plant

	Cost	Depreciation
	$m	$m
At 1 October 20X4	97.20	32.50
Addition at cost (W1)	21.50	
Disposals (W2)	(15.00)	(9.00)
Depreciation charge for year (W3)		20.74
Balance at 30 September 20X5	103.70	44.24

267

Workings:

(W1) Addition at cost

	$million
Basic cost	20.00
Installation	1.00
Testing	0.50
	21.50

(W2) Disposal

The accumulated depreciation on the plant disposed of = 20% of $15 million for three years = $9 million. (**Note:** The asset was held at the year ends 30 September 20X2, 20X3 and 20X4; therefore depreciation has been charged for three years.)

(W3) Annual depreciation charge

The depreciation charge for the year is 20% of the corrected cost of plant at the year end i.e. 20% × $103.7 million = $20.74 million.

308 BI (NOV 05 EXAM)

Building

	$
Cost	1,000,000
Y/e 30/9/X3 – Depreciation (1,000,000/20)	(50,000)
Y/e 30/9/X4 – Depreciation (1,000,000/20)	(50,000)
CV	900,000
Revaluation	1,800,000
Credit to revaluation reserve	900,000

Following the revaluation, depreciation must be calculated on the revalued figure. There seems to have been no change to the estimate of the building's life, so 18 years of life remain.

Y/e 30/9/X5	$
Valuation b/f	1,800,000
Depreciation (1,800,000/18)	(100,000)
CV	1,700,000
Revaluation	1,500,000
Debit to revaluation reserve	200,000

As the building had previously been revalued, the impairment loss can be debited to the revaluation reserve rather than being charged to the statement of profit or loss.

Future depreciation will be based on the revalued figure: $1,500,000/17 years = $88,235 p.a.

Brand

The brand must be valued at the lower of carrying amount ($250,000) and recoverable amount ($200,000), i.e. $200,000. Recoverable amount is the higher of (a) fair value less costs to sell ($200,000) and (b) value in use ($150,000).

Working:

	$
Cost	500,000
Accumulated amortisation (500,000 × 5/10)	(250,000)
Carrying amount	250,000

The impairment loss of $50,000 ($250,000 − $200,000) must be charged to the statement of profit or loss in the year ended 30 September 20X5.

309 REVALUATION (NOV 06 EXAM)

	A	B
1.9.W6 Cost	200,000	120,000
Useful economic life	20	15
At first revaluation – 31.8.X1 – CV	200,000 × 15/20 =150,000	120,000 × 10/15 = 80,000
Revaluation gain/(loss)	30,000	(5,000)
Valuation carried forward	180,000	75,000
At second revaluation – 31.8.X6 – CV	180,000 × 10/15 = 120,000	75,000 × 5/10 = 37,500
Revaluation gain/(loss)	(20,000)	(7,500)
Revaluation	100,000	30,000

The impairment on B of $7,500 goes to the statement of profit or loss, as there is no revaluation reserve in respect of that building.

The impairment on A is less than the revaluation reserve of $30,000, so the impairment is booked against the revaluation reserve, leaving a balance on that reserve of $10,000.

310 USEFUL ECONOMIC LIFE

Memo

To: Transport Manager

From: Trainee Management Accountant

Date:

Subject: **Useful economic life of vehicle**

A requirement of IAS 16 *Property, Plant and Equipment* is that the useful economic life (and the residual value) of each item of property, plant and equipment should be reviewed at least once each year. If there is a change in the estimate, a change in accounting estimate should be made in accordance with IAS 8 *Accounting Policies, Changes in Accounting Estimates and Errors*.

The delivery vehicle is currently valued at cost less accumulated depreciation. At 1 April 20X2, the asset had been held for two years, and its expected useful life was four years. Its carrying value was therefore $10,000, which is $20,000 cost less two years of accumulated depreciation of $5,000 per year.

At 31 March 20X3, the revision to the estimated useful life means that from 1 April 20X2, the asset had four more years of expected useful life. From that date, the asset should therefore be depreciated over its remaining revised expected useful life. The annual depreciation charge from 1 April 20X2 should therefore be $2,500 (= $10,000/4 years).

This means that for the year to 31 March 20X3, the annual depreciation charge should be $2,500. The carrying value of the asset at the beginning of the year, as indicated above, is $10,000. The carrying value at 31 March 20X3 will be:

	$
Vehicle at cost	20,000
Less accumulated depreciation	12,500
Carrying value	7,500

311 DECOMMISSIONING

Memo

To: Production Manager

From: Trainee Management Accountant

Date:

Subject: **Decommissioning costs**

It is a requirement of IAS 16 *Property, Plant and Equipment* that the cost of an item of property, plant or equipment should, on initial recognition of the cost, include an estimate of the future costs of decommissioning work and restoring the site on which the asset is located, if there is an obligation to do this work. For the oil well a future obligation exists, therefore a cost for the future decommissioning work and land restoration must be included in the cost of the asset from 1 March 20X3.

This obligation for future decommissioning costs and land restoration should be measured in accordance with IAS 37 *Provisions, Contingent Liabilities and Contingent Assets*. This states that, when the time value of money is material, which it is in this case, the amount of the future obligation should be discounted to a present value. The discount rate should be a pre-tax rate.

The cost of the new oil well from 1 March 20X3 must therefore include an amount for future decommissioning costs, equal to $20 million discounted from Year 20 to a present value equivalent. There should be a corresponding liability in the statement of financial position for the discounted value of the provision.

The asset should be depreciated in accordance with our normal accounting policies, and normal rules of valuation of the asset will apply. For example, the asset will be subject to regular impairment reviews.

There should be an annual review of the provision, and any adjustments to the present value of the provision will be made through the statement of profit or loss. If there is no inflation and no change in the estimate of costs, the provision should be $20 million by the end of Year 20.

Signed: Trainee Management Accountant

312 HOTELS

Memo

To: Accountant

From:

Date:

Subject: Accounting treatment of revaluations

(a) The carrying amount or carrying value of Hotel K at 30 September is $430,000, which is $110,000 higher than its current valuation of $320,000. In compliance with the new accounting policy, Hotel K should be revalued to $320,000. The reduction in the statement of financial position valuation of $110,000 represents an impairment loss. This loss should be recognised as a charge in the statement of profit or loss for the year to 30 September 20X4.

> *Tutorial note*
>
> *The hotel has not previously been revalued. If there had been a previous revaluation, the impairment loss could have been set off against the amount of the earlier revaluations of the same property by means of a reduction in the revaluation reserve, rather than treated as a charge in the statement of profit or loss. However, this situation does not apply in this case.*

(b) Hotel G should be revalued to $650,000 and Hotel H to $820,000 from 1 January 20X4. The valuations should separate the value of the land from the value of the buildings, and depreciation from 1 January 20X4 should be based on the new valuation of the buildings and the estimated remaining useful life of the buildings (50 years for Hotel G and 30 years for Hotel H). A similar accounting treatment should apply to Hotel K from 1 January 20X4.

The transfer to the revaluation reserve for Hotels G and H should be the difference between their carrying amount at 1 January 20X4 (before the revaluation) and their revalued amount. The carrying value of the hotels is their cost less accumulated depreciation to 1 January 20X4. The carrying value of the hotels is reduced by a depreciation charge for the first three months of the year (1 October – 31 December 20X3).

In this way, there will be a depreciation charge for the hotels in the statement of profit or loss for the full 12 months of the year, the first three months based on the old valuation and the following nine months based on the new valuation.

(c) The carrying value of each hotel at 30 September 20X4 should be the revalued amounts less accumulated depreciation since the revaluations (for the nine months from 1 January 20X4).

313 DEVELOPMENT COSTS (1) (MAY 06 EXAM)

(a) Under IAS 38 *Intangible Assets,* development expenditure can be regarded as an intangible asset if and only if, an entity can demonstrate all of the following:

- the technical feasibility of completing the asset so that it can be used or sold
- the intention to complete the asset to use it or sell it
- the ability to use or sell the asset
- how the asset will generate future economic benefits
- the availability of technical, financial and other resources to complete the project to make and use or sell the asset
- the ability to reliably measure the expenditure on the development of the asset.

(b) As all of the above criteria seem to have been met by CD's new process:

CD will treat the $180,000 development cost as an intangible non-current asset in its statement of financial position at 30 April 20X6. Amortisation will start from 1 May 20X6 when the new process starts operation.

314 DEVELOPMENT COSTS (2) (MAY 08 EXAM)

This question required students to whether the expenditure gives rise to an asset under IAS 38. For an asset to be recognised as an intangible asset there must be a probable flow of benefit to the enterprise and you must be able to make a reliable estimate of cost.

- Item i) can be recognised as an intangible asset if the author expects the book to be successful and profitable and it is probable. The cost would not be amortised until the book is actually published.
- Item ii) did not have any additional sales and therefore there was no probable flow of a benefit to the enterprise. They also stated that no reliable estimate could be made, therefore the expense must be written off direct to the statement of profit or loss.
- Item iii) is very difficult to measure whether there will be a probable benefit as a result of the advertising to improve the corporate image. It would also be hard to make a reliable estimate of cost and therefore should also be written off to the statement of profit or loss as an expense.

315 HF ERRORS (MAY 09 EXAM)

Item 1 relates to IAS 2 that states inventory should be valued at the lower of cost or NRV. The inventory has been overvalued by $500 and should be adjusted, however it is not material (only 3% of revenue) so it would be acceptable to adjust in the next set of accounts.

Item 2 relates to IAS 38 that states development costs can only be capitalised if they meet the criteria of the standard. If the project has now been abandoned it does not meet the criteria and should be written off from the statement of financial position against profit. The CV of $600,000 is material and should be done immediately.

Item 3 relates to IAS 37 that states if a present obligation exists and it can be reliably measured and it is probable to occur a provision should be made. This seems to be the case so a full provision is needed for the £5,000,000. The entries should be to debit the asset account and credit the provision. The cost will then be depreciated as part of the asset on the statement of financial position and written off over the 20 years.

Ideally the provision should be discounted to present value and then unwound over the 20 year period.

If the directors do not agree on these changes a modified report will be issued with a qualified opinion to explain the material misstatements.

316 REDEEMABLE SHARES (1) (MAY 06 EXAM)

(a)

The total finance cost is:	$
Issue costs	192,800
Annual dividend (200,000 × $10 × 5%) × 5	500,000
Redemption cost (200,000 × $10 × 15%)	300,000
	992,800

(b)

	Balance b/fwd $	Finance cost 10% $	Dividend paid $	Balance c/fwd $
31/3/X6	*1,807,200	180,720	–100,000	1,887,920
31/3/X7	1,887,920	188,792	–100,000	1,976,712
31/3/X8	1,976,712	197,671	–100,000	2,074,383
31/3/X9	2,074,383	207,438	–100,000	2,181,821
31/3/Y0	2,181,821	218,179	–100,000	2,300,000

*Note: The opening balance represents the net proceeds, i.e. $2,000,000 less $192,800 issue costs.

317 REDEEMABLE SHARES (2) (MAY 08 EXAM)

Tutorial note

This was an unusual question that required the application of the sum of the digits methods to allocate the finance cost.

Cash received	$10,000,000
Issue costs	$601,500
Cash raised	$9,398,500
Total finance cost =	
Issue costs	$601,500
Annual interest	$2,000,000
Redemption cost	$1,000,000
	$3,601,500

Sum of the digits = 4 × 5/2 = 10

Year 1	4/10 × 3,601,500	$1,440,600
Year 2	3/10 × 3,601,500	$1,080,450
Year 3	2/10 × 3,601,500	$ 720,300
Year 4	1/10 × 3,601,500	$ 360,150

Statement of profit or loss for the year ended 30/4/X8

Finance cost $1,080,450

Statement of financial position as at 30/4/X8

Non-current liability $10,919,550

(9,398,500 + 1,440,600 − 500,000 + 1,080,450 − 500,000)

318 REDEEMABLE SHARES (3) (MAY 13 EXAM)

(i) IAS 32 *Financial Instruments*: Presentation requires shares to be classified as debt (financial liability) or equity according to their substance rather than legal form.

A financial liability is defined as a contractual obligation to deliver cash or other financial asset to another entity.

Cumulative redeemable preferred shares meet the definition of financial liability and therefore must be classified as debt and included in the statement of financial position under non-current liabilities.

(ii) IAS 39 *Financial Instruments*: Recognition and Measurement: The cumulative redeemable preferred shares will initially be measured at the fair value of the consideration received. That is issue price less issue costs, ($500,000 – $20,000 = $480,000).

The charge to profit or loss will be based on the effective interest rate which includes any issue costs, dividends paid and redemption costs.

319 SHARE ISSUES (AUG 13 EXAM)

(i) Bonus issue of shares is an issue of shares to existing shareholders for free. A bonus issue is used to capitalise reserves, it does not raise new capital.

A rights issue is an issue of shares below full market price to existing shareholders. A rights issue is made to raise new capital from existing shareholders. They are issued at a discount to current market price to encourage the shareholders to subscribe for the rights issue.

(ii) Number of shares issued: 5,000,000/5 = 1,000,000

Transaction value: 1,000,000 shares at $3.50 = $3,500,000

Accounting entries required:

	Debit	Credit
Cash	$3,500,000	
Share capital		$1,000,000
Share premium		$2,500,000

320 CB IMPORTERS (MAY 06 EXAM)

A customer with whom an entity transacts a significant volume of business is not a related party merely by virtue of the resulting economic dependence. XC is therefore not a related party and the negotiated discount does not need to be disclosed.

A party is related to an entity if it has an interest in the entity that gives it significant influence over the entity, such as being a member of the key management personnel of the entity.

As founder member and major shareholder holding 40% of the equity, George is able to exert significant influence and is a related party of CB.

George is also a related party as he is CB's president. He is a member of the key management personnel of CB.

The sale of the property for $500,000 will need to be disclosed, along with its valuation as a related party transaction.

Providers of finance are not related parties simply because of their normal dealings with the entity. However, if a party is a close member of the family of any individual categorised as a related party, they are also a related party. As Arnold is George's son and George is a related party, Arnold is also a related party. The loan from FC will need to be disclosed, along with the details of Arnold and his involvement in the arrangements.

321 RELATED PARTIES (NOV 07 EXAM)

A related party is:

- an entity that directly, or indirectly through one or more intermediaries, controls, is controlled by, or is under the same control as a second entity; or
- an entity that has an interest in the second entity that gives it significant influence; or
- an entity that has joint control over the second entity; or
- an associate
- a joint venture in which the entity is a venturer
- a member of the key management personnel of the entity or parent
- any close relation of the personnel in any of the above.

A related party transaction is a transfer of resources or obligations between related parties, regardless of whether a price is charged.

322 AE (MAY 05 EXAM)

Statement of profit or loss:	$000	$000
Revenue		60,000
Costs incurred to 31 March 20X5	24,000	
Costs to completion	19,000	
		43,000
Profit		17,000
Recognise 50% profit		8,500
Revenue recognised 50% of contract value 60,000/2		30,000
Statement of financial position :		
Total contact costs incurred		24,000
Recognised profit		8,500
		32,500
Less: Progress payments received		25,000
Gross amount due from customer		7,500

Statement of profit or loss for the year to 31 March 20X5

	$000
Revenue from long-term contract	30,000
Cost of sales (balance)	21,500
Profit	8,500

Statement of financial position as at 31 March 20X5

	$000
Receivables	
Long-term contract – gross amounts due from customer	7,500

323 HS (MAY 09 EXAM)

The overall contract is profitable:

	$
Contract value	300
Costs incurred to date	170
Estimated cost to complete	100
Profit	30

Stage of completion: work certified/contract value = 165/300 = 55%

Statement of profit or loss:

Revenue (55% × 300)	165
COS (55% × 270)	148.5
Profit	16.5

Statement of financial position:

Cost incurred	170
Profit (IS)	16.5
Less: progress payments	130
Amounts due from customers (asset)	56.5

324 CC (MAY 10 EXAM)

Total contract	$m	$m
Revenue		63
Costs incurred to 31 March 20X9	18	
Costs incurred to 31 March 20Y0	26	
Costs to completion	20	
		64
Overall loss on contract		(1)

Statement of profit or loss and other comprehensive income YE 31/03/X9

	$m
Revenue	22
Cost of sales	(18)
Profit	4

Statement of profit or loss and other comprehensive income YE 31/03/Y0

	$m
Revenue (75% × 63) less 22 already recognised	25
Cost of sales (balancing figure)	(30)
Loss (overall loss of $1 plus removal of $4 profit already recognized in the previous year)	(5)

Statement of financial position

	$m
Total contact costs incurred (18 + 26)	44
Overall loss recognized to date	(1)
Less amounts invoiced (22 + 15)	(37)
	6

325 INTANGIBLES (NOV 09 EXAM)

(i) Goodwill – purchased goodwill is the price paid over the value of the net assets of the business. In this scenario JX has paid $700,000 for a business worth $650,000, hence creating $50,000 of goodwill.

This will be shown in JX's statement of financial position at 31 October 20X9 and will be subject to an impairment review by IFRS 3 *Business Combinations* each year.

(ii) The development expenditure appears to meet the criteria of IAS 38 to defer expenditure, i.e. expect to complete, able to use or sell, profitable, etc.

Therefore, this will be shown in JX's statement of financial position at 31 October 20X9 at $590,000 ($90,000 purchased and $500,000 spent to complete) and it will be amortised over five years, beginning on 1 November 20X9.

(iii) Brand Z was acquired as part of JX's business. IAS 38 sets out the conditions under which an intangible asset (such as a brand) can be recognised:

- it must be probable that future economic benefits will flow to the business, and
- the cost of the asset can be measured reliably.

In the situation in the question, both conditions apply. Presumably the valuation of $200,000 on purchase is a reliable measurement of the fair value of the brand at this date, so Brand Z can be recognised as a purchased intangible non-current asset in JX's statement of financial position.

In JX's statement of financial position at 31 October 20X9, the brand will be shown as:

Non-current assets	Cost $000	Accumulated amortisation $000	Carrying value $000
Purchased brand	200	–	200

The brand cannot be shown at its revalued amount of $250,000 unless an active market exists, which we have no evidence of. The brand will be amortised over its useful life.

326 EARTHQUAKE (NOV 10 EXAM)

(i) IAS 37 *Provisions, Contingent Liabilities and Contingent Assets* requires that future costs of reinstatement be provided for as soon as they become an unavoidable commitment. The mine's license requires the work to be done, so there is a commitment as soon as the mine starts operations.

(ii) The earthquake occurred after the end of the accounting period. Assets and liabilities at 31 August 20X9 were not affected. The earthquake is indicative of conditions that arose after the reporting period and does not give any further evidence in relation to assets and liabilities in existence at the reporting date. Therefore according to IAS 10 *Events after the Reporting Period* it will be classified as a non-adjusting event after the reporting period. The cost of the repairs will be charged to the Statement of profit or loss and other comprehensive income in the period when it is incurred. Due to the impact on MN, i.e. closure and loss of earnings for 6 months, the earthquake and an estimate of its effect will need to be disclosed by way of a note in MN's financial statements for the year ended 31 August 20X9.

327 SHOE FACTORY (MAY 10 EXAM)

Under IFRS 5 *Non-current Assets Held for Sale and Discontinued Operations* it specifies that discontinued operations must be shown separately from continued operations. A discontinued operation is defined as either an operation that has been disposed of or is classified as held for sale at the accounting date.

Based on the scenario, the shoe factory has not yet closed and does not meet the criteria of an asset held for sale, i.e. available for immediate sale in its present condition, the sale is highly probable, a reasonable price has been set and the sale is expected to be completed in the next year. The scenario clearly states AD has not yet attempted to find a buyer.

Therefore, AD should continue to show the shoe factory under continuing operations in the current accounting period.

CIMA's Code of Ethics for Professional Accountants states five fundamental principles that accountants are required to comply with.

If AD's management do not follow the requirements of IFRS 5 and exclude the results of the shoe factory from their accounts, they will be breaching three of these principles:

- Objectivity – Accounts should not show a bias opinion and should not be influenced by other people. Professional judgement should be applied at all times, i.e. following the rules of IFRS 5.
- Integrity – An accountant should remain honest at all times and would not be doing this if they exclude the shoe factory from the accounts.
- Professional behaviour – Accountants should always comply with the accounting standard rules when preparing accounts. This would not be done if we do not apply IFRS 5.

328 OPERATING SEGMENTS (NOV 12 EXAM)

IFRS 8 *Operating segments* defines an operating segment as a component of an entity:

- That engages in business activities, earning revenues and incurring expenses
- Whose operating results are regularly reviewed by the entity's chief operating decision maker to make decisions about resources to be allocated to the segment and assess its performance.

A segment will be identified as a reportable segment if it contributes more than 10% of:

- Revenue
- Profits
- Losses
- Assets

In addition the reportable segments must in aggregate account for a minimum of 75% of total revenue. Additional reportable segments must be identified, even if they do not meet the 10% rule, until 75% of revenue is accounted for by reportable segments.

329 FINANCE LEASE (1)

The cost of the asset is $88,300. It is assumed that the expected residual value is 0, and that the straight-line method of depreciation is used. The annual depreciation charge is therefore $88,300/5 years = **$17,660**.

		$
Total lease payments (5 years × $21,000)		105,000
Asset cost		88,300
Finance charges on the lease		16,700
Sum-of-the-digits		5 + 4 + 3 + 2 + 1 = 15
(lease payments annual in arrears)		or (5 × 6)/2)=15

		$
Finance charge in Year 1	(5/15 × $16,700)	5,567
Finance charge in Year 2	(4/15× $16,700)	4,453
Finance charge in Year 3	(3/15× $16,700)	3,340

ANSWERS TO SECTION B-TYPE QUESTIONS : SECTION 5

Year	Opening liability for lease $	Finance charge $	Lease payments $	Closing liability for lease $
1	88,300	5,567	(21,000)	72,867
2	72,867	4,453	(21,000)	56,320
3	56,320	3,340	(21,000)	38,660

Statement of profit or loss extracts

Year 1 $
Depreciation 17,660
Finance charge 5,567

Year 2
Depreciation 17,660
Finance charge 4,453

Statement of financial position extracts	End of Year 1 $	End of Year 2 $
Non-current assets at cost (leased)	88,300	88,300
Accumulated depreciation	17,660	35,320
Carrying value	70,640	52,980
Liabilities: amounts due under finance lease		
Non-current liability	56,320	38,660
Current liability	16,547	17,660

330 FINANCE LEASE (2) (MAY 05 EXAM)

(a) The finance cost in the statement of profit or loss for the year ended 31 March 20X5 is $9,067.

(b) **Statement of financial position as at 31 March 20X5 – extract**

	$
Non-current assets – tangible	
Finance lease	116,000
Less: Depreciation (116,000/5 × 2 years)	46,400
	69,600
Non-current liabilities	
Amounts due under finance lease	$53,200
Current liabilities	
Amounts due under finance lease ($76,400 – $53,200)	$23,200

Workings:

	$
Total payments under the lease ($30,000 × 5)	150,000
Fair value of the asset	116,000
Finance cost	34,000

Five years sum of digits: 5 + 4 + 3 + 2 + 1 = 15

Year	Proportion	Finance cost
		$
20X3/X4	5/15 × $34,000	11,333
20X4/X5	4/15 × $34,000	9,067
20X5/X6	3/15 × $34,000	6,800

Year	Balance b/fwd	Finance charge	Repayment	Balance c/fwd
	$	$	$	$
20X3/X4	116,000	11,333	(30,000)	97,333
20X4/X5	97,333	9,067	(30,000)	76,400
20X5/X6	76,400	6,800	(30,000)	53,200

331 FINANCE LEASE (3) (MAY 07 EXAM)

(i) Finance charge for year ended 31 March 2007 = $72,000

(ii)

	$000
Current liability (606 − 378) =	228
Non-current liability	378

Working:

Year ended 31 March	Bal b/fwd	Payment	Sub-total	Interest	Bal c/fwd
	$000	$000	$000	$000	$000
2006	900	(228)	672	90	762
2007	762	(228)	534	72	606
2008	606	(228)	378	51	429
2009	429	(228)	201	27	228
2010	228	(228)	0	0	0

332 CLOSURE (1) (MAY 07 EXAM)

IFRS 5 defines a 'discontinued activity' as one that:
- represents a major line of business
- is part of a single co-ordinated plan, and
  - has either been discontinued by the year end or the assets transferred to 'held for sale'.
  - DP seems to have satisfied these criteria as the directors are committed to the factory closure, but it has not been completed by the year end.

The assets for sale should therefore be classified as non-current assets 'held for sale' and shown separately on the statement of financial position in the year to 31 March 20X7.

The total cost of the manufacturing facility for the year ended 31 March 20X7 must be shown separately in the statement of profit or loss under the heading 'discontinued activities'. The total cost must include the turnover and operating costs of the manufacturing facility for the year, together with the closure costs of $620,000 incurred to date and the $70,000 loss incurred on the disposal of the plant and equipment.

Assets classified as 'held for sale' are not depreciated. Non-current assets classified as 'held for sale' must be carried at the lower of carrying value or fair value less costs to sell. Therefore the carrying value of $750,000 will be shown as 'held for sale'.

333 CLOSURE (2) (NOV 07 EXAM)

(i) EK can treat the sale of its retailing division as a 'discontinued operation' as defined by IFRS 5 *Non-current Assets Held for Sale and Discontinued Operations* as it is 'held for sale'. There is a plan to dispose of the separate major line of business as a single transaction, such that the economic value of the assets will be realised by selling, rather than continuing to use them.

(ii) The assets should be recognised at the lower of:
- the value under normal accounting standards, i.e. $443,000
- the value on sale, being the fair value less the costs of sale, i.e. $423,000 less $25,000.

Therefore, EK should value the assets at $398,000.

This results in an impairment loss of $$45,000 ($443,000 − $398,000), which should be recognised as an expense to the statement of profit or loss.

Once this valuation exercise has been performed, no depreciation or amortisation should be recognised.

The trading performance of the continuing divisions should be shown in the statement of profit or loss (or disclosed by way of note), as well as the overall performance, so that readers can evaluate the likely impact of the disposal.

334 WZ (SEP 11 EXAM)

According to CIMA's Code of ethics for professional accountants WZ is in a position where he may be compromising his integrity and objectivity.

Integrity – This principle imposes an obligation to be truthful and honest on the accountant. A professional accountant should not be associated with reports and other information where she/he believes that the information contains misleading statements. This seems to be the case with the revised treatment of the property, WZ believes that the revised financial statements will not follow IFRS 5 and may not show a true and fair view of the situation.

Objectivity – A professional accountant should not allow conflict of interest or undue influence of others to override professional or business judgements or to compromise her/his professional judgements. The management board is overriding WZ's professional and business judgement as it is imposing its business judgement over the professional accountant's (WZ) professional judgement.

If WZ were to accept the change outsiders may interpret this as a lack of professional judgement by WZ as IFRS 5 will not be applied correctly.

The possible options for WZ in this situation would be:

- To try and persuade the management board that IFRS 5 must be followed and the property treated correctly in the financial statements.
- To refuse to remain associated with the financial statements if IFRS 5 is not followed and to disassociate himself from them as much as possible.
- To consider reporting the situation to the external auditors or other appropriate authorities possibly after taking legal advice.
- To consider resignation from his post as a professional accountant.

335 LP (FEB 13)

A single figure should be shown on the statement of profit or loss and other comprehensive income, comprising the loss after tax and loss incurred on the disposal of assets. Therefore a separate section "Discontinued operations" will be shown after the section of the statement of profit or loss and other comprehensive income headed "Continuing operations". The heading will be loss for the period from discontinued operations and the amount shown will be ($42,000). The notes to the statement of comprehensive income will need to disclose each of the amounts included in the loss after tax, i.e.

	$000
Revenue	95
Operating expenses	(110)
Operating loss	(15)
Loss on disposal of assets	(30)
Tax refund	3
Loss	(42)

Comparative information for prior periods must be restated using the current classification, that is division C results for prior periods will be shown as discontinued operations.

The restructuring expense is not included in discontinued operations as according to IFRS 5 *Non-current assets held for sale and discontinued operations* this is an expense that relates to ongoing operations and should be included under continuing operations. As the $75,000 restructuring is a material item in the context of continuing operations, it will need to be shown as a separate item on the statement of profit or loss and other comprehensive income as required by IAS 1 *Presentation of financial statements*..

336 REVENUE RECOGNITION (1) (NOV 07 EXAM)

(i) The criteria for income recognition under IAS 18 *Revenue Recognition* are:
- the risks and rewards of ownership must have passed to the purchaser
- the seller no longer controls the goods
- the revenue can be measured reliably
- there is reasonable certainty of payment
- the related costs can be measured reliably.

(ii) The payment made by the supermarket covered the six months to 28 February 20X8 so that, at the year end, EJ had supplied two months' worth. Accordingly, EJ should recognise revenue of $150,000 × 2/6 = 50,000.

The related costs are $20,000 per month, so $40,000.

Accordingly, EJ should include a gross profit on this contract in its results for the year to 31 October 20X7 of $10,000.

337 REVENUE RECOGNITION (2) (NOV 09 EXAM)

(i) The criteria for income recognition of services under IAS 18 *Revenue Recognition* are:
- the revenue can be measured reliably
- the stage of completion can be measured reliably
- there is reasonable certainty of payment
- the related costs can be measured reliably.

(ii) It looks like all of the criteria for recognition has been met and therefore a proportion of the revenue should be recognised.

The contract is for two years and at the accounting date it has been running for six months.

Therefore, we should recognise 6/24 × $400,000 = $100,000 of the repairs and maintenance contract.

The balance of the contract ($300,000) would be treated as a liability on the statement of financial position, $200,000 current and $100,000 non-current.

338 DIRECT METHOD (MAY 08 EXAM)

> **Key answer tips**
>
> A straight forward statement of cash flows using the direct method.

Workings:

Receivables cash from customers = 440

(W1)

Opening balance	45
Sales for the year	445
Closing balance	(50)
	440

Cash paid to payables = 235

(W2)

Opening balance	20
Purchases (W3)	235
Closing balance	(30)
	225

(W3)

Purchases =

Cost of material used	220
Closing inventory	40
Opening inventory	(25)
	235

FC's statement of cash flow YE 31 March X7

Direct method:

Cash received from customers	440
Rent received	45
Cash paid to suppliers	(225)
Cash paid to employers	(70)
Other expenses paid	(15)
Cash generated from operations	175

ANSWERS TO SECTION B-TYPE QUESTIONS : SECTION 5

339 GK (NOV 08 EXAM)

> **Key answer tips**
>
> This question requires the student to prepare extracts from the statement of cash flows. It is very straight forward but make sure you only answer the question, more information is given than required and time could be wasted by making addition calculations not needed.

(a) **GK Statement of cash flow for the year ended 31 October 20X8 (Extract)**

Cash flows from operating activities	$000
Profit before tax	2,200
Adjust for:	
Depreciation (1,110 + 882)	1,992
Finance cost	600
Gain on disposal of plant (60 – 35)	(25)
	4,767
Increase in inventory	(250)
Increase in trade receivables	(150)
Decrease in trade payables	(70)
Cash generated from operations	4,297

(b) **GK Statement of cash flow for the year ended 31 October 20X8 (Extract)**

Cash flows from investing activities	$000
Purchase of property, plant and equipment (W1)	(1,977)
Proceeds from sale of Plant and equipment	60
Net cash used in investing activities	(1,917)

Cash flows from financing activities	
Dividends paid	(500)
Issue of share capital	4,500
Redemption of interest bearing borrowings	(4,600)
	(600)

287

(W1)

Non-current assets

	$		$
Bfwd	10,500	Depn (1,110 + 882)	1,992
Bfwd	4,550	Disposal (CV)	35
Additions	1,977	Cfwd	10,000
		Cfwd	5,000
	17,027		17,027

340 BENEFITS OF CASH FLOW (MAY 12 EXAM)

The benefits to users of financial statements of having a statement of cash flows included in them are:

- It can help users assess the liquidity and solvency of an entity. Adequate cash is required to pay debts and dividends when due, the cash flow shows the cash available.
- It helps users assess financial adaptability. If an entity is able to turn inventory into cash it can reinvest in new inventory or activities.
- It can help users to assess future cash flows. Current cash flows can be used to project future cash availability.
- It can assist users in valuing the entity if they use the discounted cash flow model.
- It provides enhanced comparability between entities as cash flows are not subjective and remain the same regardless of the accounting policies used by different entities for the same type of transactions.
- It helps users identify the differences between cash flow and profit. It can help highlight where cash is being generated and where it is being spent. May help indicate problems early on.

Tutorial note

You must make sure you answer the question set and state the benefits to the users and not just the management.

341 INVESTING ACTIVITIES (MAY 13 EXAM)

CFQ Statement of cash flow for the year ended 31 March 20X3 (Extract)

Cash flows from investing activities	$million
Purchase of property, plant and equipment (W1)	(170)
Proceeds from sale of Plant and equipment	45
Purchase of Non-current asset investments W2)	(7)
Purchase of Deferred development expenditure (W3)	(13)
Net cash used in investing activities	(145)

(W1)

Non-current assets – PPE

	$		$
Bfwd	645	Depn	120
		Disposal (CV)	60
Additions	170	Cfwd	635
	815		815

(W2)

Non-current assets – investments

	$		$
Bfwd	107	Revaluation loss	21
Additions	7	Cfwd	93
	114		114

(W3)

Non-current assets – developments

	$		$
Bfwd	24	Amortisation	8
Additions	13	Cfwd	29
	37		37

342 FINANCING ACTIVITES (AUG 13 EXAM)

SF Statement of cash flow for the year ended 31 March 20X3 (Extract)

Cash flows from financing activities	$000
Proceeds from share issue (460 + 82 – 400 – 70)	72
Proceeds from new loan (W2)	49
Repaid of loan	(25)
Payment for finance leases (W1)	(29)
Dividend paid	(19)
Net cash inflow in financing activities	48

(W1)

Finance lease payables

	$		$
Payments	29	B/fwd (60 + 6)	66
		Additions	55
C/fwd (98 + 10)	108	Finance costs	16
	137		137

(W2)

Long term borrowings

	$		$
Payments	25	B/fwd	105
C/fwd	129	Additions	49
	154		154

GROUP COMPANY FINANCIAL ACCOUNTS

343 GOODWILL (NOV 10 EXAM)

(i) The answer is $100,000

Net assets of DN	Date of acquisition
	$000
$1 equity shares	180
Share premium	40
Retained earnings	60
Fair value adjustment – land	70
	350

Goodwill

	$000
Cost of investment (180 × $2.50)	450
Net assets of HB at acquisition (as above)	350
Goodwill	100

(ii) IFRS 3 *Business Combinations* requires that goodwill is calculated and recognised in the Statement of financial position as an intangible non-current asset. Goodwill is not amortised but must be subjected to impairment reviews at least once a year.

HB should record goodwill as $100,000 in its intangible non-current assets and not provide for any amortisation. An impairment review should be carried out on or before 31 August 20X9.

344 INVESTMENTS (NOV 10 EXAM)

(i) The acquisition of 80,000 non-voting preferred shares will not give control or any influence over ABC, therefore this would be classified as a non-current asset investment in HI's financial statements.

(ii) The preferred shares will be ignored as they do not add any influence to the equity shares. The 40,000 equity shares would give a 40% holding. Without any further information, a 40% holding of equity shares would be assumed to give significant influence over the entity and would be classified as an associated entity, according to IAS 28 *Investments in Associates*.

(iii) The 70,000 equity shares will give HI a 70% interest in ABC, this would be sufficient to give control of ABC. As HI would gain control of ABC, ABC would be classified as a subsidiary, according to IAS 27 *Consolidated and Separate Financial Statements*.

Section 6

ANSWERS TO SECTION C-TYPE QUESTIONS

SINGLE COMPANY FINANCIAL ACCOUNTS

345 AF (MAY 05 EXAM)

> **Key answer tips**
>
> This is a straight forward question that requires the preparation of the two of the key financial statements, statement of profit or loss and other comprehensive income and statement of financial position. This question requires you to work through a number of notes prior to the preparation of the statements. Remember the trial balance represents what has already happened and the figures must be adjusted for the inclusion of the notes (i.e. you must consider the double entry for the notes). Most of the adjustments require the usual items, such as depreciation, taxation and interest. The only item that should cause any problem should be the operating lease. Remember with an operating lease the asset is not recognised on the statement of financial position and the amount charged to the statement of profit or loss should be equal each year over the lease period.

AF Statement of profit or loss and other comprehensive income for the year ended 31 March 20X5

	$000
Revenue	8,210
Cost of sales (W1)	(3,957)
Gross profit	4,253
Income from investments	68
Administrative expenses	(1,540)
Distribution costs	(1,590)
Profit from operations	1,191
Finance cost (1,500 × 6%)	(90)
Profit before tax	1,101
Income tax expense (250 + 100)	(350)

	$000
Profit for the period	751
Other comprehensive income:	
Revaluation gain on investments	110
Total comprehensive income for the year	861

AF Statement of financial position as at 31 March 20X5

	$000	$000	$000
Non-current assets			
Property, plant and equipment (3,594 + 1,393)			4,987
Available for sale investments			1,750
Current assets			
Inventory		1,320	
Trade receivables		1,480	
Cash and cash equivalents		822	
			3,622
Total assets			10,359
Equity and liabilities			
Equity			
Share capital		4,500	
Share premium		1,380	
Revaluation reserve (330 + 110)		440	
Retained earnings (W5)		864	
Total equity			7,184
Non-current liabilities			
6% Loan	1,500		
Deferred tax (710 + 100)	810		
Total non-current liabilities			2,310
Current liabilities			
Trade and other payables (W6)	615		
Tax payables	250		
Total current liabilities			865
Total equity and liabilities			10,359

ANSWERS TO SECTION C-TYPE QUESTIONS : SECTION 6

Workings:

			$000	$000
(W1)	**Cost of sales**			
	Cost of goods			3,463
	Add depreciation – buildings (W2)			96
	– plant and equipment (W3)			348
	Operating lease (W4)			50
				3,957

(W2)	**Buildings**			
	Land and building at cost			5,190
	Less: Depreciation for year b/f		1,500	
	Depreciation for year (5,190 – 2,000) × 3%		96	(1,596)
	Carrying value			3,594

(W3)	**Plant and equipment**			
	Plant and equipment cost			3,400
	Depreciation b/fwd		1,659	
	Depreciation for year (3,400 – 1,659) × 20%		348	2,007
	Carrying value			1,393

(W4)	**Operating lease**			
	Total payments (4 × 62,500)		250	
	Allocated evenly over 5 periods (250/5)		50 a year	

Tutorial note

The new lease is an operating lease, therefore the full cost must be charged to the statement of profit or loss over the five years of the lease. The useful economic life of the asset is irrelevant.

(W5)	**Retained earnings**		
	Balance b/fwd		388
	Profit for the year		751
			1,139
	Less: Dividend paid		(275)
			864

(W6)	**Trade and other payables**		
	Trade payables		520
	Operating lease accrual		50
	Finance cost		45
			615

PAPER F1 : FINANCIAL OPERATIONS

346 DZ (MAY 07 EXAM)

> 🔑
>
> **Key answer tips**
>
> This is a more difficult question that requires the preparation of the three key financial statements, statement of profit or loss and other comprehensive income, statement of financial position and statement of changes in equity. This question requires you to work through quite a number of notes prior to the preparation of the statements. Remember the trial balance represents what has already happened and the figures must be adjusted for the inclusion of the notes (i.e. You must consider the double entry for the notes). Many of the adjustments require the usual items, such as inventory, depreciation, taxation and interest. However, you do have a number of more complicated adjustments such as revaluations, disposals of assets, research and development. Be careful to no get bogged down with these and end up spending too much time on the adjustments. If you can't do everything, do what you can, leave it and then move on.

(a) **DZ – Property, plant and equipment**

Cost/valuation	Land	Property Land	Property Buildings	Plant & Equipment	Total
	$000	$000	$000	$000	$000
Balance at 31 March 20X6	1,250	3,500	7,700	4,180	16,630
Disposals	(1,250)	0	0	620	(1,870)
	0	3,500	7,700	3,560	14,760
Revaluation	0	600	(2,000)	0	(1,400)
	0	4,100	5,700	3,560	13,360
Depreciation					
Balance at 31 March 20X6	0	0	1,900	2,840	4,740
Disposals	0	0	0	(600)	(600)
	0	0	1,900	2,240	4,140
Revaluation adjustment	0	0	(1,900)	0	(1,900)
Charge for year	0	0	285	330	615
	0	0	285	2,570	2,855
Carrying value at 31 March 20X7	0	4,100	5,415	990	10,505
Carrying value at 31 March 20X6	1,250	3,500	5,800	1,340	11,890

Workings:

Depreciation

Buildings	5,700 × 5%	=	285

Split:	Production 80%	=	228
	Admin 20%	=	57

Machinery and equipment

Reducing balance = 3,560 − 2,240 = 1,320

1,320 @ 25% = 330

Total production depreciation = 228 + 330 = 558

> *Tutorial note*
>
> *The non-current asset note requires you to show all movements in the cost and depreciation accounts. Remember to show the disposal cost and accumulated depreciation adjustment, the actual proceeds does not appear in this statement. The depreciation will then be calculated for the year based on the assets that existed at the year end. You are also required to show the revaluation adjustment for the land and buildings, remember at the revaluation date all accumulated depreciation must be removed from the account to the revaluation reserve. Depreciation will then begin again at the revalued amount.*

(b) **DZ – Statement of profit or loss and other comprehensive income for the year ended 31 March 20X7**

		$000	$000
Revenue			8,772
Cost of sales	(W1)		(4,377)
Gross profit			4,395
Gain on disposal of non-current asset	(W2)		250
Administrative expenses	(W3)	(948)	
Distribution costs		(462)	(1,410)
Profit from operations			3,235
Finance cost			(160)
Profit before tax			3,075
Income tax expense	(W4)		(728)
Profit for the period			2,347
Other comprehensive income:			
Revaluation of land and buildings			500
Total comprehensive income			2,847

DZ – Statement of financial position at 31 March 20X7

	$000	$000	$000
Non-current assets			
Property, plant and equipment (answer (a))			10,505
Intangible assets – development costs (W5)			198
Current assets			
Inventory (W6)		435	
Trade receivables		1,059	
Cash and cash equivalents		103	
			1,597
Total assets			12,300
Equity and liabilities			
Equity			
Share capital		1,000	
Revaluation reserve		1,850	
Retained earnings		5,121	
Total equity			7,971
Non-current liabilities			
8% loan		2,000	
Deferred tax (W4)		665	
Total non-current liabilities			2,665
Current liabilities			
Trade and other payables (W7)		853	
Tax payable (W4)		811	
Total current liabilities			1,664
Total equity and liabilities			12,300

DZ – Statement of changes in equity for the year ended 31 March 20X7

	Equity shares	Revaluation reserve	Retained earnings	Total
	$000	$000	$000	$000
Balance at 1 April 20X6	1,000	2,100	2,024	5,124
Realised revaluation gain (W8)		(750)	750	0
Revaluation in year		500		500
Profit for period			2,347	2,347
Balance at 31 March 20X7	1,000	1,850	5,121	7,971

Workings:

(W1) **Cost of sales**

	$000
Inventory raw materials at 1 April 20X6	132
Purchases	2,020
	2,152
Less inventory raw materials at 31 March 20X7	(165)
	1,987
Direct labour	912
Production overheads	633
Depreciation	558
Production cost	4,090
Inventory finished goods at 1 April 20X6	240
	4,330
Less inventory finished goods at 31 March 20X7	(270)
Loss on disposal of machinery (W2)	15
Research and development cost (W5)	302
Total	4,377

(W2) Gain on disposal of non-current assets

Land –	Carrying value	1,250	
	Less – receipt	1,500	
	Gain	250	
Machinery –	Carrying value	20	
	Less – receipt	5	
	Loss	(15)	

> **Tutorial note**
>
> *The gain on the sale of the land could be deducted from expenses. However, as it is a material amount, it has been shown separately on statement of profit or loss and other comprehensive income. The loss on the disposal of the machinery has been treated as a cost of sales expense separately but could've been netted off against the gain on the land.*

(W3) Administration expenses

Per trial balance	891
Depreciation	57
	948

(W4) Income tax expense

Income tax for year		811
Previous year balance		25
		836
Deferred tax		
Balance 1 April 20X6	773	
Balance 31 March 20X7	(665)	
		(108)
Statement of profit or loss		728

(W5) Intangible assets – research and development

Cost balance 1 April 20X6	867
Add incurred in year	48
	915
Less amortisation for year at 20%	(183)
Less amortisation b/fwd at 1 April 20X6	(534)
Balance 31 March 20X7	198

Amortisation for the year	183
Research cost	119
Charge to Statement of profit or loss	302

(W6) Inventory

Raw materials	165
Finished goods	270
	435

(W7) Trade and other payables

Trade payables	773
Interest due on loan	80
	853

(W8) Realised gain on disposal

Land disposed of original cost	500
revalued amount	1,250
Realised gain	750

Tutorial note

When a revalued asset is sold the realised gain on disposal must be calculated and released from the revaluation reserve to the retained earnings.

PAPER F1 : FINANCIAL OPERATIONS

347 EY (NOV 07 EXAM)

> **Key answer tips**
>
> This is a more difficult question that requires the preparation of the three key financial statements, statement of profit or loss, statement of financial position and statement of changes in equity. This question is different to anything the examiner has ever set before because you are not given the traditional trial balance and notes to work through. You are required to calculate the figures for the financial statements by using the opening statement of financial position, cash book and notes. This means that for many entries you will need to recreate the ledgers to find out the statement of profit or loss and statement of financial position entries. This question requires the student to have a good understanding of double entry!

EY Statement of financial position at 31 October 20X7

	$000	$000	$000
Non-current assets			
Prop, plant and equipment (W5)		7,729	
Intangibles (W3)		1,100	
			8,829
Current assets			
Inventory	985		
Gross amounts due from customers (W1)	840		
Trade receivables	620		
			2,445
			11,274
Equity and liabilities			
Equity			
Share capital		3,500	
Revaluation reserve (W5)		200	
Retained earnings (SOCIE)		1,164	
			4,864
Non-current liabilities			
Loan notes (W10)	4,760		
Deferred tax (W7)	222		
		4,982	

ANSWERS TO SECTION C-TYPE QUESTIONS : SECTION 6

	$000	$000	$000
Current liabilities			
Trade and other payables	670		
Short term borrowings	208		
Tax payable (W4)	420		
Interest payable (W2)	130		
		1,428	
Total liabilities			6,410
			11,274

EY Statement of profit or loss and other comprehensive income for the year to 31 October 20X7

	$000
Revenue (W12)	8,207
Cost of sales (W11)	(6,133)
Gross profit	2,074
Distribution costs	(730)
Administrative expenses	(500)
Gain on disposal of land	200
Profit	1,044
Finance costs (W2)	(173)
Profit before tax	871
Income tax expense (W13)	(482)
Profit for the period	389
Other comprehensive income	–
Total comprehensive income	389

EY Statement of changes in equity for the year to 31 October 20X7

	Share capital $000	Revaluation reserve $000	Retained earnings $000	Total $000
Balance at 31 October 20X6	3,000	600	1,625	5,225
Realised gain on disposal of land		(400)	400	0
Profit for the period			389	389
Dividends			(750)	(750)
Issue of share capital	500		(500)	0
Balance at 31 October 20X7	3,500	200	1,164	4,864

Workings:

(W1) Government contract

	$000	$000
Contract value		1,400
Costs year 1	600	
Remaining	400	
		(1,000)
		400

Profit to recognize = 600/1000 = 60%

Revenue 1,400 × 60%	840
COS 1,000 × 60%	600
Profit	240

Gross amounts due from customers:

Cost incurred to date	600
Profit recognised	240
	840

(W2) Interest payable

	$000
B/f	117
Paid	(160)
C/f	(130)
Charge	173

(W3) Research & development

	$000
R&D year 1 – no certainty of valuable outcome – expense	300
Artificial wood – expense as not viable	800
	1,100
Amortisation on existing R&D – straight line (1000/5)	200
Total charge to the statement of profit or loss	1,300

ANSWERS TO SECTION C-TYPE QUESTIONS : SECTION 6

> *Tutorial note*
>
> *Under IAS 38 research costs must be written off to the statement of profit or loss immediately and development costs can be capitalised on the statement of financial position, provided that they meet the capitalisation criteria. The artificial wood development cost is not viable, hence does not meet capitalisation criteria and must be written off as an expense to the statement of profit or loss. You will amortise the existing development costs from last year ($1,000) but there will be no amortisation on this year's development costs ($500 above) because production has not yet begun.*

Intangibles

	$000
Cost B/fwd	1,000
Capitalised for this year	500
	1,500
Amortisation B/fwd	(200)
Amortisation on existing R&D – straight line (1000/5)	(200)
Carrying value	1,100

(W4) **Income tax**

	$000
B/f payable	670
Paid	(690)
Increase in prior year liability	20
Current year charge	420
C/f payable	420

(W5) Property, plant and equipment

	Land	Premises 6% SL	Plant 15% RB	Total
	$000	$000	$000	$000
Cost b/f	2,000	1,500	3,800	7,300
Addition		1,600	1,860	3,460
Disposal	(1,000)			(1,000)
	1,000	3,100	5,660	9,760
Depreciation b/f	0	(350)	(760)	(1,110)
	0	(186)	(735)	(921)
	0	(536)	(1,495)	(2,031)
CV c/f	1,000	2,564	4,165	7,729

Revaluation reserve:

	$000
B/f	600
Revaluation realised to retained earnings	(400)
C/f	200
Disposal proceeds	1,200
Revaluation	(400)
Cost	(600)
Profit (Show as a material item)	200

Tutorial note

The revalued land has now been sold. The profit on disposal is calculated based on the difference between proceeds and the book value (revalued amount). The revaluation reserve for the land will then be released into retained earnings.

(W6) Bonus issue 1:6

New shares = 3,000/6 = 500

Transfer from retained reserves nominal value of $500

ANSWERS TO SECTION C-TYPE QUESTIONS : SECTION 6

> *Tutorial note*
>
> *The cash book shows a dividend paid of 25 cents per share and a total of $750. This must therefore represent 3,000 shares. The equity on the statement of financial position has a balance of $3,000, therefore each share must a nominal value of $1 each. The nominal value is then used to account for the bonus issue.*

(W7) Deferred tax

	$000
B/f	180
Increase	42
C/f	222

(W8) Receivables

	$000
B/f	(753)
Received	7,500
C/f	620
Sales	7,367

(W9) Payables

	$000
B/f	573
Paid	3,000
C/f	670
Purchases	3,097

(W10) Loan notes

	$000
B/f	2,260
Additional	2,500
	4,760

(W11) Cost of sales

	$000
Depreciation (W5)	921
Amortisation	200
R&D costs (W3)	1,100
Expenditure on Government contract (W11)	600
Opening inventory	1,200
Closing inventory	(985)
Purchases (W9)	3,097
	6,133

(W12) Revenue

	$000
Sales (W8)	7,367
Government contract (W1)	840
	8,207

(W13) Tax charge

	$000
Increase in prior year charge	20
Current year charge	420
Increase in deferred tax	42
	482

348 FZ (MAY 08 EXAM)

Key answer tips

This is a difficult question that requires the preparation of the three key financial statements, statement of profit or loss, statement of financial position and statement of changes in equity. In part (a) you are required to decide how to treat items (i) and (ii) and then apply your decision to your answer in part (b). This question requires the student to have a good understanding of IFRS 5 for discontinued operations and assets held for sale but still has all of the usual favourites in the notes for adjustments for bad debts, depreciation, taxation, disposals of an asset, interest, share issues and revaluations. A well prepared student could still score well by applying their knowledge to the core areas of the questions, even if their knowledge of IFRS 5 is weak.

ANSWERS TO SECTION C-TYPE QUESTIONS : SECTION 6

(a) (i)
- The sale of the newsagent should be treated under IFRS 5 as a discontinued operation.
- Profit or loss should be shown separately in the statement of profit or loss.
- The assets meet the criteria of assets held for sale.
- Assets should be valued at the lower of carrying value or fair value less costs to sell
- Assets should not be depreciated but held for sale under NCA.

(ii)
- The cost of reorganising can only be treated as a provision under IAS 37 provided it meets the criteria that there is a probable flow of benefit, the amount can be reliably measured and that there is a present obligation (legal or constructive).
- A reorganising or restructuring provision can only be made for direct costs which existed at the reporting date; no provision can be made for future costs of the organisation.
- IAS 37 states staff retraining and relocation costs and investments in new computer systems cannot be included. These costs are deemed be future costs of the organisation
- and not liabilities at the reporting date.

(b) **Statement of profit or loss for FZ for the year ended 31 March 20X8**

	$000
Revenue (10,170 – 772)	9,398
Cost of sales (W1)	(4,363)
Gross profit	5,035
Admin expenses (W1)	(406)
Distribution costs (W1)	(384)
Operating profit	4,245
Finance costs (5% × $1,000)	(50)
Profit before tax	4,195
Income tax (W5)	(1,080)
Profit after tax from continued operations	3,115
Loss from discontinued operations (W2)	(301)
Profit for the period	2,814

Statement of financial position of FZ as at 31 March 20X8

	$000	$000
Non-current assets		
P,P & E (W3)		11,516
Current assets		
Inventory	900	
Trade receivables (929 – 62)	867	
Cash and cash equivalents	853	2,620
Non-current assets held for sale (W4)		4,800
Total assets		18,936
Equity and liabilities		
Share capital		5,000
Share premium		3,000
Revaluation reserve		190
Retained earnings		8,122
		16,312
Non-current liabilities		
Loan notes	1,000	
Deferred tax (197 + 40 increase)	237	
		4,982
Current liabilities		
Payables	417	
Tax	920	
Interest	50	
		1,387
Total Liabilities		18,936

Statement of Changes in Equity FZ YE 31 March 20X8

	Equity Shares	Share Premium	Revaluation Reserve	Retained Earnings	Total
Bal b/f @ 1 April X7	4,000	2,500	190	5,808	12,498
Share issue	1,000	500			1,500
Dividend				(500)	(500)
Profit for period				2,814	2,814
Bal c/f @ 31 March X8	5,000	3,000	190	8,122	16,312

Workings:

(W1)

	Cost of sales Discont	Contin	Admin Expenses Discont	Contin	Distri Costs Discont	Contin
TB	580	3,540	96	344	57	375
Gain on disposal						(10)
Bad debt				62		
Depn – plant		463				
Depn – building		360				
Depn – vehicle						19
Impairment goodwill	300					
Impairment of shop	160					
Total to Statement of profit or loss	**1,040**	**4,363**	**96**	**406**	**57**	**384**

(W2) **Gain on disposal**

	$000
Cost less depreciation	5
Cash received	15
	10

Discontinued activity	$000
Revenue	772
Cost of sales (W1)	(1,040)
Gross loss	(268)
Administration expenses (W1)	(96)
Distribution cost (W1)	(57)
Loss from operations	(421)
Income tax	120
Loss for the period	(301)

Tutorial note

The discontinued loss is shown separately at the bottom of the statement of profit or loss as a total because the note (xi) states minimum disclosure.

(W3) Non-current assets

Cost	Buildings	Plant	Vehicles	Total
Balance 01/04/07	12,000	2,313	147	14,460
Disposal			(57)	(57)
Balance 31/3/08	12,000	2,313	90	14,403
Depreciation				
Balance 01/04/07	720	1,310	67	2,097
Charge for the year –				
Building (3% × 12,000)	360			
Plant (20% × 2,313)		463		
Vehicles (25% × 75)			19	842
Disposal			(52)	(52)
Balance 31/3/08	1,080	1,773	34	2,887
CV 31/3/08	10,920	540	56	11,516

(W4) Non-current assets held for Sale

Newsagent at cost (TB)	6,200
Depreciation	1,240
CV	4,960
Goodwill	300
Fair value	5,000
Less: cost to sell	200
	4,800
Impairment on shop	160
Impairment on goodwill	300
SOFP value (lower)	4,800

ANSWERS TO SECTION C-TYPE QUESTIONS : **SECTION 6**

> *Tutorial note*
>
> *The newsagents shop is treated as an asset held for sale and valued at the lower of CV or net selling price. Therefore, we need to value the shop at $4,800 and the NBV of the assets needs to be reduced by $160 impairment. In addition to this the goodwill relating to the shop will be written off by impairment. This results in a total impairment of $480 to be charged to cost of sales. The asset held for sale will be removed from the non-current asset total and shown separately on the statement of financial position under the current asset total. Assets held for sale should no longer be depreciated.*

(W5) **Taxation**

Charge for the year (SOFP)	920
Increase in deferred tax (237 – 197)	40
Credit for discontinued activity	120
	1,080

349 GZ (NOV 08 EXAM) — Walk in the footsteps of a top tutor

> **Key answer tips**
>
> This is a difficult question that requires the preparation of the three key financial statements, statement of profit or loss and other comprehensive income, statement of financial position and statement of changes in equity. In part a) you are required to prepare quite a complicated non-current asset note. This involved dealing with an asset held for sale and the usual adjustments. This question required knowledge of how to deal with decommissioning costs and you needed to remember that these are debited to the asset account and credited to the provisions. However, it still had all of the usual favourites in the notes for adjustments for depreciation, taxation, disposals of an asset, interest, share issues and leased assets. A well prepared student could still score well by applying their knowledge to the core areas of the questions, even if their knowledge of IFRS 5 is weak. The main thing is to work through the notes logically and not get bogged down with the more difficult areas of the question.

PAPER F1 : FINANCIAL OPERATIONS

> **Tutor's top tips**
>
> You are required to complete the non-current asset note in a suitable format. You should not prepare ledgers or use any other format if you are to gain any marks from this part of the question. Firstly enter all of the easy figures that are given in the trial balance, i.e. Cost and depreciation bought forward. You will find it easier if you split the gold and silver mine as per note (iv) in the question. Next enter any purchases or disposals, remember you are increasing/decreasing the cost/depreciation by the actual amounts for the assets, not the cash proceeds. You have a decommissioning cost in note (ii) to add to the silver mine as this is a condition of the licence and must then adjust for the gold mine (asset held for sale). This is transferred from the non-current asset totals to show separately on the statement of financial position. Finally, calculate this year's depreciation on any assets you have remaining at the end of the year. Remember we do not depreciate assets held for sale.

GZ Financial Statements for the year ended 31 October 20X8

(a) **Note to the financial statements – Property, plant and equipment**

Cost	Silver Mine	Gold Mine	Plant & Equip't	Plant Leased	Total
Balance brought forward	–	2,623	3,025	–	5,648
Purchases	4,096	–	–	900	4,996
Disposal	–	–	(200)	–	(200)
Decommissioning provision	3,230	–	–	–	3,230
Transfer to non-current assets held for sale	–	(2,623)	–	–	(2,623)
Balance carried forward	7,326	–	2,825	900	11,051
Depreciation					
Balance brought forward	–	2,123	370	–	2,493
Disposal	–	–	(195)	–	(195)
Transfer to non-current assets held for sale	–	(2,123)	–	–	(2,123)
Charge for year (W1)	366	–	663	225	1,254
Balance carried forward	366	–	838	225	1,429
Carrying value 31 Oct 20X8	6,960	–	1,987	675	9,622
Carrying value 31 Oct 20X7	–	500	2,655	0	3,155

Gold mine = discontinued (held for sale asset)

Value at lower of:

Net selling price ($520 – $27) = $493 or

Carrying value ($2,623 – $2,123) = $500

Value at $493, impairment of $7 to COS

Decommissioning costs treated as part of the cost of the asset under IAS 16.

Dr   NCA

Cr   Provisions (NCL)

Depreciation see (W1)

Tutor's top tips

The gold mine is treated as an asset held for sale and valued at the lower of CV or net selling price. Therefore, we need to value the gold mine at $493 and the CV of the assets needs to be reduced by $7 impairment. The asset held for sale will be removed from the non-current asset total and shown separately on the statement of financial position under the current asset total.

(b) **GZ Statement of changes in equity for the year ended 31 October 20X8**

	Equity shares	Share premium	Revaluation reserve	Retained earnings	Total
	$000	$000	$000	$000	$000
Balance Bfwd	5,000	0	80	2,810	7,890
Issue of shares	1,400	420	0	0	1,820
Revaluation of investments	0	0	134	0	134
Dividend paid	0	0	0	(550)	(550)
Profit for the period	0	0	0	937	937
Balance Cfwd	6,400	420	214	3,197	10,231

Share issue:

Dr   Suspense $1,820

Cr   Shares (nominal value 1,400 × $1)

Cr   Share premium $420

Revaluation of investments:

Dr   Investments ($2,311 – $2,177) = $134

Cr   Revaluation reserve

> **Tutor's top tips**
>
> When completing the SOCIE you should firstly enter the b/fwd figures for the items from the trial balance. You should then deal with the share issue that needs to be moved from the suspense account. Remember the nominal amount will go into the share capital account and the excess will go into the premium account. Don't forget transfer this year's profit for the period (before comprehensive income) and show the distribution of profits to shareholders.

GZ – Statement of profit or loss and other comprehensive income for the year ended 31 October 20X8

	$000	$000
Revenue		9,600
Cost of sales (W2)		(6,572)
Gross profit		3,028
Administrative expenses	(1,131)	
Distribution costs	(719)	(1,850)
Profit from operations		1,178
Investment income		218
Finance cost (W6)		(131)
Profit before tax		1,265
Income tax expense (W7)		(328)
Profit for the period		937
Other comprehensive income:		
Revaluation gain on investments		134
Total comprehensive income		1,071

GZ – Statement of financial position as at 31 October 20X8

	$000	$000	$000
Non-current assets			
Property, plant and equipment (part a)			9,622
Intangibles (W3)			95
Available for sale investments			2,311
			12,028
Current assets			
Inventory		2,410	
Trade receivables		2,715	
Cash and cash equivalents		2,025	
			7,150
Non-current assets held for sale (part a)			493
Total assets			19,671
Equity and liabilities			
Equity			
Share capital		6,400	
Share premium		420	
Revaluation reserve		214	
Retained earnings		3,197	
Total equity			10,231
Non-current Liabilities			
Deferred tax (W8)		671	
Finance lease (W5)		682	
Provision for decommissioning (W4)		3,230	
Total non-current liabilities			4,583
Current liabilities			
Trade payables		2,431	
Finance lease		113	
Tax payable		375	
Interest payable (W5)		38	
Loan notes (payable 20X9)		1,900	
Total current liabilities			4,857
Total equity and liabilities			19,671

Workings – all figures in $000

(W1) Depreciation for year

Silver mine	7,326 × 5%=	366
Gold mine	Nil as held for sale	
Leased plant	900 fair value × 25% =	225
Plant and equipment	2,825 – (370 – 195) = 2,650 × 25% =	663
Total depreciation		1,254

(W2) Cost of sales

Balance per trial balance	5,245
Depreciation (W1)	1,254
Amortisation of operating licence (W3)	5
Decommissioning cost – excess (W4)	58
Loss on non-current assets held for sale (part a)	7
Loss on disposal of plant (W9)	3
	6,572

(W3) Government Operating Licence (intangible asset)

Balance per trial balance	100
Amortisation for year (100 / 20) to COS	(5)
	95

(W4) Decommissioning provision gold mine

Balance per trial balance	950
Provision utilised in year (cost $1,008)	(950)
	–
Decommissioning expenditure in year	1,008
Less utilised provision	950
COS expense	58

ANSWERS TO SECTION C-TYPE QUESTIONS : SECTION 6

(W5) Finance lease liability

Cost	900
Payments (7 × 160)	1,120
Finance cost	220

Sum of digits, 7 years = 28
n × (n + 1)/2 = (7 × 8)/2

| First 2 years | 31/10/2008 | =7/28 × 220 | 55 |
| | 31/10/2009 | =6/28 × 220 | 47 |

Year to	Cost/balance	Finance charge	Sub total	Paid	Balance
31/10/20X8	900	55	955	(160)	795
31/10/20X9	795	47	842	(160)	682

Total liability $795

NCL $682

CL ($795 − $682) = $113

Tutor's top tips

The payments for the lease are made in arrears and the total liability at the end of the year must be split between current and non-current. This is done by looking one year ahead and to get the non-current liability (how much will we still owe in one year's time?) and then deducting this from the total liability to find the amount that is current.

(W6) Finance cost

Interest due on loan (4% × $1,900) = $76	
Interest paid	38
Accrual ($76 − $38)	38
Finance lease (W5)	55
Statement of profit or loss	131

PAPER F1 : FINANCIAL OPERATIONS

> **Tutor's top tips**
>
> *The finance cost must be based on the amount due for the year. Don't forget to include the finance lease interest here.*

(W7) **Tax expense**

Balance brought forward	13
Tax for current year	375
Decrease in deferred tax	(60)
Statement of profit or loss	328

(W8) **Deferred tax**

Balance brought forward	731
Decrease in the year (credit to statement of profit or loss)	(60)
Statement of financial position	671

(W9) **Loss on disposal non-current asset**

Carrying value of equipment	
Cost	200
Depreciation	(195)
Carrying value	5
Sold for	(2)
Loss on disposal to COS	3

ANSWERS TO SECTION C-TYPE QUESTIONS : SECTION 6

350 JZ (NOV 09 EXAM)

> **Key answer tips**
>
> This is a straight forward, question that requires the preparation of the three key financial statements, statement of profit or loss and other comprehensive income, statement of financial position and statement of changes in equity. In part a) you are required to prepare a non-current asset note, requiring adjustments for a disposal and depreciation. It has all of the usual favourites in the notes for adjustments for depreciation, taxation, disposals of an asset, interest, share issues and construction contract. A well prepared student could still score well by applying their knowledge to the core areas of the question. The only problem students may find is that it is quite time consuming to complete in the required time.

JZ Financial Statements for the year ended 30 September 20X9

(a) **Note to the financial statements – Property, plant and equipment**

Cost/Valuation	Land	Buildings	Plant & Equip't	Total
Balance 01/10/X8	3,500	7,460	3,680	14,640
Purchase	–	–	300	300
Disposal	(600)	–	(720)	(1,320)
Balance 30/09/X9	2,900	7,460	3,260	13,620
Depreciation				
Balance 01/10/X8	–	1,930	1,720	3,650
Disposal	–	–	(720)	(720)
Charge for year (W1 & 3)	–	373	565	938
	–	2,303	1,565	3,868
Carrying value 30/09/X8	3,500	5,530	1,960	10,990
Carrying value 30/09/X9	2,900	5,157	1,695	9,752

321

(b) **JZ Statement of profit or loss and other comprehensive income for the year ended 30 September 20X9**

	$000
Revenue (W7)	7,825
Cost of sales (W1)	(3,190)
Gross profit	4,635
Administrative expenses (W3)	(1,157)
Distribution costs	(405)
Profit disposal of non-current asset (W4)	720
Profit from operations	3,793
Finance costs (W5)	(109)
Profit before tax	3,684
Income tax expense (W2)	(775)
Profit for the year	2,909
Other comprehensive income:	–
Total comprehensive income for the year	2,909

JZ Statement of changes in equity for the year ended 30 September 20X9

	Equity shares $000	Share premium $000	Retained earnings $000	Total $000
Balance at 01/10/X8	1,200	100	2,064	3,364
New share issue (W9)	300	150		450
Statement of profit or loss and other comprehensive income			2,909	2,909
Balance at 30/09/X9	1,500	250	4,973	6,723

JZ Statement of financial position as at 30 September 20X9

	$000	$000
Assets		
Non-current assets		
PPE (part a)		9,752
Current assets		
Inventory	212	
Receivables	937	
Amount due from customers (W6)	15	
Cash and cash equivalents	87	
		1,251
Total assets		11,003
Equity and liabilities		
Capital and reserves		
Equity share capital		1,500
Share premium account		250
Retained earnings		4,973
		6,723
Non-current liabilities		
Long-term borrowings	1,800	
Deferred tax (W2)	600	
Finance lease (W8)	199	
		2,599
Current liabilities		
Trade payables	786	
Finance lease (W8)	60	
Provision for legal claim (45 – 5) (W1)	40	
Accrued interest (W5)	45	
Income tax (W2)	795	
		1,681
Total equity and liabilities		11,003

Workings:

(W1) Cost of sales

	$000
Cost of goods sold (TB)	2,561
Depreciation on P & E (25% × $2,260)	565
Construction contract (W6)	69
Reduction in provision from $45 to $40	(5)
	3,190

NB: Carrying value of P & E = cost $3,260 − depreciation ($1,720 − $720) = $2,260

> *Tutorial note*
>
> The question is not clear how to depreciate the leased plant and machinery. In the answer above we have depreciated it in the same way as the purchased plant and machinery but it could have been written off over the lease period of 6 years. This would have given a total depreciation charge of $490 for the purchased P & E and $50 for the lease ($300/6).

(W2) Income tax

	$000
Income tax on profits for the year	795
Deferred tax decrease ($620 − $600)	(20)
	775

(W3) Administration expenses

	$000
TB	784
Depreciation on building (5% × $7,460)	373
	1,157

(W4) Loss on disposal of non-current assets

	$000
Land value	600
Proceeds	1,320
Profit	720

> **Tutorial note**
>
> JZ has also disposed of plant and equipment but no profit or loss has been made. This is because they did not receive any proceeds and the asset had a carrying value of zero at the disposal date.

(W5) Finance cost

Interest due on loan (5% × $1,800) = $90

Interest paid	45
Accrual	45

	$000
Interest due on loan	90
Interest on finance lease (W8)	19
	109

(W6) Government contract

	$000	$000
Contract value		300
Costs year 1	74	
Remaining cost to complete	124	
		(198)
Overall profitable		102

Profit to recognise = 35%	
Revenue 300 × 35% =	105
COS 198 × 35%	69
Profit	36

Gross amounts due from customers:	
Cost incurred to date	74
Profit recognised	36
Less amounts invoiced	(95)
	15

> **Tutorial note**
>
> We are making the assumption the amounts received from customers on the trial balance equals the amount invoiced to customers.

(W7) Revenue

	$000
TB	7,720
Construction contract (W6)	105
	7,825

(W8) Finance lease

Year to	Cost/balance	Paid	Sub total	Finance Charge 7.93%	Balance
30/09/X9	300	(60)	240	19	259
30/09/Y0	259	(60)	199	16	215

Current liability = $60 (payment)

Non-current liability = $199 (total liability at 30/09/X9 $259 less payment $60)

> **Tutorial note**
>
> It is important to identify payments are made in advance for the lease, hence deducted each year before interest is calculated.

(W9) Share issue

	$000
300 issued at $1	300
Premium 50% × 200	150
Total value of issue	450

ANSWERS TO SECTION C-TYPE QUESTIONS : SECTION 6

351 EZ (MAY 10 EXAM)

> **Key answer tips**
>
> This is the first question written for the new syllabus by your examiner. It is a straight forward question that requires the preparation of the three key financial statements, statement of profit or loss and other comprehensive income, statement of changes in equity and statement of financial position. This question requires you to work through a number of notes prior to the preparation of the statements. Remember the trial balance represents what has already happened and the figures must be adjusted for the inclusion of the notes (i.e. you must consider the double entry for the notes). Most of the adjustments require the usual items, such as depreciation, taxation and interest. The only items that may cause any problems could be the operating lease and the impairment on the land. Remember with an operating lease the asset is not recognised on the statement of financial position and the amount charged to the statement of profit or loss should be equal each year over the lease period. When dealing with the impairment, remember to charge the impairment to any previous revaluations first to reduce the reserve to nil and then charge any excess to a suitable expense category in the statement of profit or loss.

EZ Statement of profit or loss and other comprehensive income for the year ended 31 March 20Y0

	$000
Revenue	720
Cost of sales (W1)	(467)
Gross profit	253
Administrative expenses (W7)	(211)
Distribution costs (W8)	(93)
Loss on revaluation of land (W3)	(15)
Loss from operations	(66)
Finance costs (W5)	(10)
Loss before tax	(76)
Income tax expense (W2)	(8)
Loss for the year	(84)
Other comprehensive income:	
Revaluation loss on land (W3)	(10)
Total comprehensive loss for the year	(94)

EZ Statement of changes in equity for the year ended 31 March 20Y0

	Equity shares	Share premium	Revaluation reserve	Retained earnings	Total
	$000	$000	$000	$000	$000
Balance at 31 March 20X9	400	200	10	181	791
New share issue (W10)	200	100			300
Statement of profit or loss and other comprehensive income			(10)	(84)	(94)
Dividends paid				(92)	(92)
Balance at 31 March 20Y0	600	300	0	5	905

EZ Statement of financial position as at 31 March 20Y0

	$000	$000
Assets		
Non-current assets		
PPE (W3)		960
Current assets		
Inventory	112	
Receivables (W6)	150	
Cash and cash equivalents	22	
		284
Total assets		1,244
Equity and liabilities		
Capital and reserves		
Equity share capital		600
Share premium account		300
Revaluation reserve		0
Retained earnings		5
		905
Non-current liabilities		
Long-term borrowings	250	
Deferred tax (30 – 10) (W2)	20	
		270
Current liabilities		
Trade payables	32	
Accrued interest and lease (W5 & W9)	19	
Income tax (W2)	18	
		69
Total equity and liabilities		1,244

ANSWERS TO SECTION C-TYPE QUESTIONS : SECTION 6

Workings:

(W1) Cost of sales

	$000
Cost of goods sold (TB)	418
Depreciation (W3)	44
Loss on sale of plant (W4)	5
	467

NB: Loss on land revaluation of $15 may also have been included here.

(W2) Income tax

	$000
Income tax on profits for the year	18
Deferred tax decrease	(10)
	8

(W3) Tangible non-current assets

	Land $000	PPE $000	Total $000
Cost or valuation:			
At 31 March 20X9	700	480	1,180
Revaluation	(25)	–	(25)
Disposal	–	(37)	(37)
At 31 March 20Y0	675	443	1,118
Accumulated depreciation:			
At 31 March 20X9	–	144	144
Charge for year	–	44	44
Disposal	–	(30)	(30)
Revaluation	–	–	–
At 31 March 20Y0	0	158	158
Carrying value:			
At 31 March 20X9	700	336	1,036
At 31 March 20Y0	675	285	960

The loss on land of $25 will be charged first against the revaluation reserve to reduce it to nil ($10) and then the balance will be expenses to the statement of profit or loss ($15).

Depreciation on PPE = 10% × $443 = $44.

(W4) Loss on disposal of non-current assets

Equipment carrying value	7
Less proceeds	2
Loss	(5)

(W5) Finance cost

Interest due on loan (4% × $250) = $10

Interest paid	0
Accrual	10

(W6) Receivables

	$000
TB	275
Irrecoverable debt written off	(125)
	150

(W7) Administration expenses

	$000
TB	86
Irrecoverable debt written off	125
(may have been shown a separate item in P&L)	
	211

(W8) Distribution costs

	$000
TB	69
Lease (W9)	24
	93

(W9) Operating lease

	$000
Total payments (24 × $2,500)	60
Total life of the lease in months	30
Current year charge (60/30 × 12)	24
Amount paid already (TB)	15
Accrual	9

(W10) Share issue

	$000
200 issued at $1	200
Premium 50% × 200	100
Total value of issue	300

ANSWERS TO SECTION C-TYPE QUESTIONS : SECTION 6

352 XB (NOV 10 EXAM) — Walk in the footsteps of a top tutor

> **Key answer tips**
>
> This is a straight forward question that requires the preparation of the three key financial statements, statement of profit or loss and other comprehensive income, statement of changes in equity and statement of financial position. This question requires you to work through a number of notes prior to the preparation of the statements. Most of the adjustments require the usual items, such as depreciation, taxation and interest. The main item that may cause a problem is the calculation of the taxation in part a. It is important that you calculate the profit before tax on the statement of profit or loss first, as this will be your starting point to calculate the taxable profit. Don't forget to calculate the deferred tax as well as the current tax. This will represent the difference between the accounting book value and tax base of non-current assets.

> **CIMA examiner comments**
>
> This question produced some very good answers with some candidates scoring full marks. However a considerable number of candidates lost marks on the taxation calculations. Some ignored tax, even though the question highlighted the fact that it was worth 8 marks. Most answers attempted either deferred tax calculations or current tax calculations, but few attempted both.

(a) **XB – Statement of profit or loss and other comprehensive income for the year ended 31 October 20X9**

		$000
Revenue		690
Cost of sales	(W6)	(323)
Gross profit		367
Administrative expenses	(W7)	(202)
Distribution costs		(62)
Profit from operations		103
Finance cost	(W5)	(6)
Profit before tax		97
Income tax expense	(W4)	(34)
Profit for the period		63
Other comprehensive income:		–
Total comprehensive income for the year		63

(b) **XB – Statement of financial position at 31 October 20X9**

	$000	$000
Non-current assets		
Property, plant and equipment (W3)		882
Current assets		
Inventory	18	
Trade receivables	109	
Cash and cash equivalents	216	
		343
Total assets		1,225
Equity and liabilities		
Equity		
Share capital	630	
Share premium	99	
Retained earnings	181	
Total equity		910
Non-current liabilities		
Long-term borrowings	200	
Deferred tax (W2)	7	
Total non-current liabilities		207
Current liabilities		
Trade payables (77 – 3)	74	
Tax payables (W1)	31	
Interest accrual (W5)	3	
		108
Total equity and liabilities		1,225

XB – Statement of changes in equity for the year ended 31 October 20X9

	Equity shares $000	Share premium $000	Retained earnings $000	Total $000
Balance at 1 November 20X8	300	0	168	468
Share issue (W8)	330	99		429
Profit for the year			63	63
Dividends paid			(50)	(50)
Balance at 31 October 20X9	630	99	181	910

ANSWERS TO SECTION C-TYPE QUESTIONS : SECTION 6

Workings:

(W1) Taxation charge for the year

	$000
Profit for the year before tax	97
Add back:	
Entertaining costs	12
Political donations	5
Depreciation charge for the year (W3)	86
Less: tax depreciation (23 + 55)	(78)
Taxable profit	122
× 25%	31

Tutor's top tips

It is important you work through the statement of profit or loss up to the line profit before tax before you try to attempt the tax calculation. The profit before tax will be your starting point in order to calculate the taxable profit. Remember to check the tax rules for your country before making the adjustments.

Tax depreciation	Plant & Equipment $000
Balance at 31 October 20X8	90
Tax depreciation at 25% on balance b/fwd	(23)
Addition during the year	110
Tax depreciation at 50% on addition only	(55)
Balance at 31 October 20X9	122

Tutor's top tips

The tax rules of the country allow 50% relief for purchases made in the year but only 25% on the opening tax balance for assets acquired in previous years.

(W2) Deferred taxation

	Accounting CV $000	Tax Base $000	Difference $000	X 25% $000
Balance at 31 October 20X9 (W1) and (W3)	152	122	30	7

> **Tutor's top tips**
>
> Remember, deferred tax is calculated based on the difference between the carrying value in the accounts and the tax base. We are only interested in the plant and equipment because we do not depreciate land.

(W3) **PPE**

	Land	Plant & Equipment	Total
Cost/valuation	$000	$000	$000
Balance at 31 October 20X8	730	320	1,050
Additions	–	110	110
Balance at 31 October 20X9	760	430	1,160
Depreciation			
Balance at 31 October 20X8	0	192	192
Charge for year	0	86	86
Balance at 31 October 20X9	0	278	278
Carrying value at 31 October 20X9	730	152	882
Carrying value at 31 October 20X8	730	128	858

Depreciation on plant and equipment = 20% × 430 = 86 (COS)

(W4) **Taxation**

	$000
Tax estimate (W1)	31
Under-provision (TB)	6
Deferred tax decrease (10 – 7)(W2)	(3)
Charge to the statement of profit or loss	34
Current tax (CL)(W1)	31
Deferred tax (NCL)(W2)	7

Tutor's top tips

The tax estimate for the year represents the current liability on the SOFP and the cumulative deferred tax provision represents the non-current liability on the SOFP. Only the movement in deferred tax will show on the statement of profit or loss.

(W5) **Finance cost**

	$000
Loan $200 × 3%	6
Amount paid on TB	3
Accrual made	3

(W6) **Cost of sales**

	$000
TB	237
Depreciation of PPE (W3)	86
	323

(W7) **Administration expenses**

	$000
TB	185
Donations on TB	5
Entertaining costs on TB	12
	202

Tutor's top tips

The adjustments made to the administration expenses relate to the other costs in the trial balance. The most sensible place to put these costs would be administration.

(W8) **Share issue**

	$000
Share capital 330 × $1	330
Share premium 330 × 30%	99
Proceeds from issue	429

PAPER F1 : FINANCIAL OPERATIONS

353 MN (MAY 11 EXAM)

> **Key answer tips**
>
> This is a difficult question that requires the preparation of the three key financial statements, statement of profit or loss, statement of financial position and statement of changes in equity. This question requires the student to have a good understanding of IFRS 5 for discontinued operations and assets held for sale but still has all of the usual favourites in the notes for adjustments for, depreciation, taxation and interest. A well prepared student could still score well by applying their knowledge to the core areas of the questions, even if their knowledge of IFRS 5 is weak.

> **CIMA examiner comments**
>
> This question produced some very good answers with some candidates scoring full marks. However a considerable number of candidates lost marks on the discontinued operation and warranty calculations.

MN – Statement of profit or loss and other comprehensive income for the year ended 31 March 20X9

Continued operations

		$000
Revenue (1,120 – 80)		1,040
Cost of sales	(W5)	(553)
Gross profit		487
Administrative expenses (160 – 40)		(120)
Distribution costs (170 – 90)		(80)
Profit from operations		287
Finance cost	(W4)	(12)
Profit before tax		275
Income tax expense	(W3)	(72)
Profit for the period from continuing operations		203
Discontinued operations		
Loss for the period from discontinued operations (W6)		(189)
Other comprehensive income:		
Revaluation gain on investments		–
Total comprehensive income for the year		14

ANSWERS TO SECTION C-TYPE QUESTIONS : SECTION 6

> *Tutorial note*
>
> *Remember you must remove the elements of the discontinued operations from the main body of the statement of profit or loss. The discontinued operation will be summarised as one line at the bottom of the statement of profit or loss.*

MN – Statement of financial position as at 31 March 20X9

	$000	$000
Non-current assets		
Property, plant and equipment (W1)		1,823
Current assets		
Inventory	65	
Trade receivables	101	
		166
Non-current assets held for sale (W2)		176
Total assets		2,165
Equity and liabilities		
Equity		
Share capital	600	
Share premium	200	
Retained earnings	761	
Total equity		1,561
Non-current liabilities		
Long-term borrowings	300	
Deferred tax (W3)	78	
		378
Total non-current liabilities		
Current liabilities		
Trade payables	51	
Tax payables (W3)	67	
Provision for warranty (W7)	82	
Bank overdraft	14	
Interest accrual (W4)	12	
		226
Total equity and liabilities		2,165

PAPER F1 : FINANCIAL OPERATIONS

MN – Statement of changes in equity for the year ended 31 March 20X9

	Share capital	Share premium	Retained earnings	Total
	$000	$000	$000	$000
Balance at 1 April 20X8	600	200	777	1,577
Profit for the year			14	14
Dividends paid			(30)	(30)
Balance at 31 March 20X9	600	200	761	1,561

Workings:

(W1) PPE – continuing operations

Cost/valuation	Land	Building	Plant & Equipment	Total
	$000	$000	$000	$000
Balance at 31 March 20X8	1,220	700	240	2,160
Balance at 31 March 20X9	1,220	700	240	2,160
Depreciation				
Balance at 31 March 20X8	0	140	142	282
Charge for year	0	35	20	55
Balance at 31 March 20X9	0	175	162	337
Carrying value at 31 March 20X9	1,220	525	78	1,823
Carrying value at 31 March 20X8	1,220	560	98	1,878

Depreciation on building = 5% × cost $700 = 35 (COS)

Depreciation on plant and equipment = 20% × (240 – 142) = 20 (COS)

(W2) PPE – discontinuing operations

Cost/valuation	Land $000	Building $000	Plant & Equipment $000	Total $000
Balance at 31 March 20X8	150	40	60	250
Balance at 31 March 20X9	150	40	60	250
Depreciation				
Balance at 31 March 20X8	0	20	35	55
Charge for year	0	2	5	7
Balance at 31 March 20X9	0	22	40	62
Carrying value at 31 March 20X9	150	18	20	188
Carrying value at 31 March 20X8	150	20	25	195

Depreciation on building = 5% × cost $40 = 2 (COS)

Depreciation on plant and equipment = 20% × (60 – 35) = 5 (COS)

These assets are now classified as held for sale, i.e. valued lower of carrying value ($188) or net selling price ($176).

Therefore, these assets will be valued at $176.

Impairment of $12 (188 – 176) will be charged to COS.

(W3) Taxation – continued operations

	$000
Tax estimate (67 + 10)	77
Under-provision (TB)	–
Deferred tax decrease (83 – 78)	(5)
Charge to the statement of profit or loss	72
Current tax (CL)	67
Deferred tax (NCL)	78

Tutorial note

Don't forget you are trying to work out the tax charge in the statement of profit or loss for the continued operation. The amount in the trial balance represents the amount due, i.e. 67, this is net of the refund due on the discontinued operation of 10.

(W4) Finance cost

	$000
Loan $300 × 4%	12
Accrual made (not shown as paid on TB)	

(W5) Cost of sales – continued operations

	$000
TB (622 – 130)	492
Depreciation of PPE (W1)	55
Increase in warranty provision (W7)	6
	553

(W6) Loss from discontinued operations

	$000
Revenue	80
Cost of sales	(130)
Administration expenses	(40)
Distribution costs	(90)
Depreciation for the year (W2)	(7)
Impairment (W2)	(12)
Tax refund	10
Loss for the year	(189)

(W7) Provision for warranty

	$000
190 × 10%	19
20 × 15%	3
80 × 75%	60
Balance at 31 March 20X9 (SOFP)	82
Balance at 31 March 20X8	76
Increase to COS in IS (82 – 76)	6

ANSWERS TO SECTION C-TYPE QUESTIONS : SECTION 6

354 ZY (SEP 11 EXAM)

> **Key answer tips**
>
> This is a straight forward question that requires the preparation of the three key financial statements, statement of profit or loss, statement of financial position and statement of changes in equity. This question requires the student to have an understanding of IAS 2 and IAS 10 but still has all of the usual favourites in the notes for adjustments for, depreciation, taxation and interest. The finance lease was very similar to previous questions and as long as students had revised this topic, it should not have caused them any problems. The redeemable preference shares were unusual; however, students could still score well if they didn't remember how to deal with them.

> **CIMA examiner comments**
>
> This question produced some very good answers with some candidates scoring full marks. However a considerable number of candidates lost marks on the finance lease, the cumulative redeemable preferred shares and inventory adjustments.

ZY – Statement of profit or loss and other comprehensive income for the year ended 30 June 20X1

		$000	$000
Revenue (W6)	(W6)		2,054
Cost of sales	(W3)		(1,136)
Gross profit			918
Administrative expenses	(W3)	386	
Distribution costs		221	(607)
Profit from operations			311
Finance cost	(W8)		(29)
Profit before tax			282
Income tax expense	(W4)		(64)
Profit for the period from continuing operations			218

ZY Statement of financial position at 30 June 20X1

		$000	$000
Non-current assets			
Property, plant and equipment	(W1)		1,385
Current assets			
Inventory	(W9)	385	
Trade receivables (W5)	(W6)	202	
Cash and cash equivalents		229	816
Total assets			2,201
Equity and liabilities			
Equity			
Share capital		500	
Other components of equity		490	
Retained earnings		416	
Total equity			1,406
Non-current liabilities			
Long term borrowings		320	
4% Cumulative, Redeemable Preferred shares		150	
Finance lease	(W7)	78	
Deferred tax	(W4)	38	
Total non-current liabilities			586
Current liabilities			
Trade payables		120	
Tax payable	(W4)	56	
Finance lease	(W7)	22	
Interest payable	(W8)	11	
Total current liabilities			209
Total equity and liabilities			2,201

ZY – Statement of changes in equity for the year ended 30 June 20X1

	Equity shares $000	Share Premium $000	Revaluation reserve $000	Retained earnings $000	Total $000
Balance at 1 July 20W0	500	270	220	288	1,278
New share issue					
Profit for period				218	218
Dividend paid				(90)	(90)
Balance at 30 June 20X1	500	270	220	416	1,406

Workings:

(W1) **PPE**

Cost/valuation	Property $000	Plant & Equipment $000	Vehicle Lease $000	Total $000
Balance at 1 July 20W0	844	864	0	1,708
Addition			120	120
Disposal		(95)		(95)
Balance at 30 June 20X1	844	769	120	1733
Depreciation				
Balance at 1 July 20W0	8	249	0	257
Disposal		(95)		(95)
Charge for year (W3)	8	154	24	186
Balance at 30 June 20X1	16	308	24	348
Carrying value at 30 June 20X1	828	461	96	1,385
Carrying value at 30 June 20W0	836	615	0	1,451

Property charge = $844 × 1% = $8

Plant and equipment charge = $769 × 20% = $154

Finance lease = $120 × 20% = $24

(W2) **Gain on disposal**

	$000
Cost less depreciation	0
Cash received	10
Gain on disposal	10

(W3)

	Cost of sales $000	Administration $000
Trial balance		338
Inventory b/f	358	
Purchases	987	
Closing inventory (W9)	(385)	
Gain on disposal NCA (W2)	(10)	
Irrecoverable debt (W5)		48
Depreciation (W1)	186	
	1,136	386

(W4) Tax

	$000
Balance b/f	15
Current year estimate	56
Decrease in deferred tax (45 – 38)	7
Charge to the statement of profit or loss	64
Current tax (CL)	56
Deferred tax (NCL)	38

(W5) Trade receivables

	$000
Trial balance	280
Less bad debt (W3)	(48)
Less goods on sale or return	(30)
	202

Tutorial note

The bad debt must be written off as per IAS 10, as an adjusting event, i.e. evidence has arose to give information of conditions to suggest the amount will no longer be recoverable.

(W6) Revenue

	$000
Trial balance	2,084
Less goods on sale or return	(30)
	2,054

ANSWERS TO SECTION C-TYPE QUESTIONS : SECTION 6

(W7) Finance lease

Year to	Cost/balance	Finance Charge 7.93%	Paid	Balance
30/06/X1	120	10	(30)	100
30/06/X2	100	8	(30)	78

Current liability = $100 − $78 = $22 (total liability at the end of 30/06/X1 less NCL)

Non-current liability = $78 (amount owing at the end of 30/06/X2)

(W8) Finance cost

	$000
Interest on long term borrowings ($320 × 5%)	16
Finance charge on lease (W7)	10
Dividend on Preferred shares ($150 × 4% × 6/12)	3
Charge to the statement of profit or loss	29

Amount paid on TB $8

Accrual on SOFP for loan interest of $8 and preference dividend of $3 = $11

> **Tutorial note**
>
> Don't forget the redeemable preference shares are treated as liabilities, hence the dividend treated as a finance cost and NOT a distribution of retained earnings in the SOCIE. The shares were issued on 1 January 20X1 and therefore we only need to accrue for a dividend for six months.

(W9) Inventory @ 30 June 20X1

	$000
Balance @ 30 June 20X1	390
Inventory write down	(20)
Sale or return goods	15
Adjusted balance 30 June 20X1	385

> **Tutorial note**
>
> The inventory must be valued at the lower of cost $100 or NRV $80 ($110 − $30). Therefore, we must write the inventory down by $20.

PAPER F1 : FINANCIAL OPERATIONS

355 ABC (NOV 11) *Walk in the footsteps of a top tutor*

Key answer tips

This is a straight forward question that requires the preparation of the three key financial statements, statement of profit or loss, statement of financial position and statement of changes in equity. This question requires the student to have an understanding of IAS 10 and IAS 10 but still has all of the usual favourites in the notes for adjustments for, depreciation, disposal of an asset, taxation and interest. The construction contracts may have caused students a problem, especially as one was profitable and one was a loss making contract; however, students could still score well if they didn't remember how to deal with them.

CIMA examiner comments

This question produced some very good answers with some candidates scoring full marks. However a considerable number of candidates were unable to prepare correct calculations for the construction contracts. Some candidates also seemed unaware that the figures calculated had to be included in the financial statements.

ABC – Statement of profit or loss and other comprehensive income for the year ended 30 September 20X1

		$000	$000
Revenue	(W7)		15,900
Cost of sales	(W3)		10,931
Gross profit			4,969
Administrative expenses	(W3)	(1,045)	
Distribution costs	(W3)	(590)	(1,635)
Profit from operations			3,334
Finance cost	(W5)		(115)
Profit before tax			3,219
Income tax expense	(W6)		(944)
Profit for the period			2,275

ABC – Statement of Financial Position at 30 September 20X1

		$000	$000
Non-current assets			
Property, plant and equipment	(W2)		8,948
Current assets			
Inventory		310	
Gross amounts due from customers for contract work	(W1)	490	
Trade receivables	(W8)	785	
Cash and cash equivalents		440	
			2,025
Total assets			10,973
Equity and liabilities			
Equity			
Share capital		2,500	
Share premium		1,500	
Retained earnings		2,652	
Total equity			6,652
Non-current liabilities			
Long term borrowings		2,300	
Deferred tax	(W6)	269	
Total non-current liabilities			2,569
Current liabilities			
Trade payables		235	
Tax payable	(W6)	910	
Gross amounts due to customers for contract work	(W1)	550	
Interest payable	(W5)	57	
Total current liabilities			1,752
Total equity and liabilities			10,973

ABC – Statement of changes in equity for the year ended 30 September 20X1

	Equity shares $000	Share Premium $000	Retained Earnings $000	Total $000
Balance at 1 October 2011	2,500	1,500	627	4,627
Statement of profit or loss and other comprehensive income for year			2,275	2,275
Dividend paid			(250)	(250)
Balance at 30 September 2011	2,500	1,500	2,652	6,652

Workings:

(W1) Construction Contracts

		Contract 1		Contract 2
Overall profitability test		$000		$000
Revenue		11,000		8,000
Total cost	(3,750 + 5,400)	9,150	(2,250 + 6,750)	9,000
Profit/(loss)		1,850		(1,000)
Statement of profit or loss				
Revenue	(40% × 11,000)	4,400	(25% × 8,000)	2,000
Cost of sales	(40% × 9,150)	(3,660)	(25% × 9,000)	2,250
Profit/(Loss)		740		(250)
Expected loss on rest of contract				(750)
Total loss on Contract 2				(1,000)
Statement of financial position				
Cost incurred to date		3,750		2,250
Profit/(loss)		740		(1,000)
Cash received from clients		(4,000)		(1,800)
Amounts due from/(to) clients		490		(550)

ANSWERS TO SECTION C-TYPE QUESTIONS : **SECTION 6**

Tutor's top tips

Many students panic when they see a construction contract in a question. This question had two!

The key to success with a construction contract is to look at each contract individually and decide how it should be dealt with.

Step one: Establish whether the contract is profitable overall.

Step two: If the contract is profitable take a % of revenue and total cost to the statement of profit or loss. If the contract is a loss making one take a % of revenue to the statement of profit or loss but the cost must be amount required to ensure the whole of the loss is recognised immediately.

Step three: Identify the SOFP figures.

Tutor's top tips

Contract one was a profitable one, hence a % of overall revenue and total cost was recognised. These amounts are included in the usual revenue and cost of sales lines.

Tutor's top tips

Contract two was a loss making contract, hence a % of overall revenue is recognised but the cost of sales must be the balancing amount to ensure the total loss is recognised immediately. Therefore, if revenue is $8,000 × 25% = $2,000 and the total loss is $1,000, we must recognise cost of sales to be $3,000.

Tutor's top tips

Don't forget if the contract is profitable we recognise **a % of the profit** but if it is a loss making contract we **recognise all of the loss.**

(W2) Non-current assets

Cost	Plant and equipment	Buildings	Total
Balance b/fwd	4,930	11,000	15,930
Disposal	(75)	–	(75)
Balance c/fwd	4,855	11,000	15,855
Depreciation			
Balance b/fwd	2,156	3,750	5,906
Disposal	(65)	–	(65)
Charge for the year	691	375	1,066
Balance c/fwd	2,782	4,125	6,907
Carrying value b/fwd	2,774	7,250	10,024
Carrying value c/fwd	2,073	6,875	8,948

Depreciation on the building = $7,500 × 5% = $375

Depreciation on the plant and equipment = $2,764 × 25% = 691

Tutor's top tips

This question did not require the full preparation of the PPE note and students could approach the workings for the $8,948 in a different way.

When preparing the carrying value do not forget to remove the disposal before calculating this year's depreciation charge on the plant and equipment, i.e. cost after disposal = $4,855 – depreciation after disposal $2,156 – 65 = $2,091. Therefore, the carrying value to use for the depreciation charge for the year = cost $4,855 – depreciation of $2,091 = $ 2,764

ANSWERS TO SECTION C-TYPE QUESTIONS : SECTION 6

(W3)

	Cost of sales $000	Administration $000	Distribution $000
Trial balance	3,210	1,020	590
Depreciation – buildings (W2)	375		
Depreciation – plant and equipment (W2)	691		
Irrecoverable debt (W8)		25	
Gain on disposal of P&E (W4)	(5)		
Construction contract 1 (W1)	3,660		
Construction contract 2 (W1)	3,000		
Totals	10,931	1,045	590

(W4) **Plant and equipment disposal**

	$000
Carrying value of asset (75 – 65) (W2)	10
Proceeds	(15)
Profit on disposal	5

(W5) **Interest**

	$000
Finance cost – interest due 2,300 × 5% =	115
Paid (TB)	58
Accrual – current liability	57

> *Tutor's top tips*
>
> *The interest charged to the statement of profit or loss must be the due amount for the year. The trial balance only shows an amount of $58 being paid and therefore we are required to make an accrual or the difference. This accrual will increase the interest expense to the required amount for the year and show as a current liability on the SOFP.*

(W6) **Tax**

Statement of profit or loss tax expense	$000
Balance b/f	15
Estimate for the year	910
Increase in deferred tax	19
	944

351

Statement of financial position	$000
Current liability – tax estimate	910
Non-current liability	
Provision deferred tax b/fwd	250
Increase for the year	19
Provision deferred tax c/fwd	269

Tutor's top tips

The tax expense for the year charged to the statement of profit or loss consists of three elements, the amount of the TB (this is an under-provision from previous years), this year's estimate and the movement on the deferred tax account.

*The current liability **is always this year's estimate** and the non-current liability should be the **cumulative deferred tax provision**.*

(W7) **Revenue**

	$000
Sales revenue	9,500
Construction contract 1 revenue (W1)	4,400
Construction contract 2 revenue (W1)	2,000
Profit on disposal	15,900

(W8) **Receivables**

	$000
TB	810
Irrecoverable debt	(25)
	785

Tutor's top tips

On 1 August 20X1, ABC was informed that one of its customers, EF, had ceased trading. The liquidators advised ABC that it was very unlikely to receive payment of any of the $25,000 due from EF at 30 September 20X1. This should be treated as an adjusting event as per IAS 10. Although, ABC didn't find out until after the year end that EF had ceased trading they are required to account for the irrecoverable debt to ensure the receivables shows the correct recoverable amount for the accounting date.

ANSWERS TO SECTION C-TYPE QUESTIONS : SECTION 6

356 RTY (MAR 12)

> **Key answer tips**
>
> This is a very similar question to the May 2007 exam question DZ, requiring the preparation of the three key statements; statement of profit or loss and other comprehensive income, statement of changes in equity and statement of financial position. This question is quite heavily weighted with non-current asset notes requiring adjustments for depreciation, two disposals and a revaluation. It also includes an intangibles note dealing with research and development. Although the usual adjustments were still there for interest, irrecoverable debts and taxation, this question may have been more time consuming than recent 25 mark questions.

> **CIMA examiner comments**
>
> This question produced fewer good answers than usual with no candidate scoring full marks. A considerable number of candidates were unable to prepare correct calculations for the property, plant and equipment and depreciation charge for the year. Many candidates were unable to correctly deal with the research and development expenditure and amortisation.

		$000	$000
Revenue			9,320
Cost of sales	(W3)		(6,059)
Gross profit			3,261
Administrative expenses	(W3)	(1,225)	
Distribution costs	(W3)	(679)	(1,904)
Profit from operations			1,357
Finance cost	(W5)		(137)
Profit before tax			1,220
Income tax expense	(W6)		(755)
Profit for the period			465
Other comprehensive income			
Revaluation of property	(W7)		1,240
Total comprehensive income for the period			1,705

RTY – Statement of Financial Position at 31 January 20X2

		$000	$000
Non-current assets			
Property, plant and equipment	(W1)		14,877
Development expenditure	(W2)		272
			15,149
Current assets			
Inventory		330	
Trade receivables	(W8)	1,428	
Cash and cash equivalents		142	
			1,900
Total assets			17,049
Equity and liabilities			
Equity			
Share capital		1,375	
Share premium		2,750	
Retained earnings		3,912	
Revaluation reserve		3,340	
Total equity			11,377
Non-current liabilities			
Long term borrowings		2,740	
Deferred tax	(W6)	1,019	
Total non-current liabilities			3,759
Current liabilities			
Trade payables		1,080	
Tax payable	(W6)	765	
Interest payable	(W5)	68	
Total current liabilities			1,913
Total equity and liabilities			17,049

RTY Statement of changes in equity for year ended 31 January 20X2

	Equity Shares	Share Premium	Retained Earnings	Revaluation Reserve	Total
	$000	$000	$000	$000	$000
Balance at 1 February 20X1	1,375	2,750	2,785	2,900	9,810
Statement of profit or loss and other comprehensive income for year			465	1,240	1,705
Disposal of revalued property (W4)			800	(800)	0
Dividend paid			(138)		(138)
Balance at 31 January 20X2	1,375	2,750	3,912	3,340	11,377

Workings:

(W1) Depreciation

	Land	Buildings	Plant & equipment	Total
Cost/Valuation	$000	$000	$000	$000
Balance b/f	6,220	10,900	5,750	22,870
Revaluation	630	(2,000)	–	(1,370)
Disposal	(1,800)	–	(820)	(2,620)
Balance c/f	5,050	8,900	4,930	18,880
Depreciation				
Balance b/f	–	2,610	3,900	6,510
Disposal	–	–	(800)	(800)
Revaluation	–	(2,610)	–	(2,610)
Charge for the year	–	445	458	903
Balance c/f	–	445	3,558	4,003
Carrying value 31 Jan 20X2	5,050	8,455	1,372	14,877
Carrying value 31 Jan 20X1	6,220	16,745	1,850	16,360

Depreciation on the building = $8,900 × 5% = $445

Depreciation on the plant and equipment = $1,830 × 25% = 458.

PAPER F1 : FINANCIAL OPERATIONS

> **Tutorial note**
>
> This question did not require the full preparation of the PPE note and students could approach the workings for the $14,877 in a different way.
>
> When preparing the carrying value of the plant and equipment to calculate depreciation using the reducing balance basis, do not forget to remove the disposal, i.e. cost after disposal = $4,930 – depreciation after disposal $3,900 – 800 =$3,100. Therefore, the carrying value to use for the depreciation charge for the year = cost $4,930 – depreciation of $3,100 = $1,830.

> **Tutorial note**
>
> The revaluation occurred at the beginning of the year and we must therefore clear any opening depreciation on the building to the revaluation reserve. This year's depreciation charge should be based the revalued amount of $8,900.

(W2) Development expenditure

	$000
Cost balance 1 February 20X1	1,199
Expenditure in year	71
	1,270
Less amortisation for year at 20%	(254)
Less amortisation b/fwd at 1 February 20X1	(744)
Balance 31 January 20X2	272
Amortisation for the year	254
Research cost	163
Charge to Statement of profit or loss	417

(W3)

	Cost of sales $000	Administration $000	Distribution $000
Trial balance	4,939	1,225	679
Depreciation (W1)	903		
Research (W2)	163		
Irrecoverable debt (W8)	48		
Development amortisation (W2)	254		
Gain on disposal of non-current assets (260 – 12) (W4)	(248)		
Totals	6,059	1,225	679

> *Tutorial note*
>
> The CIMA model answer treats the irrecoverable debt as a cost of sale; however, it would be acceptable to treat this as an administration expense.

(W4) **Disposal of non-current assets**

Land	$000
Carrying value of asset	1,800
Proceeds	(2,060)
Profit on disposal	260

Plant and equipment	$000
Carrying value of asset (820 – 800) (W2)	20
Proceeds	(8)
Loss on disposal	(12)

> *Tutorial note*
>
> Don't forget to release the revaluation reserve for the land once the land has been sold. This amount of $800 ($1,800 – $1,000) will reduce the revaluation reserve and increase the retained earnings in the SOCIE.

(W5) Interest

		$000
Finance cost – interest due	2,740 × 5% =	137
Paid (TB)		69
Accrual – current liability		68

(W6) Tax

Statement of profit or loss tax expense

	$000
Balance b/f	35
Estimate for the year	765
Decrease in deferred tax	(45)
	755

Statement of financial position

	$000
Current liability – tax estimate	765
Non-current liability	
Provision deferred tax b/fwd	1,064
Decrease for the year	(45)
Provision deferred tax c/fwd	1,019

Tutorial note

The tax expense for the year charged to the statement of profit or loss consists of three elements, the amount of the TB (this is an under-provision from previous year's), this year's estimate and the movement on the deferred tax account. Don't forget that a deferred tax decrease in the provision will reduce this year's tax expense.

*The current liability **is always this year's estimate** and the non-current liability should be the **cumulative deferred tax provision**.*

(W7) Revaluation of Land and buildings

	$000
Land (W1)	630
Building (W1)(2,000 – $2,610)	610
Other comprehensive income	1,240

Tutorial note

The other comprehensive income should represent the revaluation gains and losses of assets during the year. The land has been revalued upwards by $630 and the building upwards by $610 (carrying value at the revaluation date of $10,900 – $2,610 = $8,290 to $8,900).

(W8) **Receivables**

	$000
TB	1,476
Irrecoverable debt	(48)
	1,428

Tutorial note

On 1 March 20X2, RTY was informed that one of its customers, BVC, had ceased trading. The liquidators advised RTY that it was very unlikely to receive payment of any of the $48,000 due from BVC at 31 January 20X2. This should be treated as an adjusting event as per IAS 10. Although, RTY didn't find out until after the year end that BVC had ceased trading they are required to account for the irrecoverable debt to ensure the receivables shows the correct recoverable amount for the accounting date.

357 DFG (MAY 12)

Key answer tips

This question required the preparation of the three key statements; statement of profit or loss and other comprehensive income, statement of changes in equity and statement of financial position. The non-current asset part of the question was relatively straight forward, requiring a depreciation adjustment for a change in useful life but no adjustments for revaluations or disposals. Some students may have struggled with the treatment in part a) for the revenue recognition and impairment of the patent, however, lots of easy marks could be picked up for the usual adjustments of tax, interest and depreciation.

CIMA examiner comments

This question produced some very good answers with some candidates scoring full marks. However a considerable number of candidates were unable to explain the two issues in part (a) or prepare correct calculations for the patent and depreciation of property, plant and equipment.

(a) **Item (vi) revenue recognition:**

IAS 18 specifies five conditions that must be met before revenue can be recognised. The first two conditions have not been met by this customers order as no goods have been despatched.

- that significant risks and rewards of ownership of the goods have transferred to the buyer
- the entity selling does not retain any influence or control over the goods.

If all criteria are not met under IAS 18 DFG should not recognise any revenue in its financial statements for the year ended 31 March 20X2 and should remove the sales revenue and record the deposit received as a deferred income (current liability).

Item (vii) impairment of intangible non-current assets:

An asset should be reviewed for impairment whenever circumstances indicate that an impairment may have occurred. Due to recent economic circumstances a review has been carried out of the patent. An impairment occurs where the asset's carrying value is more than the recoverable amount. The recoverable amount is the higher of its value in use and its fair value less cost to sell. The patent's carrying value at 31 March 20X2, $54,000 (after annual amortisation of $9,000) is more than the higher of its value in use of $50,000 and its fair value $47,000. Therefore an impairment has occurred and the patent must be written down by $4,000 from $54,000 to $50,000.

Tutorial note

The impairment review is done at the end of the year, therefore, we must amortise the patent for the year before we compare the carrying value to the recoverable amount to test for impairment.

(b) **DFG – Statement of profit or loss and other comprehensive income for the year ended 31 March 20X2**

		$000	$000
Revenue	(W6)		1,185
Cost of sales	(W3)		(642)
Gross profit			543
Administrative expenses	(W3)	(236)	
Distribution costs	(W3)	(90)	(326)
Profit from operations			217
Finance cost	(W4)		(14)
Profit before tax			203
Income tax expense	(W5)		(77)
Profit for the period			126
Other Comprehensive Income			
Revaluation of property			–
Total comprehensive income for the period			126

ANSWERS TO SECTION C-TYPE QUESTIONS : SECTION 6

Statement of changes in equity for the year ended 31 March 20X2

	Equity shares $000	Share premium $000	Retained earnings $000	Total $000
Balance at 1 April 20X1	550	110	121	781
Profit for period			126	126
Dividend paid			(55)	(55)
Balance at 31 March 20X2	550	110	192	852

DFG Statement of financial position at 31 March 20X2

		$000	$000
Non-current assets			
Patent	(W2)		50
Property, plant and equipment	(W1)		1,077
			1,127
Current assets			
Inventory		186	
Trade receivables		135	321
Total assets			1,448
Equity and liabilities			
Equity			
Share capital			550
Share premium			110
Retained earnings			192
Total equity			852
Non-current liabilities			
5% Loan notes		280	
Deferred tax	(W5)	90	
Total non-current liabilities			370
Current liabilities			
Trade payables		61	
Cash and cash equivalents		56	
Tax payable	(W5)	52	
Interest payable	(W4)	7	
Deferred income	(W6)	15	
Provision	(W7)	35	
Total current liabilities			226
Total equity and liabilities			1,448

Workings:

(W1) Depreciation

	Land & Buildings	Plant & equipment	Total
	$000	$000	$000
Cost			
Balance b/f	960	480	1,440
Balance c/f	960	480	1,440
Depreciation			
Balance b/f	33	234	267
Charge for the year	21	75	96
Balance c/f	54	309	363
Carrying value 31 March 20X2	906	171	1,077
Carrying value 31 March 20X1	927	246	1,173

Depreciation on the building = $960 − $260 land × 3% = $21

Depreciation on the plant and equipment = $480 −120 = $360 × 12.5% = $45

Change in life plant & equipment = $120 − depreciation for 4 years $60 ($120 × 12.5% × 4) = $60 carrying value at the change in life date. New charge = $60/2 years remaining life = $30

Total depreciation for plant and equipment = $45 + $30 = $75

Tutorial note

This question did not require the full preparation of the PPE note and students could approach the workings for the $1,077 in a different way.

The depreciation charge for the plant and equipment must be calculated in two stages: firstly a calculation for the charge for the existing equipment at 12.5%, i.e. cost less $120 and then a separate calculation for the change in life equipment. This equipment has already been depreciated for 4 years since acquisition and therefore has a remaining life of 2 years. The remaining book value at the date of the change must now be written off over these 2 years.

ANSWERS TO SECTION C-TYPE QUESTIONS : SECTION 6

(W2) **Patent**

	$000
Balance b/fwd – cost	90
Balance b/fwd – amortisation	(27)
Carrying value at 31 March 20X1	63
Amortisation for the year (27/3)	(9)
Carrying value at 31 March 20X2	54
Recoverable amount	50
Impairment charge to cost of sales	4

Tutorial note

The amortisation for the year must be deducted from the opening balance of the patent before we can test for impairment due to the date of the impairment review being 31 March 20X2. The patent was acquired 3 years ago and therefore the $27 amortisation b/fwd in the TB represents 3 years of amortisation = $9 pa.

The recoverable amount is the higher of the value in use of $50 and fair value less cost to sell of $47.

The carrying value at 31 March 20X2 is greater than the recoverable amount and we must therefore impair the patent to $50 and charge the impairment to cost of sales.

(W3)

	Cost of sales $000	Administrative expenses $000	Distribution Costs $000
Trial balance:	554	180	90
Provision (W7)		35	
Depreciation – buildings (W1)		21	
Depreciation – plant and equipment (W1)	75		
Patent amortisation/ impairment (W2 (9 + 4)	13		
	642	236	90

363

(W4) **Interest**

		$000
Finance cost – interest due	280 × 5% =	14
Paid (TB)		7
Accrual – current liability		7

(W5) **Tax**

Statement of profit or loss tax expense $000
Balance b/f	10
Estimate for the year	52
Increase in deferred tax	15
	77

Statement of financial position
Current liability – tax estimate	52
Non-current liability	
Provision deferred tax b/fwd	75
Increase for the year	15
Provision deferred tax c/fwd	90

(W6) **Revenue**

	$000
TB	1,200
Deferred income	(15)
	1,185

Tutorial note

As per part a) the deposit must be removed from revenue and treated as deferred income.

(W7) **Provision**

A provision will be made as one of DFG's customers has started litigation against DFG, claiming damages caused by an allegedly faulty product. DFG has been advised that it will probably lose the case and that the claim for $35,000 will probably succeed. As there is a probable outflow of economic benefits, the amount can be reliably estimated and DFG has a present obligation as a result of past events, this meets the criteria for a provision under IAS 37.

To make the provision DFG will increase cost of sales and create a current liability.

ANSWERS TO SECTION C-TYPE QUESTIONS : **SECTION 6**

358 QWE (AUG 12)

> **Key answer tips**
>
> This question required the preparation of the three key statements; statement of profit or loss and other comprehensive income, statement of changes in equity and statement of financial position. The non-current asset part of the question was relatively straight forward requiring the usual calculation of depreciation for the year and a disposal. There were lots of easy marks that could be picked up for the usual adjustments of tax, interest and depreciation. Very similar question to the March 12 re-sit paper. Students may struggle with the journal entries to clear the suspense account.

> **CIMA examiner comments**
>
> This question produced some very good answers with some candidates scoring full marks. However a considerable number of candidates were unable to prepare the journal entries to clear the suspense account in part (a) or prepare correct calculations for the deferred development expenditure and depreciation of property, plant and equipment.

(a) QWE Journal entries to clear suspense:

	Debit $000	Credit $000
Suspense account	15	
Plant and equipment disposal account		15
Being cash received on disposal of some plant and equipment		
Research expense account	20	
Suspense account		20
Being research cost to be treated as an expense		

> **Tutorial note**
>
> The proceeds from the disposal of the plant and equipment should be credited to the disposal account where it will be used in part b) to calculate the profit or loss on disposal. The research cost should be treated as an expense to cost of sales.

(b) **QWE – Statement of profit or loss and other comprehensive income for the year ended 31 March 20X2**

		$000	$000
Revenue			2,220
Cost of sales	(W3)		(1,675)
Gross profit			545
Administrative expenses	(W3)	(295)	
Distribution costs	(W3)	(72)	(367)
Profit from operations			178
Finance cost	(W4)		(20)
Profit before tax			158
Income tax expense	(W5)		(116)
Profit for the period			42
Other comprehensive income			
Revaluation of property			–
Total comprehensive income for the period			42

Statement of changes in equity for the year ended 31 March 20X2

	Equity shares	Share Premium	Retained Earnings	Total
	$000	$000	$000	$000
Balance at 1 April 20X1	930	310	621	1,861
Statement of profit or loss and other comprehensive income for year			42	42
Dividend paid			(62)	(62)
Balance at 31 March 20X2	930	310	601	1,841

QWE – Statement of financial position at 31 March 20X2

		$000	$000
Non-current assets			
Property, plant and equipment	(W1)		2,301
Development expenditure	(W2)		105
			2,406
Current assets			
Inventory		214	
Trade receivables	(W7)	98	
Cash and cash equivalents		42	
			354
Total assets			2,760
Equity and liabilities			
Equity			
Share capital		930	
Share premium		310	
Retained earnings		601	
Total equity			1,841
Non-current liabilities			
Long term borrowings		500	
Deferred tax	(W5)	111	
Total non-current liabilities			611
Current liabilities			
Trade payables		190	
Tax payable	(W5)	83	
Provision legal claim	(W8)	25	
Interest payable	(W4)	10	
Total current liabilities			308
Total equity and liabilities			2,760

PAPER F1 : FINANCIAL OPERATIONS

Workings:

(W1) **Depreciation**

	Land &Buildings	Plant & equipment	Total
	$000	$000	$000
Cost			
Balance b/f	2,410	560	2,970
Disposal	–	(82)	(82)
Balance c/f	2,410	478	2,888
Depreciation			
Balance b/f	386	185	571
Disposal	–	(79)	(79)
Charge for the year	48	47	95
Balance c/f	434	153	587
Carrying value 31 March 20X2	1,976	325	2,301
Carrying value 31 March 20X1	2,024	375	2,399

Depreciation on the building = $2,410 – $800 land × 3% = $48

Depreciation on the plant and equipment = $372 × 12.5% = $47

Tutorial note

This question did not require the full preparation of the PPE note and students could approach the workings for the $2,301 in a different way.

When preparing the carrying value of the plant and equipment to calculate depreciation using the reducing balance basis, do not forget to remove the disposal, i.e. cost after disposal = $478 – depreciation after disposal $185 – $79 = $106. Therefore, the carrying value to use for the depreciation charge for the year = cost $478 – depreciation of $106 = $372

(W2) **Deferred development expenditure**

	$000
Balance b/fwd – cost	150
Balance b/fwd – amortisation	(30)
Amortisation for the year (10% × $150)	(15)
Carrying value at 31 March 20X2	105

(W3)

	Cost of sales $000	Administration $000	Distribution $000
Trial balance	1,605	190	72
Amortisation development expenditure (W2)	15		
Research (from part (a))	20		
Depreciation – buildings (W1)		48	
Depreciation – plant and equipment (W1)	47		
Gain on disposal PPE (W6)	(12)		
Irrecoverable debt (W7)		32	
Legal claim (W8)		25	
Totals	1,675	295	72

(W4) **Interest**

		$000
Finance cost – interest due	500 × 4% =	20
Paid (TB)		10
Accrual – current liability		10

(W5) **Tax**

Statement of profit or loss tax expense $000
Balance b/f 8
Estimate for the year 83
Increase in deferred tax 25
                                        116

Statement of financial position
Current liability – tax estimate 83
Non-current liability
Provision deferred tax b/fwd 86
Increase for the year 25

Provision deferred tax c/fwd 111

(W6) **Disposal of non-current assets**

Plant and equipment $000
Carrying value of asset (82 – 79) (W2) 3
Proceeds (part a) (15)

Profit on disposal 12

(W7) **Receivables**

$000
TB 130
Irrecoverable debt (32)

98

PAPER F1 : FINANCIAL OPERATIONS

> **Tutorial note**
>
> On 1 August 20X2 QWE was advised that one of its customers, that had been in some financial difficulties at 31 March 20X2, had gone into liquidation and that the $32,000 balance outstanding at 31 March 20X2 was very unlikely to be paid. This should be treated as an adjusting event as per IAS 10. Although, QWE didn't find out until after the year end that the customer had ceased trading they are required to account for the irrecoverable debt to ensure the receivables shows the correct recoverable amount for the accounting date.

(W8) **Provision**

A provision will be made as one of QWE's customers has started litigation against QWE, claiming damages caused by an allegedly faulty product. QWE has been advised that it will probably lose the case and the claim for $25,000 will probably succeed.

As there is a probable outflow of economic benefits, the amount can be reliably estimated and DFG has a present obligation as a result of past events, this meets the criteria for a provision under IAS 37.

To make the provision QWE will increase administration expenses and create a current liability.

359 YZ (NOV 12)

> **Key answer tips**
>
> This question required the preparation of the three key statements; statement of profit or loss and other comprehensive income, statement of changes in equity and statement of financial position. There were lots of easy marks that could be picked up for the usual adjustments of tax, interest and depreciation. The additional adjustment for intangibles and the operating lease have now been examined many times before!

> **CIMA examiner comments**
>
> This question produced some very good answers with some candidates scoring full marks. However a considerable number of candidates were unable to correctly calculate or treat some of the adjustments required. E.g. research expenditure treated as an intangible asset; revaluation gain treated as revenue; operating lease treated as a finance lease. Many candidates did not know the components that made up Cost of Sales and did not produce a single figure for cost of sales. Many candidates included two or three figures for the various cost of sales expenses in the statement of profit or loss and other comprehensive income. E.g. production costs were shown as a separate item and not included in cost of sales in a large proportion of answers.

YZ Statement of profit or loss and other comprehensive income for the year ended 30 September 20X2

	$000
Revenue	9,820
Cost of sales (W2)	(4,287)
Gross profit	5,533
Administrative expenses (W4)	(978)
Distribution costs	(515)
Profit from operations	4,040
Finance cost (W9)	(210)
Profit before tax	3,830
Income tax expense (W5)	(698)
Profit for the period	3,132
Other comprehensive income:	
Revaluation of land (W1)	500
Total comprehensive income for the year	3,632

YZ Statement of financial position as at 30 September 20X2

	$000	$000	$000
Non-current assets			
Property, plant and equipment (W1)			13,247
Intangible assets (W6)			294
Current assets			
Inventory (W7)		422	
Trade receivables		1,130	
Cash and cash equivalents		130	
			1,682
Total assets			15,223
Equity and liabilities			
Equity			
Share capital		1,700	
Share premium		100	
Revaluation reserve		2,300	
Retained earnings		6,079	
Total equity			10,179

Non-current liabilities
7% Loan	3,000	
Deferred tax (W5)	383	
Total non-current liabilities		3,383
Current liabilities		
Trade and other payables (W6)	940	
Operating lease (W8)	6	
Tax payables (W5)	715	
Total current liabilities		1,661
Total equity and liabilities		15,223

YZ – Statement of changes in equity for the year ended 30 September 20X2

	Equity shares $000	Share premium $000	Revaluation reserve $000	Retained earnings $000	Total $000
Balance at 1 Oct 20X1	1,500	0	1,800	3,117	6,417
Share issue (W10)	200	100			300
Revaluation in year			500		500
Profit for period				3,132	3,132
Dividend paid				(170)	(170)
Balance at 30 Sept 20X2	1,700	100	2,300	6,079	10,179

Workings:

(W1) Tangible Non-current Assets

Cost/Valuation	Land $000	Buildings $000	Plant & Equip. $000	Total $000
Balance 01/10/X1	9,000	3,400	3,900	16,300
Disposals	0	0	(35)	(35)
Revaluation	500	0	0	500
Balance 30/09/X2	9,500	3,400	3,865	16,765
Depreciation				
Balance 01/10/X1	0	816	2,255	3,071
Disposals	0	0	(32)	(32)
	0	816	2,223	3,039
Charge for year	0	68	411	479
Balance 30/09/X2	0	884	2,634	3,518
Carrying value at 30/9/X2	9,500	2,516	1,231	13,247

Depreciation charge for the year:

Buildings – 3,400 × 2% = 68

Plant and equipment - 3,865 – 2,223 = 1,642 × 25% = 411

> *Tutorial note*
>
> *The question did not ask you to prepare a PPE note so alternative methods could have been used to find the carrying value at the end of the year.*

(W2) **Cost of sales**

	$000
Inventory raw materials at 30/9/X1	275
Purchases	2,220
Less inventory raw materials at 30/9/X2	(242)
Direct labour	670
Production overheads	710
Depreciation (W1)	411
Inventory finished goods at 30/9/X1	190
Less inventory finished goods at 30/9/X2	(180)
Gain on disposal of machinery (W3)	(5)
Lease (W8)	6
Research and patent amortisation (W6)	232
	4,287

(W3) **Gain on disposal**

	$000
Cost less depreciation (35 – 32)	3
Cash received	8
Gain on disposal	5

(W4) **Administration expenses**

	$000
TB	910
Depreciation (W1)	68
	978

(W5) Tax

Income statement tax expense	$000
Balance b/f	30
Estimate for the year	715
Decrease in deferred tax	(47)
	698

Statement of financial position	
Current liability – tax estimate	715
Non-current liability	
Provision deferred tax b/fwd	430
Increase for the year	(47)
Provision deferred tax c/fwd	383

(W6) Patent

	$000
Balance b/fwd – cost	420
Balance b/fwd – amortisation	(84)
Amortisation for the year (420 × 10%)	(42)
Carrying value at 30 Sept 20X2	294

Research costs of $190 expensed to COS

Total expense to COS $190 + $42 = $232

(W7) Inventory

	$000
Raw materials	242
Finished goods	180
	422

(W8) Operating lease

	$000
Total payments (8 × 3)	24
Total life of the lease in years	4
Current year charge (24/4)	6
Amount paid already (TB)	0
Accrual	6

(W9) Finance cost

	$000
Amount due $3,000 × 7%	210
TB amount paid	210
Accrual	0

(W10) Share issue

200,000 × $1 = $200,000 share capital

200,000 × $0.50 = $100,000 share premium

> **Tutorial note**
>
> The share issue has already been accounted for in the trial balance figures. However the nominal value will show as a movement in share capital and the 50% premium as a movement in share premium in the statement of changes in equity for the year.

360 CQ (FEB 13)

> **Key answer tips**
>
> This is a straight forward question that requires the preparation of the three key financial statements, statement of profit or loss and other comprehensive income, statement of financial position and statement of changes in equity. This question has all of the usual favourites in the notes for adjustments for, depreciation, taxation and interest. The finance lease was very similar to previous questions except that payments were made in advance but as long as students had revised this topic, it should not have caused them any problems.

> **CIMA examiner comments**
>
> This question produced some very good answers but there were very few candidates scoring full marks. However a considerable number of candidates were unable to correctly calculate or treat some of the adjustments required. E.g. finance lease, depreciation of non-current assets and intangible asset impairment.

PAPER F1 : FINANCIAL OPERATIONS

CQ Statement of profit or loss and other comprehensive income for the year ended 31 December 20X2

	$000
Revenue	1,992
Cost of sales (W2)	(1,107)
Gross profit	885
Administrative expenses (W2)	(407)
Distribution costs (W2)	(140)
Profit from operations	338
Finance cost (W3)	(35)
Profit before tax	303
Income tax expense (W5)	(67)
Profit for the period	236

CQ Statement of financial position as at 31 December 20X2

	$000	$000	$000
Non-current assets			
Property, plant and equipment (W1)			1,472
Intangible assets (W6)			65
Current assets			
Inventory (W7)		170	
Trade receivables		249	
Cash and cash equivalents		192	
			611
Total assets			2,148
Equity and liabilities			
Equity			
Share capital		750	
Share premium		225	
Retained earnings		374	
Total equity			1,349

Non-current liabilities
Bank loan	375	
Deferred tax (W5)	168	
Finance lease (W4)	27	
Total non-current liabilities		570
Current liabilities		
Trade and other payables	140	
Finance lease (W4)	12	
Tax payables (W5)	77	
Total current liabilities		229
Total equity and liabilities		2,148

CQ Statement of changes in equity for the year ended 31 December 20X2

	Equity shares	Share premium	Retained earnings	Total
	$000	$000	$000	$000
Balance at 1 Jan 20X2	500	150	168	818
Share issue (W8)	250	75		325
Profit for period			236	236
Dividend paid			(30)	(30)
Balance at 31 Dec 20X2	750	225	374	1,349

Workings:

(W1) Tangible non-current assets

Cost/Valuation	Land	Buildings	Plant & Equip.	Vehicles	Total
	$000	$000	$000	$000	$000
Balance 01/01/X2	1,015	400	482	0	1,897
Addition	0	0	0	46	46
Balance 31/12/X2	1,015	400	482	46	1,943
Depreciation					
Balance 01/01/X2	0	120	279	0	399
Charge for year	0	12	51	9	72
Balance 31/12/X2	0	132	330	9	471
Carrying value at 31/12/X2	1,015	268	152	37	1,472

Depreciation charge for the year:

Buildings – 400 × 3% =12

Plant and equipment – 482 – 279 = 203 × 25% = 51

Vehicle – 46/5 year lease period = 9

(W2)

	Cost of sales $000	Administrative expenses $000	Distribution Costs $000
Inventory 01/01/X2	196		
Purchases	996		
Less inventory at 31/12/X2 (W7)	(170)		
Depreciation P&E(W1)	51		
Depreciation vehicle(W1)	9		
Patent (7 + 18) (W6)	25		
Trial balance		395	140
Depreciation building (W1)		12	
	1,107	407	140

(W3) **Interest**

	$000
Finance cost – interest due 375 × 8%	30
Paid (TB)	30
Finance lease (W4)	5
Finance cost	35

(W4) **Finance Lease**

Year to	Cost/balance	Paid	Sub total	Finance Charge 15%	Balance
31/12/X2	46	(12)	34	5	39
31/12/X3	39	(12)	27	4	31

Current liability = $12 (next payment)

Non-current liability = $39 – $12 payment = $27

ANSWERS TO SECTION C-TYPE QUESTIONS : SECTION 6

> *Tutorial note*
>
> The lease payments are made in advance and must therefore be deducted from the opening balance BEFORE the interest is calculated for the year. This method of payment means the next payment will be the current liability and the balance of the total liability must be treated as non-current in the SFP. All calculations have been made to the nearest $000.

(W5) **Tax**

Income statement tax expense	$000
Balance b/f	32
Estimate for the year	77
Decrease in deferred tax	(42)
	67

Statement of financial position	$000
Current liability – tax estimate	77
Non-current liability	
Provision deferred tax b/fwd	210
Decrease for the year	(42)
Provision deferred tax c/fwd	168

(W6) **Patent**

	$000
Cost balance 1 Jan 20X2	180
Less amortisation b/fwd at 1 Jan 20X2	(90)
Less amortisation for the year (180/10)	(18)
Balance 31 Dec 20X2	72
Fair value	65
Impairment (72 – 65)	7

> *Tutorial note*
>
> The amortisation for the year must be deducted from the opening balance of the patent before we can test for impairment due to the date of the impairment review being 31 December 20X2.
>
> The carrying value at 31 December 20X2 is greater than the recoverable amount and we must therefore impair the patent to $65 and charge the impairment to cost of sales.

(W7) **Inventory**

	$000
Balance	183
Obsolete items	(13)
	170

(W8) **Share issue**

250,000 × $1 = $250,000 to share capital

250,000 × $0.30 = $75,000 to share premium

> *Tutorial note*
>
> *The share issue has already been accounted for in the trial balance figures; however, it has been accounted for incorrectly by debiting cash and crediting its own account. This total amount of $325 must be removed and correctly transferred to the share capital and share premium accounts.*

361 SA (MAY 13 EXAM)

> **Key answer tips**
>
> This question required the preparation of the three key statements; statement of profit or loss and other comprehensive income, statement of changes in equity and statement of financial position. The non-current asset part of the question was relatively straight forward, requiring an adjustment for an asset held for sale but no adjustments for revaluations or disposals. Some students may have found the discontinued operation/held for sale part of the question difficult, however, lots of easy marks could be picked up for the usual adjustments of tax, interest and depreciation.

> **CIMA examiner comments**
>
> This question was overall, reasonably well answered, but marks were not as high as in recent examinations. Many candidates were unable to correctly calculate or treat the adjustments required for non-current assets. Significant proportions of candidates were unable to correctly adjust for the discontinued operations assets and revenue/expenses and most failed to include the result in profit or loss. Very few candidates made correct adjustments to make the carrying value of the discontinued operation its fair value. There seemed to be an increased number of candidates that did not even gain marks for basic adjustments that appear in most questions of this type.

(a) The criteria that must be met before an operation can be classified as "held for sale" under IFRS 5 *Non-current assets held for sale and discontinued operations* are:
- It must be available for immediate sale in its present condition
- The sale must be highly probable, management must be committed to selling the assets and have an active programme to locate a buyer
- It must be being offered at a reasonable price
- The sale is expected within the next year

(b) **SA – Statement of profit or loss for the year ended 31 March 20X3**

Continuing operations	$000
Revenue	2,784
Cost of sales	(1,900)
Gross profit	884
Administrative expenses (W3)	(368)
Distribution costs (W3)	(20)
Profit from operations	496
Finance cost (W4)	(27)
Profit before tax	469
Income tax (W5)	(87)
Profit for the period from continuing operations	382
Discontinued operations	
Loss from discontinued operations (W6)	(284)
Profit for the period	98

Statement of changes in equity for the year ended 31 March 20X3

	Equity shares	Revaluation reserve	Retained earnings	Total
	$000	$000	$000	$000
Balance at 1 April 20X2	800	80	183	1,063
Profit for year			98	98
Dividend paid			(55)	(55)
Balance at 31 March 20X3	800	80	226	1,106

SA – Statement of financial position at 31 March 20X3

		$000	$000
Non-current assets			
Property, plant and equipment	(W1)		983
Current assets			
Inventory		68	
Trade receivables		56	
Cash and cash equivalents		202	
			326
Asset held for sale	(W2)		431
Total assets			1,740
Equity and liabilities			
Equity			
Share capital		800	
Revaluation reserve		80	
Retained earnings		226	
Total equity			1,106
Non-current liabilities			
Long term borrowings		450	
Deferred tax	(W5)	69	
Total non-current liabilities			519
Current liabilities			
Trade payables		51	
Tax payable	(W5)	50	
Interest payable	(W4)	14	
Total current liabilities			115
Total equity and liabilities			1,740

Workings:

(W1) Non-current assets (continuing operations)

Cost/valuation	Plant and equipment	Buildings	Total
Balance b/fwd	1,010	995	2,005
Assets held for sale	(180)	(460)	(640)
Balance c/fwd	830	535	1,365
Depreciation			
Balance b/fwd	360	50	410
Assets held for sale	(140)	(23)	(163)
Charge for the year	122	13	135
Balance c/fwd	342	40	382
Carrying value b/fwd	650	945	1,595
Carrying value c/fwd	488	495	983

Depreciation on the building = $535 × 2.5% = $13

Depreciation on the plant and equipment = $830 − (360 − 140) = 610 × 20% = $122

(W2) Non-current assets (discontinuing operations)

Cost	Plant and equipment	Buildings	Total
Balance b/fwd	180	460	640
Balance c/fwd	180	460	640
Depreciation			
Balance b/fwd	140	23	163
Charge for the year	8	12	20
Balance c/fwd	148	35	183
Carrying value c/fwd	32	425	457

Depreciation on the building = $460 × 2.5% = $12

Depreciation on the plant and equipment = $180 − 140 = 40 × 20% = $8

Fair value = $431

We must write down the assets held for sale to fair value = $457 − $431 = $26

PAPER F1 : FINANCIAL OPERATIONS

> **Tutorial note**
>
> The assets are treated as an asset held for sale at the year end so we are therefore required to depreciate them as normal for the year before we value you them as an asset held for sale. They are then valued at the lower of CV or net selling price. Therefore, we need to value the assets at $431 and the CV of the assets needs to be reduced by $26 impairment. The asset held for sale will be removed from the non-current asset total and shown separately on the statement of financial position under the current asset total. The depreciation charge for the year and the impairment amount should be shown as part of the calculation for the discontinued operations profit or loss.

(W3)

	Administration $000	Distribution $000
Trial balance	263	145
Less: discontinued operations	(30)	(125)
Depreciation – buildings (W1)	13	
Depreciation – plant and equipment (W1)	122	
Totals	368	20

(W4) **Interest**

	$000
Finance cost – interest due 450 × 6% =	27
Paid (TB)	13
Accrual – current liability	14

(W5) **Tax**

Income statement tax expense

	$000
Estimate for the year (continuing operations)	90
Decrease in deferred tax	(3)
	87

Statement of financial position

Current liability – tax estimate	50
Non-current liability	
Provision deferred tax b/fwd	72
Decrease for the year	(3)
Provision deferred tax c/fwd	69

(W6) Discontinued operations

	$000
Revenue	185
Cost of sales	(230)
	(45)
Administration (W3 + W2)(30 + 20)	(50)
Distribution (W3)	(125)
	(220)
Closure costs	(78)
	(298)
Tax refund	40
	(258)
Loss on adjustment in value to fair value (W2)	(26)
	(284)

Tutorial note

When we have a discontinued operation we must collect together all revenues and costs relating to the operation and show as a single figure on the face of the statement of profit or loss. This includes any impairments or depreciation on assets held for sale in W2.

362 BVQ (AUG 13 EXAM)

Key answer tips

This question required the preparation of the three key statements; statement of profit or loss and other comprehensive income, statement of changes in equity and statement of financial position. The non-current asset part of the question was probably the part students would most struggle with, requiring an adjustment for an asset held for sale, impairment and depreciation. Some students may have struggled with the calculation of the depreciation for the asset held for sale and the appropriate treatment and valuation in the SFP. The finance lease was also a little different with it having payments in advance, rather than the usual payments in arrears. However, lots of easy marks could be picked up for the usual adjustments of tax, interest and depreciation.

PAPER F1 : FINANCIAL OPERATIONS

> **CIMA examiner comments**
>
> Part (a) was not well answered; most candidates repeated the information in the question regarding economic downturn without adding anything. Very few answers gave sufficient detail for 3 marks. Part (b) produced some very good answers but there were very few candidates scoring full marks. However a considerable number of candidates were unable to correctly calculate or treat some of the adjustments required. E.g. finance lease, depreciation of non-current assets and non-current asset impairment.

(a) IAS 36 *Impairment of Assets* requires BVQ to assess at each reporting date whether there is any indication that any assets may be impaired. If any indication exists, the recoverable amount must be estimated, that is, an impairment review must be carried out.

Due to the general economic downturn property prices have reduced during the year. This could suggest that BVQ's property has suffered impairment.

BVQ has experienced a reduction in sales demand and is reducing its asset base by selling a specialised machine. This suggests that impairment may have occurred to its plant and machinery.

Therefore BVQ needed to carry out an impairment review.

(b) **BVQ – Statement of profit or loss for the year ended 31 March 20X3**

	$000
Revenue	4,364
Cost of sales	(1,873)
Gross profit	2,491
Administrative expenses (W3)	(907)
Distribution costs (W3)	(291)
Profit from operations	1,293
Loss on non-current assets held for sale (W2)	(16)
Finance cost (W4)	(50)
Profit before tax	1,227
Income tax expense (W5)	(238)
Profit for the period	989

Statement of changes in equity for the year ended 31 March 20X3

	Equity shares $000	Retained earnings $000	Total $000
Balance at 1 April 20X2	1,400	728	2,128
Profit for year		989	989
Dividend paid		(70)	(70)
Balance at 31 March 20X3	1,400	1,647	3,047

BVQ – Statement of financial position at 31 March 20X3

		$000	$000
Non-current assets			
Property, plant and equipment	(W1)		3,318
Current assets			
Inventory		198	
Trade receivables		916	
Cash and cash equivalents		118	
			1,232
Asset held for sale	(W2)		72
Total assets			4,622
Equity and liabilities			
Equity			
Share capital		1,400	
Retained earnings		1,647	
Total equity			3,047
Non-current liabilities			
Long term borrowings		600	
Deferred tax	(W5)	393	
Finance lease	(W6)	134	
Total non-current liabilities			1,127
Current liabilities			
Trade payables		176	
Tax payable	(W5)	180	
Interest payable	(W4)	18	
Finance lease	(W6)	74	
Total current liabilities			448
Total equity and liabilities			4,622

Workings:

(W1) Depreciation

	Land & buildings	Plant & equipment	Vehicles	Total
Cost/valuation	$000	$000	$000	$000
Balance b/f	2,553	3,888	324	6,765
Asset held for sale	0	(180)	0	(180)
Balance c/f	2,553	3,708	324	6,585
Depreciation				
Balance b/f	190	2,489	65	2,744
Asset held for sale	0	(92)	0	(92)
Impairment	103	0	0	103
Charge for the year	27	420	65	512
Balance c/f	320	2,817	130	
Carrying value 31 March 20X3	2,233	891	194	3,318
Carrying value 31 March 20X2	2,363	1,399	259	4,021

Depreciation on the building = $2,553 − $1,653 land × 3% = $27

Depreciation on the plant and equipment = $3,888 − $2,489 = $1,399 × 30% = $420

Vehicles = $324/5 = $65

Depreciation on the asset held for sale at 31/3/X3 = $180 × 30% = $54 + 38 (126 × 30%) = $92

Tutorial note

This question did not require the full preparation of the PPE note and students could approach the workings in a different way.

The asset held for sale does not become a held for sale asset until the last day of the year and therefore must be depreciated as normal for the current year.

(W2) Non-current assets held for Sale

Cost (W1)	180
Depreciation (W1)	(92)
CV	88
Fair value	73
Less: cost to sell	0.8
	72.2
Impairment	16
SOFP value (lower)	72

ANSWERS TO SECTION C-TYPE QUESTIONS : SECTION 6

> *Tutorial note*
>
> The asset held for sale and valued at the lower of CV or net selling price. Therefore, we need to value the asset at $72,200 (round down to $72k) and the CV of the asset needs to be reduced by $16,000 impairment. This results in a total impairment of $16,000 to be charged to the statement of profit or loss. The asset held for sale will be removed from the non-current asset total and shown separately on the statement of financial position under the current asset total.

(W3)

	Administration $000	Distribution $000
Trial balance	357	226
Less: discontinued operations		
Depreciation – buildings (W1)	27	
Depreciation – plant and equipment (W1)	420	
Depreciation – vehicles (W1)		65
Impairment on land and buildings (W1)	103	
Totals	907	291

(W4) **Interest**

		$000
Finance cost – interest due	600 × 6% =	36
Paid (TB)		18
Accrual – current liability		18
Finance cost:		
Interest due		36
Finance lease (W6)		14
		50

389

(W5) **Tax**

	$000
Income statement tax expense	
TB under provision	27
Estimate for the year (continuing operations)	180
Increase in deferred tax	31
	238

Statement of financial position

Current liability – tax estimate	180
Non-current liability	
Provision deferred tax b/fwd	362
Increase for the year	31
Provision deferred tax c/fwd	393

(W6) **Finance lease**

Year to	Cost/balance	Paid	Sub total	Finance charge 7.12%	Balance
31/3/X2	324	(74)	250	18	268
31/3/X3	268	(74)	194	14	208

Total liability at 31/3/X3 $208

NCL $134 (total liability less CL)

CL $74 (next payment)

Tutorial note

The payments for the lease are made in advance and the total liability at the end of the year must be split between current and non-current. Therefore, the next payment will treated as the current liability and the balance of the total liability must be treated as non-current. Don't forget we are in the second year of this lease!

ANSWERS TO SECTION C-TYPE QUESTIONS : SECTION 6

363 CJ (MAY 06 EXAM)

> **Key answer tips**
>
> This is a relatively straight forward statement of cash flows to prepare using the indirect method. It has all of the usual items but don't forget to split the other income between dividends received (investing activities) and the gain on the sale of investments (to calculate the proceeds from the sale of investments – investing activities).

CJ – Statement of cash flows for the year ended 31 March 20X6

	$000	$000
Cash flows from operating activities		
Profit before taxation	4,398	
Adjustments for:		
Other income	(200)	
Depreciation	4,055	
Finance cost	1,302	
Gain on disposal of plant (W2)	(23)	
	9,532	
Increase in inventory	(214)	
Increase in trade receivables	(306)	
Increase in trade and other payables (W6)	420	
Cash generated from operations	9,432	
Interest paid (W3)	(1,602)	
Income taxes paid (W4)	(1,796)	
Net cash from operating activities		6,034
Cash flows from investing activities		
Purchase of property, plant and equipment (W1)	(2,310)	
Investment income received	180	
Proceeds from sale of equipment	118	
Proceeds from disposal of available for sale investments (W5)	620	
Net cash used in investing activities		(1,392)
Cash flows from financing activities		
Proceeds from issue of share capital (W7)	10,000	
Repayment of interest bearing borrowings	(6,000)	
Equity dividends paid	(800)	
Net cash from financing activities		3,200
Net increase in cash and cash equivalents		7,842
Cash and cash equivalents at 1 April 20X5		(880)
Cash and cash equivalents at 31 March 20X6		6,962

391

Workings:

(W1)

Carrying values	Property	Plant	Available for sale investments
	$000	$000	$000
Balance b/fwd	18,000	10,000	2,100
Revaluation	1,500	0	0
	19,500	10,000	2,100
Disposal	0	(95)	(600)
Depreciation for year	(2,070)	(1,985)	0
	17,430	7,920	1,500
Acquired in year (to balance)	1,730	580	0
Balance c/fwd	19,160	8,500	1,500

Total purchases = 1,730 + 580 = 2,310

(W2) **Gain on disposal of plant**

	$000
Carrying value	95
Cash received	118
Gain	23

(W3) **Interest paid**

Balance b/fwd	650
Finance cost in statement of profit or loss	1,302
	1,952
Balance c/fwd	(350)
Interest paid in year	1,602

(W4) **Tax paid**

Balance b/fwd – Current tax	1,810	
Deferred tax	800	2,610
Statement of profit or loss charge		2,099
		4,709
Balance c/fwd – Current tax	1,914	
Deferred tax	999	2,913
Paid in year		1,796

ANSWERS TO SECTION C-TYPE QUESTIONS : SECTION 6

(W5) Proceeds from disposal of available for sale investments

Disposal per (W1)	600
Add gain on disposal	20
	620

> **Tutorial note**
>
> This is dealt with in the same way as you would deal with a gain on a non-current asset. If we know we made a gain from the sale and we know what the investments were worth (movement in the statement of financial position) the proceeds can be calculated. A gain means we sold the investments for more than the carrying value, hence added.

(W6) Increase in trade payables

Trade and other payables balance b/fwd		1,700
Less: Interest b/fwd		(650)
		1,050
Trade and other payables balance c/fwd	1,820	
Less: Interest c/fwd	(350)	1,470
Increase in trade payables		420

> **Tutorial note**
>
> We cannot simply look at the movement in the payables in the statement of financial position because it includes the movement of interest. Interest is dealt with separately in the interest paid and must be removed so it isn't double counted.

(W7) Proceeds from issue of equity share capital

Equity shares	5,000
Share premium	5,000
	10,000

393

PAPER F1 : FINANCIAL OPERATIONS

364 DN (NOV 06 EXAM)

> **Key answer tips**
>
> A very straight forward question that should not cause any problems for a well prepared student. Don't forget that if the examiner shows more than one loan on the statement of financial position you are required to show the movement on each separately in the statement of cash flows.

Statement of cash flows for the year ended 31 October 20X6

	$000	$000
Cash flows from operating activities		
Profit before tax		790
Adjustments for:		
Depreciation (100 + 230)		330
Profit on disposal		(5)
Finance cost		110
		1,225
Increase in inventories (190 – 140)		(50)
Increase in receivables (340 – 230)		(110)
Increase in payables (105 – 85)		20
Cash generated from operations		1,085
Interest paid (W8)		(130)
Tax paid (W9)		(120)
Net cash from operating activities		835
Cash flows from investing activities		
Additions to tangible assets (W1)	(677)	
Disposal proceeds in respect of tangible assets (W2)	15	
		(662)
Cash flows from financing activities		
Bank loan repaid (W3)	(2,000)	
New loan (W3)	1,500	
Share issue (W6)	600	
Dividend (W7)	(400)	
		(300)
Net decrease in cash and cash equivalents		(127)
Cash and cash equivalents at 1 November 20X5		45
iCash and cash equivalents at 31 October 20X6		(82)

394

ANSWERS TO SECTION C-TYPE QUESTIONS : SECTION 6

Workings:

(W1)

Plant and equipment (NBV)

B/f	1,405	Depreciation	230
Additions (balance)	677	Disposal	10
		c/f	1,842
	2,082		2,082

(W2)

Disposal proceeds		15,000
CV 60,000 × 1/6		(10,000)
Profit on disposal		5,000

(W3)

Bank loans

Repaid	2,000	B/f	2,000
C/f	1,500	New loan	1,500
	3,500		3,500

(W4) **Payables**

	20X6	20X5	
Trade payables	105	85	To movement on payables
Interest	55	75	To interest working
Tax	70	50	To tax working
Bank overdraft	82	0	To cash and cash equivalents

(W5)

Property

B/f	2,800		
Revaluation	400	Depreciation	100
		C/f	3,100
	3,200		3,200

(W6)

Equity and share premium

		B/f	1,000
		Proceeds from share issue	600
C/f – equity	1,300		
C/f – share premium	300		
	1,600		1,600

(W7) **Dividend**

Profit after tax	650
Movement on retained earnings 1,660 – 1,410	250
Therefore, dividend	400

Check 0.2 × 2 × 1,000 = 400

(W8)

Interest creditor

		B/f	75
Paid	130	Statement of profit or loss	110
C/f	55		
	185		185

(W9)

Tax creditor

		B/f	50
Paid	120	Statement of profit or loss	140
C/f	70		
	190		190

ANSWERS TO SECTION C-TYPE QUESTIONS : SECTION 6

365 HZ (MAY 09 EXAM)   *Walk in the footsteps of a top tutor*

Key answer tips

This is a difficult statement of cash flows to prepare using the indirect method. It requires the student to first consider the adjustments that must be made to profit and then continue with the statement of cash flows. It does have some tricky parts, such as the treatment of the redeemable preference shares, the adjustment of the provision in the statement of cash flows (not a cash item) and remembering the impairment of goodwill is dealt with the same as depreciation and amortisation. The main thing is to do the core bits of the question you able to do and then have a go at the harder areas. You could still score well if you focused on the core areas of the question.

(a) **Notes for adjustments – all figures are to the nearest $000.**

Adjustments are needed for the suspense account:

Dr Suspense	1,000
Cr Non-current liability	1,000

The issue costs should not have been charged to admin, they should be charged against the liability:

Dr Non-current liability	70
Cr Admin costs	70

Tutor's top tips

A redeemable preference share is treated as a debt and not equity, hence shown in the non-current liability section of the statement of financial position. Any issue costs must be charged to the non-current liability account and not administration expenses in the statement of profit or loss. This will increase profit by 70.

The net proceeds from the issue = 930

The profit must be increased by 70

The suspense account is removed

397

The redeemable preference shares are treated as if they were a loan, hence the finance cost must be calculated:

Costs to issue	70
Dividend ($1,000 × 5%) × 10 years	500
Redemption ($1,000 × 10%)	100
Total finance cost	670

Year to	Cost/balance	Finance charge	Paid	Balance
31/03/20X9	930	62	(50)	942
31/03/20Y0	942	63	(50)	955

The finance charge is the charge to the statement of profit or loss; the balance represents what would be shown at the end of the year on the statement of financial position.

Tutor's top tips

The redeemable preference shares are dealt with in the same way as a finance lease. The net proceeds (1,000 − issue costs of 70) are used as the base figure to calculate the charge to the statement of profit or loss using the actuarial method, i.e. 6.72% × 930 = 62. The interest is added to the liability and then reduced by the dividend paid (gross amount received of 1,000 × 5% = 50). Any dividends paid are treated as the finance cost and not a distribution of profits in the statement of changes in equity.

The final adjustment is for the write off of the development costs:

Dr Admin costs	170
Cr Development (SOFP)	170

The revised profit will be:	$000
Per Statement of profit or loss	305
Development cost write off	(170)
Issue cost adjustment	70
Finance cost of preference shares	(62)
Profit before tax	143

(b) **Statement of cash flows for HZ for the year ended 31 March 20X9**

	$000	$000
Cash flows from operating activities		
Profit before taxation (part a)	143	
Adjustments for:		
Depreciation	940	
Profit on disposal of non-current assets (128 – 98)	(30)	
Impairment of goodwill (W1)	133	
Development written off (W2)	170	
Provision (W3)	120	
Finance cost (W4)	122	
	─────	
Operating profit before working capital changes	1,598	
Increase in inventories (890 – 750)	(140)	
Increase in receivables (924 – 545)	(379)	
Increase in payables (744 – 565)	179	
	─────	
Cash generated from operations	1,258	
Interest paid (W5)	(206)	
Income taxes paid (W6)	(250)	
Net cash from operating activities		802
Cash flows from investing activities		
Purchase of plant and equipment (W7)	(480)	
Proceeds from sale of plant	128	
Purchase of development costs (W2)	(28)	
Net cash used in investing activities		(380)
Cash flows from financing activities		
Proceeds from issue of share capital (W8)	605	
Repayment of 10% loans	(1,250)	
Issue of redeemable preference shares (part a)	930	
Dividends paid	(290)	
Net cash used in financing activities		(5)
		─────
Net increase in cash and cash equivalents		417
Cash and cash equivalents at beginning of period (all cash at bank)		300
		─────
Cash and cash equivalents at end of period (all cash at bank)		717

(W1)

Goodwill

	$000		$000
Bfwd	350	Written off	133
		Cfwd	217
	─────		─────
	350		350

(W2)

Developments

	$000		$000
Bfwd	170	Written off	170
Additions	28	Cfwd	28
	198		198

(W3) A provision is included in admin expenses, this is not a cash item and must be added back to profit. All workings to the nearest $000.

(W4) The profit has a finance cost of $122 to add back. This is made up of the original finance cost of $60 + $62 from the preference shares (part a). All workings to the nearest $000.

(W5)

Interest

	$000		$000
Bank	156	Bfwd	113
Cfwd	17	Statement of profit or loss	60
	173		173

Tutor's top tips

The bank amount of $156 is added to $50 preference dividend paid = $206. Redeemable preference share dividends are classed as interest on the cash flow statement, not equity dividends paid. All workings to the nearest $000.

(W6)

Current tax

	$000		$000
Bank	250	Bfwd	247
Cfwd	117	Statement of profit or loss (182 – 62)	120
	367		367

Deferred tax

	$000		$000
		Bfwd	250
Cfwd	312	Statement of profit or loss	62
	312		312

(W7)

Property, plant and equipment

	$000		$000
Bfwd	6,250	Disposal	98
Revalued	162	Depreciation	940
Additions	480	Cfwd	5,854
	6,892		6,892

(W8) Proceeds from share issue 806,000 × $0.75 = $605

(c) **HZ – Statement of changes in equity for the year ended 31 March 20X9**

	Equity shares	Share premium	Revalue reserve	Retained earnings	Total
	$000	$000	$000	$000	$000
Balance Bfwd	2,470	530	400	1,840	5,240
Issue of shares	403	202	0	0	605
Revaluation	0	0	162	0	162
Dividend paid	0	0	0	(290)	(290)
Loss for the period (IS)	0	0	0	(39)	(39)
Balance Cfwd	2,873	732	562	1,511	5,678

Tutor's top tips

Revised Statement of profit or loss figure = part a 143 less tax in question 182 = loss 39 (assumption tax charge will not be changed). The preference dividends are not part of the SOCIE as treated as a non-current liability on the statement of financial position. Preference dividends will not be treated as a distribution of profit but as a finance cost on the statement of profit or loss. They are redeemable, hence treated as if they were a loan.

PAPER F1 : FINANCIAL OPERATIONS

366 YG (NOV 10 EXAM)

> **Key answer tips**
>
> A very straight forward question that should not cause any problems for a well prepared student. It has all of the usual items but don't forget about the intangibles (development costs) and provisions. Amortisation is treated the same as depreciation and added back to the profit before tax and the purchase or disposal of the development costs will be dealt with in the investing activities section.

> **CIMA examiner comments**
>
> This question produced some very good answers, some candidates scoring full marks on part (a), but it also produced some very poor answers scoring just a few marks. Candidates either knew how to do cash flows and scored fairly high marks or didn't really know what they were doing, suggesting that some had been question spotting and had not prepared for statements of cash flow.
>
> Part (b) Candidates usually covered confidentiality briefly but also tried to cover the rest of CIMA's Code of Ethics, such as integrity, objectivity and professional behaviour.

(a) **YG – Statement of cash flows for the year ended 31 October 20X9**

	$000	$000
Cash flows from operating activities		
Profit before taxation	266	
Adjustments for:		
Provision	(150)	
Depreciation	250	
Development amortisation	145	
Finance cost	16	
Loss on disposal of non-current asset (W2)	4	
	———	
	531	
Increase in inventory (509 – 606)	(97)	
Increase in trade receivables (372 – 456)	(84)	
Increase in trade payables (310 – 425)	115	
	———	
Cash generated from operations	465	
Interest paid (W3)	(14)	
Income taxes paid (W4)	(180)	
	———	
Net cash from operating activities		271

	$000	$000
Cash flows from investing activities		
Purchase of property, plant and equipment (W1)	(448)	
Proceeds from sale of equipment	66	
Development expenditure (W5)	(68)	
Net cash used in investing activities		(450)
Cash flows from financing activities		
Proceeds from issue of share capital (2,180 + 620 – 3,780 – 1,420)	2,400	
Repayment of interest bearing borrowings (715 – 360)	(355)	
Equity dividends paid (W6)	(82)	
Net cash from financing activities		1,963
Net increase in cash and cash equivalents		1,784
Cash and cash equivalents at 1 November 20X8		205
Cash and cash equivalents at 31 October 20X9		1,989

(W1)

Property, plant and equipment (CV)

B/f	4,248	Depreciation	250
Additions (balance)	448	Disposal	70
Revaluation	300		
		c/f	4,676
	4,996		4,996

(W2)

Proceeds	66,000
Carrying value	70,000
Loss on disposal	4,000

(W3)

Interest creditor

		B/f	3
Paid (balance)	14	Statement of profit or loss	16
C/f	5		
	19		19

(W4)

Tax creditor

Paid (balance)	180	B/f (170 + 170)	340
		Statement of profit or loss	120
C/f (70 + 210)	280		
	460		460

(W5)

Development expenditure

B/f	494	Amortisation	145
Additions (balance)	68	C/f	417
	562		562

(W6) **Dividend**

Profit after tax (IS)	146
Movement on retained earnings 1,314 – 1,250	64
Therefore, dividend (146 – 64)	82

(b) Confidentiality is one of the fundamental principles of the CIMA Code of Ethics for Professional Accountants.

A professional accountant should respect the confidentiality of information acquired as a result of business relationships and should not disclose any such information to third parties unless there is a legal or professional right or duty to disclose. If there is no right or duty to disclose, the principle of confidentiality requires the professional accountant to not disclose confidential information outside the employing entity without specific authority. In addition it is usually illegal to use this type of information for personal gain. In most countries this would be classified as insider trading. The CIMA Code requires that the professional accountant does not use confidential information to their personal advantage or the advantage of third parties.

You would therefore have to respond by either not accepting the invitation or accepting the invitation but make it clear in advance that you are unable to discuss any confidential information relating to your employer and the employer's activities.

ANSWERS TO SECTION C-TYPE QUESTIONS : SECTION 6

367 OP (MAY 11 EXAM) — Walk in the footsteps of a top tutor

Key answer tips

A very straight forward question that should not cause any problems for a well prepared student. It has all of the usual items but don't forget about the intangibles (development costs and brand) and provisions. Amortisation/impairment will be treated the same as depreciation and added back to the profit before tax and the purchase or disposal of the development costs will be dealt with in the investing activities section.

CIMA examiner comments

This question produced some very good answers, some candidates scoring full marks on part (a), but it also produced some very poor answers scoring just a few marks. Candidates either knew how to do cash flows and scored fairly high marks or didn't really know what they were doing, suggesting that some had been question spotting and had not prepared for statements of cash flow.

Q4(b) Many candidates were unable to prepare correct calculations for a finance lease with payments at the end of each period. Some candidates were also unable to state where each amount calculated should be shown in the financial statements.

(a) **OP's – Statement of cash flows for the year ended 31 March 20X9**

	$000	$000
Cash flows from operating activities		
Profit before taxation	1,089	
Adjustments for:		
Provision (0 – 40)	40	
Depreciation (25 + 17)	42	
Development amortisation	15	
Brand name impairment (40 – 30)	10	
Finance cost	15	
Loss on disposal of non-current asset	6	
	1,217	
Decrease in inventory (450 – 446)	4	
Increase in trade receivables (310 – 380)	(70)	
Increase in trade payables (95 – 150)	55	
Cash generated from operations	1,206	
Interest paid (W3)	(25)	
Income taxes paid (W4)	(280)	
Net cash from operating activities		901

405

	$000	$000
Cash flows from investing activities		
Purchase of property, plant and equipment (W1)	(432)	
Proceeds from sale of equipment (W2)	5	
Development expenditure (W5)	(10)	
Net cash used in investing activities		(437)
Cash flows from financing activities		
Proceeds from issue of share capital (200 + 100 – 400 – 200)	300	
Repayment of interest bearing borrowings (250 – 100)	(150)	
Equity dividends paid (W6)	(580)	
Net cash from financing activities		(430)
Net increase in cash and cash equivalents		34
Cash and cash equivalents at 1 April 2010		35
Cash and cash equivalents at 31 March 2011		69

(W1)

Property, plant and equipment (CV)

B/f	663	Depreciation (17 + 25)	42
Additions (balance)	432	Disposal	11
		Impairment	65
		c/f	977
	1,095		1,095

(W2)

Loss on disposal	6,000
Carrying value	11,000
Proceeds on disposal	5,000

(W3)

Interest creditor

		B/f	20
Paid (balance)	25	Statement of profit or loss	15
C/f	10		
	35		35

(W4)

Tax creditor

Paid (balance)	280	B/f (260 + 120)	380
		Statement of profit or loss	280
C/f (250 + 130)	380		
	660		660

(W5)

Development expenditure

B/f	65		
Additions (balance)	10	Amortisation	15
		C/f	60
	75		75

(W6) **Dividend**

Profit after tax (IS)	809
Movement on retained earnings 652 – 423	229
Therefore, dividend (809 – 229)	580

(b)

Year	Balance b/fwd	Finance charge 12%	Repayment	Balance c/fwd
	$	$	$	$
31/3/X2	248,610	29,833	(44,000)	234,443
31/3/X3	234,443	28,133	(44,000)	218,576

Statement of profit or loss and other comprehensive income for year ended 31 March 20X2 – extract

	$
Depreciation charge (see below)	24,861
Finance cost	29,833

Statement of financial position as at 31 March 20X2 – extract

	$
Non-current assets – tangible	
Finance lease	248,610
Less: Depreciation (248,610/10)	(24,861)
	223,749
Non-current liabilities	
Amounts due under finance lease	218,576
Current liabilities	
Amounts due under finance lease (234,443 – 218,576)	15,867

Statement of cash flows for the year ended 31 March 20X2 – extract

	$
Operating activities	
Finance cost	29,833
Depreciation	24,861
Financing activities	
Amounts paid under finance lease	(44,000)

368 UV (SEP 11 EXAM)

Key answer tips

A very straight forward question that should not cause any problems for a well prepared student. It has all of the usual items but don't forget about the intangibles (development costs) and provisions. Amortisation will be treated the same as depreciation and added back to the profit before tax and the purchase or disposal of the development costs will be dealt with in the investing activities section. The tax on the other comprehensive income item may cause a problem as it is the first time we have seen such an item but simply calculated by grossing up the income and then applying the 25% tax rate as per the question. Student's may have been surprised to see a non-current asset note as part of the question but again it was very straight forward and a lot of easy marks could be picked up by just filling in the figures from the question. It was important to tackle this part of the question before attempting the cash flow, as many of these figures are required to complete the cash flow statement.

CIMA examiner comments

This question produced some very good answers, some candidates scoring full marks on part (b), but it also produced some very poor answers scoring just a few marks. Candidates either knew how to do cash flows and scored fairly high marks or didn't really know what they were doing, suggesting that some had been question spotting and had not prepared for statements of cash flow.

ANSWERS TO SECTION C-TYPE QUESTIONS : **SECTION 6**

(a) **UV Tangible Non-current asset note**

	Property $000	Plant $000	Equipment $000	Total $000
Non-current assets				
Cost or valuation				
At 30 June 20W0	4,150	2,350	985	7,485
Additions	0	215	275	490
Disposals (60 + 30)	0	(90)	0	(90)
Adjustment on revaluation	350	0	0	350
At 30 June 20X1	4,500	2,475	1,260	8,235
Depreciation				
At 30 June 20W0	450	1,350	900	2,700
Disposals	0	(60)	0	(60)
Charge for year	50	280	40	370
Adjustment on revaluation	(450)	0	0	(450)
At 30 June 20X1	50	1,570	940	2,560
Carrying value at 30 June 20X1	4,450	905	320	5,675
Carrying value at 30 June 20W0	3,700	1,000	85	4,785

Property depreciation charge for the year $4,500/90 = $50

Tutorial note

Remember to check the date of the revaluation. As the revaluation of the property occurred at the beginning of the year we must remove the opening depreciation and transfer it to the revaluation reserve. The current year's depreciation will then be calculated on the revalued amount of $4,500,000.

PAPER F1 : FINANCIAL OPERATIONS

(b) **UV's – Statement of cash flows for the year ended 30 June 20X1**

	$000	$000
Cash flows from operating activities		
Profit before taxation	1,540	
Adjustments for:		
Provision for legal claim (105 – 75)	30	
Decrease in provision for restructuring (100 – 0)	(100)	
Depreciation (part a)	370	
Development amortization (W4)	13	
Finance cost	95	
Loss on disposal of non-current asset	15	
	1,963	
Increase in inventory (95 – 80)	(15)	
Increase in trade receivables (190 – 145)	(45)	
Decrease in trade payables (60 – 85)	(25)	
Cash generated from operations	1,878	
Interest paid (W2)	(122)	
Income taxes paid (W3)	(229)	
Net cash from operating activities		1,527
Cash flows from investing activities		
Purchase of property, plant and equipment (part a)	(490)	
Proceeds from sale of plant (W1)	15	
Development expenditure (W4)	(114)	
Net cash used in investing activities		(589)
Cash flows from financing activities		
Proceeds from issue of share capital (910 + 665 – 760 – 400)	415	
Repayment of interest bearing borrowings (1,500 – 250)	(1,250)	
Equity dividends paid (W5)	(168)	
Net cash from financing activities		(1,003)
Net decrease in cash and cash equivalents		(65)
Cash and cash equivalents at 1 July 20W0		160
Cash and cash equivalents at 30 June 20X1		95

(W1) **All *workings* to the nearest $000**

Loss on disposal	15
Carrying value	30
Proceeds on disposal	15

(W2)

Interest creditor

Paid (balance)	122	B/f	32
		Statement of profit or loss	95
C/f	5		
	127		127

(W3)

Tax creditor

Paid (balance)	229	B/f (305 + 0)	305
		Statement of profit or loss	455
C/f (321 + 410)	731	Other comprehensive income (600/75 × 25)	200
	960		960

Tutorial note

The other comprehensive income represents the revaluation of the property in part a) 350 increase in cost + 450 accumulated depreciation, net of tax, i.e. 800 – 25% = 600. The tax charge of $200 must be considered when calculating the tax paid for the year.

(W4)

Development expenditure

B/f	69		
Additions	114	Amortisation	13
		C/f	170
	183		183

(W5) **Dividend**

Profit after tax (IS)	1,085
Movement on retained earnings (2,899 – 1,982)	917
Therefore, dividend (1,085 – 917)	168

PAPER F1 : FINANCIAL OPERATIONS

GROUP COMPANY FINANCIAL ACCOUNTS

369 JASPER *Walk in the footsteps of a top tutor*

> **Key answer tips**
>
> This is a more difficult consolidated statement of financial position involving a parent, a subsidiary and an associate. Adjustments are required for the fair value, pre-acquisition reserves, inter-company sales and unrealised profit. Make sure you show all workings clearly and don't forget that the associates assets/liabilities are not added with the parent and subsidiaries in the consolidated statement of financial position. You are only required to show the investment in the associate and consider the effect it will have on reserves.

Consolidated statement of financial position as at 31 December 20X4

	$	$000
Non-current assets		
Property, plant and equipment (2,960 + 1,720 + 300)		4,980
Goodwill (W3)		200
Investment in Swede (W7)		366
		5,546
Current assets		
Inventories (625 + 320 – 50 (W6))	895	
Receivables (350 + 300 – 100 (W8))	550	
Cash at bank (55 + 120 + 100 (W8))	275	
		1,720
		7,266
Equity and liabilities		
Ordinary share capital		2,200
Reserves (W5)		3,306
		5,506
Non-current liabilities		
Loan Notes (500 + 200 – 200 (intra-group loan))		500
Current liabilities		
Bank overdraft	560	
Trade payables (500 + 200)	700	
		1,260
		7,266

ANSWERS TO SECTION C-TYPE QUESTIONS : **SECTION 6**

Workings:

(W1) **Group structure**

- Jasper owns 100% of the shares of Carrot so Carrot is a subsidiary.
- Jasper owns 30% of the shares of Swede so Swede is an associate

> *Tutor's top tips*
>
> *First establish the relationships of the companies. This is important because a subsidiary will be dealt with differently to an associate. These percentages will be used to calculate the parents share of the reserves in the consolidated statement of financial position.*

(W2) **Net assets of Carrot**

	Date of acquisition	Year end
	$000	$000
Share capital	800	800
Retained earnings	500	1,260
Fair value adjustment	300	300
	1,600	2,360

> *Tutor's top tips*
>
> *This working is important because the reserves at acquisition will be used to calculate the goodwill on the acquisition of the subsidiary. The post acquisition reserves (the difference between the reserves at year end and reserves at acquisition) will be used to calculate the reserves on the consolidated statement of financial position.*

Net assets of Swede

	Date of acquisition	Year end
	$000	$000
Share capital	800	800
Retained earnings	150	410
	950	1,210

(W3) **Goodwill (Carrot)**

	$000
Cost of investment	1,800
Net assets of Carrot at acquisition (W2)	(1,600)
Goodwill	200

> *Tutor's top tips*
>
> This is a comparison between the amount paid to acquire the subsidiary and the total net assets that existed at that date of acquisition (shares and reserves).

(W4) **Non-controlling interests**

Not relevant – we own 100% of the subsidiary

(W5) **Consolidated retained earnings**

	$000
Jasper	2,530
Carrot (2,360 – 1,600 (W2))	760
Swede – 30% × (1,210 – 950 (W2))	78
Unrealised profit adjustments (W6)	(62)
	3,306

> *Tutor's top tips*
>
> This is the total reserves that belong to the group. You will need to add the parents reserves to their share of post acquisition reserves of the subsidiary and associate. The post acquisition reserves are calculated by taking the difference in the net assets at year end and acquisition of the subsidiary/associate.

(W6) **Unrealised profit**

On sales to Carrot – 25% × $200,000 = $50,000

On sales to Swede – 25% × $160,000 × 30% = $12,000

> *Tutor's top tips*
>
> The unrealised profit on the subsidiary is deducted from the inventory total and the amount for the associate is deducted from the investment in the associate.

ANSWERS TO SECTION C-TYPE QUESTIONS : SECTION 6

(W7) Investment in Swede

	$000
Cost	300
Share of post-acquisition profits (W5)	78
Unrealised profit (W6)	(12)
	366

(W8) Inter-company trading

> **Tutor's top tips**
>
> No adjustment is made for trading balances between group companies and an associate. The $100,000 inter-company receivable is removed from the receivables of Jasper. It is not included in the payables of Carrot since Carrot made payment just before the year end. Therefore $100,000 is shown as cash in transit.

370 HOT

> **Key answer tips**
>
> This is a straight forward consolidated statement of profit or loss involving a parent, a subsidiary and an associate. Adjustments are required for the inter-company trading and unrealised profit. Make sure you show all workings clearly and don't forget that the associates income/expenses are not added with the parent and subsidiaries in the consolidated statement of profit or loss. You are only required to show the share of the associate profits.

Consolidated statement of profit or loss for the year ended 31 December 20X4

	$000
Revenue (60,000 + 45,000 – 2,000)	103,000
Cost of sales (30,000 + 22,500 – 2,000 + 150)	(50,650)
Gross profit	52,350
Other operating expenses (9,000 + 4,500)	(13,500)
Operating profit	38,850
Investment income (W4)	2,750
Interest payable (3,000 + 2,250 – 800)	(4,450)
Share of profits of Tepid (40% × 9,900)	3,960
Profit before tax	41,110
Taxation (7,600 + 5,500)	(13,100)
Profit for the year	28,010

Workings:

(W1) Group structure

Hot owns 100% of Warm

Hot owns 40% of Tepid

(W2) Inter-company sales

We must deduct the inter-company sales from the total sales and cost of sales in the consolidated statement of profit or loss for the subsidiary. We do not adjust the inter-company sales for the associate in the consolidated statement of profit or loss.

(W3) Unrealised profit

	$000	
Sales value	600	133.33%
Cost value	450	100%
Profit	150	33.33%

Tutorial note

Hot sells at a mark up of one third. This means the cost is the base figure and one third is added to it to get the selling price. If Warm still has inventory valued at 600,000 (cost to Warm = selling price), we must eliminate the profit element. Sales between a group company and an associate are not eliminated on consolidation.

(W4) Investment income

	$000
Hot + Warm	11,550
Dividend from Warm	(6,000)
Dividend from Tepid (5,000 × 40%)	(2,000)
Intra-group interest (8,000 × 10%)	(800)
Consolidated investment income	2,750

ANSWERS TO SECTION C-TYPE QUESTIONS : **SECTION 6**

371 AX GROUP (MAY 10 EXAM) *Walk in the footsteps of a top tutor*

Key answer tips

This is the first group question set by the examiner for the new syllabus. It is a straight forward question involving a parent, subsidiary and associate. Adjustments are required for the fair value, pre-acquisition reserves, inter-company sales and unrealised profit. Make sure you show all workings clearly and don't forget that the associates assets/liabilities are not added with the parent and subsidiaries in the consolidated statement of financial position. You are only required to show the investment in the associate and consider the effect it will have on reserves. Be careful when dealing with the subsidiary as pre-acquisition reserves show a DEBIT balance, hence losses at that date. The question also requires the calculation of tax for the parent using the usual techniques for calculating taxable profit and deferred taxation.

CIMA examiner comments

This question produced some very good answers, some candidates scoring full marks, but it also produced some very poor answers scoring just a few marks. The most significant mistake in this question was the incorrect treatment of the associated entity. Almost all candidates identified AA as an associated entity but some candidates then failed to treat the entity as an associate when preparing the consolidated financial statements. An associated entity's results should be consolidated as one line on the statement of profit or loss and other comprehensive income and the group's share of net assets should be shown in the statement of financial position as one line under non-current assets. Candidates used several wrong methods to consolidate AA, some used the same method as used for the subsidiary. A major display of lack of knowledge was exhibited by candidates who included a proportion of each item on each line in the consolidated statements whilst others left AA out of the consolidated financial statements altogether. All of these approaches led to relatively poor marks.

(a) **Tax on AX**

	$	$
Current tax		
Pre-tax profit in the accounts		264
Add back:		
Accounting depreciation	31	
Entertaining cost	4	
	—	35
		299
Deduct:		
Tax depreciation	(49)	
	—	(49)
Taxable profit		250
Current tax charge at 25%		62.5
Rounded to		63

Deferred tax	$
Accounting depreciation	31
Tax depreciation	49
Difference	18
× 25% tax	4.5
Rounded to	5

Summary
Charge to IS

Current tax	63
Deferred tax movement	5
	68

SOFP

Current liability – Current tax	63
Non-current liability – D tax increase	5

(b) **AX Group consolidated statement of profit or loss and other comprehensive income for the year ended 31 March 20Y0**

	$000
Revenue (820 + 285 – 55)	1,050
Cost of sales (406 + 119 – 55 + 5)	(475)
Gross profit	575
Distribution costs (48 + 22)	(70)
Administration expenses (84 + 36)	(120)
Profit from operations	385
Finance cost (18 + 5)	(23)
Share of profits of associate (51 × 22%)	11
Profit before tax	373
Taxation (68 + 16)) part a	(84)
Profit for the year	289
Other comprehensive income:	–
Total comprehensive income for the year	289

AX Group consolidated statement of financial position as at 31 March 20Y0

	$000	$000
Non-current assets		
Property, plant and equipment (1,120 + 700 + 75)		1,895
Goodwill (W3)		137
Investment in associate (W7)		156
		2,188
Current assets		
Inventories (205 + 30 – 5 (W6))	230	
Receivables (350 + 46)	396	
Cash at bank	30	
		656
		2,844
Equity and liabilities		
Equity share capital		1,500
Retained earnings (W5)		543
		2,043

Non-current liabilities

Borrowings (360 + 80)	440	
Deferred tax (120 + 16 + 5) part a	141	
		581

Current liabilities

Trade payables (92 + 29)	121	
Bank overdraft	20	
Current tax (63 + 16) part a	79	
		220
		2,844

Workings:

(W1) **Group structure**
- AX owns 100% of the shares of AS so AS is a subsidiary.
- AX owns 22% of the shares of AA so AA is an associate (120/550).

(W2) **Net assets of AS (sub)**

	Date of acquisition $000	Year end $000
Share capital	600	600
Retained losses/earnings	(72)	15
Fair value adjustment	75	75
PUP (sub sells) (W6)		(5)
	603	685

> *Tutor's top tips*
>
> Be careful when showing the reserves at acquisition for the subsidiary. The reserves show a debit balance which means they were retained losses.

Net assets of AA (associate)

	Date of acquisition $000	Year end $000
Share capital	550	550
Retained earnings	49	100
	599	650

ANSWERS TO SECTION C-TYPE QUESTIONS : SECTION 6

(W3) Goodwill (sub)

	$000
Cost of investment	740
Net assets of AS at acquisition (W2)	(603)
Goodwill	137

(W4) Non-controlling interests

Not relevant – we own 100% of the subsidiary

(W5) Consolidated retained earnings

	$000
AX (518 – 68) part a	450
AS (685 – 603 (W2))	82
AA – 22% × (650 – 599 (W2))	11
	543

(W6) Unrealised profit (sub sells)

On sales to AX – $25,000/125 × 25 = $5,000

> *Tutor's top tips*
>
> The subsidiary is selling to the parent. Therefore, the unrealised profit is deducted from the inventory total and W2.

(W7) Investment in Associate

	$000
Cost	145
Share of post-acquisition profits (W5)	11
	156

PAPER F1 : FINANCIAL OPERATIONS

372   PH GROUP (NOV 11)

> **Key answer tips**
>
> This is was a relatively straight forward group question set by the examiner involving the preparation of a consolidated statement of financial position for a parent, subsidiary and associate. Adjustments are required for the fair value, depreciation, intra-group balances, pre-acquisition reserves and unrealised profit. Make sure you show all workings clearly and don't forget that the associates assets/liabilities are not added with the parent and subsidiaries in the consolidated statement of financial position. You are only required to show the investment in the associate and consider the effect it will have on reserves.

> **CIMA examiner comments**
>
> This group question should have been expected, as groups have only been asked once before as a 25 mark question on the new syllabus. The question was very badly answered by candidates in some centres, even though it was a straight-forward question. However there were some very good answers from candidates who were prepared for it but it also produced some very poor answers with candidates scoring just a few marks. Candidates either knew how to prepare a consolidated statement of financial position and scored fairly high marks or didn't really know what they were doing, suggesting that some had been question spotting and had not prepared for a consolidated statement of financial position.

(a)   Control is the power to govern the financial and operating policies of an entity so as to obtain benefit from its activities.

There is a presumption that control exists where the investor entity owns over half of the voting power of the other entity.

IFRS 10 also sets out circumstances where control can be established with less than 50% of the equity votes:

- Where there is power over more than half the voting rights by virtue of an agreement with other investors.
- Where there is power to govern the financial and operating policies of the entity under a statute or agreement.
- Power to appoint or remove the majority of board of directors or equivalent governing body.
- Power to cast the majority of votes at meetings of the board of directors or equivalent body.

ANSWERS TO SECTION C-TYPE QUESTIONS : SECTION 6

(b) **PH Group – Consolidated statement of financial position as at 30 September 20X1**

	$000	$000
Non-current assets		
Property, plant and equipment (50,390 + 57,590 + 1,300 – 65)		109,215
Goodwill (W3)		18,610
Investment in associate (W7)		17,670
		145,495
Current assets		
Inventories (10,160 + 14,410 – 1,200) (W6))	23,370	
Receivables (21,400 + 13,200 – 90 (W9))	34,510	
Cash at bank (1,260 + 3,600 + 2,800 (W8))	7,660	
		65,540
		211,035
Equity and liabilities		
Equity share capital	126,000	
Retained earnings (W5)	34,425	
		160,425
Non-current liabilities		
Borrowings (32,700 + 12,600 – 12,600(W9))		32,700
Current liabilities		
Trade payables (12,600 + 5,400 – 90 (W9))		17,910
		211,035

Workings:

(W1) **Group structure**
- PH owns 100% of the shares of SU so SU is a subsidiary.
- PH owns 33 1/3% of the shares of AJ so AJ is an associate (8,000/24,000).

(W2) **Net assets of SU (sub)**

	Date of acquisition $000	Year end $000
Share capital	48,000	48,000
Retained losses/earnings	7,680	15,600
Fair value adjustment	1,300	1,300
Depn adjustment (1,300/20)		(65)
	56,980	64,835

> **Tutorial note**
>
> The fair value of SU's property, plant and equipment on 1 October 20X0 exceeded its book value by $1,300,000. In order to value the net assets at acquisition correctly we must adjust for this fair value. As this adjustment is made to a depreciating asset we must then take the depreciation into account at the year end, i.e. reduce the fair value by one year's depreciation because we acquired the company exactly one year ago.

Net assets of AJ (associate)

	Date of acquisition $000	Year end $000
Share capital	24,000	24,000
Retained earnings	24,990	28,800
	48,990	52,800

(W3) **Goodwill (sub)**

	$000
Cost of investment	75,590
Net assets of SU at acquisition (W2)	(56,980)
Goodwill	18,610

(W4) **Non-controlling interests**

Not relevant – we own 100% of the subsidiary

(W5) **Consolidated retained earnings**

	$000
PH	26,500
SU (64,835 – 56,980(W2))	7,855
AJ – 33 1/3% × (52,800 – 48,990 (W2))	1,270
PUP – parent sells (W6)	(1,200)
	34,425

(W6) **Unrealised profit (Parent sells)**

On sales to SU – $4,800,000/133.333 × 33.333 = $1,200,000

ANSWERS TO SECTION C-TYPE QUESTIONS : **SECTION 6**

> *Tutorial note*
>
> *The parent is selling to the subsidiary. Therefore, the unrealised profit is deducted from the inventory total and W5. PH calculates profit based on mark up method which means one third is added to the cost to get the selling price, hence the selling price represents 133 1/3%.*

(W7) **Investment in Associate**

	$000
Cost	16,400
Share of post-acquisition profits (W5)	1,270
	17,670

(W8) **Intra-group trading**

PH has a current account balance of $10,000,000.

SU has a current account balance of $7,200,000.

The difference is due to cash in transit of $2,800,000.

> *Tutorial note*
>
> *If we account for the cash by reducing the current account receivable of PH by $2,800,000 and increasing cash by $2,800,000, the new balance of $7,200,000 receivable will cancel out with SU's payable current account balance of $7,200,000.*

(W9) **Intra-group loan**

The loan of $12,600,000 must be eliminated, i.e. reduce the investment in PH and reduce the borrowings of SU. We must also eliminate the associated accrued interest of $90,000 by reducing receivables of PH and payables of SU.

373 TREE GROUP (MAR 12)

> **Key answer tips**
>
> This was a slightly harder group question set by the examiner, compared with the previous exam, involving the preparation of a consolidated statement of financial position and statement of profit or loss and other comprehensive income for a parent, subsidiary and associate. Adjustments are required for the fair value, depreciation, intra-group balances, intra-group loan/interest, pre-acquisition reserves and unrealised profit. Make sure you show all workings clearly and don't forget that the associates assets/liabilities are not added with the parent and subsidiaries in the consolidated statement of financial position. You are only required to show the investment in the associate and consider the effect it will have on reserves.

> **CIMA examiner comments**
>
> Some very good answers from candidates who were prepared for a question on consolidated financial statements but it also produced some very poor answers with candidates scoring just a few marks. Candidates either knew how to prepare a consolidated statement of financial position and scored fairly high marks or didn't really know what they were doing. Most were able to calculate the adjustments for inventory and cash in transit but many were unable to make the correct entries in the financial statements.

Tree Group Consolidated statement of profit or loss and other comprehensive income for the year ended 31 January 20X2

	$000
Revenue (2,200 + 777 – 180)	2,797
Cost of sales (1,112 + 456 – 180 + 24 + 40 (W6))	(1,452)
Gross profit	1,345
Expenses (221 + 115)	(336)
Profit from operations	1,009
Finance cost (102 + 59 – 30 (W9))	(131)
Share of profits of associate (150 × 40%)	60
Profit before tax	938
Taxation (145 + 32)	(177)
Profit for the year	761
Other comprehensive income:	–
Total comprehensive income for the year	761

ANSWERS TO SECTION C-TYPE QUESTIONS : SECTION 6

Tree Group – Consolidated statement of financial position as at 31 January 20X2

	$000	$000
Non-current assets		
Property, plant and equipment (1,535 + 1,155 + 240 – 24)		2,906
Goodwill (W3)		90
Investment in associate (W7)		610
		3,606
Current assets		
Inventories (1,360 + 411 – 40 (W6))	1,731	
Receivables (1,540 + 734)	2,274	
Cash at bank (47 + 75 + 28 (W8))	150	
		4,155
		7,761
Equity and liabilities		
Equity share capital		3,900
Retained earnings (W5)		806
		4,706
Current liabilities		
Trade payables (2,690 + 365)		3,055
		7,761

Workings:

(W1) Group structure

- Tree owns 100% of the shares of Branch so Branch is a subsidiary.
- Tree owns 40% of the shares of Leaf so Leaf is an associate (332/830).

(W2) Net assets of Branch (sub)

	Date of acquisition $000	Year end $000
Share capital	790	790
Retained losses/earnings	380	495
Fair value adjustment	240	240
Depn adjustment (240/10)		(24)
Branch accrued interest (W9)		30
	1,410	1,531

PAPER F1 : FINANCIAL OPERATIONS

> *Tutorial note*
>
> The fair value of Branch's property, plant and equipment on 1 February 20X1 exceeded its book value by $240,000. In order to value the net assets at acquisition correctly we must adjust for this fair value. As this adjustment is made to a depreciating asset we must then take the depreciation into account at the year end, i.e. reduce the fair value by one year's depreciation because we acquired the company exactly one year ago.
>
> Don't forget to increase the PPE on the consolidation by the fair value amount and reduce by the depreciation charge. The depreciation will also increase cost of sales or expenses in the statement of profit or loss and other comprehensive income.

Net assets of Leaf (associate)

	Date of acquisition $000	Year end $000
Share capital	830	830
Retained earnings	70	220
	900	1,050

(W3) **Goodwill (sub)**

	$000
Cost of investment	1,500
Net assets of Branch at acquisition (W2)	(1,410)
Goodwill	90

(W4) **Non-controlling interests**

Not relevant – we own 100% of the subsidiary

(W5) **Consolidated retained earnings**

	$000
Tree	665
Branch (1,531 – 1,410 (W2))	121
Leaf – 40% × (1,050 – 900 (W2))	60
PUP – parent sells (W6)	(40)
	806

(W6) Unrealised profit (Parent sells)

On sales to Branch – $180,000 × 2/3 left in inventory = $120,000/150 × 50 = $40,000

> **Tutorial note**
>
> The parent is selling to the subsidiary. Therefore, the unrealised profit is deducted from the inventory total and W5. Tree calculates profit based on mark up method which means 50% is added to the cost to get the selling price, hence the selling price represents 150%.
>
> We only calculate PUP on the closing inventory of inter-company sales and NOT the total sale amount.
>
> Don't forget to increase the cost of sales by the PUP amount in the statement of profit or loss and other comprehensive income as the reduction in closing inventory will cause cost of sales to increase.

(W7) Investment in Associate

	$000
Cost	550
Share of post-acquisition profits (W5)	60
	610

(W8) Intra-group trading

Tree has a current account balance of $123,000.

Branch has a current account balance of $95,000.

The difference is due to cash in transit of $28,000.

> **Tutorial note**
>
> If we account for the cash by reducing the current account receivable of Tree by $28,000 and increasing cash by $28,000, the new balance of $95,000 receivable will cancel out with Branch's payable current account balance of $95,000.

(W9) Intra-group loan

The loan of $600,000 must be eliminated, i.e. reduce the investment in Tree and reduce the borrowings of Branch. We must also eliminate the associated accrued interest made by Branch of $30,000 by reducing payables of Branch and increasing profits of Branch in (W2). No adjustments are made to Tree's accounts as they have not accrued for the interest.

374 LOCH GROUP (MAY 12)

> **Key answer tips**
>
> A very similar question to the March 2012 re-sit exam involving the preparation of a consolidated statement of financial position and statement of profit or loss and other comprehensive income for a parent, subsidiary and associate. Adjustments are required for the fair value, depreciation, intra-group balances, intra-group loan/interest, pre-acquisition reserves and unrealised profit. A well prepared student should not have any problem with this question.

> **CIMA examiner comments**
>
> The answers to the group accounts question were a significant improvement on the answers in November 2011. There were some very good answers from candidates who were prepared with some scoring full marks for part (b) although candidates in some centres were unable to gain more than half marks. Candidates either knew how to prepare a consolidated statement of financial position and consolidated statement of profit or loss and other comprehensive income and scored fairly high marks or didn't really know what they were doing, suggesting that some had been question spotting and had not prepared for a question on consolidated financial statements.

(a) Consideration for River paid in shares:

Cost $950,000; share market value $2. Therefore Loch issued 475,000 shares at a premium of $475,000.

Journal

	Dr $000	Cr $000
Investment in River	950	
Equity shares		475
Share premium		475

(b) **Loch Group consolidated statement of profit or loss and other comprehensive income for the year ended 31 March 20X2**

	$000
Revenue (1500 + 693 – 220)	1,973
Cost of sales (865 + 308 – 220 + 73 + 12 (W6))	(1,038)
Gross profit	935
Expenses (124 + 70 + 20)	(214)
Profit from operations	721
Finance cost (80 + 40 – 15 (W9))	(105)
Share of profits of associate (80 × 30%)	24
Profit before tax	640
Taxation (118 + 20)	(138)
Profit for the year	502
Other comprehensive income:	0
Total comprehensive income for the year	502

Loch Group consolidated statement of financial position as at 31 March 20X2

	$000	$000
Non-current assets		
Property, plant and equipment (1,193 + 767 + 144 – 12)		2,092
Goodwill (W3)		56
Investment in associate (W7)		247
		2,395
Current assets		
Inventories (1107 + 320 – 73 (W6))	1,354	
Receivables (1,320 + 570)	1,890	
Cash at bank (62 + 58 + 26 (W8))	146	
		3,390
		5,785
Equity and liabilities		
Equity share capital (3500 + 475 (part a))		3,975
Share premium (part a)		475
Retained earnings (W5)		602
		5,052
Current liabilities		
Trade payables (393 + 340)		733
		5,785

Workings:

(W1) Group structure

- Loch owns 100% of the shares of River so River is a subsidiary.
- Loch owns 30% of the shares of Stream so Stream is an associate (156/520).

(W2) Net assets of River (sub)

	Date of acquisition $000	Year end $000
Share capital	600	600
Retained losses/earnings	130	385
Fair value adjustment	144	144
Depn adjustment (144/12)		(12)
River accrued interest (W9)		15
	874	1,132

Tutorial note

The fair value of River's property, plant and equipment on 1 April 20X1 exceeded its carrying value by $144,000. In order to value the net assets at acquisition correctly we must adjust for this fair value. As this adjustment is made to a depreciating asset we must then take the depreciation into account at the year end, i.e. reduce the fair value by one year's depreciation because we acquired the company exactly one year ago.

Don't forget to increase the PPE on the consolidation by the fair value amount and reduce by the depreciation charge. The depreciation will also increase cost of sales or expenses in the statement of profit or loss and other comprehensive income.

Net assets of Stream (associate)

	Date of acquisition $000	Year end $000
Share capital	520	520
Retained earnings	45	125
	565	645

(W3) Goodwill (sub)

	$000
Cost of investment (part a)	950
Net assets of River acquisition (W2)	(874)
	76
Impairment	(20)
Goodwill	56

(W4) Non-controlling interests

Not relevant – we own 100% of the subsidiary

(W5) Consolidated retained earnings

	$000
Loch	413
River (1,132 – 874(W2))	258
Stream – 30% × (645 – 565 (W2))	24
Impairment (W3)	(20)
PUP – parent sells (W6)	(73)
	602

(W6) Unrealised profit (Parent sells)

On sales to River – $220,000 /150 × 50 = $73,333 (round to 73)

> **Tutorial note**
>
> The parent is selling to the subsidiary. Therefore, the unrealised profit is deducted from the inventory total and W5. Loch calculates profit based on mark up method which means 50% is added to the cost to get the selling price, hence the selling price represents 150%.
>
> Don't forget to increase the cost of sales by the PUP amount in the statement of profit or loss and other comprehensive income as the reduction in closing inventory will cause cost of sales to increase.

(W7) Investment in Associate

	$000
Cost	223
Share of post-acquisition profits (W5)	24
	247

PAPER F1 : FINANCIAL OPERATIONS

(W8) **Intra-group trading**

Loch has a current account balance of $101,000.

River has a current account balance of $75,000.

The difference is due to cash in transit of $26,000.

> *Tutorial note*
>
> *If we account for the cash by reducing the current account receivable of Loch by $26,000 and increasing cash by $26,000, the new balance of $75,000 receivable will cancel out with River's payable current account balance of $75,000.*

(W9) **Intra-group loan**

The loan of $300,000 must be eliminated, i.e. reduce the investment in Loch and reduce the borrowings of River. We must also eliminate the associated accrued interest made by River of $15,000 by reducing payables of River and increasing profits of River. No adjustments are made to Loch's accounts as they have not accrued for the interest.

375 WOOD GROUP (AUG 12) — *Walk in the footsteps of a top tutor*

Key answer tips

This is a harder re-sit exam involving the preparation of a consolidated statement of financial position and statement of profit or loss and other comprehensive income for a parent, subsidiary and associate. Adjustments are required for the fair value, depreciation, intra-group balances, intra-group loan/interest, pre-acquisition reserves and unrealised profit. Students would probably struggle with the adjustments for the inter-company sale of an asset as this is the first time it has been examined. However, lots of the usual suspects were in the question to pick up the easier marks.

CIMA examiner comments

The answer to part (a), explanation of the treatment of an inter-group transfer of a piece of machinery at a profit to the holding entity, was very poor with many candidates not attempting an answer and a large proportion of the rest explaining that the profit should be increased to record the transfer again. A number of the answers to part (b) simply added the holding entity's and subsidiary's figures together, making no attempt at any consolidation adjustments other than a goodwill calculation. There were notably fewer candidates using proportional consolidation in this examination.

(a) The sale to Plank must be recognised in the group consolidated accounts at carrying value, with no profit or loss recognised. Therefore the following adjustments need to be made:

- Cancel the profit on the sale – reduce consolidated profit for the year/consolidated retained earnings by $20,000 ($95,000 proceeds less $75,000 carrying value).
- Cancel the increase in depreciation [($95,000 – $75,000)/10], $2,000 – increase consolidated profit for the year/consolidated retained earnings by $2,000.
- Reduce consolidated non-current assets – property, plant and equipment in the statement of financial position by $20,000 – $2,000 = $18,000.

Tutor's top tips

When a non-current asset is sold to a subsidiary we must eliminate the impact the transfer has had on the group, i.e. adjust the group accounts to bring the asset back into the group at what it would have been had the sale not taken place. Therefore, we are eliminating the group profit from the statement of profit or loss, along with the additional depreciation charge of $2,000. The impact on the statement of profit or loss will be a reduction in profit of $18,000. We must also eliminate the additional increase in the SOFP, i.e. extra cost of $20,000 less additional depreciation of $2,000, a net reduction of $18,000.

An alternative approach could be:

	$
Carrying value of asset for Plank ($95,000 – depreciation for the year of $9,500)	85,500
Carrying value of asset for Wood ($75,000 – depreciation for the year of $7,500)	67,500
Change in asset value for the year	18,000

Tutor's top tips

Reduce (W5) as parent is the seller by $18,000

Reduce PPE by $18,000

Don't forget to reduce profit in the statement of profit or loss by the same amount by adjusting the cost of sales expense downwards.

(b) **Wood Group Consolidated statement of profit or loss and other comprehensive income for the year ended 31 March 20X2**

	$000
Revenue (15,500 + 6,900 – 520)	21,880
Cost of sales (8,700 + 3,080 – 520 + 260 (W6) + 90 + 20 – 2 (part a))	(11,628)
Gross profit	10,252
Expenses (1,250 + 750 + 80)	(2,080)
Profit from operations	8,172
Finance cost (810 + 440 – 155 (W9))	(1,095)
Share of profits of associate (830 × 28%)	232
Profit before tax	7,309
Taxation (1,250 + 230)	(1,480)
Profit for the year	5,829
Other comprehensive income:	0
Total comprehensive income for the year	5,829

Tutor's top tips

The cost of sales has adjustments to eliminate the inter-company sale of $520, the additional depreciation charge of $90 for the year due to the fair value adjustment, the adjustment for PUP of $260 and the adjustment of $18 regarding part a). The depreciation adjustment relating fair value could be shown in expenses as an alternative because we do not know what type of asset the adjustment relates to. However, the profit on the sale of the machinery must be shown in cost of sales as machinery is a production item.

The impairment for the year has been charged to expenses.

Don't forget to eliminate the inter-company loan interest from the finance cost.

Wood Group consolidated statement of financial position as at 31 March 20X2

	$000	$000
Non-current assets		
Property, plant and equipment		
(11,820 + 7,240 + 1,350 – 90 -20 + 2 (part a))		20,302
Goodwill (W3)		490
Investment in associate (W7)		2,652
		23,444
Current assets		
Inventories (12,060 + 3,215 – 260 (W6))	15,015	
Receivables (13,400 + 5,710 – 520 (W8))	18,590	
Cash at bank (1,730 + 510 + 210(W8))	2,450	
		36,055
		59,499
Equity and liabilities		
Equity share capital		38,900
Share premium		5,520
Retained earnings (W5)		7,739
		52,159
Current liabilities		
Trade payables (3,910 + 3,740 – 310)		7,340
		59,499

Tutor's top tips

Don't forget only the parent's share capital and premium should appear in the consolidated statement of financial position.

Workings:

(W1) Group structure

- Wood owns 100% of the shares of Plank so Plank is a subsidiary.
- Wood owns 28% of the shares of bush so Bush is an associate (1,540/5,500).

(W2) **Net assets of Plank (sub)**

	Date of acquisition $000	Year end $000
Share capital	6,000	6,000
Retained losses/earnings	1,280	3,680
Fair value adjustment	1,350	1,350
Depn adjustment (1,350/15)		(90)
Plank accrued interest (W9)		155
	8,630	11,095

Tutor's top tips

The fair value of Plank's property, plant and equipment on 1 April 20X1 exceeded its carrying value by $1,350,000. In order to value the net assets at acquisition correctly we must adjust for this fair value. As this adjustment is made to a depreciating asset we must then take the depreciation into account at the year end, i.e. reduce the fair value by one year's depreciation because we acquired the company exactly one year ago.

Don't forget to increase the PPE on the consolidation by the fair value amount and reduce by the depreciation charge. The depreciation will also increase cost of sales in the statement of profit or loss and other comprehensive income.

Net assets of Bush (associate)

	Date of acquisition $000	Year end $000
Share capital	5,500	5,500
Retained earnings	410	1,240
	5,910	6,740

(W3) **Goodwill (sub)**

	$000
Cost of investment	9,200
Net assets of Plank acquisition (W2)	(8,630)
	570
Impairment	(80)
Goodwill	490

(W4) **Non-controlling interests**

Not relevant – we own 100% of the subsidiary

(W5) **Consolidated retained earnings**

	$000
Wood (5,400 – 18 (part a))	5,382
Plank (11,095 – 8,630(W2))	2,465
Bush – 28% × (6,740 – 5,910(W2))	232
Impairment (W3)	(80)
PUP – parent sells (W6)	(260)
	7,739

Tutor's top tips

Don't forget to reduce Wood's retained earnings by the elimination of the inter-company sale of an asset as per part a).

(W6) **Unrealised profit (Parent sells)**

On sales to Plank – $520,000/200 × 100 = $260,000

Tutor's top tips

The parent is selling to the subsidiary. Therefore, the unrealised profit is deducted from the inventory total and W5. Wood calculates profit based on mark up method which means 100% is added to the cost to get the selling price; hence the selling price represents 200%.

Don't forget to increase the cost of sales by the PUP amount in the statement of profit or loss and other comprehensive income as the reduction in closing inventory will cause cost of sales to increase.

(W7) **Investment in Associate**

	$000
Cost	2,420
Share of post-acquisition profits (W5)	232
	2,652

(W8) **Intra-group trading**

Wood has a receivables balance of $520,000.

Plank has a payables balance of $310,000.

These inter-company balances must be eliminated.

Cash in transit of $210,000.

> *Tutor's top tips*
>
> *In this question we have two inter-company amounts to deal with, the amount of $520,000 as per note (vi) still in inventory and note (ix). We must eliminate $520,000 from receivables as Wood has not yet received the cheque and still thinks Plank owes this amount. However, Plank believes they have a payables balance of $310,000 due to the fact they have sent a cheque for $210,000. To conclude, we must reduce receivables by $520,000, reduce payables by $310,000 and increase cash by $210,000.*
>
> *Don't forget to eliminate the inter-company sale in the statement of profit or loss and other comprehensive income from the revenue and cost of sales expense.*

(W9) **Intra-group loan**

The loan of $3,100,000 must be eliminated, i.e. reduce the investment in Wood and reduce the borrowings of Plank. We must also eliminate the associated accrued interest made by Plank of $155,000 by reducing payables of Plank and increasing profits of Plank. No adjustments are made to Wood's accounts as they have not accrued for the interest.

> *Tutor's top tips*
>
> *In this question Plank has accrued for the loan interest due to be paid by showing this as a finance cost in the statement of profit or loss and other comprehensive income and a liability in the statement of financial position. These adjustments must be eliminated for consolidation purposes. Wood has not made any accruals for the interest due from Plank, hence no corrections needed.*

376 AZ GROUP (NOV 12)

> **Key answer tips**
>
> This is was a relatively straight forward group question set by the examiner involving the preparation of a consolidated statement of financial position for a parent, subsidiary and associate. The usual adjustments are required for the fair value, depreciation, intra-group balances, pre-acquisition reserves and unrealised profit. However, this question does require a slightly more complicated adjustment for an asset transferred within the group. Make sure you show all workings clearly and don't forget that the associates assets/liabilities are not added with the parent and subsidiaries in the consolidated statement of financial position. You are only required to show the investment in the associate and consider the effect it will have on reserves.

> **CIMA examiner comments**
>
> The answer to part (a), explanation of the meaning of fair value and calculation of fair value, was very poor with many candidates not attempting an answer and a large proportion of the rest explaining that fair value was the price paid to acquire a subsidiary. A large proportion of the answers to part (b) simply added the holding entity's and subsidiary's figures together, (sometimes including the associated entity or adding a 20% portion of the associated entity), making little attempt at any consolidation adjustments other than a goodwill calculation. There seemed to be an increase in the number of candidates not showing adequate workings. This made it more difficult for markers to award the correct marks as markers could not see how figures were arrived at.

(a) (i) According to IFRS 10 *Consolidated financial statements*, the group accounts must include net assets at their fair value at the date of acquisition. This is to reflect the cost to the group of the assets at acquisition and ensures an accurate calculation of goodwill.

Fair value is usually defined as the amount for which an asset can be exchanged between knowledgeable, willing parties in an arm's length transaction.

(ii) Fair value of net assets of PQ at acquisition

	Carrying value at 1/Oct/X0 $000	Valuation at 1/Oct/X0 $000
Property	200	300
Plant and equipment	97	117
	297	417

	At acquisition $000
Equity shares	100
Revaluation reserve	60
Share premium	50
Retained earnings	38
Fair value adjustment (417 – 297)	120
Fair value of net assets of PQ at acquisition	368

(b) **AZ Group – Consolidated statement of financial position as at 30 September 20X2**

	$000	$000
Non-current assets		
Property, plant and equipment (400 + 297 + 100 + 20 (part (a)) - 8 (W2) – 18 (W9))		791
Goodwill (W3)		112
Investment in associate (W7)		136
		1,039
Current assets		
Inventories (190 + 60 - 13) (W6))	237	
Receivables (144 + 63 – 52 – 60 (W8))	95	
Cash at bank (48 + 21 + 60(W8))	129	
		461
		1,500
Equity and liabilities		
Equity share capital	900	
Share premium	300	
Retained earnings (W5)	137	
		1,337
Current liabilities		
Trade payables (96 + 119 – 52 (W8))		163
		1,500

ANSWERS TO SECTION C-TYPE QUESTIONS : SECTION 6

Workings:

(W1) **Group structure**

- AZ owns 100% of the shares of PQ so PQ is a subsidiary.
- AZ owns 20% of the shares of SY so SY is an associate (80,000/400,000).

(W2) **Net assets of PQ (sub)**

	Date of acquisition $000	Year end $000
Share capital	100	100
Share premium	50	50
Revaluation reserve	60	60
Retained losses/earnings	38	112
Fair value adjustment	120	120
Depn adjustment (20/5 × 2)		(8)
PURP (W6)		(13)
	368	421

Tutorial note

The fair value of PQ's property, plant and equipment on 1 October 20X0 exceeded its book value by $120,000. In order to value the net assets at acquisition correctly we must adjust for this fair value. As part of this adjustment is made to a depreciating asset (P & E) we must then take the depreciation into account at the year end, i.e. reduce the fair value by two year's depreciation because we acquired the company exactly two years ago.

Net assets of SY (associate)

	Date of acquisition $000	Year end $000
Share capital	400	400
Share premium	100	100
Retained earnings (95 – 55)	40	95
	540	595

> **Tutorial note**
>
> We are not told SY's retained earnings at acquisition in the question. However, as we acquired the company exactly one year ago and we know the current year's profit we can calculate this by removing the current year profit from the closing balance.

(W3) **Goodwill (sub)**

	$000
Cost of investment	500
Net assets of PQ at acquisition (W2)	(368)
Goodwill at acquisition	132
Impairment	(20)
	112

(W4) **Non-controlling interests**

Not relevant – we own 100% of the subsidiary

(W5) **Consolidated retained earnings**

	$000
AZ	111
PQ (421 – 368(W2))	53
SY – 20% × (595 – 540 (W2))	11
Impairment	(20)
PURP on machine (W9)	(18)
	137

(W6) **Unrealised profit in inventory (sub sells)**

$52,000/133.333 × 33.333 = $13,000

> **Tutorial note**
>
> The sub is selling to the parent. Therefore, the unrealised profit is deducted from the inventory total and W2. PQ calculates profit based on mark up method which means one third is added to the cost to get the selling price, hence the selling price represents 133 1/3%.

ANSWERS TO SECTION C-TYPE QUESTIONS : SECTION 6

(W7) Investment in Associate

	$000
Cost	125
Share of post-acquisition profits (W5)	11
	136

(W8) Intra-group trading

Inter-group trading $52,000 + $60,000 = reduce receivables by $112,000 and reduce payable by $52,000 and increase cash by $60,000 (recorded by the payable but not the receivable – hence cash in transit)

> *Tutorial note*
>
> *The current account adjustment is a tricky one! Note vi) states the inventory sold by the sub to the parent has not yet been paid for, hence we need to remove the $52,000 from both the receivable and payables balances. However, in note viii) we are told AZ made a payment to PQ which had not been received. This means we have cash in transit and therefore the sub has not removed this balance from their receivables balance. Therefore, we need to increase cash and reduce receivables to account for this $60,000.*

(W9) Unrealised profit in PPE (parent sells)

	$000
CV now (74 – depn 74/4)	55.5
Original CV (50 – depn 50/4)	37.5
PURP	18

> *Tutorial note*
>
> *This is another tricky adjustment! We need to adjust PPE back to what it would've been had the transfer of the asset not taken place in the group. The easiest way to do this is to calculate the difference in carrying values at the year end. The transfer took place at the beginning of the year and we are therefore required to adjust the opening CV's by this year's depreciation charge. As it is the parent making the sale we must remove the profit from W5 and PPE.*

PAPER F1 : FINANCIAL OPERATIONS

377 TX GROUP (FEB 13)

> **Key answer tips**
>
> This is was a relatively straight forward group question set by the examiner involving the preparation of a consolidated statement of financial position for a parent, subsidiary and associate. Adjustments are required for the fair value, depreciation, intra-group balances, pre-acquisition reserves and unrealised profit. Students may have struggled with the treatment of the negative goodwill but not many marks would have lost here by applying the wrong treatment. Make sure you show all workings clearly and don't forget that the associates assets/liabilities are not added with the parent and subsidiaries in the consolidated statement of financial position. You are only required to show the investment in the associate and consider the effect it will have on reserves.

> **CIMA examiner comments**
>
> The answer to part (a), how control can be obtained without acquiring more than 50% of the equity shares, was very poor with many candidates not attempting an answer and a large proportion of the rest explaining that significant influence gave control or that control could be obtained by creating a sub-subsidiary type of arrangement.
>
> There seemed to be an increase in the number of candidates not showing adequate workings. There also seemed to be an increasing number with very untidy/difficult to follow workings. This made it more difficult for markers to award the correct marks as they could not see how figures were arrived at.

(a) IFRS 10 *Consolidated financial statements* states that the key concept that determines whether an entity is a subsidiary of another entity is that of control. Any situation that gives an entity control of another creates a parent/subsidiary relationship.

IFRS 10 provides the following instances where control can be achieved with fewer than 50% of equity shares:

- Power over more than 50% of voting rights by virtue of an agreement with other investors
- Power to govern the financial and operating policies of the entity under a statute or agreement
- Power to appoint or remove the majority of the members of the board of directors or equivalent governing body and control of the entity is by that board or body
- Power to cast the majority of votes at meetings of the board of directors or equivalent governing body and control of the entity is by that board or body

ANSWERS TO SECTION C-TYPE QUESTIONS : SECTION 6

(b) **TX Group – Consolidated statement of financial position as at 31 December 20X2**

	$000	$000
Non-current assets		
Property, plant and equipment (545 + 480 + 72 – 4 (W2))		1,093
Goodwill (W3)		0
Investment in associate (W7)		205
		1,298
Current assets		
Inventories (221 + 55 – 11) (W6))	265	
Receivables (98 + 75 – 44 – 15(W9))	114	
Cash at bank (72 + 15 (W8))	87	
		466
		1,764
Equity and liabilities		
Equity share capital	800	
Share premium	400	
Retained earnings (W5)	342	
		1,542
Current liabilities		
Trade payables (156 + 47 – 44(W9))	159	
Bank overdraft	63	
		222
		1,764

Workings:

(W1) Group structure

- TX owns 100% of the shares of SX so SX is a subsidiary.
- TX owns 30% of the shares of LW so LW is an associate (150,000/500,000).

(W2) Net assets of SX (sub)

	Date of acquisition $000	Year end $000
Share capital	360	360
Retained earnings	110	140
Fair value adjustment	72	72
Depn adjustment (72/18)		(4)
	542	568

447

> **Tutorial note**
>
> The fair value of SX's property, plant and equipment on 1 January 20X2 exceeded its book value by $72,000. In order to value the net assets at acquisition correctly we must adjust for this fair value. As this adjustment is made to a depreciating asset we must then take the depreciation into account at the year end, i.e. reduce the fair value by one year's depreciation because we acquired the company exactly one year ago.

Net assets of LW (associate)

	Date of acquisition $000	Year end $000
Share capital	500	500
Share premium	100	100
Retained earnings	70	120
	670	720

(W3) **Goodwill (sub)**

	$000
Cost of investment	530
Net assets of SU at acquisition (W2)	(542)
Goodwill	(12)

> **Tutorial note**
>
> The negative goodwill at acquisition means the parent made a bargain purchase, i.e. paid less than the subsidiary net assets were worth at acquisition. This profit should be transferred directly to retained earnings in W5.

(W4) **Non-controlling interests**

Not relevant – we own 100% of the subsidiary

ANSWERS TO SECTION C-TYPE QUESTIONS : SECTION 6

(W5) Consolidated retained earnings

	$000
TX	300
SX (568 – 542(W2))	26
LW – 30% × (720 – 670 (W2))	15
Negative goodwill (W3)	12
PUP – parent sells (W6)	(11)
	342

(W6) Unrealised profit (Parent sells)

On sales to SX – $44,000/133.333 × 33.333 = $11,000

> *Tutorial note*
>
> *The parent is selling to the subsidiary. Therefore, the unrealised profit is deducted from the inventory total and W5. PH calculates profit based on mark up method which means one third is added to the cost to get the selling price, hence the selling price represents 133 1/3%.*

(W7) Investment in Associate

	$000
Cost	190
Share of post-acquisition profits (W5)	15
	205

(W8) Intra-group trading

We need to reduce receivables by $44,000 and the $15,000 not accounted for by the parent.

We need to reduce payables by $44,000 and increase cash by $15,000 in transit.

> *Tutorial note*
>
> *The current account adjustment is a tricky one! Note iv) states the inventory sold by the sub to the parent has not yet been paid for, hence we need to remove the $44,000 from both the receivable and payables balances. However, in note v) we are told SX made a payment to TX which had not been received. This means we have cash in transit and therefore the parent has not removed this balance from their receivables balance. Therefore, we need to increase cash and reduce receivables to account for this $15,000.*

ns
PAPER F1 : FINANCIAL OPERATIONS

378 CLUB GROUP (MAY 13)

> **Key answer tips**
>
> This was a harder exam involving the preparation of a consolidated statement of financial position for a parent, subsidiary and associate. Adjustments were required for the fair value, depreciation, intra-group balances, pre-acquisition reserves and unrealised profit. Students would probably struggle with the adjustments for the inter-company sale of an asset, however, lots of the usual suspects were in the question to pick up the easier marks.

> **CIMA examiner comments**
>
> The answer to part (a), explanation of the treatment of a post acquisition increase in goodwill, was very poor with many candidates not attempting an answer and a large proportion of the rest explaining that an increase in goodwill should be added to intangible non-current assets and reserves.
>
> This time a smaller proportion of the answers to part (b) simply added the holding entity's and subsidiary's figures together, (sometimes adding a 20% portion of the associated entity), making little attempt at any consolidation adjustments other than a goodwill calculation.
>
> There seemed to be an increase in the number of candidates not showing adequate workings. There also seemed to be an increasing number with very untidy/difficult to follow workings. This made it more difficult for markers to award the correct marks as they could not see how figures were arrived at. It is essential that adequate, clear workings are shown for every question or marks could be lost. Overall there seemed to be more good answers to this question than in recent examinations.

(a) If an impairment review indicates that goodwill has increased in value, the increase is deemed to be internally generated goodwill. Internally generated goodwill is not allowed to be recognised in the financial statements.

Club will therefore not recognise the increase in goodwill and will include goodwill in its statement of financial position at its original value.

(b) **Club – Consolidated statement of financial position as at 31 March 20X3**

	$000	$000
Non-current assets		
Property, plant and equipment		
(50,050 + 30,450 + 1,200 – 200 (W2) – 20 (W9))		81,480
Goodwill (W3)		10,570
Investment in associate (W7)		8,573
		———
		100,623

450

ANSWERS TO SECTION C-TYPE QUESTIONS : SECTION 6

Current assets
Inventories (34,910 + 9,310 – 192 (W6))	44,028	
Receivables (38,790 + 16,530 – 960 – 115 (W8))	54,245	
Cash at bank (5,010 + 1,480 + 115(W8))	6,605	
		104,878
		205,501

Equity and liabilities
Equity share capital	112,620
Retained earnings (W5)	23,441
	136,061

Non-current liabilities
Borrowings (32,000 + 15,000)	47,000

Current liabilities
Trade payables (11,320 + 10,830 – 960 (W8))	21,190	
Interest (800 + 450)	1,250	
		22,440
		205,501

Workings:

(W1) **Group structure**

- Club owns 100% of the shares of Green so Green is a subsidiary.
- Club owns 25% of the shares of Tee so Tee is an associate (3,980/ 15,920).

(W2) **Net assets of Green (sub)**

	Date of acquisition	Year end
	$000	$000
Share capital	17,370	17370
Share premium	3,470	3,470
Retained earnings	3,000	10,650
Fair value adjustment	1,200	1,200
Depn adjustment (1,200/12 × 2)		(200)
	25,040	32,490

> **Tutorial note**
>
> The fair value of Green's property, plant and equipment on 1 April 20X1 exceeded its book value by $1,200,000. In order to value the net assets at acquisition correctly we must adjust for this fair value. As this adjustment is made to a depreciating asset we must then take the depreciation into account at the year end, i.e. reduce the fair value by two year's depreciation because we acquired the company exactly two years ago.

Net assets of Tee (associate)

	Date of acquisition $000	Year end $000
Share capital	15,920	15,920
Retained earnings	1,300	3,590
	17,220	19,510

(W3) **Goodwill (sub)**

	$000
Cost of investment	35,610
Net assets of SU at acquisition (W2)	(25,040)
Goodwill	10,570

(W4) **Non-controlling interests**

Not relevant – we own 100% of the subsidiary

(W5) **Consolidated retained earnings**

	$000
Club	15,630
Green (32,490 – 25,040 (W2))	7,450
Tee – 25% × (19,510 – 17,220 (W2))	573
PURP on inventory– parent sells (W6)	(192)
PURP on machine – parent sells (W9)	(20)
	23,441

ANSWERS TO SECTION C-TYPE QUESTIONS : SECTION 6

(W6) Unrealised profit (Parent sells)

On sales to Green – $960,000/133.333 × 33.333 = $240,000 × 80% = $192,000

> *Tutorial note*
>
> *The parent is selling to the subsidiary. Therefore, the unrealised profit is deducted from the inventory total and W5. Club calculates profit based on mark up method which means one third is added to the cost to get the selling price, hence the selling price represents 133 1/3%. We must then remove 80% of this profit because 20% of the goods have now been sold outside of the group.*

(W7) Investment in Associate

	$000
Cost	8,000
Share of post-acquisition profits (W5)	573
	8,573

(W8) Intra-group trading

We need to reduce receivables by $960,000 and the $115,000 not accounted for by the parent.

We need to reduce payables by $960,000 and increase cash by $115,000 in transit.

> *Tutorial note*
>
> *The current account adjustment is a tricky one! Note v) states the inventory sold by the parent to the sub has not yet been paid for, hence we need to remove the $960,000 from both the receivable and payables balances. However, in note vii) we are told Green made a payment to Club which had not been received. This means we have cash in transit and therefore the parent has not removed this balance from their receivables balance. Therefore, we need to increase cash and reduce receivables to account for this $115,000.*

(W9) Unrealised profit in PPE (parent sells)

	$000
CV now (115 – depn 115/5)	92
Original CV (90 – depn 90/5)	72
PURP	20

Tutorial note

This is another tricky adjustment! We need to adjust PPE back to what it would've been had the transfer of the asset not taken place in the group. The easiest way to do this is to calculate the difference in carrying values at the year end. The transfer took place at the beginning of the year and we are therefore required to adjust the opening CV's by this year's depreciation charge. As it is the parent making the sale we must remove the profit from W5 and PPE.

379 ROAD GROUP (AUG 13)

Key answer tips

This was a harder question involving the preparation of a consolidated statement of financial position for a parent, subsidiary and associate. Adjustments were required for the fair value, depreciation, intra-group balances, pre-acquisition reserves and unrealised profit. Students would probably struggle with the adjustments for the inter-company sale of an asset, however, lots of the usual suspects were in the question to pick up the easier marks.

CIMA examiner comments

The answer to part (a), the meaning of control, was very poor. Most candidates did state that 50% share holding was required but did not elaborate. A large proportion of the answers also stated that 20% shareholding gave significant influence therefore control.

It is essential that adequate, clear workings are shown for every question or marks could be lost.

(a) According to IFRS 10 *Consolidated Financial Statements* control is the power to govern the financial and operating policies of an entity so as to obtain benefit from its activities.

There is a presumption that control exists where the investor entity owns over half of the voting power of the other entity. Where control over another entity exists that entity is regarded as a subsidiary.

ANSWERS TO SECTION C-TYPE QUESTIONS : SECTION 6

IFRS 10 also sets out circumstances where control can be established with less than 50% of the equity votes, in each case where control exists the entity will be regarded as a subsidiary, even if less than 50% of the equity voting shares are held.

IFRS 10 provides the following instances where control can be achieved with less than 50% of equity shares:

- Power over more than 50% of voting rights by virtue of an agreement with other investors
- Power to govern the financial and operating policies of the entity under a statute or agreement
- Power to appoint or remove the majority of the members of the board of directors or equivalent governing body and control of the entity is by that board or body
- Power to cast the majority of votes at meetings of the board of directors or equivalent governing body and control of the entity is by that board or body

(b) **Road – Consolidated statement of financial position as at 31 March 20X3**

	$000	$000
Non-current assets		
Property, plant and equipment (1,840 + 1,060 + 320 (W2) – 48 – 24 (W9))		3,148
Goodwill (W3)		170
Investment in associate (W7)		330
		3,648
Current assets		
Inventories (310 + 236 – 26 (W6))	520	
Receivables (140 + 119 – 110 (W8))	149	
Cash at bank (71 + 27 + 110(W8))	208	
		877
		4,525
Equity and liabilities		
Equity share capital		2,000
Share premium		500
Retained earnings (W5)		927
		3,427
Non-current liabilities		
Borrowings (700 + 250 – 250 (W10))		700
Current liabilities		
Trade payables (270 + 128)	398	
Interest (25 – 25 (W10))	0	
		398
		4,525

Workings:

(W1) Group structure

- Road owns 100% of the shares of Street so Street is a subsidiary.
- Road owns 25% of the shares of Drive so Drive is an associate (175/700).

(W2) Net assets of Street (sub)

	Date of acquisition $000	Year end $000
Share capital	550	550
Share premium	150	150
Retained earnings	122	339
Fair value adjustment	320	320
Depn adjustment (320/20 × 3)		(48)
	1,142	1,311

Tutorial note

The fair value of Street's property, plant and equipment on 1 April 20X0 exceeded its book value by $320,000. In order to value the net assets at acquisition correctly we must adjust for this fair value. As this adjustment is made to a depreciating asset we must then take the depreciation into account at the year end, i.e. reduce the fair value by three year's depreciation because we acquired the company exactly three years ago.

Net assets of Drive (associate)

	Date of acquisition $000	Year end $000
Share capital	700	700
Share premium	200	200
Retained earnings	350	458
	1,250	1,358

(W3) Goodwill (sub)

	$000
Cost of investment	1,350
Net assets of Street at acquisition (W2)	(1,142)
Goodwill at acquisition	208
Impairment	(38)
Goodwill at reporting date	170

(W4) Non-controlling interests

Not relevant – we own 100% of the subsidiary

(W5) Consolidated retained earnings

	$000
Road	814
Street (1,311 – 1,142 (W2))	169
Drive – 25% × (1,358 – 1,250 (W2))	27
Loan interest adjustment (W10)	25
Impairment (38 (W3) + 20 (W7))	(58)
PURP on inventory– parent sells (W6)	(26)
PURP on machine – parent sells (W9)	(24)
	927

(W6) Unrealised profit (Parent sells)

On sales to Street – $220,000/125 × 25 = $44,000 × 60% = $26,400 (round to 26)

Tutorial note

The parent is selling to the subsidiary. Therefore, the unrealised profit is deducted from the inventory total and W5. Road calculates profit based on mark up method which means one 25% is added to the cost to get the selling price, hence the selling price represents 125%. We must then remove 60% of this profit because 40% of the goods have now been sold outside of the group.

(W7) Investment in Associate

	$000
Cost	323
Share of post-acquisition profits (W5)	27
Impairment	(20)
	330

(W8) Intra-group trading

We need to reduce receivables by $110,000 and increase cash by $110,000 in transit.

Tutorial note

The current account adjustment is a tricky one! Note vi) states that half the inventory sold by the parent to the sub has not yet been paid for. However, in note vii) we are told Street made a payment to Road which had not been received. This means we have cash in transit and therefore the parent has not removed this balance from their receivables balance. Hence we need to increase cash and reduce receivables to account for this $110,000.

PAPER F1 : FINANCIAL OPERATIONS

(W9) Unrealised profit in PPE (parent sells)

	$000
CV now (95 – depn 95/5)	76
Original CV (65 – depm 65/5)	(52)
PURP	24

> **Tutorial note**
>
> This is another tricky adjustment! We need to adjust the CV of PPE back to what it would have been had the transfer of the asset not taken place in the group. The easiest way to do this is to calculate the difference in carrying values at the year end. The transfer took place at the beginning of the year and we are therefore required to adjust the opening CV by this year's depreciation charge. As it is the parent making the sale we must remove the profit from W5 and PPE.

(W10) Intra-group loan

The loan of $250,000 must be eliminated, i.e. reduce the investment in Road and reduce the borrowings of Street. We must also eliminate the associated accrued interest made by Street of $25,000 by reducing payables of Street and increasing retained earnings (W5).

> **Tutor's top tips**
>
> In this question Street has accrued for the loan interest due to be paid by showing a liability in the statement of financial position. These adjustments must be eliminated for consolidation purposes. Road has not made any accruals for the interest due from Street, hence no corrections needed in their receivable accounts.

Section 7

SPECIMEN EXAM QUESTIONS

We are grateful to CIMA for their kind permission to reproduce these specimen papers.

The Chartered Institute of Management Accountants 2009

CIMA 2010 Chartered Management Accounting Qualification – Specimen Examination Paper F1 – Published November 2009

Note: *Information on relevant tax rules will be published on the CIMA website at least 6 weeks prior to the date of the examination and be reproduced within the examination paper.*

COUNTRY X – TAX REGIME FOR USE THROUGHOUT THE EXAMINATION PAPER

Relevant tax rules for years ended 30 April 2007 to 2010

Corporate profits

Unless otherwise specified, only the following rules for taxation of corporate profits will be relevant, other taxes can be ignored:

(a) Accounting rules on recognition and measurement are followed for tax purposes.

(b) All expenses other than depreciation, amortisation, entertaining, taxes paid to other public bodies and donations to political parties are tax deductible

(c) Tax depreciation is deductible as follows: 50% of additions to Property, Plant and Equipment in the accounting period in which they are recorded; 25% per year of the written-down value (i.e. cost minus previous allowances) in subsequent accounting periods except that in which the asset is disposed of. No tax depreciation is allowed on land.

(d) The corporate tax on profits is at a rate of 25%.

(e) Tax losses can be carried forward to offset against future taxable profits from the same business.

Value Added Tax

Country X has a VAT system which allows entities to reclaim input tax paid.

In country X the VAT rates are:

Zero rated   0%

Standard rated   15%

PAPER F1 : FINANCIAL OPERATIONS

CIMA 2010 Chartered Management Accounting Qualification – Specimen Examination Paper F1

Published November 2009

SECTION A – 20 MARKS

[*Note:* The indicative time for answering this section is 36 minutes]

ANSWER *ALL* TEN SUB-QUESTION IN THIS SECTION

Instructions for answering Section A:

The answers to the ten sub-questions in Section A should ALL be written in your answer book.

Your answers should be clearly numbered with the sub-question number and ruled off, so that the markers know which sub-question you are answering. **For multiple choice questions, you need only write the sub-question number and the letter of the answer option you have chosen.** You do not need to start a new page for each sub-question.

QUESTION ONE

1.1 Which of the following statements is correct?

A   Tax evasion is legally arranging affairs so as to minimise the tax liability

Tax avoidance is the illegal manipulation of the tax system to avoid paying taxes due

B   Tax evasion is legally arranging affairs so as to evade paying tax

Tax avoidance is tax planning, legally arranging affairs so as to minimise the tax liability

C   Tax evasion is using loop holes in legislation to evade paying tax

Tax avoidance is the illegal manipulation of the tax system to avoid paying taxes due

D   Tax evasion is the illegal manipulation of the tax system to avoid paying taxes due

Tax avoidance is tax planning, legally arranging affairs so as to minimise the tax liability

(2 marks)

SPECIMEN EXAM QUESTIONS : SECTION 7

1.2 A has been trading for a number of years. The tax written down value of A's property, plant and equipment was $40,000 at 31 March 2009. A did not purchase any property, plant and equipment between 1 April 2009 and 31 March 2010.

A's Statement of profit or loss for the year ended 31 March 2010 is as follows:

	$
Gross profit	270,000
Administrative expenses	(120,000)
Depreciation – property, plant and equipment	(12,000)
Distribution costs	(55,000)
	83,000
Finance cost	(11,000)
Profit before tax	72,000

Administration expenses include entertaining of $15,000.

What is A's income tax due for the year ended 31 March 2010?

- A 8,750
- B 13,750
- C 15,500
- D 22,250

(2 marks)

1.3 B buys goods from a wholesaler, paying the price of the goods plus VAT. B sells goods in its shop to customers. The customers pay the price of the goods plus VAT.

From the perspective of B, the VAT would have

- A Effective incidence
- B Formal incidence
- C Ineffective incidence
- D Informal incidence

(2 marks)

1.4 CT has taxable profits of $100,000 and pays 50% as dividends.

The total tax due is calculated as:

CT's corporate income tax ($100,000 × 25%)	$25,000
CT's shareholder's personal income tax on dividends received ($50,000 × 20%)	$10,000
Total tax due	$35,000

The tax system in use here would be classified as a:

- A Imputation tax system
- B Partial imputation tax system
- C Classical tax system
- D Split rate tax system

(2 marks)

1.5 The International Accounting Standards Board's *Conceptual Framework for Financial Reporting* sets out four qualitative characteristics, relevance and reliability are two, list the other two. **(2 marks)**

1.6 The CIMA Code of Ethics for Professional Accountants sets out four principles that a professional accountant is required to comply with. Two principles are objectivity and professional competence/due care, list the other two. **(2 marks)**

1.7 The purpose of an external audit is to:

- A check the accounts are correct and to approve them
- B enable the auditor to express an opinion as to whether the financial statements give a true and fair view of the entity's affairs
- C search for any fraud taking place in the entity
- D check that all regulations have been followed in preparing the financial statements and to authorise the financial statements **(2 marks)**

1.8 Goodwill arising on acquisition is accounted for according to IFRS 3 *Business combinations*.

Goodwill arising on acquisition is:

- A carried at cost, with an annual impairment review
- B written off against reserves on acquisition
- C amortised over its useful life
- D revalued to fair value at each year end **(2 marks)**

1.9 IT has 300 items of product ABC2 in inventory at 31 March 2010. The items were found to be damaged by a water leak. The items can be repaired and repackaged for a cost of $1.50 per item. Once repackaged, the items can be sold at the normal price of $3.50 each.

The original cost of the items was $2.20 each. The replacement cost at 31 March 2010 is $2.75 each.

What value should IT put on the inventory of ABC2 in its statement of financial position at 31 March 2010?

- A $600
- B $660
- C $810
- D $825 **(2 marks)**

1.10 (i) CD is Z's main customer.

(ii) FE is a supplier of Z.

(iii) ST is Z's chairman of the board and a major shareholder of Z.

(iv) K is Z's banker and has provided an overdraft facility and a $1,000,000 loan.

(v) JT is the owner of a building entity that has just been awarded a large building contract by Z. JT is also the son of ST.

Which 2 of the above can be regarded as a related party of Z?

A (i) and (iii)

B (ii) and (iv)

C (iii) and (v)

D (iv) and (v)

(2 marks)

(Total for Question One = 20 marks)

PAPER F1 : FINANCIAL OPERATIONS

CIMA 2010 Chartered Management Accounting Qualification –
Specimen Examination Paper F1

Published November 2009

SECTION B – 30 MARKS

[*Note:* The indicative time for answering this section is 90 minutes]

ANSWER *ALL* SIX SUB-QUESTIONS IN THIS SECTION – 5 MARKS EACH

QUESTION TWO

(a) ATOZ operates in several countries as follows:

- ATOZ was incorporated in country BCD many years ago. It has curtailed operations in BCD but still has its registered office in country BCD and carries out a small proportion (less than 10%) of its trade there.
- ATOZ buys most of its products and raw materials from country FGH.
- ATOZ generates most of its revenue in country NOP and all its senior management live there and hold all the management board meetings there.

Required:

(i) Explain why determining corporate residence is important for corporate income tax. (2 marks)

(ii) Explain which country ATOZ will be deemed to be resident in for tax purposes. (3 marks)

(Total for sub-question (a) = 5 marks)

(b) WX operates a retail business in country X and is registered for VAT purposes.

During the last VAT period WX had the following transactions:

Purchases of materials and services, all at standard VAT rate, $130,000 excluding VAT.

Purchase of new machinery, $345,000, inclusive of VAT.

Sales of goods in the period, all inclusive of VAT where applicable, were:

Sales of goods subject to VAT at standard rate $230,000

Sales of goods subject to VAT at zero rate $115,000

Assume you are WX's trainee management accountant and you have been asked to prepare the VAT return and calculate the net VAT due to/from the tax authorities at the end of the period.

Assume WX has no other transactions subject to VAT and that all VAT paid can be recovered.

Required:

(i) Explain the difference between a single stage sales tax and VAT. (2 marks)

(ii) Calculate the net VAT due to/from WX at the end of the period. (3 marks)

(Total for sub-question (b) = 5 marks)

(c) Country K uses prescriptive accounting standards. Country K's standard on intangible assets has a list of intangible assets covered by the standard and an extensive list of items that are not allowed to be recognised as assets. RS has incurred expenditure on a new product that does not appear to be specifically listed as "not allowed" by the standard. RS's management want to classify the expenditure as an intangible non-current asset in RS's statement of financial position. They argue that the type of expenditure incurred is not listed in the accounting standard as being "not allowed" therefore it is allowed to be capitalised.

RS's auditors have pointed out that the expenditure is not listed as being "allowed" and therefore should not be capitalised.

Required:

Explain the possible advantages of having accounting standards based on principles rather than being prescriptive. Use the scenario above to illustrate your answer.

(Total for sub-question (c) = 5 marks)

(d) BD is a well established double glazing business, manufacturing building extensions, doors and windows in its own manufacturing facility and installing them at customer properties.

BD's financial statements for the year ended 31 March 2009 showed the manufacturing facility and installation division as separate reportable segments.

On 1 March 2010, BD's management decided to sell its manufacturing facility and concentrate on the more profitable selling and installation side of the business.

At BD's accounting year end, 31 March 2010, BD had not found a buyer for its manufacturing facility and was continuing to run it as a going concern. The facility was available for immediate sale; the management were committed to the sale and were actively seeking a buyer. They were quite sure that the facility would be sold before 31 March 2011.

The manufacturing facility's fair value at 31 March 2010 was $2.8 million, comprising total assets with a fair value of $3.6 million and liabilities with a fair value of $0.8 million.

BD's management accountant calculated that the manufacturing facility had incurred a loss for the year of $0.5 million before tax and the estimated cost of selling the manufacturing facility was $0.2 million.

Required:

Explain, with reasons, how BD should treat the manufacturing facility in its financial statements for the year ended 31 March 2010. **(Total for sub-question (d) = 5 marks)**

(e) L leases office space and a range of office furniture and equipment to businesses. On 1 April 2009 C acquired a lease for a fully furnished office space (office space plus office furniture and equipment) and a separate lease for a computer system from L.

The office space was a lease of part of a large building and the building had an expected life of 50 years. The lease was for 5 years with rental payable monthly. The first year was rent free. The $1,000 per month rental commenced on 1 April 2010.

The computer system lease was for 3 years, the expected useful life of the system was 3 years. The $15,000 per year lease rental was due annually in arrears commencing with 31 March 2010. The interest rate implicit in the lease is 12.5% and the cost of the leased asset at 1 April 2009 was $35,720. C depreciates all equipment on the straight line basis.

Under the terms of the computer system lease agreement C is responsible for insuring, servicing and repairing the computers. However, L is responsible for insurance, maintenance and repair of the office.

C allocates the finance charge for finance leases using the actuarial method.

Required:

Explain the accounting treatment, required by international financial reporting standards, in the financial statements of C in respect of the two leases for the year ended 31 March 2010. **(Total for sub-question (e) = 5 marks)**

(f) PS issued 1,000,000 $1 cumulative, redeemable preferred shares on 1 April 2009. The shares were issued at a premium of 25% and pay a dividend of 4% per year. The issue costs incurred were $60,000. The shares are redeemable for cash of $1.50 on 31 March 2019. The effective interest rate is 5.18%. Ignore all tax implications.

The management accountant of PS has extracted the following amounts from the preferred shares ledger account, for the year ended 31 March 2010:

Account – Non-current liability – Preferred shares

Net amount received on issue	$1,190,000
Finance cost @5.18%	$61,642
Less dividend paid	($40,000)
Balance at 31 March 2010	$1,211,642

Required:

(i) **Explain the IAS 32 *Financial instruments* – presentation and IAS 39 Financial instruments – recognition and measurement requirements for the presentation and measurement of an issue of preferred shares.** **(3 marks)**

(ii) **Using the information provided above, explain the amounts that PS should include for the preferred shares in its statement of profit or loss and other comprehensive income and statement of financial position as at year ended 31 March 2010.**
(2 marks)

(Total for sub-question (f) = 5 marks)

CIMA 2010 Chartered Management Accounting Qualification –
Specimen Examination Paper F1

Published November 2009

SECTION C – 50 MARKS

[*Note:* The indicative time for this section is 90 minutes]

ANSWER *BOTH* QUESTIONS IN THIS SECTION – 25 MARKS EACH

QUESTION THREE

XY's trial balance at 31 March 2010 is shown below:

	Notes	$000	$000
Administrative expenses		303	
Available for sale investments	(ii)	564	
Cash and cash equivalents		21	
Cash received on disposal of land			48
Cost of goods sold		908	
Distribution costs		176	
Equity dividend paid	(ix)	50	
Income tax	(iii)	12	
Inventory at 31 March 2010		76	
Land at cost – 31 March 2009	(v)	782	
Long term borrowings	(viii)		280
Ordinary Shares $1 each, fully paid at 31 March 2010	(vii)		500
Property, plant and equipment – at cost 31 March 2009	(vi)	630	
Provision for deferred tax at 31 March 2009	(iv)		19
Provision for property, plant and equipment depreciation at 31 March 2009	(vi)		378
Retained earnings at 31 March 2009			321
Revaluation reserve at 31 March 2009			160
Revenue			1,770
Share premium at 31 March 2010			200
Trade payables			56
Trade receivables		210	
		3,732	3,732

PAPER F1 : FINANCIAL OPERATIONS

Additional information provided:

(i) XY trades in country X.

(ii) Available for sale investments are carried in the financial statements at market value. The market value of the available for sale investments at 31 March 2010 was $608,000. There were no purchases or sales of available for sale investments during the year.

(iii) The income tax balance in the trial balance is a result of the under-provision of tax for the year ended 31 March 2009.

(iv) The taxation due for the year ended 31 March 2010 is estimated at $96,000. The tax depreciation cumulative allowances at 31 March 2009 for property, plant and equipment were $453,000.

(v) Land sold during the year had a carrying value of $39,000. The fair value of the remaining land at 31 March 2010 was $729,000.

(vi) Property, plant and equipment is depreciated at 20% per annum straight line. Depreciation of property, plant and equipment is considered to be part of cost of sales. XY's policy is to charge a full year's depreciation in the year of acquisition and no depreciation in the year of disposal.

(vii) XY issued 100,000 equity shares on 31 October 2009 at a premium of 50%. The cash received was correctly entered into the financial records and is included in the trial balance.

(viii) Long term borrowings consist of a loan taken out on 1 April 2009 at 5% interest per year. No loan interest has been paid at 31 March 2010.

(ix) XY paid a final dividend of $50,000 for the year ended 31 March 2009.

Required:

(a) Calculate the deferred tax amounts relating to property, plant and equipment, that are required to be included in XY's statement of profit or loss and other comprehensive income for the year ended 31 March 2010 and its statement of financial position at that date.

Ignore all other deferred tax implications. **(5 marks)**

(b) Prepare XY's statement of profit or loss and other comprehensive income and statement of changes in equity for the year to 31 March 2010 and a statement of financial position at that date, in a form suitable for presentation to the shareholders and in accordance with the requirements of International Financial Reporting Standards. **(20 marks)**

Notes to the financial statements are not required, but all workings must be clearly shown. Do not prepare a statement of accounting policies. **(Total for Question Three = 25 marks)**

QUESTION FOUR

The draft summarised Statements of financial position at 31 March 2010 for three entities, P, S and A are given below:

	P $000	P $000	S $000	S $000	A $000	A $000
Non-current assets						
Property, plant and equipment	40,000		48,000		34,940	
Investments:						
40,000 Ordinary shares in S at cost	60,000					
Loan to S	10,000					
8,000 Ordinary shares in A at cost	13,000					
		123,000		48,000		34,940
Current assets						
Inventory	8,000		12,000		8,693	
Current a/c with S	8,000		0		0	
Trade receivables	17,000		11,000		10,106	
Cash and cash equivalents	1,000	34,000	3,000	26,000	3,033	21,832
Total assets		157,000		74,000		56,772
Equity and liabilities						
Equity shares of $1 each	100,000		40,000		20,000	
Retained earnings	21,000		13,000		7,800	
		121,000		53,000		27,800
Non-current liabilities						
Borrowings		26,000		10,000		10,000
Current liabilities						
Trade payables	10,000		5,000		18,972	
Current a/c with P	0		6,000		0	
		10,000		11,000		18,972
Total equity and liabilities		157,000		74,000		56,772

PAPER F1 : FINANCIAL OPERATIONS

Additional information:

(i) P's acquired all of S's equity shares on 1 April 2009 for $60,000,000 when S's retained earnings were $6,400,000. P also advanced S a ten year loan of $10,000,000 on 1 April 2009.

(ii) The fair value of S's property, plant and equipment on 1 April 2009 exceeded its book value by $1,000,000. The excess of fair value over book value was attributed to buildings owned by S. At the date of acquisition these buildings had a remaining useful life of 20 years. P's accounting policy is to depreciate buildings using the straight line basis.

(iii) At 31 March 2010 $250,000 loan interest was due and had not been paid. Both P and S had accrued this amount at the year end.

(iv) P purchased 8,000,000 of A's equity shares on 1 April 2009 for $13,000,000 when A's retained earnings were $21,000,000. P exercises significant influence over all aspects of A's strategic and operational decisions.

(v) S posted a cheque to P for $2,000,000 on 30 March 2010 which did not arrive until 7 April 2010.

(vi) No dividends are proposed by any of the entities.

(vii) P occasionally trades with S. In March 2010 P sold S goods for $4,000,000. P uses a mark up of one third on cost. On 31 March 2010 all the goods were included in S's closing inventory and the invoice for the goods was still outstanding.

(viii) P's directors do not want to consolidate A. They argue that they do not control A, therefore it does not need to be consolidated. They insist that A should appear in the consolidated statement of financial position at cost of $13,000,000.

Required:

(a) Draft a response that explains to P's directors the correct treatment of A in the consolidated financial statements. Include comments on any ethical issues involved.

(5 marks)

(b) Prepare a Consolidated Statement of Financial Position for the P Group of entities as at 31 March 2010, in accordance with the requirements of International Financial Reporting Standards. (20 marks)

Notes to the financial statements are not required but all workings must be shown.

(Total for Question Four = 25 marks)

Section 8

ANSWERS TO SPECIMEN EXAM QUESTIONS

We are grateful to CIMA for their kind permission to reproduce these specimen papers.

The Chartered Institute of Management Accountants 2009

CIMA 2010 Chartered Management Accounting Qualification – Answers for Specimen Examination Paper F1 – Published November 2009

SECTION A

QUESTION ONE

1.1 D

1.2 D

	$
Profit before tax	72,000
Add : Depreciation – property, plant and equipment	12,000
Add: Entertaining costs	15,000
Less: Tax depreciation ($40,000 × 25%)	(10,000)
	89,000
Taxed at 25%	22,250

1.3 B

1.4 C

1.5 Comparability and understandability

1.6 Integrity and confidentiality

1.7 B

1.8 A

1.9 A

Cost	$2.20
Selling price	$3.50
Repair costs	$1.50
Net realisable value	$2.00 ($3.50 − $1.50)

Use lower of cost and net realisable value = $2.00 × 300 units = $600

1.10 C

SECTION B

QUESTION TWO

(a) (i) It is important to determine corporate residence as corporate income tax is usually a residence-based tax. Whether corporate income tax will be charged depends on the residence, for tax purposes, of any particular entity.

(ii) The OECD model tax convention provides that an entities status shall be determined as follows:

(a) it shall be deemed to be a resident only of the State in which its place of effective management is situated

(b) if the State in which its place of effective management is situated cannot be determined or if its place of effective management is in neither State, it shall be deemed to be a resident only of the State with which its economic relations are closer

(c) if the State with which its economic relations are closer cannot be determined, it shall be deemed to be a resident of the State from the laws of which it derives its legal status.

ATOZ will be deemed to be resident in country NOP as that is where its place of effective management is.

(b) (i) Single-stage sales taxes apply at one level of the production/distribution chain only; they can be applied to any one of the following levels:

- the manufacturing level
- the wholesale level
- the retail level.

Tax paid by entities is not recoverable.

VAT charges tax at every level, but tax paid at one level can usually be recovered by deducting it from tax collected at the next level. The ultimate consumer bears all the tax.

(ii)

Outputs:	VAT exclusive	VAT	VAT inclusive
Standard rate (230,000/115 × 15)	200,000	30,000	230,000
Zero rate	115,000	0	115,000
Inputs:			
Materials and services	(130,000)	(19,500)	(149,500)
New machinery (345,000/115 × 15)	(300,000)	(45,000)	(345,000)
Amount due to be refunded by tax authority		(34,500)	

(c) The possible advantages of having accounting standards based on principles rather than being prescriptive include:

(i) It will be harder to construct ways of avoiding the requirements of individual standards, for example, in country K the prescriptive standard sets out definitions of what is allowed and what is not allowed, this causes problems if some items are not specified, such as in RS's case. Whereas if the standard sets out general principles, it is much harder to avoid the standard's requirements as what is included will be defined by applying the principle.

(ii) If a prescriptive standard lists items or specifies quantities they may go out of date fairly quickly and need to be regularly updated. This may be the problem with RS, the expenditure incurred may not have been required when the standard was agreed. If principles based standards are used they do not go out of date unless a principle is changed.

(iii) If an actual value is specified in a standard, it may be possible for some entities to construct various means of avoiding the application of that requirement. If a general principle is specified it will apply no matter what value is put on it

(iv) With principle based standards the requirements in certain situations will need to be applied using professional judgement, which can help ensure that the correct application is used. Whereas a prescriptive standard would require a certain treatment to be used, regardless of the situation, which could lead to similar items being treated the same way even if the circumstances are different.

(v) Principles-based GAAP should ensure that the spirit of the regulations are adhered to, whereas the prescriptive system is more likely to lead to the letter of the law being followed rather than the spirit.

(d) The manufacturing facility has been shown as a separate reportable operating segment according to IFRS 8. This means that it must be a separate operating unit whose operating results are regularly reviewed by BD's chief operating decision maker. This implies that there is discrete financial information available for the manufacturing facility's operations. It will therefore meet the IFRS 5 definition of a discontinued operation, a component of an entity classified as held for sale and is part of a single plan to dispose of a separate major line of business. The manufacturing facility loss of $0.5 million will be shown as one amount as a discontinued operation on the statement of profit or loss and other comprehensive income, at the end of the statement of profit or loss section, after profit from continuing activities and before other comprehensive income. The detailed breakdown of the loss will be given in the notes to the statement of profit or loss and other comprehensive income. The manufacturing facility has not been disposed of by the year end, so it will be classified as a "non-current asset held for sale". Non-current assets held for sale are valued in the statement of financial position at fair value less the cost to sell. The assets and liabilities have to be shown separately, so the assets of $3.4 million (assets $3.6 million less cost to sell $0.2 million) will be shown after current assets, with the heading non-current assets held for sale. The liabilities of $0.8 million will be shown under current liabilities and headed "liabilities directly associated with non-current assets classified as held for sale".

(e) **Office space – Operating lease**

Rentals due: Total payments 4 years at $1,000 × 12 = £48,000

Spread over 5 years = $48,000/5 = $9,600 p.a.

Statement of profit or loss for year to 31 March 2010 (extract)

Administrative expenses – Office rentals $9,600

Statement of financial position as at 31 March 2010 (extract)

Current liability – Accrued rentals $9,600

Computer system

Finance Charge: Allocate finance charge using actuarial method at 12.5% interest paid in arrears.

Depreciate asset using normal accounting policy.

	Opening balance	Finance charge (IS)	Paid	Closing balance (SOFP)
31/03/10	35,720	4,465	(15,000)	25,185
31/03/11	25,185	3,148	(15,000)	13,333
31/03/12	13,333	1,667	(15,000)	0

Summary of accounting entries:

Statement of profit or loss for year ended 31.03.10 (extract)

	$
Finance charges	4,465
Depreciation (35,720/3)	11,907

Statement of financial position (extract)

Non-current assets

Leased equipment under finance leases at cost	35,720
Accounting depreciation	(11,907)
Carrying value	23,813

Non-current liabilities

Obligations under finance leases	13,333

Current liabilities

Obligations under finance leases	11,852

(f) (i) IAS 32 requires the particular rights attaching to a preference share to be analysed to determine whether it exhibits the fundamental characteristic of a financial liability. There are a number of characteristics that will indicate that there is an obligation to transfer financial assets to the holder of the share, in each case the preferred share will need to be classified as debt rather than equity. If the terms of issue provide for mandatory redemption for cash the preferred shares will be treated as liabilities. If the preference shares are non-redeemable, the appropriate classification is based on an assessment of the substance of the contractual arrangements and the definitions of a financial liability and equity instrument. For example if the preferred shares are cumulative it means that a dividend will always eventually have to be paid and is therefore not discretionary. Therefore the preferred shares are classified as debt.

(ii) PS's shares provide for a cash redemption and are therefore classified as debt. In the statement of financial position the preferred shares will be shown under non-current liabilities. The dividend paid on the preferred shares will be treated as finance cost in the statement of profit or loss. PS Extracts from financial statements:

PS Statement of profit or loss and other comprehensive income for year ended 31 March 2010 (extract)

Finance expense $61,642

PS Statement of financial position as at 31 March 2010 (extract)

Non-current liabilities

Preferred shares $1,211,642

SECTION C

QUESTION THREE

(a) **Property, plant and equipment**

	Accounting carrying value	Tax base	Difference × 25%
	$000	$000	$000
Cost	630	630	
Depreciation (TB)	(378)		
Tax depreciation (note below)		(453)	
Balance at 31/03/09	252	177	19
Depreciation (20% × 630)	(126)		
Tax depreciation (25% × 177)		(44)	
Balance at 31/03/10	126	133	(2)

Note 1 – tax depreciation

Accounting depreciation 126 pa
TB accumulated depreciation 378
378/126 = purchased 3 years ago

Year 1 – 50% × 630	315
Year 2 – 25% × 315	79
Year 3 – 25% × (315 – 79)	59
Tax depreciation at 31/03/09	453

(also given in note (iv) of the question)

Statement of profit or loss and other comprehensive income (extract)

	$000
Income tax expense – deferred tax	(21)
(decrease 19 to (2))	

Statement of financial position (extract)

Current assets – deferred tax	2

(b) **XY – Statement of profit or loss and other comprehensive income for the year ended 31 March 2010**

		$000
Revenue		1,770
Cost of sales	(W5)	(1,039)
Gross profit		745
Administrative expenses		(303)
Distribution costs		(176)
Profit from operations		252
Finance cost	(W3)	(14)
Profit before tax		238
Income tax expense	(W2)	(87)
Profit for the period		151
Other comprehensive income:		
Revaluation gain on investments	(W6)	44
Total comprehensive income for the year		195

XY – Statement of financial position as at 31 March 2010

	$000	$000
Non-current assets		
Property, plant and equipment (W1)		855
Available for sale investments		608
		1,463
Current assets		
Inventory	76	
Trade receivables	210	
Deferred tax asset (part a)	2	
Cash and cash equivalent	21	
		309
Total assets		1,772
Equity and liabilities		
Equity		
Share capital	500	
Share premium	200	
Revaluation reserve	204	
Retained earnings	422	
Total equity		1,326

	$000	$000
Non-current liabilities		
Long-term borrowings	280	
Total non-current liabilities		280
Current liabilities		
Trade payables	56	
Tax payables (W2)	96	
Interest accrual (W3)	14	
		166
Total equity and liabilities		10,359

XY – Statement of changes in equity for the year ended 31 March 2010

	Share capital	Share premium	Revaluation reserve	Retained earnings	Total
	$000	$000	$000	$000	$000
Balance at 1 April 2009	400	150	160	332	1,031
Share issue (W7)	100	50			150
Revaluation of investments (W6)			44		44
Profit for the year				151	151
Dividends paid				(50)	(50)
Balance at 31 March 2010	500	200	204	422	1,326

Workings:

(W1) PPE

	$000
Land b/wd	782
Disposal	(39)
Land at cost	743
Fair value	729
Impairment (assumption not revalued in the past)	14
PPE cost b/wd	630
Depreciation b/fwd	(378)
Charge for the year (20% × 630)	(126)
Carrying value 31/03/10	126
Total PPE (729 + 126)	855

(W2) Taxation

	$000
Tax estimate	96
Under-provision (TB)	12
Deferred tax decrease (part a)	(21)
Land at cost	743
Fair value	729
Charge to the statement of profit or loss	87
Current tax (CL)	96
Deferred tax asset (part a)	2

(W3) Finance cost

	$000
Loan $280 × 5%	14
Accrual made (not shown as paid on TB)	

(W4) Land disposal

	$000
Carrying value	39
Proceeds	48
Profit on disposal	9

(W5) Cost of sales

	$000
TB	908
Depreciation of PPE (W1)	126
Profit on sale of land	(9)
Land impairment	14
	1,039

(W6) Available for sale investments

	$000
TB	564
Market value	608
Revaluation gain	44

(W7) Share issue

	$000
100,000 shares × $1	100
Premium 50%	50

QUESTION FOUR

(a)   Draft

To P's Directors

From Management Accountant

Treatment of A in the P Group Consolidated Financial Statements

Entities should be consolidated according to the requirements of International Financial Reporting Standards and not according to whether the entity makes a profit or loss during the year. P owns 40% of the equity shares in A and exercises significant influence over all aspects of A's strategic and operational decisions. P does not control A as it only holds 40% of the shares/votes. P would need >50% of the equity shares to be able to exercise control over A. The argument that A does not need to be consolidated is partially correct; A cannot be consolidated as a subsidiary. Instead A will need to be consolidated as an associated entity using the equity method, as P exercises significant influence over all aspects of A's strategic and operational decisions. Equity accounting recognises the post acquisition profits and losses of the associated entity and includes the group share instead of simply recording dividends received from the associated entity. To treat A as a simple investment at cost could be construed as unethical as it would not follow the requirements of international financial reporting standards. The CIMA Code of Ethics for Professional Accountants requires an accountant to have integrity. Integrity implies fair dealing and truthfulness. A professional accountant should not be associated with financial reports that they believe omits or obscures information required to be included where such omission or obscurity would be misleading. Treating A as an investment would obscure the full extent of P's commitment to its associate and could therefore be unethical. We cannot therefore allow A to be treated as an investment.

(b)

(W1) Group holdings:

P in S – 40,000,000/40,000,000 = 100% Treat as wholly owned subsidiary

P in A – 8,000,000/20,000,000 = 40% Treat as an associate

(W2) Net assets of S

	Date of acquisition $000	Year end $000
Share capital	40,000	40,000
Retained earnings	6,400	13,000
Fair value adjustment	1,000	1,000
Depreciation adjustment		(50)
	47,400	53,950

The property has a useful life of 20 years, excess depreciation is therefore $1,000,000/20 = $50,000.

Net assets of A

	Date of acquisition $000	Year end $000
Share capital	20,000	20,000
Retained earnings	21,000	7,800
	41,000	27,800

(W3) Goodwill (S)

	$000
Cost of investment	60,000
Net assets of S at acquisition (W2)	(47,400)
Goodwill	12,600

(W4) N/A

(W5) Consolidated retained earnings

	$000
P	21,000
S (53,950 – 47,400 (W2))	6,550
A – 40% × (27,800 – 41,000(W2))	(5,280)
Unrealised profit adjustments (W6)	(1,000)
	21,270

(W6) **Unrealised profit**

Parent sells to subsidiary – 4,000/133.33 × 33.33 = 1,000 PUP

Reduce (W5) and inventory

(W7) **Investment in Associate**

	$000
Cost	13,000
Share of post-acquisition losses (W5)	(5,280)
	7,720

(W8) **Current accounts**

P receivable balance $8,000

S payable balance $6,000

Cash in transit $2,000

(W9) **Inter-company loan**

Reduce investments $10,000

Reduce non-current liabilities $10,000

Loan interest accrued of $250

Reduce receivables $250

Reduce payables $250

P Group – Consolidated statement of financial position as at 31 March 2010

	$	$000
Non-current assets		
Property, plant and equipment (40,000 + 48,000 + 1,000 – 50)		88,950
Goodwill (W3)		12,600
Investment in associate (W7)		7,720
		109,270
Current assets		
Inventories (8,000 + 12,000 – 1,000 (W6))	19,000	
Receivables (17,000 + 11,000 – 250 (W9))	27,750	
Cash at bank (1,000 + 3,000 + 2,000 (W8))	6,000	
		52,750
		162,020
Equity and liabilities		
Ordinary share capital		100,000
Reserves (W5)		21,270
		121,270
Non-current liabilities		
Loan Notes (26,000 + 10,000 – 10,000 (intra-group loan))		26,000
Current liabilities		
Trade payables (10,000 + 5,000 – 250)		14,750
		162,020

DO NOT OPEN THIS QUESTION PAPER UNTIL YOU ARE TOLD TO DO SO.

CIMA

Financial Pillar

F1 – Financial Operations

21 November 2013 – Thursday Morning Session

Instructions to candidates

You are allowed three hours to answer this question paper.

You are allowed 20 minutes reading time **before the examination begins** during which you should read the question paper and, if you wish, highlight and/or make notes on the question paper. However, you will **not** be allowed, **under any circumstances**, to open the answer book and start writing or use your calculator during this reading time.

You are strongly advised to carefully read ALL the question requirements before attempting the question concerned (that is all parts and/or sub-questions).

ALL answers must be written in the answer book. Answers written on the question paper will **not** be submitted for marking.

You should show all workings as marks are available for the method you use.

ALL QUESTIONS ARE COMPULSORY.

Section A comprises 10 sub-questions and is on pages 3 to 5.

Section B comprises 6 sub-questions and is on pages 6 to 8.

Section C comprises 2 questions and is on pages 10 to 13.

The country 'Tax Regime' for the paper is provided on page 2. Maths tables and formulae are provided on pages 17 and 18.

References to IFRS in this paper refer to International Financial Reporting Standards or International Accounting Standards as issued or adopted by the International Accounting Standards Board.

The list of verbs as published in the syllabus is given for reference on page 19.

Write your candidate number, the paper number and examination subject title in the spaces provided on the front of the answer book. Also write your contact ID and name in the space provided in the right hand margin and seal to close.

Tick the appropriate boxes on the front of the answer book to indicate the questions you have answered.

F1 – Financial Operations

TURN OVER

© The Chartered Institute of Management Accountants 2013

COUNTRY X - TAX REGIME FOR USE THROUGHOUT THE EXAMINATION PAPER

Relevant Tax Rules for Years Ended 31 March 2007 to 2014

Corporate Profits

Unless otherwise specified, only the following rules for taxation of corporate profits will be relevant, other taxes can be ignored:

- Accounting rules on recognition and measurement are followed for tax purposes.
- All expenses other than depreciation, amortisation, entertaining, taxes paid to other public bodies and donations to political parties are tax deductible.
- Tax depreciation is deductible as follows:
    - 50% of additions to property, plant and equipment in the accounting period in which they are recorded;
    - 25% per year of the written-down value (i.e. cost minus previous allowances) in subsequent accounting periods except that in which the asset is disposed of;
    - No tax depreciation is allowed on land.
- The corporate tax on profits is at a rate of 25%.
- No indexation is allowable on the sale of land.
- Tax losses can be carried forward to offset against future taxable profits from the same business.

Value Added Tax

Country X has a VAT system which allows entities to reclaim input tax paid.
In country X the VAT rates are:

Zero rated	0%
Standard rated	15%
Exempt goods	0%

SECTION A – 20 MARKS

[You are advised to spend no longer than 36 minutes on this section]

ANSWER *ALL* TEN SUB-QUESTIONS IN THIS SECTION

Instructions for answering Section A:

The answers to the ten sub-questions in Section A should ALL be written in your answer book.

Your answers should be clearly numbered with the sub-question number and then ruled off, so that the markers know which sub-question you are answering. **For multiple choice questions, you need only write the sub-question number and the letter of the answer option you have chosen.** You do not need to start a new page for each sub-question.

Question One

1.1　Which ONE of the following is regarded as a direct tax?

A　Value added tax

B　Capital gains tax

C　Excise duties

D　Property tax

(2 marks)

1.2　In many countries employees' earnings have tax deducted by their employers before being paid to them. This is sometimes referred to as "Pay-as-you-earn".

Identify TWO advantages of "Pay-as-you-earn" to *employees*.

(2 marks)

TURN OVER

1.3 UI has the following details:

(i) Incorporated in Country A.
(ii) Senior management hold regular board meetings in Country B and exercise control from there, but there are no sales or purchases made in Country B.
(iii) Carries out its main business activities in Country C.

Assume all three countries have double taxation treaties with each other, based on the OECD model tax convention.

In which country/countries will UI be deemed to be resident for tax purposes?

A   Country A

B   Country B

C   Country C

D   Countries B and C

(2 marks)

1.4 DF, a small entity resident in Country X, purchased its only item of plant on 1 October 2011 for $200,000.

DF charges depreciation on a straight line basis over 5 years.

DF's deferred tax balance as at 30 September 2013, in accordance with IAS 12 *Income Taxes* is:

A $3,750

B $11,250

C $18,750

D $45,000

(2 marks)

1.5 GH is registered for VAT in Country X and is partially exempt for VAT purposes.

GH's sales for the last VAT period, excluding VAT, were:

	$
Goods at standard rate	15,000
Goods exempt from VAT	10,000

During the period GH purchased materials and services costing a total of $12,075, including VAT at standard rate. These materials and services were used to produce standard rated goods and exempt goods.
Assume that GH had no other VAT related transactions in the period.

Calculate the net VAT due to/from GH for the VAT period.

(2 marks)

November 2013   Financial Operations

1.6 **Identify** TWO advantages of having an ethical code for accountants.

(2 marks)

1.7 **Identify** any TWO responsibilities of the IFRS Foundation.

(2 marks)

1.8 The IASB's *Conceptual Framework for Financial Reporting (2010) (Framework)* identifies faithful representation as a fundamental qualitative characteristic of financial information.

Which ONE of the following is NOT a characteristic of faithful representation?

A Free from error

B Verifiable

C Neutral

D Complete

(2 marks)

1.9 **Identify** TWO actions required under IAS 1 *(Revised) Presentation of Financial Statements* to ensure that "Financial statements shall present fairly the financial position, financial performance and cash flows of an entity."

(2 marks)

1.10 The IASB's Framework states that "materiality is an entity-specific aspect of relevance".

Describe the term "materiality" as used in the Framework.

(2 marks)

(Total for Section A = 20 marks)

Reminder

All answers to Section A must be written in your answer book.

Answers or notes to Section A written on the question paper will **not** be submitted for marking.

End of Section A   TURN OVER

Financial Operations   November 2013

SECTION B – 30 MARKS

[You are advised to spend no longer than 9 minutes on each sub-question in this section.]

ANSWER *ALL* SIX SUB-QUESTIONS IN THIS SECTION – 5 MARKS EACH

Question Two

(a)

An investment in another entity's equity is classified as an investment in a subsidiary, if the investor can exercise control over the investee.

AB acquired 4,000 of the 10,000 equity voting shares and 8,000 of the 10,000 non-voting preference shares of CD.

AB acquired 4,000 of the 10,000 equity voting shares of EF and had a signed agreement giving it the power to appoint or remove all of the directors of EF.

Required:

Explain whether CD and/or EF should be classified as subsidiaries/a subsidiary of AB. You should refer to the provisions of IFRS 10 *Consolidated Financial Statements* in your answer.

(Total for sub-question (a) = 5 marks)

(b)

YZ purchased 100% of the equity shares in WX on 1 October 2012.

YZ and WX trade with each other. During the year ended 30 September 2013 YZ sold WX inventory at a sales price of $28,000. YZ applied a mark up on cost of $33^{1}/_{3}\%$.

At 30 September 2013 WX still owed YZ $10,000 of the cost and had remaining in inventory $6,000 of the goods purchased from YZ.

Required:

Prepare the journal entries to make the required adjustment in YZ's consolidated financial statements for the year ended 30 September 2013 for the above.

(Total for sub-question (b) = 5 marks)

(c)

UV purchased an asset for $50,000 on 1 October 2009, incurring import duties of $8,000. UV depreciated the asset at 10% per year on a straight line basis.

UV sold the asset for $80,000 on 30 September 2013, incurring costs of $2,000. The asset was subject to capital gains tax of 25% and the indexation factor from 1 October 2009 to 30 September 2013 was 14%.

Required:

(i) **Explain** the purpose of "indexation" when used in the calculation of capital gains tax.
(2 marks)

(ii) **Calculate** the capital gains tax arising on the disposal of UV's asset.
(3 marks)

(Total for sub-question (c) = 5 marks)

(d)

TY is resident in Country X.

TY's statement of profit or loss for year ended 30 September 2013 was as follows:

	$
Revenue	950,000
Cost of sales	(550,000)
Gross profit	400,000
Administrative expenses	(132,000)
Taxes paid to other public bodies	(1,900)
Entertaining expenses	(1,200)
Depreciation of plant and equipment	(47,500)
Distribution costs	(42,000)
	175,400
Finance cost	(3,500)
Profit before tax	171,900

TY has accumulated tax losses of $125,000 brought forward from 2011/12.

TY owns plant and equipment purchased on 1 October 2010 at a cost of $385,000 and plant purchased on 1 October 2012 at a cost of $90,000. TY charges depreciation at 10% per year on a straight line basis on all non-current assets.

Required:

Calculate the tax payable by TY for the year ended 30 September 2013.

(Total for sub-question (d) = 5 marks)

TURN OVER

(e)

You are a trainee accountant working for JHG, which owns a number of subsidiary entities.

A new Chief Executive has recently been appointed and has raised the following queries:

- JHG is a member of a tax group. What is a tax group?
- What are the benefits to JHG and its subsidiaries of being in a tax group?

Required:

Prepare a short briefing note that answers the Chief Executive's questions.

(Total for sub-question (e) = 5 marks)

(f)

Required:

Explain the typical duties of an external auditor of an entity.

(Total for sub-question (f) = 5 marks)

(Total for Section B = 30 marks)

End of Section B

Section C starts on page 10

This page is blank

Section C starts on page 10

SECTION C – 50 MARKS

[You are advised to spend no longer than 45 minutes on each question in this section.]

ANSWER BOTH QUESTIONS FROM THIS SECTION – 25 MARKS EACH

Question Three

RDX's trial balance at 30 September 2013 is shown below:

	Notes	$000	$000
5% Loan notes (issued 2010, redeemable 2020)	(ix)		1,480
Administrative expenses		779	
Cash received on sale of equipment	(v)		23
Cash and cash equivalents		207	
Cost of sales		4,080	
Distribution costs		650	
Equity dividend paid 1 February 2013	(vii)	335	
Income tax	(ii)	24	
Inventory at 30 September 2013	(i)	1,055	
Land and buildings at cost at 1 October 2012		5,180	
Loan interest paid		37	
Equity shares $1 each, fully paid at 1 October 2012			5,650
RDX ordinary shares purchased	(viii)	135	
Plant and equipment at cost at 1 October 2012	(v)	4,520	
Provision for deferred tax at 1 October 2012	(iii)		282
Provision for buildings depreciation at 1 October 2012	(iv)		262
Provision for plant and equipment depreciation at 1 October 2012	(vi)		2,260
Retained earnings at 1 October 2012			1,990
Sales revenue			6,780
Share premium			565
Trade payables			300
Trade receivables	(x)	2,590	
		19,592	19,592

Notes:

(i) RDX has always valued its inventories using a manual system. On 1 October 2012 RDX purchased and installed a computerised inventory system and changed its inventory valuation method to the industry standard method.

The impact on inventory valuation due to the change in policy was calculated as:

Inventory value increase at 30 September 2012 by $148,000.
Inventory value increase up to 30 September 2013 by $210,000.

(ii) The income tax balance in the trial balance is a result of the under provision for the year ended 30 September 2012.

(iii) The tax due for the year ended 30 September 2013 is estimated at $160,000 and the deferred tax provision should be decreased by $30,000.

(iv) Depreciation is charged on buildings using the straight line method at 3% per annum. The cost of land included in land and buildings is $3,000,000. Buildings depreciation is treated as an administrative expense.

(v) During the year RDX disposed of old equipment for $23,000. The original cost of the equipment sold was $57,000 and its book value at 30 September 2012 was $6,000.

(vi) Plant and equipment is depreciated at 20% per annum using the reducing balance method. Depreciation of plant and equipment is considered to be part of cost of sales. RDX's policy is to charge a full year's depreciation in the year of acquisition and no depreciation in the year of disposal.

(vii) During the year RDX paid a dividend of $335,000 for the year ended 30 September 2012.

(viii) RDX purchased and cancelled 100,000 of its own equity shares on 30 September 2013 for $135,000. These shares had originally been issued at a 10% premium.

(ix) Long term borrowings consist of loan notes issued on 1 April 2010 at 5% interest per annum.

(x) On 22 October 2013 RDX discovered that ZZZ, one of its customers, had gone into liquidation. RDX has been informed that it will receive none of the outstanding balance of $230,000 at 30 September 2013.

Required:

(a) **Explain** how the change in inventory accounting policy should be recorded in RDX's financial statements for the year ended 30 September 2013, in accordance with IAS 8 *Accounting Policies, Changes in Accounting Estimates and Errors.*

(3 marks)

(b) **Prepare** RDX's statement of profit or loss and statement of changes in equity for the year to 30 September 2013 AND the statement of financial position at that date, in accordance with the requirements of International Financial Reporting Standards.

Notes to the financial statements are not required, but all workings must be clearly shown. Do NOT prepare a statement of accounting policies.

(22 marks)

(Total for Question Three = 25 marks)

Section C continues on page 12

TURN OVER

Question Four

The financial statements of AWX for the year ended 31 March 2012 and 31 March 2013 are given below:

AWX Statement of Financial Position as at:

	Notes	31 March 2013 $000	$000	31 March 2012 $000	$000
Non-current Assets					
Property, plant and equipment	(i) (ii)	4,191		4,500	
Intangible assets	(iv)	156		315	
			4,347		4,815
Current Assets					
Inventories		738		805	
Trade receivables		564		480	
Cash and cash equivalents		515		265	
			1,817		1,550
Total Assets			6,164		6,365
Equity and Liabilities					
Equity shares of $1 each		2,180		2,180	
Preference shares	(v)	700		--	
Share premium		968		968	
Revaluation reserve		469		353	
Retained earnings	(vii)	901		727	
			5,218		4,228
Non-current liabilities					
9% loan notes	(vi)	-		1,100	
Deferred tax		225		220	
			225		1,320
Current liabilities					
Trade payables		535		500	
Tax payable		84		218	
Provisions		90		-	
Interest payable		12		99	
			721		817
Total Equity and Liabilities			6,164		6,365

Statement of Profit or Loss for the year ended 31 March 2013

	Notes	$000
Revenue		6,858
Cost of sales	(iii)	(3,552)
Gross profit		3,306
Administrative expenses	(viii)	(2,042)
Distribution costs		(816)
		448
Finance cost		(40)
		408
Income tax expense		(124)
Profit for the year		284

Notes:

(i) Property, plant and equipment includes properties which were revalued upwards during the year.

(ii) Property, plant and equipment disposed of in the year had a net book value of $70,000; cash received on their disposal was $92,000.

(iii) Depreciation charged for the year was $675,000.

(iv) There were no additions or disposals of intangible assets during the year.

(v) On 1 April 2012, AWX issued 700,000 5% cumulative $1 preference shares at par, redeemable at 10% premium on 1 April 2022. Issue costs of $50,000 have been paid by AWX and included in administrative expenses. The effective rate of interest is 6·74%. The cash received for the issue of the preference shares has been debited to cash and credited to equity.

(vi) On 1 May 2012, AWX purchased and cancelled all its 9% loan notes at par plus accrued interest (included in finance costs).

(vii) Equity dividends paid during the year were $75,000 and preference share dividends paid were $35,000.

(viii) AWX has been advised that it is probably going to lose a court case and at 31 March 2013 has provided $90,000 for the estimated cost of this case.

Required:

(a) (i) **Explain** how AWX should treat its preference shares in its financial statements for the year ended 31 March 2013 according to IAS 32 *Financial Instruments: Presentation* AND,
 (ii) **Calculate** AWX's revised profit before tax for the year ended 31 March 2013 in accordance with IAS 39 *Financial Instruments: Recognition and Measurement.*

(6 marks)

(b) **Prepare** AWX's Statement of cash flows, using the indirect method, for the year ended 31 March 2013 in accordance with IAS 7 *Statement of Cash Flows.*

(19 marks)

Notes to the financial statements are not required, but all workings must be clearly shown.

(Total for Question Four = 25 marks)

(Total for Section C = 50 marks)

End of Question Paper
Maths Tables and Formulae are on Pages 17 and 18

This page is blank

This page is blank

This page is blank

MATHS TABLES AND FORMULAE

Present value table

Present value of $1, that is $(1 + r)^{-n}$ where r = interest rate; n = number of periods until payment or receipt.

Periods (n)	1%	2%	3%	4%	5%	6%	7%	8%	9%	10%
1	0.990	0.980	0.971	0.962	0.952	0.943	0.935	0.926	0.917	0.909
2	0.980	0.961	0.943	0.925	0.907	0.890	0.873	0.857	0.842	0.826
3	0.971	0.942	0.915	0.889	0.864	0.840	0.816	0.794	0.772	0.751
4	0.961	0.924	0.888	0.855	0.823	0.792	0.763	0.735	0.708	0.683
5	0.951	0.906	0.863	0.822	0.784	0.747	0.713	0.681	0.650	0.621
6	0.942	0.888	0.837	0.790	0.746	0.705	0.666	0.630	0.596	0.564
7	0.933	0.871	0.813	0.760	0.711	0.665	0.623	0.583	0.547	0.513
8	0.923	0.853	0.789	0.731	0.677	0.627	0.582	0.540	0.502	0.467
9	0.914	0.837	0.766	0.703	0.645	0.592	0.544	0.500	0.460	0.424
10	0.905	0.820	0.744	0.676	0.614	0.558	0.508	0.463	0.422	0.386
11	0.896	0.804	0.722	0.650	0.585	0.527	0.475	0.429	0.388	0.350
12	0.887	0.788	0.701	0.625	0.557	0.497	0.444	0.397	0.356	0.319
13	0.879	0.773	0.681	0.601	0.530	0.469	0.415	0.368	0.326	0.290
14	0.870	0.758	0.661	0.577	0.505	0.442	0.388	0.340	0.299	0.263
15	0.861	0.743	0.642	0.555	0.481	0.417	0.362	0.315	0.275	0.239
16	0.853	0.728	0.623	0.534	0.458	0.394	0.339	0.292	0.252	0.218
17	0.844	0.714	0.605	0.513	0.436	0.371	0.317	0.270	0.231	0.198
18	0.836	0.700	0.587	0.494	0.416	0.350	0.296	0.250	0.212	0.180
19	0.828	0.686	0.570	0.475	0.396	0.331	0.277	0.232	0.194	0.164
20	0.820	0.673	0.554	0.456	0.377	0.312	0.258	0.215	0.178	0.149

Periods (n)	11%	12%	13%	14%	15%	16%	17%	18%	19%	20%
1	0.901	0.893	0.885	0.877	0.870	0.862	0.855	0.847	0.840	0.833
2	0.812	0.797	0.783	0.769	0.756	0.743	0.731	0.718	0.706	0.694
3	0.731	0.712	0.693	0.675	0.658	0.641	0.624	0.609	0.593	0.579
4	0.659	0.636	0.613	0.592	0.572	0.552	0.534	0.516	0.499	0.482
5	0.593	0.567	0.543	0.519	0.497	0.476	0.456	0.437	0.419	0.402
6	0.535	0.507	0.480	0.456	0.432	0.410	0.390	0.370	0.352	0.335
7	0.482	0.452	0.425	0.400	0.376	0.354	0.333	0.314	0.296	0.279
8	0.434	0.404	0.376	0.351	0.327	0.305	0.285	0.266	0.249	0.233
9	0.391	0.361	0.333	0.308	0.284	0.263	0.243	0.225	0.209	0.194
10	0.352	0.322	0.295	0.270	0.247	0.227	0.208	0.191	0.176	0.162
11	0.317	0.287	0.261	0.237	0.215	0.195	0.178	0.162	0.148	0.135
12	0.286	0.257	0.231	0.208	0.187	0.168	0.152	0.137	0.124	0.112
13	0.258	0.229	0.204	0.182	0.163	0.145	0.130	0.116	0.104	0.093
14	0.232	0.205	0.181	0.160	0.141	0.125	0.111	0.099	0.088	0.078
15	0.209	0.183	0.160	0.140	0.123	0.108	0.095	0.084	0.079	0.065
16	0.188	0.163	0.141	0.123	0.107	0.093	0.081	0.071	0.062	0.054
17	0.170	0.146	0.125	0.108	0.093	0.080	0.069	0.060	0.052	0.045
18	0.153	0.130	0.111	0.095	0.081	0.069	0.059	0.051	0.044	0.038
19	0.138	0.116	0.098	0.083	0.070	0.060	0.051	0.043	0.037	0.031
20	0.124	0.104	0.087	0.073	0.061	0.051	0.043	0.037	0.031	0.026

Cumulative present value of $1 per annum, Receivable or Payable at the end of each year for n years

$$\frac{1-(1+r)^{-n}}{r}$$

Periods (n)	1%	2%	3%	4%	5%	6%	7%	8%	9%	10%
1	0.990	0.980	0.971	0.962	0.952	0.943	0.935	0.926	0.917	0.909
2	1.970	1.942	1.913	1.886	1.859	1.833	1.808	1.783	1.759	1.736
3	2.941	2.884	2.829	2.775	2.723	2.673	2.624	2.577	2.531	2.487
4	3.902	3.808	3.717	3.630	3.546	3.465	3.387	3.312	3.240	3.170
5	4.853	4.713	4.580	4.452	4.329	4.212	4.100	3.993	3.890	3.791
6	5.795	5.601	5.417	5.242	5.076	4.917	4.767	4.623	4.486	4.355
7	6.728	6.472	6.230	6.002	5.786	5.582	5.389	5.206	5.033	4.868
8	7.652	7.325	7.020	6.733	6.463	6.210	5.971	5.747	5.535	5.335
9	8.566	8.162	7.786	7.435	7.108	6.802	6.515	6.247	5.995	5.759
10	9.471	8.983	8.530	8.111	7.722	7.360	7.024	6.710	6.418	6.145
11	10.368	9.787	9.253	8.760	8.306	7.887	7.499	7.139	6.805	6.495
12	11.255	10.575	9.954	9.385	8.863	8.384	7.943	7.536	7.161	6.814
13	12.134	11.348	10.635	9.986	9.394	8.853	8.358	7.904	7.487	7.103
14	13.004	12.106	11.296	10.563	9.899	9.295	8.745	8.244	7.786	7.367
15	13.865	12.849	11.938	11.118	10.380	9.712	9.108	8.559	8.061	7.606
16	14.718	13.578	12.561	11.652	10.838	10.106	9.447	8.851	8.313	7.824
17	15.562	14.292	13.166	12.166	11.274	10.477	9.763	9.122	8.544	8.022
18	16.398	14.992	13.754	12.659	11.690	10.828	10.059	9.372	8.756	8.201
19	17.226	15.679	14.324	13.134	12.085	11.158	10.336	9.604	8.950	8.365
20	18.046	16.351	14.878	13.590	12.462	11.470	10.594	9.818	9.129	8.514

Periods (n)	11%	12%	13%	14%	15%	16%	17%	18%	19%	20%
1	0.901	0.893	0.885	0.877	0.870	0.862	0.855	0.847	0.840	0.833
2	1.713	1.690	1.668	1.647	1.626	1.605	1.585	1.566	1.547	1.528
3	2.444	2.402	2.361	2.322	2.283	2.246	2.210	2.174	2.140	2.106
4	3.102	3.037	2.974	2.914	2.855	2.798	2.743	2.690	2.639	2.589
5	3.696	3.605	3.517	3.433	3.352	3.274	3.199	3.127	3.058	2.991
6	4.231	4.111	3.998	3.889	3.784	3.685	3.589	3.498	3.410	3.326
7	4.712	4.564	4.423	4.288	4.160	4.039	3.922	3.812	3.706	3.605
8	5.146	4.968	4.799	4.639	4.487	4.344	4.207	4.078	3.954	3.837
9	5.537	5.328	5.132	4.946	4.772	4.607	4.451	4.303	4.163	4.031
10	5.889	5.650	5.426	5.216	5.019	4.833	4.659	4.494	4.339	4.192
11	6.207	5.938	5.687	5.453	5.234	5.029	4.836	4.656	4.486	4.327
12	6.492	6.194	5.918	5.660	5.421	5.197	4.988	4.793	4.611	4.439
13	6.750	6.424	6.122	5.842	5.583	5.342	5.118	4.910	4.715	4.533
14	6.982	6.628	6.302	6.002	5.724	5.468	5.229	5.008	4.802	4.611
15	7.191	6.811	6.462	6.142	5.847	5.575	5.324	5.092	4.876	4.675
16	7.379	6.974	6.604	6.265	5.954	5.668	5.405	5.162	4.938	4.730
17	7.549	7.120	6.729	6.373	6.047	5.749	5.475	5.222	4.990	4.775
18	7.702	7.250	6.840	6.467	6.128	5.818	5.534	5.273	5.033	4.812
19	7.839	7.366	6.938	6.550	6.198	5.877	5.584	5.316	5.070	4.843
20	7.963	7.469	7.025	6.623	6.259	5.929	5.628	5.353	5.101	4.870

FORMULAE

Annuity

Present value of an annuity of $1 per annum, receivable or payable for n years, commencing in one year, discounted at r% per annum:

$$PV = \frac{1}{r}\left[1 - \frac{1}{[1+r]^n}\right]$$

Perpetuity

Present value of $1 per annum, payable or receivable in perpetuity, commencing in one year, discounted at r% per annum:

$$PV = \frac{1}{r}$$

LIST OF VERBS USED IN THE QUESTION REQUIREMENTS

A list of the learning objectives and verbs that appear in the syllabus and in the question requirements for each question in this paper.

It is important that you answer the question according to the definition of the verb.

LEARNING OBJECTIVE	VERBS USED	DEFINITION
Level 1 - KNOWLEDGE What you are expected to know.	List State Define	Make a list of Express, fully or clearly, the details/facts of Give the exact meaning of
Level 2 - COMPREHENSION What you are expected to understand.	Describe Distinguish Explain Identify Illustrate	Communicate the key features Highlight the differences between Make clear or intelligible/State the meaning or purpose of Recognise, establish or select after consideration Use an example to describe or explain something
Level 3 - APPLICATION How you are expected to apply your knowledge.	Apply Calculate Demonstrate Prepare Reconcile Solve Tabulate	Put to practical use Ascertain or reckon mathematically Prove with certainty or to exhibit by practical means Make or get ready for use Make or prove consistent/compatible Find an answer to Arrange in a table
Level 4 - ANALYSIS How are you expected to analyse the detail of what you have learned.	Analyse Categorise Compare and contrast Construct Discuss Interpret Prioritise Produce	Examine in detail the structure of Place into a defined class or division Show the similarities and/or differences between Build up or compile Examine in detail by argument Translate into intelligible or familiar terms Place in order of priority or sequence for action Create or bring into existence
Level 5 - EVALUATION How are you expected to use your learning to evaluate, make decisions or recommendations.	Advise Evaluate Recommend	Counsel, inform or notify Appraise or assess the value of Advise on a course of action

Financial Pillar

Operational Level Paper

F1 – Financial Operations

November 2013

Thursday Morning Session

The Examiner's Answers
F1 - Financial Operations
November 2013

Some of the answers that follow are fuller and more comprehensive than would be expected from a well-prepared candidate. They have been written in this way to aid teaching, study and revision for tutors and candidates alike.

SECTION A

Answers to Question One

> **Rationale**
>
> **Question One** consists of 10 objective test sub-questions. These are drawn from all sections of the syllabus. They are designed to examine breadth across the syllabus and thus cover many learning outcomes.

1.1 **B**

1.2 Advantages to employees:
- Will not get into trouble for late payment of tax
- Do not usually have to prepare a self assessment tax return
- Tax is collected gradually over the year, easier to bear than one large payment
- Any other relevant advantage to the employee

Any two from the above

1.3 **B**

1.4
	Accounting $	Tax $
Cost	200,000	200,000
Acc depreciation	40,000	
First year allowance		100,000
	160,000	100,000
Depreciation	40,000	
Annual allowance		25,000
	120,000	75,000
Temporary difference	120,000 – 75,000 = 45,000	
Deferred tax	45,000 x 25% = 11,250	

Answer: B

1.5 Exempt as proportion of total outputs: 10/25 = 40%
VAT on inputs = 12,075 x 15/115 = 1,575
Excluding exempt proportion: 1,575 x 60% = 945
VAT on outputs, 15,000 x 15% = 2,250

Amount payable = 2,250 – 945 = 1,305

1.6 Advantages of an ethical code for accountants include:

- it identifies fundamental principles of professional ethics for professional accountants and provides a conceptual framework for applying those principles.
- it provides guidance on the fundamental principles.
- it helps members identify threats to compliance with fundamental principles and provides examples of safeguards that may be appropriate.

Any two from the above

1.7 The responsibilities of the IFRS Foundation include:

- Appoint members of the IASB, the IFRIC and the IFRS Advisory Council
- Review the strategy of the IASB and its effectiveness
- Approve the annual budget and determine the funding of the IASB
- Promoting the IASB and the application of IFRS/IAS
- Reviewing broad strategic issues affecting accounting standards

Any two from the above.

1.8 **B**

1.9 In order to ensure that *"Financial statements shall present fairly the financial position, financial performance and cash flows of an entity"* as required by IAS 1 (Revised) *Presentation of Financial Statements* an entity should:

- Show a faithful representation of the effects of transactions
- Select and apply accounting policies in accordance with IAS 8
- Present information that is relevant, reliable, comparable and understandable
- Provide additional disclosures if the requirements of an IFRS are insufficient to enable users to understand the full effect of a transaction.

Any two from the above.

1.10 Information is material if omitting it or misstating it could influence decisions that users make on the basis of financial information about a specific reporting entity.

SECTION B

Answers to Question Two

(a)

> **Rationale**
>
> To test candidates' knowledge of the concept of control in the context of consolidated financial statements.
>
> Tests learning outcome C1b.
>
> **Suggested Approach**
>
> Define the meaning of control according to IFRS 10 *Consolidated Financial Statements*.
> Explain the level of control AB has over CD and conclude CD is not a subsidiary of AB.
> Explain the level of control AB has over EF and conclude EF is a subsidiary of AB.

According to IFRS 10 *Consolidated financial statements* a subsidiary is an entity that is controlled by another entity. IFRS 10 defines *control* as the power to govern the financial and operating policies of an entity so as to obtain benefit from its activities.

There is a presumption that control exists where an investor entity owns 50% or more of the voting rights of the entity. A parent/subsidiary relationship can also be created when the parent entity owns less than 50% of voting rights but is able to exercise control through another means.

CD is not a subsidiary of AB.
AB has acquired 40% of the voting rights and 80% of the non-voting shares. Overall AB is only able to exercise control over 40% of CD's voting rights so cannot exercise control.

EF is a subsidiary of AB.
AB has acquired 40% of the voting rights of EF. AB also has the power to remove and appoint all of EF's directors. AB can therefore control the management of EF and can exercise control of EF. As a result EF is a subsidiary of AB.

(b)

Rationale
To test the candidates' understanding of the treatment in consolidated financial statements of unrealised profit arising from intra-group transactions. Tests learning outcome C1c.
Suggested Approach
Calculate the value of the unrealised profit in inventory. Prepare the journal entries to remove the revenue, cost of sales and unrealised profit from the consolidated financial statements.

Mark-up on cost $33^1/_3\%$ = $(33^1/_3 / 133^1/_3)$ 25% profit margin.

Goods left in inventory $6,000, PUP = $6,000 x 25% = $1,500

Journal:

	Dr $	Cr $
Consolidated revenue	28,000	
Consolidated cost of sales		28,000
Consolidated cost of sales	1,500	
Consolidated inventory (SoFP)		1,500
Consolidated trade payables	10,000	
Trade receivables		10,000

(c)

Rationale
To test candidates' understanding of a capital gain and their ability to calculate the gain in a given scenario, and the tax consequently due. Tests learning outcome A1e.
Suggested Approach
Explain the purpose of indexation. Calculate the capital gains tax payable by UV, taking account of indexation of the asset.

(i) Indexation of the cost of an asset is allowed to adjust for the effects of inflation.
An index provided by the Government is applied to the cost of the asset to increase it by the amount of inflation between the point of purchase and the point of sale.
Indexation reduces the taxable gain in times of inflation.

(ii) Capital gains tax due on the disposal of UV's asset is $2,970.

Selling price		80,000
Less selling costs		2,000
		78,000
Less cost of asset	50,000	
Add buying costs	8,000	
	58,000	
Add indexation allowance		
(58,000 x 14%)	8,120	
		66,120
Taxable gain		11,880
Tax due @ 25% = (11,880 x 25%) =		2,970

Financial Operations 5 November 2013

(d)

Rationale
Test candidates' understanding of corporate income tax calculations. Tests learning outcome A3a.
Suggested Approach
Calculate TY's annual accounting depreciation and tax depreciation. Use profit before tax and adjust it for taxes paid to other public bodies, entertaining, accounting depreciation and tax depreciation to calculate taxable profits. Calculate tax payable at 25%.

Accounting depreciation:
Plant and equipment - $385,000 x 10% = $38,500
Plant - $90,000 x 10% = $9,000
  $47,500

Tax depreciation:
Allowance for plant –
First year $90,000 x 50% = $45,000

Allowances for plant & equipment -
Year to Sept 2011- first year $385,000 x 50% = $192,500
Year to Sept 2012 – writing down allowance (385,000 – 192,500) x 25% = $48,125
Year to Sept 2013 - writing down allowance (385,000 – 192,500 – 48,125) x 25% = $36,094

TY Tax computation for year to 30 September 2013:
                                                              $
Profit before tax   171,900
Add:
Taxes paid to other public bodies   1,900
Entertaining expenses   1,200
Accounting depreciation   47,500
Less:
Tax depreciation – plant   (45,000)
Tax depreciation – plant & equipment   (36,094)
                                                              141,406
Less losses brought forward   (125,000)
Taxable profit   16,406

Tax due at 25% = ($16,406 x 25%) = $4,101.50

(e)

> **Rationale**
>
> To test candidates' understanding of tax consolidation and the benefits of group loss relief.
>
> Tests learning outcome A3a.
>
> **Suggested Approach**
>
> Explain the concept of a tax group.
> Explain the benefits of being in a tax group.

A tax group is a number of entities related through equity ownership, that meet criteria set out by the tax authorities to be treated as a group for tax purposes. Some countries allow foreign entities to be included in the tax group.

The rules relating to tax groups vary from country to country, but are often different to the criteria used for a group used for accounting consolidation purposes. As a result a tax group of entities may not be the same as the entities recognised as a group for accounting consolidation purposes. Each member of the tax group still prepares its own tax computation and pays its own tax liability.

The benefits to a group of entities such as JHG being part of a tax group include:

- It can bring benefits such as group relief and transfer of assets within the group without paying tax.
- It may save tax – it may be possible to transfer a tax loss to an entity that pays tax at a higher rate.
- Cash flow advantages – by transferring a tax loss the group can get immediate reduction in tax payable. If no group relief was possible the group could wait several years before the tax loss could be used by the entity incurring the loss.

(f)

Rationale
To test candidates' knowledge of the duties of an external auditor.
Tests learning outcome B1g.

Suggested Approach
Explain the typical duties of an external auditor.

The primary duty of the external auditor is to report to the shareholders of the entity as to whether the financial statements show a true and fair view and have been prepared in accordance with an applicable reporting framework.

Auditors also have a duty to report any problems to shareholders. The exact reporting requirements may vary from country to country but usually include:
- That the financial statements are in agreement with the underlying accounting records
- That proper accounting records have been kept
- That all information and explanations requested has been received
- That all documents and information from branch offices have been received
- That the directors' report (if required) is consistent with the financial statements

SECTION C

Question Three

> **Rationale**
>
> To test candidates' ability to prepare a set of financial statements for a single entity, including the application of a number of IFRS/IAS.
>
> Tests learning outcome C1a.
>
> **Suggested Approach**
>
> Explain how a change in policy is dealt with according to IAS 8.
> Prepare the non-current asset depreciation calculations.
> Prepare workings for Cost of sales, administration and distribution.
> Prepare all other required workings.
> Prepare the statement of profit or loss.
> Prepare the statement of financial position.
> Prepare the statement of changes in equity.

(a)

On 1 October 2012 RDX changed its accounting policy for the treatment of inventory to the industry standard method. In accordance with IAS 8 *Accounting Policies, Changes in Accounting Estimates and Errors* the change must be reported retrospectively as a prior period adjustment. The change is in line with the industry standard, so it should be consistent with IAS 2 *Inventories* and generally accepted accounting practice and should improve the comparability of the financial statements.

The $148,000 change for the year ended 30 September 2012 should be adjusted in the statement of changes in equity against the retained earnings balance at 1 October 2012. The increase in opening inventory will increase cost of sales for the year ended 30 September 2013.

No change needs to be made to the statement of profit or loss for the year ended 30 September 2013 as all inventory sold will have been charged using the new valuation method.

(b)

RDX - Statement of profit or loss for the year ended 30 September 2013

		$000	$000
Revenue			6,780
Cost of sales	W2		(4,662)
Gross Profit			2,118
Administrative expenses	W2	(1,074)	
Distribution costs		(650)	(1,724)
Profit from operations			394
Finance cost	W3		(74)
Profit before tax			320
Income tax expense	W4		(154)
Profit for the period			166

Financial Operations   November 2013

RDX Statement of financial position as at 30 September 2013

	$000	$000	$000
Non-current assets			
Property, plant and equipment			6,656
Current Assets			
Inventory		1,055	
Trade receivables (W7)		2,360	
Cash and cash equivalents		207	
			3,622
Total Assets			10,278
Equity and liabilities			
Equity	5,550		
Share premium	555		
Capital reserve	100		
Retained earnings	1,844		
Total equity			8,049
Non-current Liabilities			
Loan notes		1,480	
Deferred tax (W5)		252	
Total non-current liabilities			1,732
Current liabilities			
Trade payables		300	
Tax payable		160	
Interest payable		37	
Total current liabilities			497
Total equity and liabilities			10,278

RDX Statement of changes in equity for the year ended 30 September 2013

	Equity shares $000	Share premium $000	Retained earnings $000	Capital reserve $000	Total $000
Balance at 30 September 2012	5,650	565	1,990	0	8,205
Restatement due to change in inventory policy			148		148
Adjusted balance	5,650	565	2,138		8,353
Shares purchased during year (W8)	(100)	(10)	(25)		(135)
Capital redemption transfer			(100)	100	0
Profit for period			166		166
Dividend paid			(335)		(335)
Balance at 30 September 2013	5,550	555	1,844	100	8,049

Workings - All figures in $000

W1 – Tangible Non-current Assets

Cost/Valuation	Land $000	Buildings $000	Plant & Equip. $000	Total $000
Balance 1/10/12	3,000	2,180	4,520	9,700
Disposals			(57)	(57)
	3,000	2,180	4,463	9,643
Depreciation				
Balance 1/10/12		(262)	(2,260)	(2,522)
Disposals			51	51
Charge for year		(65)	(451)	(516)
		(327)	(2,660)	(2,987)
Net book value at 30/9/13	3,000	1,853	1,803	6,656

Depreciation
Buildings 3% straight line
2,180 x 3% = 65

Plant and equipment 20% reducing balance
4,463-(2,260-51) = 2,254 x 20% = 451

(W2)

	Cost of sales	*Administration*
Balance 30/9/2013	4,080	779
Depreciation – plant and equipment (W1)	451	
Depreciation – buildings (W1)		65
Bad debt		230
Gain on disposal (W6)	(17)	
Inventory policy adjustments	148	
Totals	4,662	1,074

(W3) Finance charge

Years loan interest (1,480 x 5%)=	74
Paid	(37)
Current liability	37

(W4) Tax

Last Year b/f	24
Current year	160
	184
Decrease in deferred tax	(30)
	154

(W5) Deferred tax

Per trial balance	282
Decrease in year	(30)
	252

(W6) Gain on disposal of asset

Cost	57
Depreciation	(51)
Carrying value	6
Cash received	23
Gain	17

(W7) Trade Receivables

Balance per trial balance	2,590
Bad debt	(230)
	2,360

(W8) Shares repurchased in year
The shares were originally issued at 10% (565/5,650) premium.
Therefore on cancellation, only 10% can be deducted from share premium.

Entries required to cancel shares are:
Debit Equity shares	100
Debit Share premium	10
Debit Retained earnings	25
	135

In the SoCIE transfer 100 from retained earnings to capital reserve to maintain capital.

Question Four

Rationale

(a) To test candidates' knowledge of the required treatment of preference shares according to IAS 32 *Financial Instruments: Presentation*.
Tests learning outcome C2b.

(b) To test candidates' ability to prepare a statement of cash flows for a single entity.
Tests learning outcome C1a.

Suggested Approach

(a)(i) Explain the IAS 32 required treatment of preference shares.

(a)(ii) Use the answer to part (i) to calculate a revised profit before tax for AWX.

(b) Prepare workings for cash received/paid for all cash movements.
Prepare statement of cash flows.

(a) (i)

IAS 32 defines an equity instrument as one that evidences a residual interest in the assets of an entity after deducting all its liabilities.
IAS 32 defines a financial liability as a contractual obligation to deliver cash or other financial asset to another.

The IAS 32 definitions mean that cumulative, redeemable preference shares are classified as a financial liability rather than equity. AWX's preference shares must therefore be treated as debt in the statement of financial position. The value of the liability in the statement of financial position will be the proceeds of the issue less cost of the issue.
The preference share dividend will be treated as a finance expense in the statement of profit or loss and statement of cash flows.

(ii) The required adjustments to AWX's profit are:

Adjusted profit before tax	$000
Per draft income statement	408
Add back preference share issue costs	50
Less preference share finance cost (650 x 6·74%)	(44)
Profit before tax	414

(b)

AWX – Statement of Cash Flows for the year ended 31 March 2013

	$000	$000
Cash flows from operating activities		
Profit before tax	414	
Adjustments for:		
Depreciation	675	
Impairment of intangible assets (W1)	159	
Provision for legal claim	90	
Finance cost (W2)	84	
Gain on disposal of property, plant & equipment (W3)	(22)	
Operating profit before working capital changes		1,400
Decrease in inventory	67	
Increase in trade receivables	(84)	
Increase in trade payables	35	
		18
Cash generated from operations		1,418
Interest paid (W4)	(162)	
Income taxes paid (W6)	(253)	
		(415)
Net cash from operating activities		1,003
Cash flows from investing activities		
Purchase of property, plant and equipment (W7)	(320)	
Proceeds from sale of property, plant and equipment (W3)	92	
Net cash used in investing activities		(228)
Cash flows from financing activities		
Proceeds from issue of preference shares (W8)	650	
Repayment of loans	(1,100)	
Equity dividends paid *	(75)	
Net cash used in financing activities		(525)
Net increase in cash and cash equivalents		250
Cash and cash equivalents at 1 April 2012		265
Cash and cash equivalents at 31 March 2013		515

* this could also be shown as an operating cash flow

Workings, all figures in $000

W1 – Intangible assets
Balance b/fwd	315
Impaired in year (balance)	(159)
Balance c/fwd	156

W2 – Finance cost
Balance per Income Statement	40
Preference shares finance charge	44
Balance c/fwd	84

W3 – Gain on disposal of property plant and equipment
Net book value of assets sold	70
Cash received	(92)
Gain	22

W4 – Interest paid
Balance b/fwd	99
Income statement	40
Balance c/fwd	(12)
Interest paid	127
Preference shares dividend paid (classified as interest per IAS 32)	35
	162

W5 – Deferred Tax

Balance b/fwd	220
Income Statement (to balance)	5
Balance c/fwd	225

W6 – Income Taxes paid

Balance b/fwd		218
Income Statement – total	124	
Less deferred tax (W5)	(5)	119
		337
Tax paid (balance)		(253)
Balance c/fwd		84

W7 – Purchase of property, plant and equipment

Balance b/fwd	4,500
Disposals (NBV)	(70)
	4,430
Revaluation (469-353)	116
	4,546
Depreciation for year	(675)
	3,871
Balance c/fwd	4,191
Total PPE purchased in year	320

W8 – Proceeds from issue of preference share capital

Issue of preference shares	700
Less issue costs	(50)
Cash received	650